An Historical Presentation of Augustinism and Pelagianism From the Original Sources

AN

HISTORICAL PRESENTATION

OF

AUGUSTINISM AND PELAGIANISM

FROM THE

ORIGINAL SOURCES,

BY

G. F. WIGGERS, D. D.

PROFESSOR OF THEOLOGY IN THE UNIVERSITY OF ROSTOCK, ETC.

———————

TRANSLATED FROM THE GERMAN,

WITH NOTES AND ADDITIONS,

BY

Rev. RALPH EMERSON,

PROF OF ECCL HIST. IN THE THEOL SEM ANDOVER, MS

═══════

ANDOVER:

PUBLISHED BY GOULD, NEWMAN & SAXTON,

NEW YORK

CORNER OF FULTON AND NASSAU STS.

1840.

D

CONTENTS.

TRANSLATOR'S PREFACE.

" Names are things." And hence the peculiarly imperative duty, when speaking of *men*, large classes of men, and especially of *christian* men, that the right appellations be employed.—But what *kinds* of things, and of what power, are names ? *Instruments*, it may in the first place be replied ; and some of them for moral and religious as well as for scientific investigation ;—lenses, for instance, and of the most diverse and most magic power ; enlarging, or diminishing ; beautifying, or deforming ; multiplying, illuminating, or obscuring; and investing objects with all imaginable hues   And again, they are weapons ;—shields of adamant ;—Damascus blades. Wise men know well their power. And good men wish to use them, and to see them used, only aright ; and high-minded men, in the best sense of the term, scorn to use them, and blush to see them used, in any other way.—Names, too, have been the *causes* as well as the implements of war, arraying brother against brother, and that in the household of faith. Who will doubt this that has heard the thunder of such wars, or read their history ?

Whoever, then, shall kindly and dispassionately afford some real aid in fixing the just import of names employed in waging holy or unholy warfare, and thus shall aid those, whose business it may be, more justly to assign the names—and others to appreciate them—may well hope to be regarded as a son of peace, however humble his labor.

And here it may just be remarked, that often it is as important to ascertain the genuine import of a good as of a bad name—the nature of a shield, as of a spear.

For the last score of years, the terms *Pelagian* and *Pelagianism* have been very freely used. Opposite terms have also been assumed or applied with perhaps equal frequency. But with how much justness, in either case, it would here be premature to inquire. We must first ascertain the true *import* of such names.

And who can object to this inquiry ? or who quake in prospect of

its results ? Honest and ingenuous men will even court for themselves their proper appellations, if fairly understood, come these appellations from what source they may.   None but a poor Christian
will bestow a wrong appellation, on any man · and none but a bad
man will kill even a bad man, with an unlawful weapon.

Hence there are probably three classes of men who will like to
read such a work as this   First, those who have been called Pelagians.   For they will honestly wish to know whether they ought any
longer to reject the appellation: and how far, if *at all*, they should
own its justness.   Secondly, those who have called them Pelagians ·
as they will wish to know whether in whole or in part they have
rightly bestowed the appellation;—and whether, to any extent, it
may also be applicable to themselves.   Thirdly, those who have
neither given nor received the name, but who would fain be better
able to judge of the propriety with which it has been so currently
applied and so promptly rejected, on the right and on the left.

The work here presented is considered, by theologians in Germany and elsewhere, as affording the best means of settling such
questions, short of a laborious investigation of the original sources,
such as our author went through in collecting the materials for his
book.

But these considerations, important as they may be to the peace
and prosperity of the church, afford neither the only nor the chief
motives for presenting this work to the English reader

" Ancient Christianity," for better or for worse, must soon become
more perfectly known to the protestant world.   And good it is that it
should be so, painful and surprising in themselves as may be some of
the disclosures.   Such advocates of patristic authority as have recently appeared in England, will spare no pains in accomplishing
one part of this labor   Nor less prompt or less able will be their
antagonists, in performing the other part of the Herculean task, if we
may judge from recent specimens of their zeal and power.   Consequences of the most serious nature, in England as well as in this
country, are now seen to be most intimately connected with the
historical disclosures that shall be made.   Indeed some of the grand
questions of protestantism, now, as in the time of the Reformation,
(though in a different attitude), are in no small degree agitated as
questions of early ecclesiastical history.

In the progress of this quickened discussion, and with the means and motives that now exist for its prosecution, we may well expect that at least the external institutions and the ethics of the early church, will soon become more fully known. These two branches are so obviously and intimately connected, that they will of course continue to be prosecuted together.

But there is another and more difficult and, I may add, more important branch of investigation, which has hitherto received far less attention from those who speak the English language : and yet its connection with the others, though not so obvious, is no less real and important. I mean the ancient history of the more abstract doctrines of Christianity. The researches in all three of these departments, should proceed with equal step, since such are their relations that no one of them can be fairly investigated or thoroughly understood, apart from the others.

While, then, the history of rites, institutions, modes of church government, and modes of social or *unsocial* life, together with the doctrines of morality, are laid open to the light, the more abstract doctrines touching the nature of man and the government of God, and upon which all are in a manner based, should be simultaneously disclosed. Otherwise, real noon-day will beam upon neither.

England is now awakened to the performance of the one part. Germany, for the passing age, has been assiduously laboring on the other. The present, therefore, seems peculiarly the juncture for availing ourselves of the more ripened results to which these laborious Germans have arrived in respect to the history of such doctrines.—The work here presented contains a minute and well authenticated account of those doctrines as first more fully developed and received in the church. The period, too, of this development was the same as that which is the most deeply interesting in respect to the other branch of research

But a still further and more permanent interest attaching to such a work, is found in the intrinsic value of doctrinal history itself, and especially the history of such a period. On this topic I must dwell a moment, as it has furnished in fact my chief motive to the labor of this translation.

The Bible, indeed, is so plain in its great outlines of truth and duty, that the fool need not err in those matters with which only the simple have to do. And so are the laws of a well-governed christian nation so right and simple in their main requisitions, that few

honest-hearted men are found in transgression. But both human
and divine laws have also much to do with far other-hearted men.
These simple laws have yet a keen eye on the wily transgressor.
His waywardness is to be met; the point of his offending, discrimi-
nated; his punishment, adjusted to his guilt; his reformation to be
wisely sought and future crime to be forefended. If one, then, is
to become deeply versed in all the bearings of these simple laws of
God, or of his country, so as to guide his own conduct in critical cases and to become a guide and a defender or a reprover of others,
he has before him, not only the task of a nice and discriminating
study of all the existing statutes, but also of the history of the interpretation of those statutes. And nearly as well might the barrister
think himself prepared for his office by the mere reading of enact-
ments, without a knowledge of common law, as the theologian think
himself master of all the important questions that can fairly be started
on the interpretation of the Bible, without a good knowledge of the
great doctrinal controversies that have actually arisen in the church.
It is reported as the saying of the greatest living oracle of American
law, that no man can certainly foretell the practical operation of any
law—so many and diverse may be its occult bearings. And, although the like uncertainty does not shroud the divine law, yet who
could imagine beforehand a hundreth part of the important questions
that have been discussed, and that may yet continue to be discussed,
respecting the full import and application of these laws? Some of
them, too, questions on which have hung the welfare of ages! And
divine as is the law, and therefore wholly good, the interpretation is
human, and we need not be startled at the limited comparison here
made of it to human laws. And although the adjudications of councils and the dicta of individual theologians, have none of the force
of common law, yet who will not be greatly guided in the right and
admonished of the wrong constructions, by the attentive study of
what they have done, and of the practical bearings of their decisions? Or who will disregard these ancient monuments? Just as well
may we put out all human lights and march back again into the dark
ages!

Nor let it be said that much of the history of christian doctrine, is
the history of those ages. For those dark ages themselves are now
a light to us—one immense light-house, to warn from those fatal
rocks amid which the shattered church was dashing for a thousand

years. It were suicidal in her now to close her eyes to that costly beacon which Providence has erected for her future safety.

Nor should the young theologian imagine that he can now summarily and safely take the mere *results* of all past discussions, as he finds them embodied in the excellent though imperfect doctrinal formulas, to which a large part of the church has been led as the fruit of long ages of toil and contest, and that he shall thus be well prepared for his work, as a guide and a guardian to the church for days to come   He cannot even well understand the formulas themselves, without a knowledge of their history, and of the times in which they were drawn up, and of the errors against which they were intended to guard.   Much less will he be adequate to the high but most delicate office of timely espying and judiciously remedying those incipient *tendencies* to such errors which, though with shifting form, are continually re-appearing.   If a timid or an ambitious alarmist, he may cry *wolf*, when no wolf is coming :—or if of an opposite character, he may be dumb when the monster is just crouching to leap the walls of his fold.

But, again ; and in a different view, for him who would know what truth is.   How is truth best elicited ? and best learned ?   Didactic reading is good.   And meditation thereon is excellent.   And the guidance of a living Gamaliel, (if a Gamaliel he be), is admirable. But with and above all these, to the mind of some independence and judgment, is discussion ;—at once the light and life of truth ;—*discussion*, as forensic, as diologistic even, as it can be made.   So the young lawyers are taught by their seniors to believe and to practice, and to hold their moot courts, and when they can, to frequent the more solemn halls of justice where real questions of life and death are pending.

But who shall write or speak the dialogue for the young divine ? Not himself, if he would gain the highest good, and not rivet himself in prejudice : not one man for both parties ; nor yet two men of the same party, if truth is to be saved from the peril of betrayal or feeble defence, and to shine with new splendor.   *Hearty* combatants must tread the stage.   Nor should they, for his highest good, be those of his own land or period, lest party spirit prejudice his judgment.   Away in space and time should they belong, the farther off the better ; and all the better, too, the more diverse the modes of speech and illustration.   Let there come up before him some old

2

Romans . and though they come with something of their gladiato-
rial zeal, and deal their mighty thrusts, at least his interest will be
kept the more awake.

And such, indeed, is what the modern listener will sometimes
think he *has* before him, in these ancient and robust personages of
the Latin church. And, what he might hardly expect, from their
lips will he hear about all that has ever yet been uttered on either
side of the specific questions they discuss;—and that, sometimes,
with a zest and freshness which nothing but the strength of feeling
and the novelty of the debate, would inspire. And often—so Dr.
Wiggers has drawn up his book—the matter comes almost in the
shape of dialogue

Nor am I quite alone in all these views. Says Dr W. in the preface to his volume on the history of semipelagianism, " a satisfying
knowledge of christian doctrine can be gained only in the historical
way, and the rich contents of the articles of faith, received by our
church [the Lutheran], first come up vividly to view, and are perceived in all their blessed fulness, when we see how they speak
themselves forth, in conflict with error, precisely in *this* and in no
other manner. By this means, as effectual preparation is made
against a shallow rationalism, as against a frozen belief in the letter,
so killing to spiritual life "

It was with the hope of promoting such an object as this, that our
author also wrote the present work , and it is with the like hope,
that this translation has been made. May the author of truth and
protector of the church, bless it to this goodly issue.

But I must turn from these general views of the subject itself, to
some brief notices of the life of Dr. W. For the few facts I can here
present, I am indebted in part to the kindness of Prof. Sears of New-
ton Theological Seminary, whose residence in Germany afforded
him the best means of information.

Prof. Wiggers was born at Biestow, near Rostock, in 1777. His
education was completed at Gottingen, where he enjoyed the instruction of the excellent G J Planck, then professor of divinity in
the university there, and whose works on doctrinal history, have been
productive of such lasting fame to himself and such benefit to the
cause of " Protestant Theology." It was from an attendance on the
lectures of Dr P , that our author's early taste for historical research,
appears to have received both its encouragement and its happy di-

rection. After finishing his studies at Göttingen, he was *privatdocent* at Rostock , and in 1810, was professor ordinarius of theology in the University of Rostock, and also director of the pedagogical seminary. The highly honorary title of *Consistorialrath*, or Counsellor of the Consistory, which is conferred by the government, he enjoyed in 1813. Other 'marks of respect and esteem received from his countrymen, need not here be detailed.

His publications have been somewhat numerous, and such as have required historical research　None of them, however, so far as I can learn, have yet appeared in English.　To some of these, he occasionally refers in the progress of this history . and for this, as well as for other reasons, it may be well here to present the titles of a part of them.

His principal works are the following ·　Examen Argumentorum Platonis pro Immortalitate Animi Humani. Rostock 1803, 4to — Commentatio in Platonis Eutyphronem. Rostock 1804, 8vo.—De Joh. Cassiano Massil., qui semipelagianismi Auctor vulgo perhibitur, Commentationes tres. Rostock 1804 ss, 4to.—Socrates als Mensch, als Burger, und als Philosoph, oder Versuch einer Characteristik des Socrates. Rostock 1807.—Dissertatio De Juliano Apostata, Religionis Christianae et Christianorum Persecutore. Rostockii 1811, 4to.—Versuch einer pragmatischen Darstellung des Augustinismus und Pelagianismus nach ihrer geschichtlichen Entwickelung　Von Gustav Friedrich Wiggers, Grossherzoglich Mecklenburgischem Consistorialrathe, Doctor und Professor der Theologie auf der Universität zu Rostock.　In zwei Theilen. Hamburg 1833.

The last is the title of our present work as found in the edition I have used.　As a literal version of it would have been too barbarous to an English ear, I have taken a liberty in forming the English title that I have nowhere else indulged.—This work was published in 1821, and was followed, in 1833, by what Dr. W. calls " the second part" of the history, but which he also more specifically entitles, Versuch einer pragmatischen Darstellung des Semipelagianismus in seinem Kampfe gegen den Augustinismus bis zur zweiten Synode zu Orange.

The following extract from the preface to this last part, may show how the first had then, for twelve years, been regarded in Germany. " The reception which the first part of my history of Augustinism has found, can be no otherwise than grateful to me.　All the reviewers,—even those the most diverse in their religious views, and some of whom have wished I had spoken with rather more affection of Augustine, while others, on the contrary, have thought they saw too great a predilection in his favor,—have fully justified my historical presentation as being in accordance with the original sources "

To this I may add the following remarks with which Prof. Sears commences an article. on the same work in the Christian Review, No. IX. Sept. 1838. " It is pleasing to see a man of great talents and profound learning, who is every way qualified to represent the present improved state of philological and historical criticism in Germany, applying all his energies and resources to produce a complete history of the Pelagian controversy. It may be safely affirmed, that the subject has never before been treated with such ability and success. The work of Vossius was, indeed, very learned and valuable, as well as that of Norisius ; but neither of them penetrates so deeply into the original sources of information, nor so completely exhausts the various topics connected with the discussion. Though the writer evidently finds the sentiments of Pelagius most congenial to his own, yet he appears to be free from polemical zeal, and writes, for the most part, with the fairness and candor becoming a historian. None but a warm partisan will find frequent occasion for dissatisfaction with him in this respect."

No candid reader of the entire work, I think, can fail to pronounce this criticism of Prof Sears, as just as it is discriminating. Till near the close of the volume, however, he might be left to infer that Dr. W. is much more inclined to the positive part of Pelagianism, than he there allows us to suppose. And in his history of semipelagianism, he shows still more clearly his evangelical views on many points —and especially in respect to the Trinity and the agency of the Divine Spirit. But while he notices freely what he regards as erroneous either in Augustine or in the Pelagians, it seems nowhere his object to obtrude his own tenets. In this excellent trait, he resembles his illustrious preceptor.

In those instances where I have found any reason to suppose Dr. W. has failed of a just presentation of the views on either side, it has been my earnest endeavor to afford the means of correcting the mistake. In order to accomplish this object, I have taken the liberty, in very many passages, of giving a more extended extract from the

original sources—often without troubling the reader with the notice
of so harmless a fact. In other cases, I have added a note. In others,
as the surest and most concise mode of correction, I have silently substituted the entire passage, from the original source, instead of our author's summary of its contents. (His summaries *generally* embody
an exact translation of the essential words, and are distinguished from
the full citations only by the omission of quotation marks). But
the principal additions I have made to the work, are included in
brackets, and interspersed in their proper places in the text, as being
more convenient for the reader than to have them in an appendix.—
But while I made such additions, in no case have I omitted or cur-
tailed any of the citations or the remarks of our author.

Most of the quotations I have translated from the originals; but
in some instances the books have not been at hand, or the case was
too plain to require the labor of searching perhaps a folio page in order to find half a sentence.

Mistakes in translation I have doubtless made ; but I have certainly taken much pains to avoid them. Always, my first object has
been, in simple and perspicuous language, to give exactly the thought
of the author ;—my second, to do the least possible violence to our
own idiom. But who—I may well venture to put the question to
men of some skill who have tried the experiment—has succeeded,
even to his *own* satisfaction, in attaining both these objects ? and especially if he has had to translate a modern German author. Many
who have not tried the experiment, for any practical purpose, may
continue to think it one of the easiest, as well as the most inglorious,
of literary labors. And some men may, indeed, have *made* it a sufficiently easy task for themselves, to write what they have entitled
translations into *English* ; and may perhaps have been well pleased
with the work of their own hands. But if we may form any opinion,
on such a subject, from the history of *biblical* translation, we may at
least suppose it no very easy thing to make a perfect translation of
any foreign author—though simple, in thought and style, as the
apostle John. If experienced biblical scholars, with the help of all
who have preceded them, can still find any just occasion for devot-
ing whole years to the more exact translation of but portions of the
scriptures, how can it be expected that he, who makes the first translation of any work, should leave no errors for the keen eye of the

critic to detect ? Job, had he lived in our age, might perhaps have said, ' O that mine enemy had *translated* a book !'

Citations of Latin or Greek, which Dr. W. often makes without translating, I have translated, and have then generally omitted the originals as superfluous. And in other cases I have just as freely added the original words, where I have supposed they could be of any use. In the marking of emphatic words in a citation, I have also exercised my own judgment.

Mistakes in the references I have often silently corrected ; but when unable to find the passages, I have given the references as I found them. Many of the scripture references are to the passages as found in the Septuagint or in the Vulgate.

It may be superfluous for me to add, in respect to my own faith, that it is neither that of Augustine, nor of Pelagius, nor of Dr. Wiggers ; nor can I be held responsible for any of their opinions. My object like that of the book itself, has been, not so much to teach, as to show what has been taught, and how it has been supported.

R. EMERSON.

Andover, April 11, 1840.

AUTHOR'S PREFACE.

————

NOTWITHSTANDING the many valuable works on the subject, I
have long been convinced that it would well repay the labor, to attempt once more the exhibition of Augustinism and Pelagianism,
from the original sources. I was led to this conviction by G. J.
Planck's excellent lectures on doctrinal history ;—and gladly do I
seize this opportunity publicly to declare my grateful respect to this
my very worthy teacher

No sooner, then, had both my inclination and office led me particularly to the study of historical theology, than I determined to undertake this labor.

For a complete survey of the progress of the controversy, I first
read cursorily, and in chronological order, the controversial writings
of Augustine against the Pelagians. I then read them a second time,
and very carefully took extracts. After this I read his other chief
works, extracting from them what seemed needful for my purpose.
I then turned to the few extant writings of Pelagius, studying and extracting as before ; and then, to all the remaining productions (partly
in the smallest fragments) both of the disciples and the opponents of
Pelagius, as Caelestius, Julian, Jerome, Marius Mercator, and others ;
and also to the very important ordinances of the emperors and the
canons and decrees of councils, etc., that pertain to the subject.

After this, I went to the construction of my work, and in such a
manner as, without looking at any later writers, to draw from the
sources with which, by long intercourse, I had gained a familiar acquaintance. But before I had completed my labor in this respect, I
compared all that has been written of importance on the subject in

ancient and in later times, and profited much by the information thus gained

Two things I had much at heart in writing my book; the one, an exact presentation of the matter itself, and consequently an accurate account of what Augustine and the Pelagians have actually taught; the other,—what is particularly missed in my predecessors—an accurate development of the external and internal connection of each system: of the external, as the doctrine came forth in the controversy and by the controversy; of the internal, as a necessary connection found in each system.

Whether I have accomplished this, so far as the sources allow, I must leave to the decision of competent judges. Every correction, by men who have investigated the sources themselves, will be heartily welcome to me.

As it is very common, in the union contests, to refer back to Augustine as Calvin's champion for the doctrine of election by grace, my work will not fail of a certain degree of interest arising from the times. It will be found that Augustine thought differently from Calvin in many respects. The latter admitted predestination in an extent in which the former never taught nor could teach it For as Augustine attributed freedom of will to the first man before the fall, he could not regard the fall itself together with all the misery arising from it, as absolutely predestinated by God.

Should my work meet with approbation, I shall proceed with the history of Augustinism and Pelagianism after the period indicated in the introduction, for which I have already collected no inconsiderable materials.

G. F. WIGGERS.

Rostock, April 7, 1821.

INTRODUCTION.

AMONG all the doctrinal controversies in the christian church, the Pelagian certainly take the first place, if we regard the importance and the consequences of their results to christian doctrine. All that part of doctrine which is commonly and not unfitly called *anthropological*, the doctrines of the necessity of baptism to salvation, of original sin, of free will, of grace, of universal or of limited redemption, of predestination, in short, all the doctrines which constitute the peculiarities of the occidental system, were modelled by these controversies and received among the tenets of the eastern as well as the western church. On the other hand, these doctrines have truly a very great importance in themselves. The doctrine of freedom, to mention only this, was always the rock of peril, not only for theologians, but also for philosophers, and it is not a little interesting to see in what diverse manners this difficult doctrine was apprehended, assailed, and defended by such sagacious men as Augustine and Pelagius How important the other doctrines are for every thinking man, needs not be shown. For as they stand in the most necessary connection with the nature and the destiny of man, here and hereafter, they are in themselves of the greatest interest, aside from all other considerations.

From this exalted interest, which is intrinsic and peculiar to Augustinism and Pelagianism, it may easily be seen why the Pelagian disputes were continually renewed in the church, though under different forms. Even after the reformation, we find them again in the contests of Baius, in the contests of Molina, in the contests occasioned by the decrees of the synod of Dort, in the contests of the Jansenists with the Jesuits And still to the present time, the whole christian world is divided between two opposite views respecting the contested doctrines, of which the one is more allied to the Augustinian, the other to the Pelagian. In its essential ideas, the Augustinian is the supernatural doctrine of the Lutheran system. The mystics gladly allied themselves to the Augustinian theory. The Pelagian

3

view was eagerly embraced and warmly defended by the so-called rationalists. No one therefore can properly understand the ecclesiastical system of doctrine in this respect, or comprehend the present state of doctrinal science, who is not familiar with the history of Augustinism.

The history of these contests has moreover a peculiar charm from the fact that the doctrines to which they relate, were first systematically developed by these disputes. Men went deeper into the subject than they had before been accustomed to do, and developed all the consequences that stood in connection with it Hence, during this contest, these doctrines acquired nearly if not quite all the modes of statement which were afterwards received into the system of our church. This excites beforehand a prepossession in favor of the man who knew how to give a form to his system which men should acknowledge as the true one more than a thousand years after.

A great many acute writers have busied themselves from the beginning with the history of these disputes, at least the earlier history of them A polemic interest must have caused many of them to cultivate more carefully this part of doctrinal history. The labors of a Gerhard John Vossius, a Cornelius Jansenius, the Augustinian Noris, the Jesuit Garnier, and others, were valuable. Christian William Francis Walch, who very diligently availed himself of the labors of his predecessors, has surpassed them all. But in him, as well as in them, there is a want of the *pragmatic** mode of treatment ; and it is difficult to obtain a clear view of the whole connection of the controversy and of the doctrines discussed in it. Nor does Walch's work embrace the later history of Augustinism. Some small historical inadvertences of the worthy man, which cannot be surprising in a work of such compass as Walch's History of Heresies, I shall silently correct. Shrockh's work affords, for the most part, only extracts from the writings of Augustine and his opponents , which, however useful in themselves, by no means discharge the task of the historian. Also in the most recent times, Munscher, Wunderman,

---

* I trust the reader will pardon this use of an old word in a new sense, as we need this new sense, and as he will not be further troubled in this way in the present translation The German lexicons do not contain the word " pragmatisch ," but our author doubtless means by it here, (as in his title page, where I have not ventured to render it separately,) a treatment *according to the order of actual development* —TR

and others have devoted their useful labors to the exhibition of the Augustino-Pelagian controversies. But notwithstanding these useful preparatory labors, we need not wonder that an opportunity is still left to the historian for acquiring merit, not only in respect to the pragmatic treatment, but also in the historical exhibition of the materials themselves. The very circumstance, also, that lasting hostile parties were formed of the adherents and the opponents of Augustinism, has hindered the calm historical investigation of what Augustine and his opponents actually taught ; and this is one of the leading causes why we are not yet, even in the latest times, completely agreed respecting Augustinism and Pelagianism, as soon as we go into a minute representation of the peculiarities of each system. Never can a doctrinal history be written which answers to its ideal but when the materials are drawn from the sources and wrought in the truly pragmatic and likewise exhausting method.

An historical presentation of Augustinism, professing to bring its history down to the time of the reformation, must fix upon certain periods through which the contest continued and in which it often assumed quite an altered form. The following may be conveniently fixed upon as such periods.

Period first. From the first appearance of Pelagius and Caelestius in Africa, in the beginning of the fifth century, to the condemnation of the Caelestians at the third general council at Ephesus in the year 431.

Period second. From the development of what was afterwards called semipelagianism, by Cassian and his adherents, to the condemnation of the alleged semipelagian opinions in Gaul at the second council of Orange (concilio Arausicano secundo) 529.

Period third. The continuance and further spread of the true semipelagian mode of thinking in the west, (but which was given out as the genuine Augustinian,) and the introduction of semipelagianism into the doctrinal system of the east, (which however, strikingly enough, was ascribed to Augustine himself and not to Cassian,) to the condemnation of Augustine in the person of the monk Gotteschalcus by a council at Mentz, 848, and by a council at Chiersey (Carisiacum,) 849.

Period fourth. The reign of semipelagianism through the whole middle age to the time of Luther.

The present development of Augustinism is limited to the first period. This, notwithstanding its brevity, is unquestionably the richest, partly because of the ample sources remaining to us, and which so sadly fail in the third period, and partly because in this period the doctrines, which were afterwards either adopted or rejected, received their complete form in the most essential part.

AUGUSTINISM AND PELAGIANISM.

FROM THE FIRST APPEARANCE OF PELAGIUS AND CAELESTIUS IN AFRICA, IN THE BEGINNING OF THE FIFTH CENTURY, TO THE CONDEMNATION OF THE CAELESTIANS AT THE THIRD GENERAL COUNCIL AT EPHESUS IN THE YEAR 431.

CHAPTER I.

Sketch of the principal men who appeared in the Pelagian controversy, Augustine on the one side, and Pelagius, Caelestius and Julian on the other.

To spread the proper light over this controversy, it will be necessary first to become acquainted with the persons who acted the most important parts in it. Among them all, Augustine stands as chief. We therefore begin with him. Here we cannot undertake to give all the particular circumstances in the lives of Augustine and of the other personages involved in these disputes, and consequently their complete biographies. A separate book would be required for this purpose. Only the most interesting external and internal facts in their lives, so far as the sources allow, must here be selected, and consequently that which is best fitted to sketch before the reader the image of what was personal in these men. Much in this controversy will thus be better understood and more correctly appreciated.

AUGUSTINE.

There are two principal sources from which to draw the needful data for a sketch of Augustine. One is the biography left us by Possidius, bishop of Calama in Numidia, not far from Hippo Regius, who was his disciple and friend, and who, according to his own de-

claration, had lived nearly forty years in the most familiar intercourse with him   It is printed in the tenth volume of Augustine's
works, the Benedictine edition published at Venice, which, as may
here be observed, is the edition we shall uniformly follow in our citations   He wrote it about the year 432; and therefore not long
after the death of Augustine. Possidius, however, has confined himself to merely the external facts in Augustine's life ; and even these
he has not fully given. Thus he passes over whatever, in his opinion,
can cast a shade upon the life of his hero   A richer fountain is that
which flows from Augustine's Confessions, written by himself about
the year 400. With an amiable frankness and impartiality, he confesses all the errors and missteps of his youth. We look deep into
his inmost soul, without being disturbed, as in the case of Rousseau,
by proud self praises and sophistical reasoning. These confessions,
written in thirteen books and containing indeed much foreign matter,
extend from his early youth to his baptism and the death of his mother which soon ensued. They are found in the first part of Augustine's works in the edition above mentioned. The later events of
his life must be supplied from Possidius's biography , though in part
they may also be learned from his own later writings, which I have
diligently used for this purpose, and from cotemporary writers.*

Aurelius Augustine was born, Nov. 13, 354, at Tagaste, a muni-
cipal town in the northern part of Numidia in Africa, and distinguished only as his birth place. His father, Patricius, was a magis-
trate of that town   Patricius was not born a Christian, but came

---

* Much preparatory work was performed by the Benedictines in their Life
of Augustine   This Life, on account of its tedious prolixity, could attract
but few readers   The Jansenist Tillemont has left us a no less diffuse biography of Augustine, which fills the whole of the thirteenth volume of his
justly esteemed Memoirs. Schoenemann, in his Bibliotheca Patrum Latinorum, has well collected in a brief space much of Augustine's history , only he is disproportionately minute in relating his disputes with the Donatists   We also here and there meet with inaccuracies   The latest biogra-
pher of Augustine, is Stollberg in his well known history of the religion of
Jesus Christ, in the addenda to parts 13, 14, 15   Full of spirit and truly pious sentiment, he narrates the life of the famous man , but discreet criticism
might warn us against much which he adopts and against many of his own
opinions which he has interwoven

[The reader is also referred to Milner's Church History, where the life of
Augustine is sketched with uncommon interest , and also to Neander.—
Tr]

over to the christian faith, towards the end of his life, and was a catechumen when Augustine was in his sixteenth year He possessed
no property, but was a man of a naturally frank and liberal cast of
mind.   The defective part of his character was impetuosity and passion.   Augustine rarely mentions his ,father ; but much more frequently his mother, Monica, who was born a Christian and who bore
with meekness the rough exterior of her husband.   He dwells on
her piety, her prayers, her tears, her sighs for the conversion of her
son   The latter he regarded as the result of the tears of faith which
she daily shed.   She endeavored to form the mind of the boy, from
early youth, to christian piety and virtue.   But she found great im-
pediments in his violent temper, on which the disposition of his father and the hot climate of Africa might have an effect.   Even in
the first years of childhood, he was admitted into the class of catechumens, by the sign of the cross and sacrament of salt, i e. mystical or consecrated salt *   In a severe cholic, which came upon him
while yet a boy, he earnestly requested baptism.   His mother, however, deferred it, because, according to what Augustine himself declares as then a very common way of thinking (Conff. I. 11), she
feared he might afterwards have still greater need of this cleansing
rite, and his sins after baptism might produce a greater disadvantage
to his future salvation.

The boy was early instructed in what was then regarded as a liberal education ; but, though naturally of good parts, he showed no
interest in elementary instruction.   The sports of youth, in which he
ambitiously strove to surpass his schoolmates, possessed a greater
charm for his jovial spirit, and on this account he had often to suffer

* According to the fifth canon of the third council of Carthage (379), catechumens received the sacrament of salt " What the catechumens receive," says Augustine (De Peccatorum Mer et Rem 11. 26,) " although not
the body of Christ, is still holy, and more holy than food by which we are
nourished, because it is a sacrament "—We may just remark here the more
extended import of the term *sacrament*, according to which it indicated "every mystical and sacred sign ' In this sense Augustine received as sacra-
ments the exorcism, afflation, and the renunciation of the devil, then practiced at baptism. De Peccato Orig 40   In a still more extended sense, he
took *sacramenta* for sacred observances, and reckoned among them, in respect to the regulations of the law in the Old Testament, " circumcision of
the flesh, the temporal sabbath, new moons, sacrifices, and all the innumerable observances of this kind." Exps. Ep, ad Galatas, c, 3. 1. Op. T. III,
P. II

corporal punishment. He betook himself to God in earnest prayer, of whose help and aid he had heard from other people besides his mother, and entreated him to preserve him from being beaten in school. It is worthy of remark and important in respect to the formation of his system, and consequently also in respect to the state of our present system of doctrine, that he early conceived an aversion to the Greek language, which himself explains from the difficulty he found in learning a foreign language. Still Augustine was not in the sequel so utterly unskilled in Greek as some represent him. His writings prove this. Thus he quotes, for instance (Contra Jul. I. 5), a couple of passages translated by him from the discourses of Basil In quoting proof texts from the bible, he indeed commonly confined himself to the Vulgate ; still he sometimes argues from the original of the New Testament, and quotes variations of the Greek manuscripts. It is, however, certain, that he never went far in the Greek language Latin, which was his mother tongue, he learned naturally and without difficulty by the practice of daily life, " amid the blandishments of nurses and the jestings of the pleasant and the mirth of the sportive," as himself says in his Confessions, I 14. On this account the grammatical learning of it must have cost him little trouble. But the reading of the Latin poets, particularly Virgil, was peculiarly alluring to his youthful spirit, and put his lively imagination in great activity. By reciting passages from these poets, he gained an applause beyond the rest of his schoolfellows of equal age, and was pronounced a boy of good promise. Hebrew he never learned. " I am ignorant of the Hebrew language," said he in a letter to bishop Memorius. Opp. T. II p. 272.

At Madaura, a town likewise in Numidia, he was for a long time instructed in rhetoric and literature. But in this neighboring town, enough could not be done for the formation of the young Augustine as a rhetorician, for which the ambition of his father designed him. A high school was then flourishing in the more distant city of Car-thage. Thither he was sent, in his seventeenth year, although the requisite expense surpassed the limited means of his father Between leaving Madaura and his journey to Carthage, he spent a year, his sixteenth, in his father's house. Here he allowed his studies to rest, and gave himself up to wantonness and extravagance. Impetuous sensuality took the most powerful possession of him. The admonitions of his mother, who would withdraw him from this slippery path, he regarded as womanish. Her prayer, her entreaty could not guard him against it; nay, he even sought a preeminence by boasting, before the striplings of his own age, of excesses which he had not in fact committed. Yet he never indulged a hard, unfriendly word against his mother.

Augustine had not been long at Carthage, when his father died The activity of his mother, however, succeeded in preventing any interruption of his studies in consequence of his father's death. By the aid of his countryman, Romanianus, to whom he ever cherished a lively gratitude, provision was made, not only for his inevitable wants, but even for all that embellishes and renders life agreeable. In other respects his residence at Carthage was not fitted to bring him back to the path of chastity and sobriety, from which he had so sadly swerved in the paternal mansion. Allured by the charms of the city and the bad example of his schoolmates, he now abandoned himself entirely to the sensual propensity of his nature. Love and public shows compassed him with the net of their enticing charms. Even during divine service in the church, so himself tells us, a fleshly passion seized him He implored God to give him chastity, but not immediately. For he wished his sensual desire to be first satisfied, and not immediately extirpated. He had not yet reached his eighteenth year, when his concubine bore him a son, named Adeodatus.

In respect to science, his inclination was chiefly to forensic eloquence, in which he distinguished himself. Hence pride and arrogance filled his heart. He had no taste for the pugnacious manners of his schoolfellows, who were hence called *eversores ;* but he was foolishly enough ashamed of being more mannerly than they. During his residence at Carthage, taken with the reading of Cicero's Hortensius, he was suddenly so incited to the study of philosophy as immediately to lay aside his rhetorical exercises and to throw from him whatever was not connected with the study. But the early impressions of his mother's christian training, still rang in his soul, and he was a long time undecided where to seek the wisdom for which he thirsted, whether in our holy scriptures or in the schools of the Greek and Roman philosophers. But suddenly an irresistible antipathy seized him against the plain, unadorned style of the scriptures, which seemed to form too glaring a contrast with the luxurious fullness of the Ciceronian eloquence which he wished to adopt

4

for himself   Now his resolution was fully taken to devote himself
to philosophy.   He entered on this course without employing a
teacher, and read by himself the Categories of Aristotle and other
writings of the ancients   But when he found himself not satisfied
by all the wisdom of the philosophers he read, when Aristotle as little as any of the others, could appease the thirst of his spirit for wisdom and knowledge and the longing of his heart for the supply of
its wants, he turned to a sect which was then extensively spread.
This sect had concealed itself under the veil of secresy, and seemed
to form a kind of secret community.   And for this reason, it must
have excited his curiosity in a high degree. Its members called themselves Manichaeans   Secret wisdom was promised to the novices,
which could only be imparted to them after passing through several
degrees and stages   Animated by the hope of here finding new explanations of the mysterious, he joined this sect,* to the great grief
of his mother who shed scalding tears over her lost son, calling
him the son of tears.   For nine years, from the nineteenth to
the twenty-eighth of his life, he remained their scholar, in hope of
finally being admitted to the mysteries.   Augustine also ensnared
his friends, and Romanianus and Alypius among the rest, in the
Manichaean errors into which himself had fallen.   Although he now
at last saw the vanity and baselessness of their opinions, and became
perhaps tired of the years of probation imposed on him before reach-
ing a higher grade, yet their doctrine seemed, unconsciously to himself, to have become very firmly interwoven with his mode of thinking, and to have left echoes that were afterwards heard in several of
the external parts of his system as presented in opposition to the Pelagians. His opponents therefore were probably not in the wrong,
when they subsequently believed they found traces of the Manichaean doctrine of the evil nature of matter and of substantial original
sin, in his doctrine of the total corruption of man in his natural state
and the want of all freedom to good, which he set up against Pelagius, and which to be sure, in several essential points, was different
from Manichaeism   For, in a certain respect, as will subsequently
appear, Augustine's doctrine of original sin might be called a more

* In respect to the Manichaean doctrine, the words are worthy of notice
(Conff IV 1) Per idem tempus . deceptis —Generally the doctrine
of the Manichaeans, in respect to minute particulars, might be more accurately presented from Augustine's works, than has yet been done

refined Manichaeism, though we should not, with Herder (Ideen der Philosophie der Geschichte der Menschheit, Th. IV. S. 145), so denominate Augustinism as a whole.)

During this period, Augustine first went to his native town, Tagaste, where he taught grammar, and from which, smitten with sore grief for the death of a friend, and allured by the hope of finding a more splendid theatre for his vocation, he returned to Carthage There he taught rhetoric, and strove in literary contests for the applause of the multitude While he despised the haruspices, he yet sought counsel of the astrologers, who were then called mathematicians, and procured the future to be foretold him by them. Judicious people, among the rest Vindicianus, a physician, endeavored, but in vain, to withdraw him from this folly ; and he was not till afterwards cured of this disease. He also, like his mother, placed great value upon revelations and dreams. Here, in his twenty-sixth and twenty-seventh years, he wrote his first work, *De Apto et Pulchro*, but which was no longer extant when he composed his Confessions.

It was also at Carthage, in his twenty-ninth year, that he withdrew from the sect of the Manichaeans, to whom he had been lukewarm for some time, and the groundlessness of whose doctrine he exposed Still he did not yet entirely abandon it, but chose to enjoy it till he should find something better.

Rome then promised a greater sphere of action for a public teacher, more honor and profit.* Hence Augustine was easily persuaded by some of his friends to go to Rome, and secretly withdrew from the embraces of his mother, in 383 Scarcely had he arrived in Rome, when he was seized with a severe sickness that brought him near the grave. But he recovered; and being in the house of a Manichaean, he was again brought into nearer intimacy with these heretics. He now immediately opened his lectures on rhetoric. He was, however, but little satisfied with the conduct of his hearers, and therefore not unwillingly embraced a prospect that was opened to him, and went to Milan, where he was established as a public teacher of rhetoric, in the year 384)

---

* Augustine denies that these were his chief motives for going to Rome, though they were urged by his friends ⁄ The grand reason was, that greater order and less rudeness prevailed in the schools at Rome than at Carthage. Conff. V 8.—Tr.

His residence in this place was fraught with the most important consequences to him.　Here lived the pious Ambrose, who received him kindly　Augustine became fond of him, and took delight in the eloquence of the man　After hearing one passage after another of scripture explained and applied by him, he perceived that the catholic system of doctrine could be defended against the Manichaeans.　Now he abandoned this sect entirely.　But as he still doubted of all, he determined to remain a catechumen till something certain should be manifest to him.　About this time his mother, who could not console herself for the absence of her son, came to Milan　Great was her joy on finding the change in her son's mind　Still Augustine was now as little of a catholic as a Manichaean, which he himself declared to his mother.　The eloquent discourses of Ambrose, however, cleared up to him more and more the doctrine of the church, and he perceived the necessity of faith and of the authority of holy writ.

Thus was Augustine now gained indeed to christianity ; but doubts still weighed on his soul.　He had not a full conviction of what he should adopt as true ; and above all, speculation on the origin of evil gave him great uneasiness.　His heart was also still encompassed by the allurements of honor, of gain, and of sensual love.　He provided another concubine, after the first had returned to Africa. But he was recalled from the abyss of sensual delights, by the fear of death and the future judgment—a fear which, though through various opinions, never left him.*　He intended to live in common with his friends ; but soon renounced this purpose.　By studying the Platonists, with which he was then much occupied and which he read in a Latin translation, he came, as he thought, upon the track of truth.　But while he had perhaps become the better instructed, he had also become more inflated by the study　In his younger years, the philosophy of the Platonists generally afforded him much satisfaction ; and in his earlier writings, there are not wanting views and ideas which he had borrowed from new-platonism　But in his later years, when he thought less liberally of heathen philosophy, he recalled the praise he had bestowed on Plato and the Platonists.　Retract I. 1.　When he had finished reading the Platonists, he went

---

* Conff V1　Nec me revocabat a profundiore voluptatum carnalium gurgite, nisi metus mortis et futuri judicii tui, qui per varias quidem opiniones, nunquam tamen recessit de pectore meo

to the scriptures. It may be regarded as rather an indication and a consequence of his former mode of theological speculation, that he made Paul's epistles the object of his study. He now came to see indeed, as he assures us in his Confessions (VII. 21.), the harmony of Paul's doctrines with each other and with the teaching of the prophets and of the law, which he had before misapprehended. Yet the obscure language of these epistles and the apparently hard doctrines of election and reprobation in the epistle to the Romans, must naturally have only increased the doubt and disquietude of heart in one who was seeking consolation and rest in christianity. Worldly concerns, it is true, had no longer any charm for him; but love still held his heart a captive. In this disquietude, and impelled by his longing for a better mode of life, he went to Simplicianus, formerly a rhetorician and a zealous Christian, and who afterwards succeeded Ambrose in the episcopal chair at Milan. With some emotion, he heard from him the account of the conversion of Victorinus Soon after this, a certain Pontitianus described to him the life of St. Anthony and the conversion of two high-commissaries (agentes in rebus). This made the most lively impression on his heart. He betook himself to a garden, where his friend Alypius followed him, who had been present at the conversation. A violent contest arose between his sensual and his spiritual nature He knew the better; and yet sensuality and the power of habit, held him a prisoner in their chains He fell into a violent passion. He tore his hair; smote his forehead; grasped his knees. He then withdrew a little from Alypius and cast himself under a figtree A flood of tears broke forth; and he implored the divine mercy for grace. Augustine believed he heard a divine voice, calling to him in the words, Tolle, lege; Tolle, lege (Take up, read; Take up, read). He dried his tears; rose up; went forth where Alypius sat, and where he had been reading the book of the Apostle. He seized and opened it; and the first words on which his eyes fell, were Rom 13 13, " Not in rioting and drunkenness, not in chambering and wantonness, not in strife and envying. But put ye on the Lord Jesus Christ, and make not provision for the flesh to fulfil the lusts thereof."*—Now his

* Here I give our common version of the passage instead of a translation of the Latin version which our author quotes. But where matters of *doctrine* are concerned, it will generally be needful to translate from the Latin, as the variations are often such as to affect the argument in question —TR.

heart was completely changed and converted to God.   He went with Alypius to his mother.   With joy she learned the change which had taken place in her son.   Now Augustine was at rest.   External things no longer troubled his heart, and he began quietly to meditate on the manner in which he should direct his future life.

The first result of these meditations, was the resolution to re-renounce all earthly cares.   He gave up the plan of marrying, which he had cherished.   A repugnance to literary fame, took possession of him.   Henceforth, he sought no wealth, no worldly honor. In the vintage vacation that soon followed in 386, he gave up the office of teacher ; and thus freed from the chains of his profession and his lusts, he retired, with some of his relatives and friends, to the rural solitude of the villa of Cassiciacum, which belonged to his friend Verecundus.   Here he spent his pious and learned leisure in prayers and sighs for the pardon of his sins, in familiar conversations with his mother and friends on religious and also on philosophical subjects, for the last of which he still ever cherished a fondness and for which his mother had also a relish, in zealous study, and partly also in the instruction of two youths from his native town [His books against the academies, his book on holy living, his soliloquies, and other works, were the fruits of this leisure.]   At this time, as well as afterwards, he expected through the efficacy of prayer, to experience effects resembling the miraculous.—As yet, Augustine had not been fully introduced into the christian church by baptism. Leaving therefore his rural seclusion, he went to Milan to be baptized by Ambrose *   This took place at the vigils of Easter, the night preceding April 25, 387.   Augustine now felt spiritual joy ; and the anguish for the life he had previously led, vanished.

A short time after, he formed the resolution of returning to Africa, in company with his mother, his friends Alypius and Evodius, his brother Navigius, and his son Adeodatus, where he wished to live with his beloved mother and his friends in the mutual practice of devotion.   But on the way, he met a heavy blow.   His mother was suddenly seized with a disease, of which she died on the ninth day, and in the fifty-sixth year of her age   How deep an impression this loss made upon him, he tells us in the ninth book of his

---

* Aug Contra Julianum, I. 3 " Ambrose I revere as a father , for he begat me in Christ Jesus through the gospel, and from him as a minister of Christ, I received the laver of regeneration "

Confessions, c. 12 He speaks of his mother with much filial affection ; recounts her great deserts in regard to himself ; and con-
cludes with a hearty prayer for her, c. 13.

Being now deprived of this gentle companion of his journey, he
put off his return to Africa, and went to Rome. Here he again met
his old friends the Manichaeans, who sought to renew the intercourse
which had been interrupted by his absence. But Augustine avoided them, and earnestly reproached them for their errors and their
bad lives. This gave occasion to many a dispute. Finally it came
to open war, which Augustine carried on against them both orally
and by writing, with the greatest vehemence, to the end of his life.
He composed several pieces against them during his present residence at Rome, which gained him great repute in the catholic
church. ⟮Here he also wrote the first book on freewill, a work which
he afterwards completed while a presbyter at Hippo, and in which
he endeavored to refute the theory of the Manichaeans on the origin
of evil. The Manichaeans derived evil from a distinct nature which
was coeternal with God , Augustine, from the freewill of man Had
he written this work during his disputes with the Pelagians, it would
certainly have received a different shape. The Pelagians were disposed to find in it their own doctrine of freewill, and the natural
competency of man to good ; and it was difficult for Augustine,
nay impossible, to harmonize his subsequent doctrine of the entire
incompetency of man to the practice of good and the theory of grace
grounded upon it, with those earlier opinions which he had presented
here and in other writings against the Manichaeans, and to turn from
himself the reproach of inconsistency and contradiction.* And subsequently the semi-pelagians, so called, believed, and not without
reason, that Augustine's opinion of predestination might be refuted
from this work.⟯

In the autumn of 388, Augustine left Rome, and landed in Africa near the close of the winter. He went by Carthage to Tagaste,
his birthplace, to his house and the lands inherited from his father.

---

* This assertion, though true in itself, seems hardly consonant with the
position before assumed, that Augustine's hard doctrines in respect to human freedom, were the lingering " echoes" of his Manichaeism Had the
order of his works indeed been reversed, it would then have been more philosophical than it now is, to charge him with some remaining taint from this
source.—TR

These he sold and gave the money to the poor, but he still lived upon them after they were sold, and, as he expresses himself in a letter to Albina (Opp. II 370), consecrated himself to the free service
of God (ad Dei liberam servitutem), i. e he became a monk. Here
he spent three years, remote from all worldly occupations, with some
friends, in monastic seclusion, in prayers, fastings, pious meditation
and conversation.   The place where they lived together, he called
a monastery.   In the mean time, however, his fame was increased
both by the mode of life he led and by the writings he put forth at
this time.   Whether it was through fear of being made a bishop
against his will, as Possidius seems to have heard from him (c. 4),
that he avoided all places where a bishopric was vacant, must remain undecided.   Enough, that he came to Hippo Regius, towards
the end of the year 391, with the pious design, as Possidius relates
(c. 3), of converting a high commissary. He attended on the
preaching of Valerius, the bishop of the place , and here, amid a
tumult, and in spite of all his resistance, he was drawn to the presbytery, and brought to the bishop for ordination.

He actually entered on his office about the time of Easter, 392,
after making preparation for it for some time   On becoming a presbyter, he erected a monastery within the precincts of the church and
lived there, as Possidius says, with the servants of God (the monks)
according to the mode and rule established under the apostles, as
had before been done at Tagaste.   No one was allowed to possess
anything as his own, but they had all things common.*   But he was
by no means the founder of a new order of monks, as later ages
have made him. This monastery became a seminary for supplying
the church.   He also instituted a nunnery at Hippo, over which his
sister presided for several years.   Nor did he now cease to increase
his fame by his writings. Publicly and in his own house he taught
and preached, even in the presence of the bishop, (which, as Possidius relates, the custom of the African church did not formerly allow), against the Donatists, Manichaeans, and heathen, with great

---

* Factus presbyter monasterium intra ecclesiam mox instituit, et cum
Dei servis vivere coepit secundum modum et regulam sub sanctis Apostolis
constitutam , maxime ut nemo quidquam proprium in illa societate haberet,
sed eis essent omnia communia, et distribueretur unicuique sicut opus erat ,
quod jam prior ipse fecerat, dum de transmarinis ad sua remeasset   Possidius, c 5.

success and much applause, and enjoyed great respect even among all the bishops. A distinguished proof of this was afforded by their giving him the honorable appointment, at the general synod of Africa, of preaching in their assembly on the public confession of faith. In the sequel, Valerius wished for him as a colleague and fellow bishop. After many objections on the part of Augustine, he finally yielded, and was ordained near the close of the year 395 or in the beginning of the next. In this elevation, he acquired the highest authority by his shining talents, in so much that the whole occidental church regarded his decisions as oracles of orthodoxy and cheerfully submitted to them.

In this sphere, Augustine was uncommonly active. He preached with zeal and touching eloquence*—he wrote—he exhorted to genuine piety, the empty semblance of which he abhorred—he decided cases in law, as was the custom of the age—he attended councils, at which he took the chief part—he defended what he regarded as the orthodox doctrines against the heretics—and discharged the other duties which his episcopal office required of him. The number of his works, which indeed are not free from repetition and prolixity, is great. Even in the episcopal house, which he now occupied, he instituted a monastery with his clergy; and with them he lived in common, and maintained a rigid discipline Women were excluded from the episcopal residence—even his beloved sister. He contended against himself and with the sensual passions which often grew up again in him, and sought in devout prayer the means of resisting the temptations to sensuality, and was thus led to the more hearty love of God He experienced a lively joy in the increase and wider spread of the faith which he held as orthodox; while on the other hand, the errors of the brethren and the transgressions of the vicious caused him much affliction. He was fired with zeal and wrote against the Manichaeans, and entreated the emperor to let the laws

---

* How solicitous Augustine was really to benefit his hearers, may be seen from a passage where he complains because his words so poorly expressed his ideas and feelings ' My sermon almost always dissatisfies me. For I am anxious for a better, which I often enjoy inwardly before beginning to develop it in audible words, but when I fall short in the exhibition of what I had thus perceived, I am greatly grieved that my tongue is inadequate to the expression of my heart For I wish my hearer to understand all that I understand, and I perceive I have not so spoken as to accomplish this," etc. De Catechizandis Rudibus, c 2 Opp T VI

take their course against them in their former power. He had to
sustain a hard and bitter contest with the Donatists, whom he at length
completely conquered in the famous conference at Carthage, in 411,
by which he restored again the unity of the catholic church. In this
contest Augustine, alas, showed himself very passionate. He pro-
voked the Donatist clergy by incessant challenges to disputation, in
which he was conscious of his superiority. He endeavored, by various insinuations, to degrade them in the estimation of their people.
And, although at first he was for milder measures, he afterwards
persuaded the emperor Honorius to cruel and persecuting laws.*
A spirit of inquisition may not indeed have been the moving cause
with Augustine, but, (as he himself gives us to understand in the
letter to Vincentius just quoted), a zeal for their conversion, which
rested on the view, that the virtue and salvation of men depend on a
connection with the true church, and the adoption of her faith. But
this zeal for making converts, was not of the right kind. He now
calmly beheld how many thousands of these unhappy people, persecuted by the severity of the laws and destitute of shelter and the
means of sustaining their wretched existence, destroyed their own
lives from mere despair † We ought not, however, to overlook the

* In his letter to Vincentius, (c 5 Opp T II 237), Augustine says, " My
opinion at first was, that no one should be forced to the unity of Christ,
but that our weapons should be words, assailing them in discussion and conquering by reason, lest we should have but pretended catholics of those we
had before known as open heretics But this opinion of mine was changed,
not by the arguments of its opposers, but by facts," etc —And further on
(p 239) , " Let the lions [the kings] be turned to crush the bones of the
slanderers, and let not Daniel himself intercede," etc   Only he would not
have the Donatists punished with death In 412, he thus wrote to Marcellinus, who had been present as imperial commissioner at the conference at
Carthage "Though they confess such great crimes, yet I beg that their
punishment may not be death, both for the sake of our conscience and as a
commendation of the catholic clemency " Ep. 139

† On this subject, he expresses himself (Contra Gaudentium I, 29 Opp
IX 652) in the following manner " If you suppose we ought to be moved
because so many thousands die in this way, how much consolation do you
think we ought to have because far and incomparably more thousands are
freed from such great madness of the Donatist party, where not only the error of the nefarious division but even madness itself was the law ?"—In a
letter to the tribune Boniface (Ep 185 c 8 Opp II 656, 657), he says
" If you were to behold at one view the congregations of these people in

spirit of the Donatists with which *they* also persecuted the catholics, and the truly jacobinic principles and disposition of the Circumcelliones who were connected with them or rather came forth from the midst of them.

About this time the great contest began with Pelagius, which in the sequel is to be minutely presented in respect to both history and doctrine.

Augustine died at Hippo, August 28, 430, in the seventy-sixth year of his age—with deep repentance of the faults he had committed and amid the reading of David's penitential Psalms—when Hippo was besieged by the Vandals, and when he had not yet finished his great work against Julian. He left to the church a more than adequate clergy and full convents both male and female.

This summary account of his life is sufficient for a preliminary sketch of what was personal in a man whose entire character is seldom understood. Still the following features of his life, taken chiefly from Possidius, may serve to fill out and more accurately define the picture.

In his exterior, he was as far removed from pomp as from cynic negligence. By nature he was, indeed, fond of enjoying many dishes,* and therefore strove against the propensity and labored to be temperate. He did not frequent feasts; yet he practised hospitality

---

very many regions of Africa, who have been freed from that perdition, you would then say, it would have been too great a cruelty if these had been left to be ruined eternally and tormented in everlasting fire, merely through fear that desperate men, even in multitudes beyond all possible estimation, should be burnt in their own voluntary fires."—With these expressions, Augustine's exhortations to the love and gentleness which ought to be shown towards heretics and particularly towards the Donatists, form indeed a wide contrast. [Yet not quite so *guilty* "a contrast" as the language of our author would seem to imply, as may be apparent to any one who carefully studies the language of Augustine and the new circumstances of the church at the early period of her alliance with the temporal power. Complete religious toleration is even now but just born on earth, and is the child of long and dear bought experience—not of abstract theory. Had we been in Augustine's day, perhaps few of us should have learned so much of the forbearing spirit, the true philosophy of the gospel, as he displayed.—Tr.]

* Ebrietas longe est a me. Crapula autem nonnunquam subrepit servo tuo. Conff. X 31. We may see the sense in which *crapula* is here used for indulgence in food—a sense which is elsewhere found in the fathers as well as in Julian. C. Jul. IV 14.

himself towards strangers, and loved scientific conversation at meals.
He could not endure that evil should be said of the absent, and therefore, as Possidius relates (c 22), he once very severely reproved
some of his intimate fellow bishops who had transgressed this rule
On his table might be read the words, " Whoever loves to assail the
life of the absent, may know this table to be unfit for him." (l. c.).
He had formed many rules of life for himself, by which he was ben-
efitted, and which proved him a correct judge. To the poor, he
gave freely of his property and the revenues of the church, which,
however, he did not manage himself, as he wished to keep his mind
free from worldly cares   He caused a *xenodochium* to be erected
at the expense of the church who had appointed a special collection
for the purpose. With the remainder of the money he caused a
basilica to be built.*   A great inclination to melancholy remained
with him through life, which in his last years must have been aggra-
vated by his horror at the devastations which the Vandals were
spreading in Africa   Nor did Augustine keep himself free from the
superstitious mode of thinking that belonged to his age, of which his
writings afford sufficient proofs. He had, from his youth up, a certain tenderness of feeling; and in the sequel, through his habit of
praying for others, he was not lightly troublesome to any one.

   From all this, the following characteristic of Augustine is manifest. [The most distinctive and the most interesting thing, and that
by which his individuality is the most strikingly indicated, is the
union of mysticism with scholasticism, i. e. the endeavor by feeling to
reach the Infinite, with the endeavor to reduce the Infinite to our comprehension. In this respect, Augustine is altogether remarkable, a
peculiar phenomenon, one might say, of christian antiquity. Certainly we find no father in whom we meet with just as many proofs of

---

* The *xenodochium*, as we may infer from the derivation of the word and
from its use in this place, was a building for the entertainment of strangers.
—*Basilica*, anciently the royal abode   In the early periods of Rome, the
basilicae were splendid public buildings, of an oblong shape, adorned with
statues and columns, where the citizens assembled for public consultation,
merchants exposed their goods for sale, and young orators practiced decla-
mation   Constantine gave some of these basilicae at Rome to the Christians
as places of worship   Hence new churches, especially if built in the same
shape, were also called basilicae. The term was also used for cathedral, or
metropolitan church —TR.

a mystic way of thinking as of the prevalence of intellect. How can
any one express himself in a more mystical way than to speak of the
embraces of God, and of sucking his milk.* And how clearly do we
hear the mere mental philosopher, when he disputes with the Donatists, and still more when he seeks to prove " the servile will" in opposition to the Pelagians. The ecstasies also, of which the vestiges
are found in his Confessions, and which put him in the condition of
those who have prophetic visions, show what a dominion fancy, the
mother of mysticism, had over him. It might indeed be objected that
we ought to consider the age of Augustine But even in his later age,
during his contests with the Pelagians, striking traces are seen of the
mystic mode of thinking, particularly in his assertions respecting the
grace of God. Fancy, therefore, and sagacity were combined in
him in a manner wholly peculiar, without our being able to say that
either preponderated over the other. This peculiar combination by
which he was at once a mystic and a scholastic, is the greatest sin-
gularity in Augustine.—In full accordance with this peculiarity, or
sufficiently explained by it, are both his earnest effort for truth and
his devout disposition, his deep religious feeling, which speaks forth
in so lovely a manner, particularly where he is not acting the polemic, e g. in the Confessions, and which must have made him ab-
hor that pride of human virtue which ascribes a merit to its own
works †

Augustine had by nature an excessive propensity to the pleasures
of sense, of which he often complains himself, and which was also
confirmed by the early errors of his youth. This propensity must

* Only a passage or two can here find a place from the Confessions which
Augustine wrote when he had already reached the age of forty-six, and
when the fire of youth had consequently abated Il 2 —felicior expectarem
amplexus tuos IV. 1 Quid sum, cum mihi bene est, *nisi sugens lac tuum,*
aut *fruens te cibo* qui non corrumpitur XIII 8 Da mihi te Deus meus,
redde te mihi; te enim amo, et si parum est, amem validius Non possum
metiri, ut sciam, quantum desit mihi amoris ad id quod sat est, ut *currat vita mea in amplexus tuos,* nec avertatur donec abscondatur in abscondito vul-
tus tui Hoc tantum scio, quia male mihi est praeter te, non solum extra
me, sed et in meipso, et omnis mihi copia quae Deus non est, egestas est 29.
Audivi Dominus meus, *et elinxi stillam dulcedinis* ex tua veritate

† The like combination of acuteness, fancy, and humility, is strikingly
visible in President Edwards—the modern Augustine—though we need not
call either of them a mystic.—Tr.

in due time have led him to mysticism. For when it afterwards became more intellectual, his fancy must needs have revelled in a world above sense; and this readily affords a psychological explanation of the fact, that his love to God was never entirely free from a tinge of sensuous love. As a necessary consequence, the new platonic philosophy which, from its mystic tendency, was well adapted to his mind, confirmed him still more in this mode of thinking.

From what has been said, we may readily infer, that Augustine possessed much natural kindness and a delicate susceptibility for friendship. But the acuteness of his understanding inclined him freely to admit consequences from principles once established, even when repugnant to his moral feeling Hence was he so formidable a disputant. The study of Aristotle's works had certainly a very salutary influence on his consecutive mode of thinking. Against the justness of his conclusions, no objection can easily be made, if we only admit the principles.

A high degree of self-importance, however, belonged to the compound of Augustine's character. Hence the arrogance with which he treated his opponents, the ambition and the intolerance which often cast so deep a shade on his life. For though he sometimes speaks very modestly of himself and the value of his works, as when he says, in his book on the gift of Perseverance (c. 21), that he would have us adopt his opinion only when we perceive that he has not erred, and though he greatly censures in others the want of moderation towards opponents, yet his contests, particularly with the Pelagians, prove how little himself could endure contradiction, especially in his later years, and that behind those assertions of modesty and humility there lay concealed a hidden pride. In his Retractations, indeed, as well as in his book On the Predestination of the Saints, he takes back many of his earlier opinions * These, however, at least in part, were opinions which could not be reconciled

---

* Augustine allows, (De Praed Sanct. c. 3.) that at first he had not decided right on the doctrine of grace, and that he was afterwards convinced that even the commencement of faith is a gift of God, by Paul's declaration (1 Cor 4 7), "But what hast thou which thou hast not received? And if thou hast received it, why dost thou glory as if thou hadst not received it?" He however maintained this latter doctrine before the beginning of the Pelagian disputes, and even in the first of the two books which, at the commencement of his episcopate, he wrote to Simplicianus, and therefore about the year 395 c. 21.

with his later system which he set up against Pelagius and his adherents. That self-love, pride, and vanity belonged to him by nature,
himself acknowledges with great ingenuousness in many parts of his
writings. This too exalted self-esteem made him intolerant; and it
explains how, with so much natural kindness and so much philan-
thropy, he could yet so severely persecute those who differed from
him in opinion. For not only did he strive with all his power to effect the destruction of the still remaining vestiges of heathenism in
Africa and to induce the emperor Honorius to severe laws for this
purpose, but he also directed his persecuting zeal against the christian heretics We ought not indeed here to forget, that an over-
strained zeal for what he regarded as truth and for the welfare of
the catholic church, from which he was anxious to remove every
heresy, had a great share in this matter; and that he regarded precisely *his own* as the only christian opinions and sought to give them
authority—the ground of which, however, lay always in a great excess of self-esteem, though he may himself have attained no clear
consciousness of it.

If we contemplate Augustine as a scholar, our judgment of him
will vary according to the different demands we make of a theologian. If we compare the famous bishop with learned theologians of
the present time, he can scarcely deserve the name of such an one.
For we shall not readily reckon among learned theologians any one
who knows nothing at all of Hebrew and but little of Greek. But if
we estimate Augustine according to his own period, as it is proper
we should, he was by all means a learned man, and was surpassed
by but few, and among the Latin fathers perhaps only by Jerome,
though by him in a high degree. Thus much, however, is certain,
Augustine had more genius than learning, more wit and penetration
than fundamental science. Augustine's was a philosophical and
especially a logical mind. His works sufficiently prove his talent
for system-making and a logical development of ideas. We also
find in them much philosophical speculation peculiar to himself.
But the value of those speculations is not to be highly rated, since
he was far from being so much of a metaphysician in general as he
was of a logician. Nor was he wanting in a knowledge of philosophical systems and the speculations of others. His weakest point
as a scholar, was in a knowledge of languages. In this he was surpassed even by Pelagius, who was only a layman. For although,

as before remarked, he was not entirely ignorant of Greek, his knowledge of it was very limited, and we meet with a multitude of oversights on this account. Hence he generally used only the Latin translation of the bible, which is so often faulty, and even in the New Testament, he recurs but seldom to the original text. His ignorance and incapacity in expounding the scriptures, at least of the Old Testament, he himself acknowledges, Retract. I. 18. Hence he very often founds his arguments from the sacred books on erroneous interpretations. He also employed philosophical reasons to support his positive doctrines and strove, to unite the rational with the revealed belief, as christian theologians had already attempted to do from the time of Justin. His supernatural system he defended not only with exegetical but also with philosophical weapons.—His knowledge of the opinions of the earlier fathers often failed him. In a letter to Jerome, (Ep. 67, in the Vallarsic edition of Jerome's works,) he frankly confesses, that he knows not the errors charged upon Origen, and begs Jerome to point them out to him.—His taste was not sufficiently formed by the study of the classics. Hence his style, (though we find some good remarks of his on grammar, and his ability for eloquence, is sufficiently manifest in particular passages), was on the whole defective in purity and elegance, as could not but be expected in an age when the study of Cicero already began to be regarded as a sin. He also believed that rhetorical euphony was rather hurtful than beneficial to the presentation of christian truths, as they thus lose their dignity. In other respects, he did not despise the liberal arts, but believed they could be profitably used only when those who practise them are inspired by the christian spirit. Ep. 101 to Memorius.

PELAGIUS AND CAELESTIUS.

After Augustine, Pelagius is the most powerful in the Pelagian controversies. The sources from which biographical notices of him are to be drawn, are confined to occasional declarations of Augustine and of some cotemporary writers. With these may likewise be connected the few biographical accounts which remain of the life of Caelestius, who is the third man in importance in this contest.*

---

* Compare the preface of the Benedictines to part tenth of Augustine's works, G J Vossii Historia Pelagiana, Opp. VI. 554, Walch s Ketzerge-

Of the early circumstances of the life of Pelagius, we know just nothing at all. Even his native land is uncertain. Generally he is regarded as a Briton, to which Mercator's declaration leads, who calls him " a Briton by nation," in his Commonitorium, appendix to part tenth of Augustine's works, ed Ben. p. 63. According to Augustine, he had the surname of *Brito*.* But he was then not a Briton but an inhabitant of Little Britain or Britany. At least this is the common import of the word *Brito*. He is also called Brito in Prosper's Chronicon, Jerome's Works, VIII. 835. By *Brito*, however, Prosper might understand only a Briton, since he derives the Pelagian heresy from Britain, in other passages, e. g , Contra Collatorem, c. 21. Vossius endeavored to prove him a Scotchman. So much is certain, that Pelagius was a monk ; and therefore a layman, as all monks still were at that time. But he belonged to no monastic community, nor was he an eremite. Augustine derived the Pelagian heresy from some who were a kind of monks, (a quibusdam velut monachis). De Gest Pel. c. 35. Perhaps Augustine intended that neither Pelagius nor Caelestius belonged to any particular monastic community, and had not bound themselves to a definite residence in any cloister.

In his exterior, Pelagius cannot have been repulsive. This is apparent even from the unfriendly description of his opponent Orosius, in his Apologeticus. He was of an imposing figure. He bore himself erect, and did not neglect his dress.

About the commencement of the fifth century, he came to Rome, where he long remained. There he lived in intercourse with very upright people, and there as well as abroad was much esteemed for the integrity of his character and the purity of his morals. " That you regard Pelagius as a beloved servant of God, I know," writes Augustine to his friend Paulinus, bishop of Nola, in the middle of the year 417.† And several years earlier, (about the year 405), Chrysos-

---

schichte, Theil IV , Schoenemann, Bibliotheca Historico-literaria Patrum Latinorum, T II Sec 7, 8.

* Ep to Paulinus, 186, Opp II 663 Compare the note of the Benedictines on this passage.

† Ep 186 " I have read some writings of Pelagius, a holy man, as I hear, and a Christian of no small progress," says Augustine De Pec Mer III. 1. ' But still," he adds (c 3), " we ought attentively to consider, that he is a good and commendable man, as they say who have known him ' And in

6

tom thus expressed himself, in his fourth letter to Olympias : " I have been sorely troubled respecting the monk Pelagius Think how many crowns they deserve who bravely stand the conflict, when men who have lived so long in the practice of piety and continence, allow themselves, as we see, to be seduced." These words cannot well refer to the Pelagian heresy, as that was not as yet the subject of discourse, but they properly refer to the fact that Pelagius had abandoned the party that defended the innocence of Chrysostom, and this was probably the cause why he bemoaned his fall That these words refer to some other Pelagius, I cannot, with Walch and others, consider as so clearly proved. From the very epistle of Chrysostom here cited, which he wrote during his exile in Armenia, it is not improbable that Pelagius had lived in the East before his residence at Rome.

It was the most anxious care of Pelagius to rouse to virtue ; and this he did with a zeal peculiar to himself * Two youths of noble extraction, Timasius and James, were moved by his exhortations to renounce worldly cares and devote themselves and their property to God, as we read in a letter of Augustine and three other bishops to pope Innocent I Ep. 177. in Opp. II 624. At Rome, Pelagius found all, even the clergy, extremely corrupt. Pure Christianity had most shamefully degenerated It had become partly a superstitious round of ceremonies, and partly an object of speculation and controversy to the learned, and had no influence on the formation and improvement of the heart. Pelagius, (who had to do, not with theoretical opinions, but with a practical Christianity, and to whom, as well as to his disciples, even their antagonist Augustine not only everywhere does justice in respect to their talents, but also always speaks with respect of their moral character, at least in his earlier writings against them), sought to employ his stay at Rome in elevating and improving his neighbors He also found in his own situation a more

---

II. 16, he says, " Hence even they who contend against these things, though they are commendable for morality and chastity of life, and hesitate not to do what the Lord commanded the rich man who inquired what he should do to obtain eternal life, viz if he would be perfect, he should sell all that he had and give to the poor and transfer his treasure to heaven, still no one of them dares to say that himself is without sin " Comp De Gestis Pelagii, c. 22, 25

* De Gestis Pelagii, c. 25,—' all who heard his vehement and in a manner ardent exhortations to a good life "

urgent demand for this.   Pelagius made the correct remark—a proof
of his knowledge of man and his psychological ken—that we must
quicken in men the consciousness of freedom, for no one will have
the resolution to tread the path of virtue if he does not entertain the
hope that he can   In the first chapter of his letter to Demetrias, he
expresses himself on this point in a remarkable manner.   " As often," he there says, " as I have to speak of the commencement of
morality and the conduct of a holy life, it is my custom first to set
forth the power and quality of human nature and to show what it
can effect ; and then to incite the mind of the hearer to the kinds of
virtue, lest it should be of no use for one to be exhorted to those
things which he may perhaps have supposed impossible for him.
For never can we enter the path of virtue unless we are led by hope
as a companion ; since all effort of seeking perishes through despair of attaining."   That God's grace and its salutary influence on
the heart of man are not hereby excluded, is plain, and will appear
still more manifest from the ensuing presentation of the Pelagian
system.   But Pelagius did not thereupon proceed to making prose-
lytes or to instituting a school, just as he universally did nothing by
which the peace and happiness of the church could be disturbed.
He conversed with his friends or with the people on virtue and a
holy life as opportunity presented itself unsought *   This, among
the Latins, was altogether a new method   In this spirit also were
several works composed by him, e. g. the Libri Exhortatorii or Con-
solatorii to a widow.

Perhaps it cannot be certainly decided whether or how far Pelagius was first led to his opinions by Rufinus—by whom some understand the famous presbyter of Aquileia who lived with him on the
most friendly terms, and others, in consequence of Mercator's assertion (Com. Ap. p. 63), a Syrian of this name. All or *at least the
greater part* of the fathers of the Greek church, before Augustine,
denied any real original sin ; and hence it may well be, that the
same presbyter Rufinus, who came from the East to Rome, towards
the close of the fourth century, (and who may have introduced into

* Might we not expect so holy a man as he, and with a zeal for reforming
men so " peculiarly his own" as our author represents, to have done a little
more than this for the promotion of virtue ? And may we not conclude
from some notices in this work, that he actually did a *little* more than this,
both to reform men and also to gain adherents ?—Tr

Stepsis, in respect to many doctrines, the freer spirit of Origen, whom he greatly admired), brought Pelagius to his view of the moral state of man, or confirmed him in it. This seems also to be confirmed by what Caelestius afterwards said in his own defence at the synod of Carthage in 412, that he had heard Rufinus maintain, that there is no propagation of sin by generation. Aug de Pec Orig 3. --Besides, Mercator might call the presbyter Rufinus a Syrian, because the latter had lived thirty years in Syria and the East.

Pelagius made the first manifestation against Augustine at Rome, when a bishop had quoted from Augustine's Confessions the following words addressed to God: "Give what thou commandest, and command what thou wilt" Pelagius said, he could not endure this. And as he protested with some vehemence, he came very near having a contest with the bishop   Aug de Dono Perseverantiae, c. 20.

It was also at Rome, and when, by his own assertion in the preface, age was approaching and consequently his powers sinking, that he wrote his Expositions of Paul's Epistles, a work so famous in the Pelagian disputes   In this work, however, he did not bring forward his doubts of original sin as being his own doubts, but as objections of the opposers of the doctrine

Here he connected himself with the future monk Caelestius, whom some consider as a Campanian; others, as a Scotchman or an Irishman; and others still, as an African. According to Mercator (Com p. 64), Caelestius was of illustrious birth, and, what is not here unimportant to remark was in the practice of the law when he united with Pelagius. He was *auditorialis scholasticus.*

Caelestius, who was different from Pelagius in age, was no less so in character.   Younger in years, he was far more passionate than the grave Pelagius, now approaching to old age.   The latter hated all strife; never put forth theoretical propositions for disputation; and would not have the authority of a teacher. The latter contended with zeal for the practical doctrines of Pelagius, and in his own feeling of their truth would fain have them acknowledged as true by others, in which he also succeeded with many. Hence Jerome said of him, in a letter to Ctesiphon, in 415 "Although a scholar of Pelagius, he is yet the master and leader of the whole host." Also, according to the account of the author of the Praedestinatus (in the above mentioned appendix to the works of Augustine, p 65), Caelestius was the first who came out as a writer against the propagation of sin by generation, and published a book *Contra Traducem Peccati*, even before the appearance of Pelagius' exposition of Romans, and therefore probably soon after the year 400. Caelestius took up the doctrines of Pelagius rather in their theoretical than their practical aspect, in which alone Pelagius would have them considered; and it seemed to him that there was more to be done for the dialectical defence of their theoretical accuracy than for their practical application. By this difference of character in the two men, the judgment may be sufficiently explained which Augustine passes upon them, in which he is probably not altogether unjust towards Pelagius. "What is the difference," says he in his work on Original Sin, c 12, "between Pelagius and Caelestius, but that the latter was the more open, the former the more concealed, this the more wilful, that the more deceitful, or at least this the more frank, that the more cunning?" For it cannot be denied, as is clear from the narrative of the controversy, that Pelagius was not always sufficiently sincere. He did not express his opinions without ambiguity. Nay, he sometimes condemned opinions at the synods, which were manifestly his own; in all which, indeed, his love of peace and the small value he placed on theoretical opinions, might have much to do. Prosper, also, in his poem on the despisers of grace, calls him "the British serpent" (coluber Britannus). De Ingratis, Ap. p. 67.

Augustine does not exclude Caelestius from the good testimony which he bears to the Pelagians in respect to external morality. He also gives him the praise of an acute mind. He calls him "a man of the most penetrating genius, who, if he should be put right, would certainly be of the greatest service" Contra Duas Epistolas Pelagianorum, II 3 But he also calls him "a man whom the wind of false doctrine has inflated" De Pec. Orig c 7. Marius Mercator, in a passage before cited, ascribes to him "incredible loquacity."— But thus much is manifest from the whole, that Caelestius had also much zeal for a pure biblical Christianity and for a practical system of morals, though he was not so anxious as Pelagius for its application *—The connection between Pelagius and Caelestius was after-

* Gennadius (De Script Eccl c 44) writes concerning Caelestius as follows "Caelestius, before running into the Pelagian doctrine, and while yet a young man, wrote three letters to his parents from the monastery (de monasterio), in the form of small books which are needful to all who seek God. For the moral diction in them contained nothing of the evil after-

wards interrupted by their separation, and we do not find that after this separation, which will be noticed in connection with the breaking out of the Pelagian affair in Africa, they ever again met each other, or had any further intercourse.

In the years 409 and 410, multitudes of all classes and conditions left Rome, from the consternation, which the third approach of Alaric, king of the Goths, had spread there. The greater part fled to Sicily. It may be that Pelagius now came here with his friend. In this way we may easily account for the commotions which arose soon after in Sicily, on account of some teachers whose affinity to the Pelagians is clear enough, and concerning which Augustine, the oracle of orthodoxy, was consulted by a certain Hilary. See the letter of Hilary to Augustine, 156, in the second part of Augustine's works. The 157th contains Augustine's answer and refutation of the alleged errors spread in Sicily. Both were probably written about the year 414.—Still it may very well be, that Caelestius, on his journey from Carthage to Ephesus, in 412, passed through Sicily, and there spread more widely his opinions, and with so much the greater zeal, as he had already become a martyr to them —From the residence of Caelestius in Sicily, it is also manifest, how the " *Definitions*," ascribed to him came from this place into the hands of the Gallic bishops Eutropius and Paul, who sent them to Augustine for refutation. De Perf. Just Hom I

In 411, Pelagius and Caelestius came to Africa But the history of the Pelagian controversies, which begin with their arrival in Africa, will hereafter be fully related

Pelagius, who was already advanced in age, soon disappears from the history. The last fact, which Mercator briefly states, is, that he was driven from Jerusalem. Ap p. 72. When this happened, whether in 417, as some would have it, or in 421. as others believe, cannot be determined. Of the time or place of his death, no vestige is found in the old writers He cannot, however, have left the stage when Augustine wrote his second book against Julian, about the

---

wards disclosed, but was throughout an incitement to virtue " *De monasterio* here means either *from the cloister*, in which he might be without being a monk, for, according to Mercator, he was *auditorialis scholasticus* when he became connected with the Pelagians, and worldly occupations were interdicted to monks , or it indicates the subject on which he wrote. The first is to me the most probable His parents may have sent him to the cloister to be brought up and instructed

year 421. For in it (c. 10), he blames the arrogance of Julian who boasted of defending forsaken truth, thereby putting himself above Pelagius and Caelestius, her only other teachers, just as though they were already gone, and he was left alone to defend truth which he considered forsaken.

The latter part of the life of Caelestius is involved in the same uncertainty, though his history is continued to a later time. About the year 429, he was banished from Constantinople by order of the emperor. To this refers the confidential letter written to Caelestius about the end of the year 430, by Nestorius, who seems to have stood in a peculiar relation to Caelestius, and who had doubtless applied to him for the purpose of obtaining the protection of the emperor. This letter has been preserved in a Latin translation by Marius Mercator and may be found in his works. Ed Garnier, I. 71. In it he mentions an "occidental council," which, as Walch in his History of Heresies (V. 439), justly supposes, was no other than the council which the Romish bishop Caelestius held against Nestorius in 430

How dissimilar Augustine and Pelagius were, is sufficiently apparent from what has already been said. Their characters were diametrically opposite. Pelagius was a quiet man, as free from mysticism as from aspiring ambition; and in this respect, his mode of thought and of action must have been wholly different from that of Augustine. But Pelagius must also have surpassed Augustine in liberal education, which appears in the greater elegance and purity of his style. He was, as will hereafter be shown, a better expositor and a more sober philosopher. Both therefore thought differently, according to their totally different spiritual physiognomy; and both, moreover, must have come into conflict just as soon as an external occasion should be presented   Whether truth or error triumphed in the contest of these men, the sequel will show

JULIAN.

As it concerns the sources for literary notices of his life, these again are confined to occasional declarations in the works of Augustine and of some other writers of the same or a little later period. They have been diligently collected by the Benedictines in their pre-

face to Augustine's Unfinished Work, by Vossius, Walch, Schóne-
mann, and others, on this well known work.

Julian, one of the most famous disciples of Pelagius and the keen-
est opponent of Augustine, who in dialectic skill even surpassed
Caelestius, was a son of the subsequent bishop Memor and Juliana,
both of whom stood in high repute for piety.   Even Augustine held
a friendly connection with Memor. and was thus also favorably inclined towards his son, whom he had besides learned to prize on account of his distinguished talents   " I," says Augustine with an
untranslatable play upon words, " am certainly not unmindful of
your father Memor of blessed memory (certe beatae memoriae Me-
moris patris tui non immemor), who formed no small friendship with
me by epistolary correspondence and caused you yourself to be very
dear to me " Contra Jul I. 4. Comp. Ep. 101, to Memor   Julian
married early.   He had, however, before entered the priesthood
and attained the office of reader.   From this he soon rose to that of
deacon.   It appears from a passage in Augustine, that now, being
received among the higher clergy, he practised continence. C. Jul.
III 21.   Julian finally reached the episcopal dignity, and that at Eclanum, which was formerly attached to Apulia but afterwards to
Campania.

Julian perhaps became acquainted with Caelestius and his opinions at Rome, where he resided for the first time when Zosimus was
bishop there Mercator Com. Ap 115 He remained, according to
Mercator, (p. 71), in the orthodox church and in communion with
the Romish bishop, till the death of Innocent who had ordained him ;
though, from a passage in Augustine (C. Jul I. 4), it may almost be
presumed that he was already inclined to Pelagianism during the life
of Innocent   But we first find him a decided Pelagian in the year
418, when he refused to subscribe the famous *tractoria* of Zosimus
which contained the condemnation of the Pelagian doctrine and,
with it, of Pelagius and Caelestius.

Julian, as well as all who had the like boldness, was deposed and
banished from Italy   With them he left the west and repaired directly to Constantinople.   But here too he had no good fortune
The bishop Atticus banished him and his companions from the city.
Julian now turned to Cilicia, to his friend Theodore, bishop of Mopseusta.   Many of the bishops exiled with him, when they saw the

affair took an unfavorable turn, abandoned him, fled to the apostolic chair for grace, and were reinstated. But Julian was of too exalted a character to deny his convictions for the sake of temporal advantage.

He was now greatly enraged at Augustine, who led at his will the emperor Honorius and the bishop of Rome, and gave laws to the church. Unmindful of the old friendship, he not only assailed him, about 419, in four books which he wrote against Augustine's first book On Marriage and Concupiscence, but he also wrote, in Cilicia, about 421 or a little later, his great work against him in eight books. Scarcely had he left Cilicia, however, when Theodore, according to Mercator's account (Com. 116), pronounced condemnation upon him at a Cilician provincial synod. In 428, when Nestorius had become bishop of Constantinople, or 429, he returned to this city, in hope of obtaining from the emperor, by the application of the new bishop, what he had lost in the west At least the letters of Nestorius to the Romish bishop Caelestine, of which we shall speak in the sequel, are proofs of the abundant complaints which Julian and the other deposed bishops of the west, presented to Theodosius II, and the Constantinopolitan bishop. In the mean time the busy Marius Mercator—one knows not whether of his own accord or induced by Augustine, whose zealous armor-bearer he was, and who might be apprehensive that Julian's heresies would take root in Constantinople—hastened to this metropolis and presented, in 429, to Theodosius and the Constantinopolitan church, a *commonitorium* [admonitory letter] composed by himself, and thus caused as well Julian and his companions as also Caelestius soon after to be banished from the city by an imperial decree Thereupon, at the third ecumenic council at Ephesus, 431, where Mercator was also present, Julian, together with Caelestius and the rest of the Pelagians, was condemned. From this time forth, the name of Julian gradually vanishes from the history, and we know nothing of his subsequent condition in life or the time of his death. Only thus much does Prosper furthermore relate, that Julian made a fresh attempt, in 439, under pretence of repentance, to be restored to communion and to regain his lost bishopric ; but that pope Sixtus III opposed his efforts. According to Gennadius (De Viris Illustribus c. 45), he died under the reign of Valentinian III, the son of Constantius, and therefore previous to the year 455.

7

Julian was an acute, philosophic genius, an adroit dialectician, and therefore by far the most formidable antagonist of Augustine. In the knowledge of languages and in classical cultivation, he far surpassed the bishop of Hippo. Besides this he was not destitute of eloquence, but was also just as often a sophist. Of his arrogance he gives proofs enough ; and we can therefore readily trust Augustine's assurance, who calls him " a most confident youth." C. Jul II. 8 But with still greater insolence, does Julian treat the consecrated bishop, calling him, among other things, " the most senseless and stupid of all men," (hominum omnium amentissimum et hardissimum, Op Imp II 29 III 145), and " a worshipper of the devil," (diaboli cultorem, C Jul III 18), and passes the most unfavorable judgment upon his writings Op Imp I. 8. He may nevertheless have possessed a kind of natural generosity In a time of famine, as Gennadius says in the same work, he gave all that he had to the poor.

Thus much however is certain, that the practical importance of Pelagianism did not escape even Julian. He speaks out plainly on this point, in a passage thus presented by Augustine. " As if agreeing with the holy scriptures and the soundest reason, and *for the purpose of inciting men to zeal in virtue*, you maintain," says Augustine, " that there is no evil in the nature of man, inculcating that there is no summit of virtue so lofty that, by God's aid, a believing mind may not reach it · and you say that there is no necessity of evil in the flesh in order that every one being commendably constituted (laudibiliter conditus) may blush to live basely, and so shame may oppose improper conduct by reminding man of the nobility of his nature " C. Jul. III. 26.

CHAPTER II.

Chief sources of information respecting the controversies between Augustine and the Pelagians

As the chief personages involved in these controversies, have now been depicted, it is proper that the principal sources should be adduced from which a knowledge of these controversies may be derived. They are

I. The few writings of Pelagius that have come down to our time   Of these, we possess the following.

1. Commentarii in Epistolas Pauli   These were written before the year 410, and contain remarks on the thirteen epistles of Paul. Those on the epistle to the Romans must naturally be the most important for a knowledge of the Pelagian doctrine. This commentary, by an odd mistake in the manuscripts, came among the works of Jerome, and is even now printed with them, although ascribed almost universally to Pelagius   In the Vallarsic edition of Jerome, it forms the conclusion   It is also appended to the Antwerp edition of Augustine's works, XII p. 315   As early as the sixth century, Cassiodorus conceived it to be a work of Pelagius, and inspection proves it to be so.   Augustine, Mercator, and others quote passages from this commentary and attribute them to Pelagius; and the sentiments they contain, which are wholly Pelagian, fully evince their author.   But as it was formerly ascribed to Jerome, it is no wonder that we meet with interpolations in several passages where orthodoxy was offended   See the *admonitio* in the above mentioned edition of Jerome's works, XI. 134, and the preface of the Benedictines to P X of Augustine's works.   And especially do we meet with interpolations in abundance in the Exposition of the Epistle to the Romans which Cassiodorus purged from the Pelagian poison, according to his own confession   See Inst Div Scrip c. 8. p. 380, 381 T II. Opp ed Paris, 1600   Compare Walch's History of Heresies, P. IV. p. 547 sqq —Still there are passages enough remaining which show Pelagianism on the face of them.

2 A letter or book to the nun Demetrias, De Virginitate, written about the year 413   This letter also was falsely ascribed to Jerome. By Vallarsius it is attached to the works of this father, T XI. P. I. p. 1,

and is also found in the appendix to the] second part of Augustine's
works. That Pelagius was the author, admits of no doubt, since, in a
passage of his letter to pope Innocent, which Augustine has preserved
in his letter De Gratia Christi c 37, he mentions himself as its author.
Augustine also adduces passages from this letter, e. g., De Gratia
Christi, c 38, and ascribes them to Pelagius Comp the *admonitio*
concerning this letter, by Vallarsius in the passage referred to. It
was also published separately by Semler with the letters of Augustine, Jerome, and others pertaining to it. Halae, 1775–8. Whitby's
tract on the imputation of Adam's sin, is appended, in which much
is found respecting the opinions of the ancient fathers on that subject.

3 A confession of faith (Libellus Fidei), which Pelagius sent to
pope Innocent at Rome, 417, but which was first delivered to Zosimus   This in like manner strayed, under the title Symboli Expla-
natio ad Damasum, among the works of Jerome, to whom it was
ascribed   It is also printed among his works in the edition of Vallarsius, T XI. P. II. p 201.   It is likewise found in the oft-cited appendix to the tenth part of Augustine's works, as well as in the fourth
part of the Mansic Collection of Councils, p 355 ; and with learned
remarks, in Wall's History of Infant Baptism, translated into Latin
by Schlosser, I 372. Bremae, 1748 —That it is a formal confession
of faith by Pelagius, is now generally acknowledged. Augustine
refuted it in his book On the Grace of Christ, and quoted many passages from it which are found verbatim in this symbol. Cap. 30, 32
sqq —Walch has also admitted it into his Bibliotheca Symbolica, p
192. See this writer in regard to the interpolations of this confession, p. 196, 197.

4. Here also is most probably to be reckoned the Epistola ad Ce-
lantiam Matronam de Ratione pie Vivendi, which has likewise been
preserved among Jerome's works, ep 148, in Val. ed. Erasmus
ascribed it to bishop Paulinus of Nola ; and Vallarsius is inclined to
impute it to Sulpitius Severus. But the language and mode of treatment are Pelagian. Hence Semler, who receives it into the work
above cited, not unjustly attributes it to Pelagius himself   Thus
much is at least certain, it is written wholly in the spirit of Pelagius.
Probably it was composed before the Pelagian controversy broke out,
but the year cannot be determined. It contains rules of living for
Celantia, the wife of a rich and distinguished man

This, however, is all that has reached our time entire of the works of Pelagius. Among the lost are his Capitula, his book De Natura, four books De Libero Arbitrio, the noted letter to pope Innocent I, with which he accompanied his confession of faith, and other writings. In the works, however, of Augustine against Pelagius and Caelestius, all or at least the greatest part of which have come down to us, not only is the substance of the book De Natura and of the letter of Pelagius to be seen, but they are often quoted verbatim. Quotations of this kind are found from the book De Natura in the book De Natura et Gratia, and fragments from the letter to Innocent in the books De Gratia Christi and De Peccato Originali Fragments also from the books on freewill we find in the books De Gratia Christi and De Peccato Originali. From the Capitula or eclogues, which contain a collection of scripture passages on moral subjects, there are fragments in the first book of Jerome's dialogue against the Pelagians, and in Augustine, particularly De Gestis Pelagii.

Nothing entire of the works of Caelestius, has reached our time. Some fragments, however, are found in Augustine, e g of the Definitions attributed to Caelestius in the book De Perfectione Justitiae Hominis; and of the important Libellus Fidei, which he presented to Zosimus, in the book De Peccato Originali. See Walch's Bibl. Symb. Vetus, p. 198.—Of Julian's works also there exist only fragments, the most important of which are contained in Augustine's books against Julian and in the Opus Imperfectum The Libellus Fidei, which was attributed to him by Garnier (Diss. Septem Quibus Integra Continetur Historia Pelagiana, in the first part of his edition of Mercator's works, p. 319), and by the Benedictines (Ap p 110), is not from him but probably from some bishops inclined to Pelagianism in the diocese of Aquileia. Comp. Rubeis Tract. de Pec. Orig c XI. p 39 sqq. Venetiis 1757. Walch's History of Heresies, IV. 676, and his Bib Symb. Vet. p. 199.

II. Augustine's controversial works against the Pelagians. In the Benedictine edition, they constitute the tenth volume, where they are arranged according to the probable order of time They are the following.

In 412, when Caelestius was first condemned at a Carthaginian synod, Augustine wrote three books, De Peccatorum Meretis et Remissione et de Baptismo Parvulorum, ad Marcellinum.

Towards the end of 412, De Spiritu et Litera, ad Marcellinum Li-

ber Unus   Here he answered some doubts which arose to Marcellinus on reading the first work.

In 415, he answered Pelagius' book on nature in a piece De Natura et Gratia   In this work, are exact quotations from that alleged
work of Pelagius.

Towards the end of the same year, appeared Ad Episcopos Eu-
tropium et Paulum Epistola seu Liber de Perfectione Justitiae Hominis, against the alleged Definitions of Caelestius

In the beginning of 417, De Gestis Pelagii ad Aurelium Episco-
pium   In this book the conduct of Pelagius at Diospolis is related
and proved. Augustine endeavors to show, that the Pelagian doctrines were not there approved of.   In this work, he first came out
publicly as a determined enemy of Pelagius, without respect or reserve   Probably the propitious result of this synod for Pelagius,
had produced this effect   In the previous works, which were directed against the Pelagian doctrine, Augustine either did not mention
Pelagius by name or else with esteem and respect, because he cherished the hope of his coming over to his system, and hence he would
not provoke him   "Lest," writes he to Paulinus (Ep. 186), " being offended he should be rendered still more insane." On this
point he also explains himself in this book, c 23, 25

In 418, De Gratia Christi et de Peccato Originali contra Pelagium
et Caelestium Libri duo   A main work   In this, Augustine refers
only to the works acknowledged by Pelagius himself in his letter to
the Romish bishop already mentioned.

At the close of this year, or in 419, the first book De Nuptiis et
Concupiscentia, with a letter to Comes Valerius   Against this book,
Julian wrote four books, which however are all lost but the extracts
given by Augustine.   The extracts from the first book were sent to
Augustine by Comes Valerius, which he answered in 420   But in
using these extracts, we must be cautious, because, by Augustine's
own confession (Retract II 62 Op. Imp. I. 16), much was altered
in them which Julian had not so written   This answer, connected
with the first book, completes the two books on marriage and concupiscence

Towards the close of 419, four books De Anima et ejus Origine.
These books are directed against Vincentius Victor, a young scholar
of Mauritania, who had found Augustine's assertions on the subject
offensive   This work is not written particularly against the Pela-

gians, but is of much importance respecting the system which Augustine developed, since the question of the propagation of souls, stands in so close a connection with the Augustinian doctrine of original sin as propagated by generation. Hence the Benedictines have assigned a place to these books among Augustine's controversial works against the Pelagians Besides, in these books, other matters are also discussed pertaining to the Pelagian disputes, e g. the object of infant baptism.

In 420, four books, Contra Duas Epistolas Pelagianorum ad Bonifacium Romanae Ecclesiae Episcopum. In these, Augustine answered two Pelagian epistles, of which Julian was regarded as the author One of them had been sent to Rome, the other was that which was sent to bishop Rufus at Thessalonica, in the name of Julian and seventeen other bishops who had refused to sign the Tractoria Both letters had been sent to Augustine by Boniface.

In the mean time, Augustine had now received, through bishop Claudius, those four books of Julian complete, instead of merely the extracts before sent him He therefore resolved on a complete refutation; and so there were forthcoming, in 421, six more books, Contra Julianum, to which was prefixed a letter to bishop Claudius. Augustine himself appears to have placed a great value on this work, and calls it (Retract II. 62) " so great and elaborate a work." It is considered one of the most perfect which he produced in this controversy.

In 426 or 427, De Gratia et Libero Arbitrio ad Valentinum et cum illo Monachos (Adrumetinos) Liber Unus. This piece he accompanied with two letters to them Adrumetum was a seaport in Africa, and the chief city of the Byzacene province, [now a part of Tunis.]

Soon after appeared a book by him addressed to them, De Correptione et Gratia, [in which he shows the consistency between " rebuke and grace."—Tr.]

In 428 or 429, he wrote two books, De Praedestinatione Sanctorum, against what have since been called the semi-pelagians, who arose in Gaul and particularly at Marseilles, and of whom he had received information through Prosper and Hilary. Only the first book, however, now commonly bears this title ; and the second, the inscription De Dono Perseverantiae. In these books, there reigns a tone of gentleness and mildness which is strikingly in contrast with

what we find in other writings of Augustine   Perhaps he intended
to win those monks by mildness, who differed from him on a doctrine against which their moral sense must have revolted.

Julian had written eight books against Augustine's second book on
marriage and concupiscence.   These Augustine designed to refute
in the same number of books.   But he did not finish this work, in
which the vestiges of decaying age cannot be mistaken.   For death
overtook him at the sixth book, in 430   Hence this book bears the
title Opus Imperfectum   Here again are extracts from Julian's
books, but which extend only to the sixth book.   These extracts,
as well as the books De Nupt. et Conc., are translated in an abridged form by G. H K. Rosenmuller, under the title, Julian's Refutation of Augustine's Books on Marriage and Lust, in a German Translation by Rosenmuller. Leipzig, 1796.

Here also come the *letters* of Augustine written on this subject,
among the most important of which, are those to Honoratus (Ep.
140, written about 412), to Hilary at Syracuse (157, about 414), also Epp 178, 179, 190, 191, 193, and that to the then Romish presbyter, afterwards pope Sixtus (194, about 418).   They are in the
second volume of the Benedictine edition of Augustine, where are
also to be found the letters of Innocent I, of Jerome, and others,
concerning Pelagianism.   Here also belongs the 88th chapter of
Augustine's book on heresies, written or at least finished about 428,
which he sent to the Carthaginian deacon Quodvultdeus.   It forms
the commencement of the eighth volume of the above mentioned
edition of Augustine   His sermons preached against the Pelagians,
also here deserve to be mentioned, of which several have reached
us.   To these belong sermons 170, 174, 176, some parts of 293,
and particularly sermon 294 on infant baptism.   They are found in
the fifth volume of his works.

III. Public documents, (which are partly acts of councils and partly civil ordinances,) and the accounts and controversial pieces of cotemporary writers, as Prosper, Jerome, Mercator, Orosius, and others.
The Benedictines have furnished, in the appendix to the tenth part
of Augustine's works, a valuable collection both of public documents
and of accounts of cotemporary writers on this subject, and also of
extracts from their writings against the Pelagians

Thus much as to the sources.

CHAPTER III.

Commencement of the Controversy.

WITH success and much applause Pelagius and Caelestius had spread their doctrines in Italy and particularly at Rome, and no one had there found anything heretical in them. The contrary ensued, when they both came into Africa, about the year 411. The fame of Pelagius had resounded in Africa during his residence at Rome ; and Augustine had already become uneasy respecting what Pelagius might be teaching in regard to grace. Still he was not disposed to write against him till he should first have a personal interview, or should find proofs of the error in his writings De Gestis Pel. c. 22. The two friends had not been long in Africa before they were there regarded as heretics. They immediately repaired to Hippo, probably to visit the famous Augustine. But he was now at Carthage, busily engaged in the affair of the Donatists. Without tarrying at Hippo, they hastened to Carthage. Pelagius, however, staid here but a short time, where Augustine saw him only once or twice, as he affirms in the passage just cited. Leaving Caelestius behind, he sailed for Palestine. Just before his departure for the east, Pelagius wrote to Augustine. We have not the letter itself, but Augustine tells us (c 26) it contained much compliment. A polite answer was returned, which we have, Ep 146 c 27, 28. The illustrious bishop there calls the monk, who had before fallen into the suspicion of heresy with him, dominum dilectissimum et desideratissimum fratrem

Throughout the whole of doctrinal and ecclesiastical history, there is occasion enough for the humiliating but true remark, that it is not the mere conviction of the truth of doctrines, which has caused the contests, but selfish interest has commonly been mingled and has incited men to seek in their opponents for errors, which they have there soon found. The truth of this remark is confirmed in the present controversy.

Caelestius, who remained at Carthage, sought for admission there among the clergy and for the office of presbyter. Ep 157. c. 3. Ep. 175. This was against the interest of the clergy of the place, especially of Paulinus, a deacon from Milan, who was unwilling to

8

have any one promoted to the presbytery before himself. Paulinus had been deacon of the church at Milan under saint Ambrose, and was not deficient in authority and influence. He sought to ruin Caelestius This could be effected only by accusing him of heterodoxy. He therefore complained of him to Aurelius, bishop of Carthage. The bishop assembled a council at Carthage early in the year 412. Paulinus appeared as his accuser, and presented six or seven propositions, professedly drawn from his writings and alleged as heretical. These propositions, which Caelestius at least did not wholly disown nor condemn, were pronounced heterodox All hope of his becoming a presbyter at Carthage, was now blasted. He was condemned and excommunicated from the church.

At this council at Carthage against Caelestius, Augustine was not present. De Gestis Pel. II. Retractt II 33 Yet soon after, in the same year, he came out as a writer against the Pelagian doctrines, after having assailed them in preaching and conversation

But about what doctrine did the controversy begin ᵓ and what was the heresy first charged on Caelestius ᵓ This is the question which must here first be answered.

It is difficult to say whether the contest began with infant baptism or with original sin Some would conclude, from a passage in Augustine, that it began with infant baptism. " A short time ago, when I was at Carthage," says he, (De Pec. Meritis, III. 6,) " I heard the passing remark from some," (Augustine here forbears naming the Pelagians,) " that infants are not baptized for the forgiveness of sins, but as an act of consecration to Christianity" (ut sanctificentur in Christo) But this passage, strictly taken, will not authorize the conclusion. So much, however, is certain ; from the close connection between the doctrine of infant baptism with that of original sin, the controversy on both doctrines must have been nearly simultaneous [For if children just born were baptized for the remission of sin, then original sin appeared to be proved, since they could not have committed any actual transgression · and again, if original sin was proved, then children should be baptized for the remission of sin.] Accordingly we find Augustine treating of both doctrines together, in his first work, just as was done in the heresies alleged against Caelestius at the council at Carthage. These heretical propositions are reckoned either six or seven, accordingly as some of them are combined or divided. They are preserved by Augustine,

(De Gestis Pel. c 11, with which compare his work on original sin, c. 2, 3, 4 and 11,) and also by Marius Mercator in both his Commonitoria. Augustine and Mercator agree in the essentials, and the differences are unimportant. These propositions, in Mercator's account in his Commonitorium, presented to the emperor Theodosius II, (in which he appeals to the acts of the synod,) do not contain the declaration, that " infants, though unbaptized, are saved," which Mercator himself attributes to Caelestius in his other Commonitorium. The omission was the fault of the transcriber, as will appear from the seven particulars which Mercator thus mentions :

1. Adam was created mortal, and would have died, whether he had sinned or not.

2 Adam's sin injured himself only, and not the human race

3. Infants are born in the same state in which Adam was before the fall.

4. Men neither die in consequence of Adam's death or fall, nor rise again in consequence of Christ's resurrection.

5. Infants, though not baptized, have eternal life.

6. The law is as good a means of salvation (lex sic mittit ad regnum coelorum) as the gospel.

7. Even before the advent of Christ, there were men who lived without sin.

In his second Commonitorium, composed about the year 431, Mercator brings together the last two propositions, in the following manner . Men can live without sin, and easily keep God's commands, since, even before the advent of Christ, there were men without sin, and since the law is as good a means of salvation as the gospel. But as Mercator appeals directly to the synodical acts, in the first Commonitorium, presented to Theodosius and the Constantinopolitan clergy, it is proper to credit the second account. Orosius, in his Apology, p 591, quotes, as a position of Caelestius, the words, " man can live without sin, and easily keep God's commands," with the not unimportant addition " *if he will ;*" and subjoins, that it was condemned by the council at Carthage. It may be that this proposition, (which, if we place no emphasis on the phrase *if he will*, may be regarded as a corollary from the proposition " before Christ's advent, were men without sin,") was condemned by the synod ; though the authority of Orosius, which is of no weight, will not justify this assumption. It is not found among the charges by Paulinus, if we are to follow the account quoted from Mercator.

These charges, at least the second and third, Caelestius would neither directly disown nor condemn, as we see from the transactions respecting both, which are given by Augustine (De Pec Orig. c. 3, 4,) with protocol preciseness, from the Carthaginian acts. In respect to the second, that Adam's sin injured himself only and not his posterity, he replied, that he had said he had doubts on the doctrine of the propagation of sin by generation, for he had heard from presbyters of the orthodox church, that they varied from that doctrine Still he would gladly be taught by those to whom God had given better discernment. Respecting the third accusation, that new born infants are in the same state as Adam was before the fall, Caelestius answered, that concerning the propagation of sin by generation, he had already declared he had received it from some teachers of the orthodox church, that it was rejected by others ; but at all events, this proposition implied no heresy, but was a point about which various opinions might be held. But he had always said, that children needed baptism, and it was a duty to baptize them. This, however, was only a shift by which Caelestius endeavored to escape the reproach of heresy. How he explained himself on the other points of complaint, we know not, for the written statement which he presented to the synod, and which is frequently mentioned, is not extant. Augustine, however, informs us, (Ep. 157 § 22, De Pec Orig. c. 19, and C Jul III 3,) as does the synodical letter, (§ 6) that he was compelled, in view of infant baptism, to grant that redemption is necessary for children.

Against those charges in which were already contained, at least in the germ, the greater part of the doctrines on which Pelagius and Caelestius' afterwards came into controversy with Augustine, an equal number of opposite propositions were now declared as orthodox at the Carthaginian synod. This is certainly the import of the rather dark words of Mercator in his Commonitorium (Ap. p. 69), De quibus omnibus capitulis, etc.

CHAPTER IV

The Pelagian doctrine on baptism, and particularly on infant
baptism ; and Augustine's doctrine on the same

The doctrine of infant baptism was, therefore, as we have seen, either the first on which the controversy began, or at least one of the first. We shall begin with this.

That the doctrine of the Pelagians on infant baptism, differed from the Augustinian theory in an essential point, is certain. But it is really difficult to show definitely in what the Pelagian view consisted ; for according to existing accounts, the Pelagians expressed themselves diversely as to the object of baptism. From the passage already adduced (De Peccat. Mer. III. 6,) it appears that some Pelagians, (whether Pelagius and Caelestius themselves, is not certain,) had maintained, that children were not baptized for the forgiveness of sins, but as an act of christian consecration. In the same piece, (I. 17, 34,) Augustine speaks of those whom he plainly enough distinguishes from Pelagius and Caelestius and the other Pelagians, who conceded that the pardon of sin is the object of infant baptism, but who came, by a singular conceit, to ascribe actual sins to newly born infants which were to be remitted through baptism. That there were people, in the time of Augustine, who thought so unphilosophically as even to ascribe sins as well as merits of their own to small children, is seen from a letter written by Alypius and Augustine to Paulinus in the year 417. Ep. 186 c 4. It may be, that these people called themselves Pelagians and were inclined to favor Pelagianism in other points, as this might be inferred from the same epistle ; but this doctrine of theirs must not be called Pelagian, since Pelagius no more acknowledged it than did Caelestius and Julian. Augustine himself says of Pelagius (De Pec. Orig. 21,) that he saw that small children, dying without baptism, had committed nothing wrong, and hence he did not dare to say they had gone to eternal death. Caelestius granted to the synod at Carthage, that redemption is needful for children, and that baptism is therefore indispensable for them ; but the forgiveness of sins, as Augustine adds, he would not any more clearly declare. De Pec. Mer I. 34, 36. Julian finally even spoke against that doctrine (Op. Imp. I. 54), since he acknowledged no "merit of acts" in children, nor either "praise" or "crime of will."

They made a familiar distinction, (which Augustine mentions in his first work against the Pelagians, just quoted, and to which he frequently refers,) between salvation or eternal life, and the kingdom of heaven   The former with them was salvation in general, the latter, the salvation of Christians   The first could be gained by the unbaptized, the last, only by the baptized   and the object of baptism was to make men partakers of the kingdom of heaven, the salvation of Christians.   In this way, after the example of several of the fathers, they believed they had found a point of reconciliation between the orthodox idea which attributed such importance to infant baptism, and the shocking idea which lies in the damnation of the unbaptized children of Christians, and of all who are not Christians, even those most esteemed for their virtues.   The great value of baptism thus remained secure, and yet the entrance to salvation was not closed against such as were not christian.   " But they object," (it is said I. 18,) " and believe they have presented something worthy of attention and examination, when they assert, that infants receive baptism, not for the forgiveness of their sin, but that they who have not the spiritual sonship, may be created in Christ and become partakers of the kingdom of heaven "   And in the same work (20), " they are startled at the declaration of the Lord, that no one who is not born again can see the kingdom of God.   When he explains this, he says, if one is not born of water and the spirit, he cannot enter the kingdom of heaven.   And hence they venture to attribute salvation and eternal life to unbaptized infants as a reward of innocence ; but, as they are not baptized, they are excluded from the kingdom of heaven   A new and singular supposition, just as though there could be salvation and eternal life out of the heritage of Christ, out of the kingdom of heaven '"   Here we see, then, what brought them to the admission of this famous distinction.   The Pelagians could not admit the damnation of unbaptized children.   It was contrary to all moral feeling.   Actual transgressions they could not have committed, and original sin, the Pelagians denied.   Again, they had doubts about promising the kingdom of heaven to the unbaptized, for Christ had said, Whoever is not born again of water and the Spirit, shall not enter the kingdom of heaven.   It was from this dilemma, as will afterwards be shown, that the very untenable distinction between eternal life and the kingdom of heaven, was to free them. Comp Sermo 294.) Pelagius, indeed, at the synod of Diospolis, 415, would not own the proposition as his, that " infants, though not baptized, have eternal life." Pelagius may not have expressed himself in exactly this definite way, as he was not generally fond of stating his doctrines in direct contradiction to the assertions of his opponent, (De Pec. Orig. 18); still the proposition in the sense intended, is altogether Pelagian, since the Pelagians, as we shall soon see, by no means admitted the damnation of unbaptized infants ; nor could they, since they did not admit Augustine's doctrine of original sin.

But subsequently the Pelagians, compelled by the objections of their opponent, Jerome, who reproached them with a departure from the commonly received symbol of faith, conceded the object of infant baptism to be the remission of sins, only they denied that original sin was thereby forgiven them. Hence they referred the remission of sins, not to sins already committed, but to such as would afterwards be committed by the children baptized. In the remarkable confession of faith which Caelestius presented for his justification to the Romish bishop Zosimus, 417, it is said : " We profess, that according to the rule of the catholic church and by the import of the gospel, children ought to be baptized for the forgiveness of sins, because the Lord has decided that the kingdom of heaven can be given only to the baptized. Since the powers of nature are not adequate to this, it must be conferred by the free gift of grace. But the baptism of children for the forgiveness of sins, does not allow me, on that account, to maintain any transmission of sin by generation, (peccatum ex traduce).—That confession is necessary, that we may not seem to adopt different sorts of baptism " De Pec. Orig. 5, 6.— Also in the confession of Pelagius, it is said . " We adopt *one* baptism, which, as we say, ought to be administered in the same words to children as to adults." Still more plainly did he declare himself in a conference with Melania and others, which Augustine mentions (De Gratia Christi, 32), viz that children receive baptism for the forgiveness of sins ; but in which he entered no further into the nature of those sins. But in his letter to Innocent, with which he accompanied that confession, he complains of being calumniated, as though he denied baptism as a sacrament for children, and promised the kingdom of heaven to some without the redemption of Christ. He had, however, heard of one heretic so wicked as not to maintain

this. Ib. 30. De Pec Orig 18. "They say," writes Augustine to
Sixtus, 418, (Ep 194 c 10,) "that the children indeed answer truly by the mouth of those who hold them, that they believe in a forgiveness of sins, but not because they are to be forgiven *them*, but
because they believe that in the church sins are to be forgiven in
baptism to those in whom they are found, and not to those who have
none. And therefore they did not mean that they were so baptized
for the forgiveness of sins as if there were occasion for redemption
to those who, according to their opinion, have no sin, but because
they, although without sin, are baptized with a baptism by which the
forgiveness of sin is imparted to every sinner " Ep. 193 c. 2)

With the distinction which the Pelagians admitted between salvation in general and the salvation of Christians, they were consistent
in presenting " the adoption of children among the sons of God," as
the object of baptism. Contra Duas Epp Pelagg II 6, it is said :
" Although you deny that they have original sin which is forgiven
in baptism ; yet you by no means deny that by that bath of regeneration, the adoption of the sons of men to sons of God, follows ;
nay, you expressly approve it " Compare the same work, IV. 2,
where the opinion is quoted from the second letter of the Pelagians,
" that baptism is necessary for every age, whereby every creature
may be adopted among the children of God, not because they derive anything from their parents which must be expiated (sit expian-
dum) by the bath of regeneration " In reference to this, they could
say, " that by baptism men are perfectly regenerated," as was cus-
tomary. Ib IV. 7.

But the manner is very remarkable in which Julian speaks (according to Op Imp. I. 53, 54) concerning the baptism both of adults
and children. According to this main passage, the Pelagians held
baptism to be salutary for every age, and heaped everlasting curses
on those who were not of this opinion   In that passage Julian says ·
" We therefore so strongly hold the grace of baptism to be useful to
all ages, that we would smite with an eternal anathema all who do
not think it necessary even for small children (ut cunctos qui illam
non necessariam etiam parvulis putant, eterno feriamus anathemate).
But we believe this grace" (he here calls baptism a grace) " rich in
spiritual gifts, which grace, abounding in benefits and venerable for
its powers, effects a cure. according to the kinds of infirmity and the
diversities of human condition, by a single virtue comprising both

remedies and positive benefits. When applied, it is not to be changed according to the circumstances,* for it now dispenses its benefits according to the capacity of the recipients. For as all the arts, instead of being increased or diminished according to the diversity of the materials on which they are exercised, remain always the same, so also, according to the apostle, there is one faith, *one* baptism; but the operations are various. This grace, which washes away the spots of wickedness, does not conflict with justice. It produces no sins, but it purifies from sins. It forgives the guilty, but it makes not the innocent guilty. For Christ, who is the redeemer of his work, by continual manifestations of grace increases the benefits towards his image; and those whom he had made good by creation, he makes better by renovation and adoption. Whoever therefore thinks that this grace" (baptism), " by which the guilty obtains pardon, by which we are spiritually enlightened, are adopted as children of God, made citizens of the heavenly Jerusalem, sanctified, placed among the number of Christ's members, and made partakers of the kingdom of heaven, is to be denied to any one, deserves the malediction of all the righteous.—Thus have I, in this confession, reproved on the one hand those who suppose baptism not needful for children, and on the other you who dare to assign it an import that stains the righteousness of God. [I protest that I hold no otherwise than that this mystery, baptism, should be administered at every age in the same words in which it was instituted, without being changed by the variety of circumstances; that by it, a sinner from a wicked becomes a perfectly good man, but an innocent person who has no evil of his own will, becomes from a good a better person, that is, a best (optimum).] Both indeed become members of Christ by baptism; only the one had before led a wicked life, the other was of an uncorrupted nature."—With this may be compared another development of Julian's, in which he exhibits the differences of the Pelagian and the Augustinian views from each other. " That we must all be regenerated by baptism, we testify by word and deed. But we do not baptize for the purpose of freeing from the claim (jure) of the devil; but that those who are the work of God, may become

---

* This refers to the " one baptism" in Pelagius' confession of faith. [Both he and his followers denied that they had any occasion for changing the formula of baptism in the case of infants, as will be seen in the sequel —TR]

his children (pignora) ; that those who are born inferior (viliter), but not punishable (noxie), may be regenerated preciously (pretiose) and not blasphemously (calumniose) ; that those who have come forth from God's plastic tuition, may be still further advanced by his mysteries ; and that those who bear the work of nature, may attain to the gifts of grace, and that their Lord who has made them good by creation, may make them better by renovation and adoption '' Op imp V 9.

Here we may introduce what Augustine, in his book on heresies, points out as heretical in the Pelagian doctrine on infant baptism. In the 88th heresy, he says . " The Pelagians maintain, that infants are so born without any shackles whatever of original sin, that there is nothing at all to be forgiven them through the second birth, but that they are baptized for the purpose of admission into the kingdom of God, through regeneration to the filial state ; and therefore they are changed from good to better, but are not by that renovation freed from any evil at all of the old imputation. For they promise them, even if unbaptized, an eternal and blessed life, though out of the kingdom of God."

The passages now quoted, which might easily be increased by those of like import, will place the reader in a condition to judge for himself how manifold is the importance which the Pelagians attributed to baptism in general and to infant baptism in particular , and with what propriety they could say, that God, by a treasure of ineffable benefits, anticipates the will of the child; and how limited are the representations which are commonly made of the Pelagian theory in this respect.—From these passages, it follows,

1. That the Pelagians, in respect to adults whom they cannot easily acquit of actual sin, concede that *they* obtain the pardon of sin through baptism The author of the Hypomnesticon,* (commonly, Hypognosticon,) V. 8, admits that the Pelagians expressly maintain, that " adults are baptized for the pardon of sins, because they can sin by the use of freewill " Hence Julian also could say, in a letter ascribed to him " We condemn those who say that baptism does not remove all sins, for we know that a perfect purification

---

* A work in six books, directed more particularly against Julian, though without naming him, and written about the year 419, probably by pope Sixtus while a presbyter at Rome, and in compliance with Augustine's request See Augustine's Works, XII 251 —Tr

is conferred by the mysteries." C. Duas Epp. Pel. I 23   Op. Imp.
II 108

2 The object of infant baptism, (which they granted was attained
by adults through baptism, in connection with pardon,) they placed
in this, that the baptized were thus consecrated to christianity   " In
addition to its natural good," says Julian, " comes also the blessing
of sanctification " C. Jul. VI 17   But this consecration to christianity must not be referred, as is often done, merely to a reception to
the church, as if the Pelagians had regarded infant baptism as only
a ceremony of initiation into christianity.   They regarded it, even
from the first, as a sacrament, by which those who receive it obtain
a higher blessing, the salvation of Christians   For in that first piece
of Augustine against them, in which he says that they regard " sanctification in Christ" as the object of infant baptism, it is also mentioned, that they consider children as becoming partakers of the
kingdom of heaven by baptism   The " sanctification in Christ,"
was therefore with them the communication of the benefits which
christianity imparted, and to which " spiritual illumination" also belongs, and is perfectly synonymous with participation in the kingdom of heaven, " adoption among the sons of God, renovation," and
the attainment of a better condition.   But,

3. In process of time, the Pelagians, as well Pelagius and Caelestius as Julian, (that they might not destroy the unity of baptism, nor
use one form of baptism for adults and another for infants,) expressly admitted, that children too are baptized for the remission of sins.
This they could always do in accordance with their theory of baptism.   For as they held to but one form of the sacrament, by which
all who received it became partakers of the benefits of christianity,
the pardon of sins could not be excluded But as they did not and
could not rationally admit actual sin in infants, they referred this
pardon, not to sins which the children *had* committed, but to such
as they would at some time commit after baptism   The author of
the Hypomnesticon (l c) makes the Pelagians say, that " children
are baptized only for the purpose of their adoption as children of
God   For grace finds in them something to adopt ; but the fountain finds nothing to wash away.   They are immersed for the pardon of sins, merely in respect to the formula of the symbol, that the
received custom may be observed."

4. The Pelagians always denied the necessity of baptism, as well

for children as adults, in the sense that original sin would thereby be
pardoned, and that the unbaptized would be eternally punished for
original sin from which they were not freed by baptism. "Since
Jesus did not declare, say they [the Pelagians], If one is not born
of water and the spirit, he shall not have eternal life ; but only, He
shall not enter the kingdom of heaven, therefore children must be
baptized, that they may be with Christ in the kingdom of God, where
they will not be if not baptized ; although, if dying without baptism,
they will have eternal life, because they are shackled with no fetters
of sin. De Pec. Mer. I. 30. This is also set forth by Augustine as
the exact point of strife between him and the Pelagians in this view.
"The Pelagians do not deny the sacrament of baptism to infants ;
and they do not promise the kingdom of heaven to any without the
redemption of Christ —But it is objected to them, that they will not
own that unbaptized children are subject to the condemnation of the
first man, and that original sin passes over to them, from which they
must be cleansed by regeneration" (baptism) ; " while they maintain that they are to be baptized only for the attainment of the kingdom of heaven, just as if, out of the kingdom of heaven, those could
have anything but eternal death who cannot have eternal life without
partaking of the body and blood of the Lord.) This is objected to
them in respect to the baptism of children.—That children cannot
enter the kingdom of heaven without baptism, they have indeed never denied. But the question does not respect this ; but the question is respecting purification from original sin in the baptized." De
Pec. Orig. 17, 18, 19 Comp C Duas Epp Pel I. 23.

This is the Pelagian doctrine on baptism. The Augustinian doctrine is quite different, and may easily be presented, as Augustine
discloses it with great clearness It may be reduced to the following points

1 On baptism in general, Augustine thus explained himself. He
ascribed to it such an efficacy as to free the baptized from the imputation of all sin, as well original sin (by which, according to the
Augustinian theory, man in his natural state is subject to the devil),
as from actual sins here committed, whether wilful or not, and whether of thought, word, or deed The baptized triumphs over the allurements and temptations of sensual passions, and his prayer for
the pardon of sins is heard. He obtains salvation. Nay, at a future
day, by a resurrection from all evil and therefore from all base pas-

sions and the infirmity which here always cleaves to him, he shall
become completely free, so that he can never more sin   For the
body, also, baptism has a sanctifying effect, so that, through the pardon of sins, not only is it no longer subjected to the burden of all its
past sins, but not even to the sensual lust that is in it, although its
corruption, which burdens even the soul, will not here be removed.
Thus fully did Augustine declare himself on baptism. C Duas Epp.
Pel. I. 14. III. 3. C. Jul. II 5. VI. 13, 14, 18. De Pec. Orig. 40.
The guilt (reatus) of concupiscence is forgiven through baptism by
which the pardon of all sins is obtained, so that it will not be reckoned as sin, although for this life it remains in its effect. De Nupt
et Conc. I. 26.   Not only all sins, but absolutely all evil to the
man, were to be removed by the laver of holy baptism, by which
Christ purifies his church that he may present it to himself without
spot or wrinkle, though not indeed in this world, but in the future.
At the resurrection was to ensue a perfect deliverance from sensual
concupiscence. /The sins of believers were to be pardoned through
baptism, as well those committed before the rite as those committed
afterwards from weakness or ignorance. Without baptism, neither
would sorrow, nor the daily prayer for the pardon of sins, nor rich
alms and benefactions avail anything I 33, 34] Baptism is an impartation (dispensatio) of the grace of Christ, which all require who
need deliverance from the power of the devil, redemption, pardon,
salvation, illumination] De Pec Mer I. 26   According to Augustine, baptism has therefore a very comprehensive advantage. By
this only can a man enjoy the fruits of Christ's redemption ; or, (as
he well expressed himself, from the immediate connection in which
the supper stood with baptism, in his time, at least in the west,*) by

* That in the west, the eucharist was given even to children directly after
baptism, in Augustine s time, may be seen from several passages in his
works, as Op Imp 11 30). The letter of the Romish bishop Innocent 1, to
the council at Mila, refers to the same practice, and is found among Augustine's letters, Ep 182   Hence those passages of scripture which speak of
the eucharist and its benefits, Augustine could also apply to baptism, because this together with that formed as it were but one act, and he could attribute the same effects to the eucharist that he ascribed to bapt.sm C Duas
Epp. Pelagg. IV 4 De Pec Mer I 24   But the condition of salvation he
connected appropriately, not with the supper, but with baptism, for, according to Augustine's idea of the mystical affinity of baptism with the eucharist, baptism made the man already a member of Christ's body and a parta-

it he participates in the flesh and blood of Christ. C Duas Epp. Pel. I.
22. By it, his death proves a blessing to him. " Though Christ has
died but once, yet he nevertheless dies for every one, when the individual, of whatever age he may be, is baptized into his death ; that
is, the person is then profited by the death of him who was without
sin, when himself, being baptized into his death, is dead unto sin,
whereas he was before dead in sin " In Augustine's view, baptism
was the means, not only of obtaining the pardon of all sin, but of
being freed from all evil.

2 The object of infant baptism in particular, was in his view to
free from the imputation of original sin and from the power of the
devil, into which man came by Adam's sin.   According to the
church formulary, children were baptized " for the remission of
sins."   Actual sin (peccatum proprium), new born children could
not commit   It is therefore original sin which they are forgiven,
through baptism, and by which the devil is expelled from them.
They are therefore blown upon and exorcised, and likewise renounce him.   The grace of God is imparted to them in baptism in
a mysterious manner   The exhibition of his doctrine on infant baptism, is one chief object of Augustine's first piece against the Pelagians   " As children," says he (De Pec. Mer. I. 19), " are subject
to no sins of their own life, the hereditary disease in them is healed
by his grace who makes them well by the laver of regeneration.—
But who does not know, that what the infant obtained through baptism, profits him nothing in riper years, provided he does not believe,
nor keep himself free from forbidden passions ?   But if he dies after
baptism, the imputation to which he was subjected by original sin,
is forgiven, and he will be perfected in that light of truth which illuminates the righteous in the presence of the Creator." " Children
born of parents ever so holy and righteous, are not free from the imputation of original sin, if not baptized in Christ." III. 12.   " Whoever is carnally born of this disobedience of the flesh, this law of sin
and death, must be spiritually born again, that he may not only be
introduced into the kingdom of God, but also be freed from the condemnation of sin.   They are therefore as truly born in the flesh
subject to the sin and death of the first man, as they are regenerated

ker of the body and blood of Christ Ep 186 c 8 De Pec. Mer I 20, and
the note of the Benedictines on the passage III 4

in baptism to a connection with the righteousness and eternal life of the other man." I. 16. " By baptism, the chain of guilt (reatus) is broken, by which the devil held the soul ; and the partition is broken down by which he separated man from his maker." I. 39. " As the necessity of infant baptism is admitted by them, who cannot rise up against the authority of the whole church, which has doubtless come through Christ and the Apostles ; so must they likewise admit that children need the benefits of the Mediator that, being cleansed by the sacrament and the charity of believers, and thus incorporated with the body of Christ, which is the church, they may be reconciled with God, may become alive in him, well, free, redeemed, enlightened. From what else are they redeemed but the death, the vice, the imputation, the subjection, the darkness of sin ? Now, since of their age, they have committed no sin in their own life, there remains only original sin " I 26. " Christ infuses the most hidden grace of his spirit in a secret manner into the children " I. 9. Hence Augustine makes the change of man's nature to commence in baptism (II. 27) ; and hence he says (Ep. 187), that the Holy Ghost dwells in baptized children, though they are not conscious of it.

In other works, Augustine frequently recurs to his theory of the object of infant baptism But it is only his doctrine of the power of the devil as dispelled by baptism, that is more fully developed and presented in them He speaks thus, De Nupt. et Conc. I. 20 : " The power of the devil is really exorcised from infants, and they also renounce it by the heart and mouth of those who carry them to baptism, since they cannot by their own, by which they, delivered from the power of darkness, may be transferred into the kingdom of their Lord. Now what is it in them by which they are held in the devil's power until delivered by Christ's baptism ? what, but sin ? For the devil finds nothing else by which he can subject human nature to his sway, which the good Author had instituted right But infants have committed no sin of their own in their life. Hence there remains original sin, by which they are captive under the power of the devil, if they are not delivered by the laver of regeneration and the blood of Christ, and pass into the kingdom of their redeemer, the power of their jailer being frustrated and ability being given them of becoming the children of God, who were the children of this world." In the same work (II. 18) he says . " From this true and well grounded apostolic and catholic faith, Julian has departed with the

Pelagians, since he does not think that those who are born are under the power of the devil ; so that infants are not to be brought to Christ that they may be delivered from the power of darkness and brought into his kingdom. And so he impeaches the church, spread throughout the whole world, in which everywhere all infants, who are to be baptized, are blown upon simply that the prince of this world may be cast out, by whom the vessels of wrath are necessarily possessed as born from Adam, if they are not born again in Christ and transferred into his kingdom as made vessels of mercy through grace." Com. De Pec. Orig. 40, Op. Imp. II. 224, and countless other passages — Augustine also indeed expresses himself thus ; in baptism " they renounce this world," which with him must be synonymous with the renunciation of the devil, since he considered the devil as the prince of this world " The reprobate inheritance which comes from Adam, is renounced through the grace of Christ, when the world is renounced, where the children of Adam are necessarily subjected to a grievous yoke, and not indeed unrighteously, from the day they come forth from their mother to the day of burial in the mother of of all. Hence the holy mysteries show clearly enough what is done when the infants renounce." Op. Imp. III. 42.

Thus Augustine explained himself as to the object of infant baptism. It has therefore a necessary effect to purify from sin, and every child that dies after baptism and before the use of reason, and so before pollution by wilful sins, must inherit salvation. " Children who can neither will nor refuse either good or evil, are nevertheless compelled to be holy and righteous when, struggling and crying with tears against it, they are regenerated by holy baptism. For doubtless, dying before the use of reason, they will be holy and righteous in the kingdom of God through grace, to which they come, not by their ability (sua possibilitate), but by necessity." Op. Imp. V 64. Grace once attained can be lost again only by special wickedness in advancing years. Ep 93 2

3 But if baptism is the absolute condition of pardon and salvation, it follows, that the unbaptized cannot be saved, nor escape the punishment of the future world. Hence all christian children, dying before baptism, as well as all the heathen, even those most highly valued for their virtues, must be eternally doomed.

This inference is of such a kind that every other part of his whole system, ought to have been given up, simply to avoid a consequence so strikingly severe and so injurious to the justice of God. But Augustine was, on the one hand, far too obstinate to renounce his position of the absolute necessity of baptism to salvation, and on the other, far too consistent to deny any conclusion which necessarily flowed from that position And if this consequence was not adduced by the Pelagians against the soundness of his view of the object of infant baptism, he himself recognized it. For a while, it may have pained him to admit the damnation of all christian children, as he shows in several passages of his writings For example he says (De Pec. Mer. I 16), we may justly conclude that infants dying without baptism, will be in the mildest punishment (in mitissima damnatione) , and (Ep. 186. c 8) they will be punished more lightly (tolerabilius) than those who have committed sins of their own. Still he says (De Pec Mer. I 28), in opposition to the eternal life of the Pelagians, " there is no middle place, so that he who is not with Christ, must be with the devil " He says (III. 4), " as nothing else is done for children in baptism but their being incorporated into the church, that is, connected with the body and members of Christ, it follows, that when this is not done for them, they belong to perdition ;" and according to the above passage from Ep. 186, they will be punished with eternal death He maintains (De Anima IV. 11) that those condemned to eternal death, are condemned not merely for known sin, but, if they as children have not committed such sin, for original sin According to Augustine, therefore, christian children, dying unbaptized, do not escape the positive punishment of Adam's sin in the eternal life He says (C. Jul VI. 3) that unbaptized children, according to Mark 16: 16, are condemned because they believe not Comp. Ep. 217. c 5 Faith with him was the condition of salvation , and unbelief makes children of the devil. C Duas Ep. Pelagg. III 3. But in baptism, according to Augustine's theory, (which need not here be regarded as further differing from the other, as there was no contest between him and the Pelagians on this point), the church believed for the children; or the children themselves believed " by the hearts and mouths of those who presented them," whom he considered as the representatives of the church, as he says in the above cited passage (C Jul VI. 3), and also as in other places, and appeals to the consent of the Pelagians on the point. Comp Epist. 193. c. 2. 194 c. 10 In like manner he also ascribes to the children the penitence which precedes faith and

10

is alluded to in " the renunciation."—" If the child," he further says
(Op Imp III. 199), " is not delivered from the power of the devil
but remains under it, why dost thou wonder, O Julian, that he, who
is not allowed to enter the kingdom of God, should be with the devil
in eternal fire ?" etc.   With this is also to be compared Ep. 215,
where he shows, that unbaptized children, who have as little of sins
as of merits of their own, are condemned for original sin ; but adults,
who use their free will and add their own to the original sin, will be
punished, not only for 'original sin, but also for their actual transgressions

The doom of the heathen is very summarily conceded by this
christian bishop.   Those who never heard anything of Christ, and
whose ignorance was not culpable, he nevertheless admits must burn
forever in hell.   " That ignorance also which does not pertain to
those who are unwilling to know, but to those who are as it were
honestly ignorant, excuses no one so far that he is not to burn in eternal
fire (sempiterno igne non ardeat), although he has not believed because he has not heard at all what to believe ; but perhaps he will
burn the more gently (mitius).   For it is not said without cause,
Pour out thy wrath on the nations that know thee not ; and that which
the apostle says, When he shall come in a flame of fire to execute
vengeance on them that know not God " De Gratia et Lib. Arb 3 *

This view of Augustine's, however, is somewhat mitigated, at least
at first sight, since, as we shall afterwards see, he allowed no real
virtues in the heathen, just because they did not believe   Hence
God would be unrighteous, said he, were he to admit any to his kingdom but the truly righteous.   Still the heathen, who by nature had
lived conformably to the law, would be punished more tolerably ;
Fabricius more tolerably than Cataline, etc. C Jul. IV 3.   Nor did
he allow the heathen who lived righteously, to go unrewarded ; but
he limited the reward to this life ; a " temporal reward " See Vossius (Hist Pel. p 678), where some pertinent passages are collected
from Augustine's writings. Compare also Augustine's fifth book De
Civitate Dei, where he speaks of the temporal reward granted by
God to the Romans for their good morals.

4. From the condemnation that would befall the unbaptized, Au-

---

* Here, as in some other places, I have thought it better to give the entire
passage from Augustine, in the place of our author's more summary statement of his views.—Tr

gustine excepts however the believer among the worshippers of the true God before the time of Christ, and likewise the unbaptized martyrs.

Augustine allows the believers before Christ to have been saved by the faith by which we must be saved. " That faith has saved the righteous of old, which also saves us ; i. e faith in the mediator between God and men, the man Christ Jesus, faith in his blood, his cross, his death, and his resurrection." De Nat. et Gr 44. " The righteous of old lived according to the same faith as we do, since they believed that the incarnation, suffering, and resurrection of Jesus, *would* take place, which we believe have taken place." C. Duas Epp. Pel III. 4   Augustine must therefore have excepted *these* unbaptized persons from condemnation.   The unbaptized martyrs also received the bloody baptism by their death, which was the belief of the church before Augustine.   This was regarded as a substitute for water baptism.   Augustine explains himself on this point, in his work on the soul and its origin, I. 9   " Since it is said by Christ, If one is not born again of water and the Spirit, he cannot enter into the kingdom of God ; and in another place, Whoever has lost his life for my sake, shall find it again, no man becomes a member of Christ except by baptism into Christ or by death for Christ."

Earlier, however, in his controversial writings against the Donatists, Augustine had conceded, that faith and conversion of heart, supply the place of baptism in Christians, if, through distress of the times, recourse cannot be had to the rite itself: only there must be no contempt of the ordinance. De Baptismo contra Donatistas, IV. 22   A conclusion which doubtless Augustine would not subsequently have ventured to make, during the Pelagian controversy.

[NOTE. Strongly as some of the preceding citations may *seem* to militate against such a " conclusion," it still appears to me by no means certain that Augustine would not have continued to the end to make it ; and that too in perfect consistency with his bold and groundless assumption that no unbaptized child and no adult heathen can be saved. For however great the stress he lays on baptism as a *means* of regeneration, " a sacrament of remission," etc., he probably nowhere intends to *confound* it with regeneration or spiritual renovation. In the case of infants he seems all along to suppose, what so many others have since believed, that at the time of baptism or

very soon after, God's Spirit works the inward change on the heart
which is indicated as needful by the outward rite   This is apparent,
for instance, even from one of the passages cited in part by our author from a work written against the Pelagians, and therefore " during the controversy "   After asserting that " Christ's grace internally produces our illumination and justification, by the operation of
which the same apostle says, Neither is he that planteth anything
nor he that watereth, but God who giveth the increase," Augustine
immediately adds : " For by this grace [the inward working of his
spirit], Christ also incorporates baptized children with his own body,
who as yet certainly cannot imitate any one   As therefore he in
whom all are made alive, besides affording an example of righteousness for their imitation, gives also to believers the most occult grace
of his spirit, which he latently infuses also *into the children*, so he in
whom all die, besides being an example to all who voluntarily transgress the Lord's commandment, has infected in himself with the occult disease of his carnal concupiscence, all descending from his
stock " De Pec Mer I 9 —From such passages as this, it seems
evident that Augustine still held to the distinction he had before made
between the effect of mere baptism as an external rite, and the inward work of divine grace   This distinction he made as clearly
perhaps as anywhere, in his work on baptism, written against the
Donatists about the year 400   There and in other works, he prefers
to call baptism " the *sacrament* of grace," " the *sacrament* of the remission of sins," and " the sacrament of regeneration," instead of calling it directly grace and remission and regeneration—thus leaving the
way open for him to deny, as he does most expressly deny, the actual conferment of saving grace on those who do not worthily receive the ordinance.   See De Bap. V. 21.

But his views on the important subject of baptismal regeneration
and also on the possibility of being saved without baptism, are very
clearly displayed in the following remarkable passage from the same
work   I need only premise, that he considered both faith and baptism requisite to salvation in cases where they are practicable, but
that either is sufficient where the individual cannot have both.
Speaking of the thief on the cross, he says : " As the thief who by
necessity went without baptism, was saved because by his piety he
had it spiritually, so where the person is baptized, though by necessity destitute of that [faith] which the thief had, he is saved.   This

the whole body of the church holds as delivered to them, in as much as small infants are baptized who certainly cannot believe with the heart unto righteousness and confess with the mouth to salvation, as the thief could —As in Abraham the righteousness of faith preceded, and circumcision, the seal of the righteousness of faith followed, so in Cornelius the spiritual sanctification by the gift of the Holy Spirit, preceded, and the sacrament of regeneration by the laver of baptism, followed As in Isaac, who was circumcised the eighth day, the seal of the righteousness of faith preceded, and as he was the follower of his father's faith, the righteousness itself, the seal of which had preceded in his infancy, came after, so in baptized infants, the sacrament of regeneration precedes, and if they practise christian piety, conversion of heart, the mystery of which preceded in their body, will follow And as in the case of the thief, the mercy of the Almighty made up what was lacking of the sacrament of baptism, because it was lacking, not through pride or contempt, but necessity, so in infants dying after baptism, the same grace of the Almighty should be believed to make up for their not being able, from the want of age and not from a wicked will, to believe with the heart unto righteousness and to confess with the mouth unto salvation — From all this it appears that the sacrament of baptism is one thing, and the conversion of the heart another , but the salvation of a person is completed by both of them.   And if one of these be wanting, we are not to think it follows that the other is wanting, since one may be without the other in an infant and the other was with the first in the thief, God Almighty making up in each case what was not wilfully wanting." De Bap. IV 23, 24.

From this and other passages that might be adduced, there is probably more reason to suppose that Augustine wavered in respect to the *time* when the spirit changes the hearts of baptized children, than on either of the other points here brought to view —In respect to the salvation of even the best of the heathen, we may readily see where Augustine's principles would lead him, as they could have neither baptism nor faith in Christ of whom they had not heard ; and so of unbaptized infants —Tr.]

The contest which arose between the bishop of Hippo and the Pelagians in respect to baptism, (a matter in which Augustine had

already so directly controverted himself, during the vehement Donatist disputes,) concerned therefore more especially *infant* baptism ;
and the chief point in which their theories differed, was this, that
Augustine maintained that baptism is administered to infants for the
forgiveness of original sin, by which they are under the power of
the devil ; and that if this is not forgiven through baptism, they will
be eternally condemned ;—whereas the Pelagians rejected both these
positions, and assumed as the object of infant baptism, a higher degree of felicity, the salvation of Christians

On this point, many things were now put forth on both sides.
The Pelagians represented it as abominable, and prejudicial to the
justice of God, that infants, who had never sinned, should be eternally damned for another's sin.   Julian expressed himself very
strongly on the point. " The children, you say" (Augustine), " do
not bear the blame of their own but of another's sins.   What sort of
sin can that be ?—What an unfeeling wretch, cruel, forgetful of God
and of righteousness, an inhuman barbarian, is he who would make
such innocent creatures as little children, bear the consequences of
transgressions which they never committed, and never could commit ? God—you answer What God ? for there are gods many
and lords many, but we worship but one God, and one Lord, Jesus
Christ. What God dost thou make the malefactor ?   Here, most
holy priest and most learned orator, thou fabricatest something more
mournful and frightful than the brimstone in the valley of Amsanc-
tus, or the pit of Avernus —God himself, say you, who commendeth
his love towards us, who even spared not his own son, but hath given
him up for us all, he so determines ; he is himself the persecutor of
those that are born ; he himself consigns to eternal fire, for an evil
will, the children who, as he knows, can have had neither a good
nor an evil will," etc * Op Imp I 48. To an objection of this kind,
Augustine could answer nothing further than by appealing to his
theory of original sin, according to which all men have sinned in
Adam, and therefore belong to a condemned mass—to passages of
scripture which he interpreted in his own way—to the unsearcha-

---

* Had our author adduced this passage in full instead of abridging it somewhat, it would have appeared still more vituperative —Such a spirit as Julian here and elsewhere exhibits, is deserving of at least as deep moral censure as Augustine can merit for honestly holding to any of his severe doctrines —Tr.

bleness of God's decrees—and to the opinions of earlier fathers in the church.—But why some children die without baptism, and others not, Augustine declared to be indeed inexplicable. Yet it can be nothing unrighteous, he added, for there can be no unrighteousness with God. Here he took refuge in Paul's declaration—O, the depth of the riches both of the wisdom and knowledge of God De Pec. Mer. I. 21.

Again, Augustine replied to the Pelagians, What is that "eternal life" which you allow to children who die before baptism, if they do not go to heaven ? De Pec. Mer. I. 20, 28. To this Pelagius answered : " Where they do not go, I know, but where they do go, I know not." De Pec. Orig 21. " If one asks them whether the unbaptized, (who therefore are not fellow heirs with Christ and will not inherit the kingdom of heaven,) obtain at least the benefit of eternal felicity by the resurrection, they are sorely in difficulty and find no escape." De Pec Mer. I. 18. Hence Augustine playfully calls the " eternal life" of the Pelagians, locum aliquem *secundae* felicitatis. Op. Imp. I. 130.

And as his opponents found something unrighteous in one child's dying without baptism while another does not, if baptism is an indispensable condition of salvation, Augustine sought to put them into difficulty by the question, How is it right, then, that one child gains by baptism the salvation of Christians, and another, who has not received baptism, is excluded from the kingdom of God ? De Pec. Mer. I. 21, 30. Op. Imp. VI. 20. What merit have those infants who are received by baptism as children of God, acquired for themselves above such as die without obtaining this favor ? C Jul IV. 8. Why, (as Augustine more definitely expresses himself, C. Duas Epp. Pel., in order to foreclose all escape to the Pelagians,) why is one twin brother accepted by baptism as a child of God, and the other not ? " The unbaptized twin brother comes to you, and inquires softly, why he is separated from his brother's good fortune ? why he is punished with this bad lot, that, while the other is to be received as a child of God, he does not receive the sacrament which is needful to every age ? This objection was in fact of no small weight, and showed the untenableness of the distinction which the Pelagians made between " eternal life" and " the kingdom of heaven " Hence he could not be satisfactorily answered by them, since they admitted no unconditional predestination, and no irrespective grace of God ;

and so I find no attempt made to answer him. For it was justly
mentioned here, and in his work on predestination (13), that they
could not reply that, in the case of him who died before baptism,
God had regard to acts which he would have committed if he had
lived, since this sin cannot be considered as having taken place, and
of course cannot be punished   And as he remarks expressly, in the
next passage, that the Pelagians could not make this answer, and
had not made it, therefore the assertion (in Ep 194. c 9, written
about the year 418), which he adduces as Pelagian, viz. that
" God foresees in those he takes away, how each one would have
lived, if he had lived, and hence suffers him to die without baptism
who, he knows, would have lived badly ; while he does not, in this
way, punish in him the bad deeds he had done, but which he would
have done," is probably to be regarded as only a *possible* answer of
the Pelagians, which Augustine notices beforehand ; or, as Augustine asserts (c 10), that he heard this expression from Pelagians, it
may be considered as only a conceit of some Pelagians, minorum
gentium (of inferior order), and not of Pelagius himself, of Caelestius, and of Julian, the representatives of Pelagianism. For if they
could bring themselves to this hypothesis, they might just as well
allow infants, dying before baptism, to be eternally damned ; as with
this hypothesis, they might then, in like manner, defend the justice
of God   But that, on the question why this child dies before baptism, but that does not, and this is therefore saved but that is not, it
must by no means be answered, that God therein regards the life
which it would have lived in riper years, says Augustine in another
work not directed against Pelagianism   For if God has regard to
the good life any one would lead if he remained in life, so must he
also have had regard to the bad life any one would have led, and
must have damned him for it.   And yet it was said (Sap. 4 11) of
the early death of many a righteous person, " he was removed, lest
wickedness should change his mind." De Gen. ad Lit X. 16. Comp.
Ep. 217 c. 5 De Anima et ejus Origine, I. 12 III. 10.—Augustine
also remarked, that we elsewhere meet with appearances which we
know not how to reconcile with our ideas of God's justice, and where
we must take refuge in the incomprehensibility of God. How, for
instance, can we call it right, that the one, according to the above
quoted declaration of the Book of Wisdom, is taken away, so that
wickedness may not change his mind, but the other lives and be-

comes ungodly ! Would they not both go to heaven, if they were taken away ? etc. De Pec. Mer I. 21. Ep 194.

Against Julian, who represented renovation (innovatio) and adoption as the object of infant baptism, but would yet allow of no original sin, Augustine made this objection, How does Christ *renew* those whom he finds but just born, if they bring no *old* sin with them ? Op Imp. III. 151. This could prove at most, that the expression *innovatio* was not fitly chosen

Still more insignificant is that which Augustine suggested against Caelestius, who had granted, at the Carthaginian synod, that, as children should be baptized, redemption is also necessary for them. Although he would not declare himself expressly in regard to original sin, yet he conceded a redemption for children, and cramped himself not a little by the term *redemptio.* " For from what should children be redeemed, if not from the power of the devil, in which they could not be if they were not held by original sin ?" etc Ep 157. 22 —From the term redemption, there followed not necessarily the freeing from the power of the devil, in which mankind might be by original sin Also, in the Pelagian sense, a redemption could always find place, since baptism was to confer the benefits of christianity, and by the same to effect a deliverance from a less happy condition.

The Pelagians, moreover, found a difficulty in its being necessary for the children of baptized parents to be baptized for the forgiveness of original sin, and therefore that the original sin, which ought to be removed by baptism, should be propagated by baptized parents. " If a sinner," say they, " begets a sinner, so that the guilt of original sin must be remitted to the child, by the reception of baptism, so must also a righteous person beget a righteous " De Pec Mer. II 9. " If even his own sins do not injure the parent, after his conversion, how much less can they injure his child." II 27. " If the body of a baptized person is a temple of God, how can a human being be formed within it who is under the dominion of the devil ?" C Jul VI. 14.—Upon this, Augustine knew of much to reply, on his theory of concupiscence remaining in the baptized after baptism, the guilt of which is indeed removed, but itself still remains active. The righteous begets, not as *righteous*, but as *impelled by sensual lust*, which is never wholly removed The body of the mother is a temple of God through grace, but not by nature. He also sought, by

11

examples from the visible world, to render intelligible the possibility
that original sin should be propagated by the baptized. The fore-
skin, which is removed by circumcision, remains in those who are
begotten by the circumcised. The chaff, which is separated with so
much care, remains in the product that arises from the purified wheat.
Augustine also pressed the Pelagians with the like difficulty on their
own supposition, according to which christian children must be born
of christian parents, and therefore baptism is superfluous to them ;
for how could *they* still admit, that the sons of the baptized must be
baptized in order thereby to become Christians ? Ll. cc., De Pec.
Mer III 8, 9. Comp. serm. 294, which was preached at Carthage
not long after the composition of the first controversial piece by Augustine.

In this and similar ways, was the contest carried on by both sides,
respecting the object of infant baptism   Yet this question always
remained as only a secondary point.   The main thing with Augustine, was original sin, for which he believed a weighty argument to
be found in infant baptism. " Baptism, which is granted for the
remission of sins, has a false object, with those who have no sin "
De Praedest. Sanct. 13.   He ever used infant baptism only as an
argument to prove his main point, and therefore touched upon it only so far as it stood in connection with the doctrine of original sin.
This doctrine we may consider as peculiarly the central point of the
whole Augustinian system.   As Augustine would not relinquish this,
he could not acknowledge any other theory of infant baptism but the
one he held.   But again ; if the Pelagians would remain true to their
view of the uncorruptedness of man, with which Augustine's original
sin stood in such contrast, they could allow every other object of infant baptism to be valid except the Augustinian   But they always
had to regard baptism as a sacrament, and to assign it a higher object than that of consecration to christianity ; and they dared not deny the necessity of infant baptism, if they would not become offensive to their age.

With what interest, now, the doctrine of original sin was assailed
and defended, by the one side and the other, and objections were
received and encountered in defence, we may anticipate beforehand.

CHAPTER V.

Pelagian view of original sin. Opposite theory of Augustine on the same.

According to the Pelagian doctrine, there is absolutely no original sin, i. e. no sin which passes, by generation, from the first man to his posterity, and of which they have to bear the punishment. This is a main point in which Pelagianism differs from Augustinism, as is shown by all the memorials of those contests now extant In these, it is worthy of remark, that the Pelagians, when they speak of Augustine's original sin, instead of the term *original sin*, used by Augustine, employ rather the expression *natural sin* (peccatum naturale), or the expression *natural evil* (malum naturale, Op. Imp. I. 101), probably in order to render the more striking the contradiction that is involved in a *natural sin* And on this account, Augustine protested against this expression, and when it was used by the Pelagians, commonly substituted his own *peccatum originale* There may be, says he, indeed, a sin of nature (peccatum naturae), but not a natural sin (peccatum naturale) In a certain sense, however, he defended this term (Op. Imp. V. 9, 40), only he regarded the expression, *original sin*, as more definite, because by it, the idea of God being the author of any sin, is removed. Augustine employed the expression *original sin*, besides, as synonymous with *hereditary evil* (hereditarium vitium, Ep. 194 c. 6), and also originale vitium. Ep. 157. c. 3.

We have already seen, that it was brought as an objection to Caelestius at Carthage, that he denied original sin ; and that he did not directly deny the objection, though he would not condemn the doctrine. [But in his confession of faith already mentioned, he denied it flatly " A sin propagated by generation (peccatum ex traduce), is totally contrary to the catholic faith Sin is not born with man, but is committed afterwards by man It is not the fault of nature, but of free will.—The mystery of baptism must not be so interpreted as to imply, to the prejudice of the Creator, that evil is transferred by nature to man, before it is committed by him " De Pec. Orig 6.— That Pelagius also admitted of no original sin, in the sense declared,

is proved by his explanation of Paul's epistles, before composed at
Rome, in which he expressly refers that passage in Romans to the
imitation of Adam's sin, in which, according to Augustine's accepta-
tion, it is said, that in Adam all his posterity sinned. Afterwards,
however, (as he would not own as his those propositions which were
charged upon Caelestius, at the synod of Diospolis, but condemned
such as taught anything in that way, viz that " Adam would have
died, whether he had sinned or not · His sin injured himself only,
not his posterity   And newborn infants are in the same condition as
Adam was before the fall," De Pec. Orig. 11), he might indeed
consider Adam's death as a punishment for *himself*, though only as
a natural necessity for his *posterity*. [Respecting both the other propositions, he explained himself against his scholar, after that synod
(De Pec. Orig 15), and condemned the propositions, because Adam
did injure his posterity, in as much as he gave them the first example
of sin ; and because new born infants are so far in a different condition from that of Adam before transgression, that they cannot yet
perform what is commanded, but he could ; and they cannot yet use
that free intelligent will, without which no command could have been
given to Adam —A transfer of Adam's sin, and an imputation of it,
and consequently original sin, Pelagius did not admit, and did not
explain himself in favor of it at Diospolis   But Julian was most zealous, as appears from the passages already quoted respecting the object of baptism, against the assumption that man comes into the world
corrupted through Adam's sin, and loaded with its guilt and punishment.   (" We believe that God has made men, and without any fault
at all, full of natural innocence, and capable of voluntary virtues."
Op Imp III 82.)

    The Pelagian idea of original sin may be reduced still more defi-
nitely to the following propositions.

    1 A propagation of sin by generation, is by no means to be ad-
mitted. This physical propagation of sin, can be admitted only when
we grant the propagation of the soul by generation   But this is a
heretical error   Consequently there is no original sin ; and nothing
in the moral nature of man has been corrupted by Adam's sin.

    Besides the passages already adduced, the following may suffice
as proof, that this was a Pelagian tenet.

    In his commentary on Romans 7 8, Pelagius remarks : " They
are insane who teach, that the sin of Adam comes on us by propa-

gation (per traducem)." In another passage, (which indeed is not
now to be found in that very interpolated work, but which Augustine
quotes from it verbatim, De Pec. Mer III. 3), Pelagius says "The
soul does not come by propagation, but only the flesh, and so this
only has the propagated sin (traducem peccati), and this only deserves punishment. But it is unjust, that the soul born to-day, that
has not come from the substance of Adam, should bear so old and
extrinsic a sin" And the Pelagians discarded the propagation of
souls by generation, which seemed to lead to materialism, and assumed, that every soul is created immediately by God. In Pelagius's confession of faith, it is said "We believe that souls are given
by God, and say, that they are made by himself." From the first
book of Pelagius on free will, Augustine quotes the following declaration of his opponent (De Pec. Orig. 13) : "All good and evil, by
which we are praise or blameworthy, do not originate together with
us, but are done by us. We are born capable of each, but not filled with either. And as we are produced without virtue, so are we
also without vice ; and before the action of his own free will, there
is in man only what God made." But the transmission of sin (peccatum ex traduce), was most vehemently and keenly assailed by Julian who, on account of this assumption, gave Augustine the nick-
name of *Traducianus.* Augustine's second book against Julian, and
also the first book of his Imperfect Work, are filled with acute arguments of that Pelagian against the propagation of sin by physical
generation, to which Augustine could make no very pertinent reply.

2. Adam's transgression was imputed to himself, but not to his
posterity. A reckoning of Adam's sin as that of his posterity, would
conflict with the divine rectitude. Hence bodily death is no punishment of Adam's imputed sin, but a necessity of nature.

From the commentary of Pelagius on Romans, Augustine quotes
his words thus (De Pec. Mer. III. 3). "It can in no way be conceded that God, who pardons a man's own sins, may impute to him
the sins of another." In his book "on nature," Pelagius says :
"How can the sin be imputed by God to the man, which he has
not known as his own ?" De Nat. et Gr 30 —If God is just, (this is
amply shown by Julian, according to the first book of the Imperfect
Work), he can attribute no foreign blame to infants.—" Children
(filii), so long as they are children, that is, before they do anything
by their own will, cannot be punishable (rei)." Op. Imp. II. 42.—

" According to the Apostle, by one man, sin came into the world, and death by sin : because the world has regarded him as a criminal and as one condemned to perpetual death   But death has come upon all men, because the same sentence reaches all transgressors of the succeeding period ; yet neither holy men nor the innocent have had to endure this death, but only such as have imitated him by transgression " II. 66   The Pelagians, therefore, could regard the bodily death of Adam's descendants no otherwise than as a natural necessity. ⌈ And if Pelagius himself admitted that it may have been a punishment in the case of Adam, (as we should rather believe by his explanation at Diospolis, though a passage quoted by Augustine from the writings of Pelagius, is against this view, De Nat. et Gr. 21) ; yet his adherents were of a different opinion, and believed that Adam was *created* mortal.   But all must have agreed in this, that the bodily death which comes on Adam's *posterity*, is not a punishment of his sin, but a necessity of nature.' " The words—till thou return to the earth from which thou wast taken, for earth thou art and to earth shalt again return—belong not to the curse, but are rather words of consolation to the man   The sufferings, toils, and griefs shall not endure forever, but shall one day end.   If the dissolution of the body was a part of the punishment of sin, it would not have been said—thou shalt return to the earth, *for earth thou art ;* but, thou shalt return to the earth, *because thou hast sinned and broken my command.*" Op Imp. VI 27. ⌈" If therefore fruitfulness, according to the testimony of Christ (Matt. 22· 30) who instituted it, was produced in order to replace what death takes away, and this was ordained as the design of marriage before the fall, it is manifest that mortality has no respect to the transgression, but to nature, to which marriage also has respect "⌉ VI 30   " Adam himself, say the Pelagians, would have died, as to the body, though he had not sinned ; and hence he did not die in consequence of his guilt, but by the necessity of nature."   Aug. de Haer. c. 88, and in innumerable other places.

3. Now, as sin itself has no more passed over to Adam's posterity, than has the punishment of sin, so every man, in respect to his *moral* nature, is born in just the same state in which Adam was first created.

Augustine quotes (De Nat. et Gr. 21) from Pelagius's book, a passage in which it is said : " What do you seek ?   They [infants] are well, for whom you seek a physician. Not only are Adam's descendants no weaker than he, but they have even fulfilled more commands, since he neglected to fulfil so much as one." In the letter to Demetrias, Pelagius depicts the prerogatives of human nature, without making any distinction between Adam's state before the fall and after it. Take only the description of conscience, in the fourth chapter. "A good conscience itself decides respecting the goodness of nature. Is it not a testimony which nature herself gives of her goodness, when she shows her displeasure at evil?—There is in our heart, so to express myself, a certain natural holiness, which keeps watch, as it were, in the castle of the soul, and judges of good and evil."—"Human nature," says Julian (C Jul. III. 4) "is adorned in infants with the dowry of innocence." "Freewill is as yet in its original uncorrupted state, and nature is to be regarded as innocent in every one, before his own will can show itself." Op Imp II 20. According to Julian, the sinner becomes, by baptism, from a bad person a perfectly good one, but the innocent, who has no evil of his own will, becomes from a good a still better person. "That has corrupted *the innocence which he received at his origin*, by bad action; but this, without praise or blame of his will, has only what he has received from God his creator. He is more fortunate as, in his early and uncorrupted age, he cannot have corrupted the goodness of his simplicity. He has no merit of acts, but only retains what he has possessed by the good pleasure of so great an architect." I 54.

But with this Pelagian view of the uncorrupted state of man's nature, the admission of a moral corruption of men in their present condition, by the continued habit of sinning, stood in no contradiction. This Pelagius taught expressly. According to the eighth chapter of his letter to Demetrias, he explicitly admits, that, by the protracted *habit* of sinning, sin appears in a measure to have gained a dominion over human nature, and consequently renders the practice of virtue difficult. "While nature was yet new, and a long continued habit of sinning had not spread as it were a mist over human reason, nature was left without a [written] law, to which the Lord, when it was oppressed by too many vices and stained with the mist of ignorance, applied the file of the law, in order that, by its frequent admonitions, nature might be cleansed again and return to its lustre. And there is no other difficulty of doing well, but the long continued habit of vice, which has contaminated us from youth

up, and corrupted us for many years, and holds us afterwards so
bound and subjugated to herself, that she seems, in a measure, to
have the force of nature " Here Pelagius also mentions the bad education by which we are led to evil —But this habit of sinning, however, affects only adults, and that by their own fault. (According to
the Pelagian theory, man is *born* in the same state, in respect to his
moral nature, in which Adam was created by God.)

———————

This was the Pelagian doctrine on original sin.   On the contrary,
Augustine's theory was as follows.

1. Adam's sin has been propagated among all men, and will always be propagated, and that by sensual lust in procreation (concupiscentia), by which man in his natural state, is subjected to the
devil.

2. The propagation of Adam's sin among his posterity, is a punishment of the same sin   The sin was the punishment of the sin
The corruption of human nature, in the whole race, was the righteous punishment of the transgression of the first man. in whom all
men already existed

3. The other penalties of Adam's sin, bodily death, the toil of labor, the shame of nakedness, sensual lust, pains of parturition, etc.,
also came upon his posterity ; and, moreover, the physical punishment of Adam's sin, just as much as the moral, was a *positive* penalty.

4. And as not only Adam's sin as a punishment, but also the other
penalties came upon his posterity, there hence follows from it the
entire moral and physical corruption of human nature.   From that
source, every man brings into the world a nature already so corrupt,
that he is not only more inclined to evil than to good, but he can do
nothing but sin, and is, on this account, subject to the righteous sentence of condemnation.

5 This original sin, however, is nothing substantial, but is a quality of the affections (affectionalis qualitas), and a vice indeed (vitium), a weakness (languor)

This is Augustine's theory of original sin, which is seldom understood in its whole bearing.   It is contained in his first work against
the Pelagians, at least in the greater part of its grand principles,
though we must not deny, that it reached so perfect a form only in
the progress of the conflict.

That Adam's sin has passed over to his descendants by propagation, and not by imitation, as the Pelagians would have it, Augustine maintains in that piece (e g. De Pec. Mer. I 9), against the Pelagians ; and endeavors to prove this by the notable passage in Rom. 5: 12. Comp. Op. Imp II 57, where he says; " The race are propagated by generation, bringing original sin with them, since the vice propagates the vice, though God creates nature (vitio propagante vitium, Deo creante naturam) ; quam naturam conjuges, etiam bene utentes vitio, non possunt tamen ita generare ut possit esse sine vitio ;* which vice in the children He, who was born without the vice, removes,—Julian to the contrary notwithstanding " And, as consonant with this, Augustine says, " ut crederemus etiam semen hominis posse vitium de gignentibus trahere." C. Jul. VI. 7.—That this propagation is effected by " the lust of the flesh," is also set forth in De Pec Mer I 29. " He in whom all die,—has, with the secret, consuming poison of his fleshly lust, infected in himself all who come from his stock." I. 9 —This doctrine is fully and plainly presented in his two books De Nuptiis et Concupiscentia. Among other things, he says : " Sensual lust, which is expiated only by the sacrament of regeneration, propagates by generation† the bond of sin to posterity, if they are not freed from that bond by regeneration." I. 23. " By this fleshly lust—a daughter of sin, as it were, and, if complied with in base things, the mother of many sins—the progeny is subjected to original sin, if not regenerated in him whom the virgin conceived without that sensual passion , on which account, he alone was born without sin, when he condescended to be born in the flesh." I. 24 He therefore makes Christ an exception from original sin, because he was conceived by a virgin without this concupiscence. And for this reason, Christ himself was also free from it II. 5 ‡ Original sin propagates itself by concupiscence. Op. Imp

* Here, and in other passages that follow, I prefer to give Augustine's Latin, though Wiggers has seen fit to translate such passages in full for his German readers —Tr

† The connection shows, that we are here to read *generatione* not *regeneratione*

‡ He also excepted the soul of Christ from the *traducianism of the soul*, which he was inclined to adopt respecting the rest of men De Gen ad Lit X 19, 20 Comp Ep 164 c 7 190 c 11, where he leaves the propagation of the soul of Christ still doubtful, but declares it inadmissible to

VI. 22. [Hence Augustine could say of carnal generation, that it produces children of death, of wrath; that it holds man in bondage under the condemned origin, etc. De Pec. Mer. III. 2. De Pec. Orig. 38.]

This carnal lust, Augustine derives from the devil, and hence allows all men to be under the power of the devil, while in their natural state. A multitude of proof passages could be produced. "Whatever arises by means of this wound (lust) inflicted on the human race by the devil, is under the power of the devil. He plucks justly as it were, the fruit of his own tree; not because human nature is from him, (which comes only from God), but vice, which is not from God" De Nupt. et Conc. I. 23 "Sensual lust springs not from the Father, but from the world, whose prince is the devil." II. 5 ["Before spiritual regeneration, they, who are born of carnal intercourse, are under the dominion of the devil, because they spring from the concupiscence by which the flesh lusteth against the spirit," etc. C. Jul IV. 4. "That discord produced by concupiscence between the flesh and spirit, is attributed, by the orthodox to *the evil counsellor* and transgressing man" Op Imp. IV 27. Hence Augustine could say: "When passion conquers, the devil conquers; when passion is conquered, the devil is conquered" C. Jul V 7 — Therefore Augustine also speaks of wounds inflicted on human nature by the devil, and calls him directly a maimer Ep. 194. c 6. See also De Nupt et Conc. I. 23, as just quoted. And, in fine, the whole unhappy condition in which man is found since the fall, according to Augustine's theory, must have appeared to him as the work of the devil, because he regarded him as the seducer of the first man. Hence he said, e g. that the devil plunged men into (physical) death De Trin IV. 13. "Corruption is propagated by the persuasion of the devil, by which corruption all are born under sin." De Nupt. et Conc II 33.

The transfer of Adam's sin to his descendants, was, according to Augustine, a part of the punishment which God laid on Adam and his race for his transgression. Many passages may be adduced in proof, that this was Augustine's opinion. But in none could it be more plainly declared, than where it is said (Op Imp I 47) ["We must distinguish three things, sin, the punishment of sin, and that

---

doubt whether the soul of Christ received no sin from Adam   Christ purified it by receiving it.

which in such a manner is sin, that it is at the same time also the punishment of sin }—Of the third kind is original sin, which is so sin that it is also itself the punishment of sin; which is indeed in children just born, but begins to appear in them as they grow up and have the needful wisdom. Yet the source of this sin descends from the will of him that sinned. For it was Adam, and in him we all were. Adam perished; and in him we have all perished."* With this compare De Perfect. Justit. 4. "It is not merely a voluntary and possible sin from which one has the freedom to abstain, but even a necessary sin, from which he has not the freedom to abstain; which is not only sin, but also the punishment of sin." Op Imp. V. 59. "By the first pair, so great a sin was committed, that by it human nature was changed for the worse, an obligation (obligatione) of sin and a necessity of death being transmitted to posterity." De Civ Dei, XIV. 1 (In this sense, Augustine said, that God punished sins by sins. De Nat et Gr. 22. C. Jul. V. 3, in which he appeals to several passages of Scripture)

The most signal moral punishment of Adam's transgression, was therefore the sin itself, or the moral corruption, that passed over to his posterity, by which Adam was also punished in his descendants.†

Besides this, Augustine admitted several other punishments, moral as well as physical, which pertained to Adam's offence, and passed over to his posterity It is worth remarking here, that Augustine did not regard the physical punishment of sin as a natural consequence of Adam's transgression in eating the forbidden fruit, by which man's body has lost its original and excellent state. For he considered the fruit as not pernicious in itself—in a place of such great felicity, God could have planted nothing bad—but it was noxious only as being forbidden. De Civ. Dei, XIV 12 ‡ The physical punishment, Augustine regarded as a positive punishment, by which God would show man his authority. By that small command not to

* The last two sentences, Augustine borrowed from Ambrose, Lib. 7. in Luc XV 24 Comp Op Imp IV 104

† Not, however, that we are punished for the sin of Adam as a separate individual from us, as we shall by and by see.—TR.

‡ Some have maintained, that the fruit of the tree of knowledge, was literally a poison, infecting the whole race and inflaming our bodily passions so as to render them ungovernable, and that the tree of life afforded a literal remedy. See Storr and Flatt.—TR.

eat of the forbidden tree, God designed to show his sovereignty.
And by it, also, obedience was made a duty, which is the mother of
all other virtues. By the transgression of the command, therefore,
the principle of all virtue was abandoned "In this command, obedience was commended; and this virtue is, in a measure, the mother and protector of all virtues, in an intelligent creature." Augustine knew no other way of explaining how such great consequences,
even to the physical state of man, could arise from the single sin of
Adam "As by that sin, so by *the curse*, has the whole nature been
changed for the worse." C Jul. III 26   Still he could always say,
even in respect to the physical state of man, that man is corrupted
"by his own vice," or "by the vice by which he voluntarily fell"
(vitio quo voluntate prolapsus est, De Pec Mer II 4), in as much
as Adam sinned from freewill, and the physical corruption of man
was connected with Adam's transgression, as a positive punishment.)

But the moral punishment of Adam's sin, was also a *positive* punishment of it [An entire moral ruin of man, did not follow from the
nature of Adam's transgression, but God had annexed this to it as a
punishment, and it was made a condition by the prohibition. God
punished sin with sin. The sinfulness (vitiositas) of the whole human race, is penal (poenalis).) "If Christ therefore is the one in
whom all are justified, because not the mere imitation of him makes
them just, but grace regenerating by the Spirit; so is Adam therefore the one in whom all have sinned, because not the mere imitation of him makes them sinners, but the punishment generating by
the flesh (poena per carnem generans) " De Pec Mer I 15

Among the punishments which Augustine believed to come on
Adam's race, besides sin itself, are the following.

1. Temporal death   "If Adam had not sinned, he would not
have been despoiled of his body, but would have been clothed with
immortality and incorruptibility, that what is mortal should be swal-
lowed up of life, i. e. pass from the animal to the spiritual state.—
But besides what an avenging God says, Earth thou art, and to earth
shalt thou return, (which I know not how to understand except of the
death of the body), there are also other testimonies by which it most
evidently appears, that the human race had to fear, on account of
sin, not only the death of the spirit, but also that of the body " De
Pec. Mer. I. 2, 4. "The body still bears the deserts of sin, because
it is subject to the condition of death." I. 7. " By the punishment

of transgression, Adam lost immortality." Op. Imp. VI. 30. "The first man sinned so grievously, that by this sin, the nature, not only of one single man but of the whole human race, was changed, and fell from the possibility of immortality to the certainty of death" VI. 12. "God had so made the first pair, that if they were obedient, the immortality of angels and a happy eternity would have resulted to them, without the intervention of death, but if disobedient, death was to be their punishment by the most righteous condemnation." De Civ. Dei, XIII. 1. "The first pair were so constituted, that if they had not sinned, they would have suffered no kind of death; but these first sinners were so punished with death, that whatever sprang from their stock, was subject to the same punishment. For nothing could originate from them different from what they were themselves. Because according to the greatness of the guilt, the condemnation changed nature for the worse; so that what was before inflicted penally on the first sinners, followed naturally to those born afterwards." XIII. 3. "The death of the body is a punishment, since the spirit, because it voluntarily left God, leaves the body against its will; so that, as the spirit left God because it chose to, it leaves the body although it chooses not to." De Trin IV. 13. Comp. De Gen. ad Lit. IX 10.

2. Concupiscence and the insubordination of the members Sometimes Augustine uses concupiscence in the wider sense for sinful passions in general, for example, De Perf. Just. Hom. 6, where he explains it as the love of sin; and, Op Imp. IV. 28, where he says, that the concupiscence of the flesh does not *in solam voluptatem genitalium aestuare*, but is found in every corporeal sense; and sometimes in the more restricted sense, in which the word is frequently used by him for sexual desire [In both senses, however, he regarded it as an evil which has come to our nature as a punishment of the fall. "The lust of the flesh, against which the good spirit lusts, is both sin, because it has in it disobedience to the dominion of the spirit, and also the punishment of sin, because it is in consequence of the transgressions of him that was disobedient; and is likewise a cause of sin, by the defection of him that consents, or the infection of him that is born." C. Jul. V. 3.] "We are ashamed of that of which the first pair were ashamed when they covered their nakedness. This" (of which they were ashamed, concupiscence) "is the punishment of sin, the guilt and the sign of sin, the inclination and the

tinder to sin, the law in the members warring against the law of the
mind, the disobedience of ourselves against ourselves, which is given
as a most righteous retribution to the disobedient." De Nupt. et
Conc. II 9 In the regenerated, however, concupiscence is not a
sin, if they do not consent to unlawful acts, and do not surrender
their members to the accomplishment of them.   But according to
the use of language, it is called sin, because it arises from sin, and
when victorious it brings forth sin I 23.   " Fleshly concupiscence
is not to be imputed to marriage, but to be suffered (toleranda). For
it is not a good coming from natural marriage, but an evil accruing
from the ancient sin" De Nupt et Conc. I. 17.   " After the first
transgression of God's law, man began to have another law in his
members warring against his spirit, and experienced the justly retri-
buted disobedience of his flesh." I. 6.   " If Julian will not allow,
that sensual concupiscence is a vice, yet let him at least admit that,
by the disobedience of the first pair, this concupiscence was vitiated,
so that, instead of acting moderately and obediently, it acts extrava-
gantly and disobediently ; ita ut ipsis quoque pudicis ad nutum non
obtemperet conjugatis, sed et quando non est necessaria moveatur,
et quando necessaria est, aliquando citius, aliquando tardius, non eorum sequatur nutus, sed suos exserat motus.   Hanc ergo ejus inobedientiam inobedientes illi tunc homines receperunt, et in nos pro-
pagine transfuderunt   Neque enim ad eorum nutum, sed utique in-
ordinate movebatur, quando membra prius glorianda, tunc jam pudenda texerunt." II 35.   " Thou art not willing, Julian, to be wise
with Ambrose, and to grant, that the evil by which the flesh lusteth
against the spirit, has entered into nature by the transgression of the
first man." Op. Imp. II. 15.   " Sensual lust belongs to the *nature*
of brutes ; but is a punishment in man." IV. 41.   " The devil re-
commended disobedience to the human mind, from which a *penal*
and shameful disobedience of the flesh would ensue ; whence original sin would be contracted, by which every one that should be born,
would be subject to the devil, and perish with the same devil, unless
regenerated " IV. 68.   " The disobedience of the members was
given to the first disobedient pair, as a righteous punishment," etc.
C. Duas Epp. Pel. I. 15.

On this concupiscence, which Augustine sometimes denominates
lust (libido), he expatiates with great particularity, as the Pelagians
made many objections to it.   In contrast to the Pelagian conclusions,

he calls it " a disease—a wound inflicted on nature through the trea-
cherous counsel given by the devil—a vice of nature—a deformity—
an evil that comes from the depravity of our nature which is vitiated
by sin." C. Jul. III. 15, 26 , V. 7. Op. Imp. IV. 33; V. 20. " No
man is now born without concupiscence." I. 72. He says concerning it, that Julian must grant it to be either a *vice* or *something vitiated* (Op. Imp. II. 218); or, as he elsewhere expresses himself, it
either *springs from sin* or is *corrupted by sin.* IV. 41. According
to Augustine, it is a *quality* (qualitas). C. Jul. VI. 18. [The guilt of
concupiscence made man guilty from his origin (originaliter hominem reum faciebat). VI. 5. Hence unbaptized children are punishable on account of concupiscence. It brings them into condemnation, though they die in childhood Its criminality (reatus) indeed
is forgiven in baptism ; but itself remains, even after baptism, for
conflict (ad agonem) ; though it does not injure those who withstand
it, just as it does not injure children who die after baptism, in whom
this conflict does not take place ; and it ceases after this life] But it
carries those who comply with it, to eternal perdition, if they are not
healed by repentance, deeds of charity, and the heavenly priest that
intercedes for us, etc. De Pec. Mer. II. 4, 33 ; De Nupt. et Conc. I.
31; C. Duas Epp. Pel. I. 13 ; C. Jul. II 3 , Op. Imp. I. 101. It is
always an evil, even in the continent who keep it in subjection, and in
the married who apply it to good, i. e. to the procreation of children.
C. Jul. IV. 2, and in many other passages. Augustine also found a
connection between mortality and concupiscence ' Before the fall,
and before there was any necessity of dying, concupiscence had no
existence , but after the body had acquired a sickly and dying nature, (which likewise belongs to the flesh of animals), it received also, on this account, the movement by which the carnal desire originates in animals, whereby those that are born, succeed the dying.'
De Gen. ad Lit. XI 32.

Finally, Augustine explains himself to this effect, that carnal concupiscence has its seat in the body as well as in the soul " The
cause of fleshly lust is not in the soul alone, and still much less in
the body alone. For it arises from both ; from the soul, because
without it no delight is felt ; and from the flesh, because without
this, no *fleshly* delight is felt," etc. X. 12. " And there are other
desires of the soul which are called fleshly, because the soul lusts

according to the flesh when it so lusts that the spirit, that is, its better and superior part, ought to resist it " C Jul V. 7.

3. The shame of nakedness. " Nam quare illud opus conjugatorum subtrahitur et absconditur etiam oculis filiorum, nisi quia non possunt esse in laudenda commixtione, sine pudenda libidine ? De hac erubuerunt etiam qui primi pudenda texerunt, quae prius pudenda non fuerunt, sed tanquam Dei opera praedicanda et glorianda. Tunc ergo texerunt, quando erubuerunt : tunc autem erubuerunt, quando post inobedientiam suam inobedientia membra senserunt " De Nupt. et Conc. II. 5. " Nec mirum si pudet laudentes, quod videmus ipsos pudere generantes.—In Paradiso autem si peccatum non praecessisset, non esset quidem sine utriusque sexus commixtione generatio, sed esset sine confusione commixtio. Esset quippe in coeundo tranquilla membrorum obedientia, non pudenda carnis concupiscentia." II. 22. Comp. II. 9   The shame of nakedness is also depicted in Op. Imp VI. 25. Comp. De Gen. ad Lit. XI. 32.

4. The pains of parturition., " We say, that the pain of childbirth, is a punishment of sin. For we know that God has said it without any ambiguity , and said it only to her that transgressed his command ; and said it only because he was offended at the transgression of his command."—' These pains came on Eve as a punishment of her crime, and not from the condition of nature ; and we do not know that brutes suffer in this way.' Op Imp. VI 26, and in other passages

5. The toil of laborers, as well as the thorns and thistles which the earth brought forth after the fall. Augustine, in his work against Julian (VI 27), endeavors to prove at large, that the toil of men engaged in labor, is a punishment of Adam's sin on his posterity ; and appeals to the well known words in Genesis, In the sweat of thy face shalt thou eat thy bread. " Do you so insult and despise the severity of God, as to maintain, that what was ordained as a punishment, is a gift of nature ?"   Among the toils of labor, he also reckons the " studies of learners," or, as he also says, " the torments of learners," and " the anxious cares ," so that no one is free from this sweat. VI. 9, 13, 29. Comp. De Pec. Mer. II. 34. " You maintain [Julian], that likewise thorns and thistles were produced before man sinned, although God does not name these among the first productions, but threatens them as the punishment of sin." Op. Imp. VI.

27. In an earlier work, however, (De Gen. ad Lit. III. 18), Augustine is doubtful whether thorns and thistles, which have their use, were not in existence before the fall of man. But he adds, that it was only after this time, that they grew as a nuisance to man in cultivating the field. "We may believe it as belonging to the completion of the punishment, that these sprung up on fields in which man was now penally laboring, though they might grow elsewhere as food for the fowls and the flocks, or for the use of man himself."

6. According to Augustine, all other moral and physical evils of man, were also a punishment of Adam's sin. The loss of personal beauty, is such a punishment. De Pec. Mer. I. 16. The corruptible body would not clog the soul, if there had been no sin. Op. Imp. VI 14. Our bodies would not have been born with defects, and there would have been no human monsters, if Adam had not corrupted our nature by his sin, and that had not been punished in his posterity. Op. Imp I. 116; II. 123; III 95, 104; V. 8. The sickly and dying nature of the human body, proceeds from the lapse of the first man. De Gen. ad Lit XI. 32. The faults of the mind with which many are born, as weakness, waywardness, stupidity of mind, are a consequence of original sin, a punishment of Adam's sin. C. Jul. III. 4; Op Imp. III. 161; IV. 134, 136; V. 11 Discernment and courage are so seldom found, because nature is corrupted by sin. IV. 1, 3. Ignorance, as soon as it is involuntary, is a punishment of Adam's sin. Ep. 194. c 6 Blindness of the heart, is a punishment of that sin. "The blindness of the heart, which only God the illuminator removes, is at once sin, in as much as there is not faith in God, and also the punishment of sin, in as much as the proud heart is punished in a fit way, and likewise the cause of sin, since something of evil is committed by the error of a blind heart. C. Jul. V. 3; De Nat. et Gr. 22; Op. Imp I 17.—The baptized, too, are not without the evil of ignorance. Although this may perhaps wholly cease in this life, yet concupiscence though weakened, will never be wholly removed. C. Jul. VI 16. The violence of habit, is a violence that comes as a punishment of that highest and greatest sin of the first man Op. Imp V. 59 The dominion of the man over the woman, is a punishment incurred by the same sin. De Gen. ad Lit. XI. 37. Fear and pain are punishments of original sin, which also remain in those whose sins are forgiven, that their faith in a future world, where these will not come, may be proved,

Op. Imp. VI. 17. " Human nature would have been propagated in paradise, according to the prolific blessing of God, although no one had sinned, until the number of the saints foreknown by God should be completed. But those infants would not have wept in paradise, nor have been dumb, nor would they at any time have been unable to use their reason, nor would they have lain feeble and inert without the use of their limbs, nor have been afflicted with diseases, nor have been injured by wild beasts, nor killed by poison, nor wounded by any accident, or deprived of any sense or any part of the body, nor vexed by demons, nor ruled by blows as they rose to childhood ; nor would they have gained instruction by labor , nor would any have been born with so vain and obtuse a mind that they could be improved neither by any labor nor suffering ; but, except in the size of their bodies, *propter incapaces uteros matrum*, they would have been born in all respects as Adam was created." Op Imp III 198. " But, in my opinion, so great weakness of the flesh, shows almost any punishment." De Pec. Mer. I. 37.—" There comes not, however, upon individuals, what the whole apostate creature has deserved ; and no individual endures so much as the whole mass deserve to suffer, but God has arranged all in measure, weight, and number, and suffers no one to endure any evil which he does not deserve."* Op. Imp II 87

[According to Augustine's theory, therefore, the nature of man, both in a physical and a moral view, is totally corrupted by Adam's sin. In the last respect, it is so deeply corrupted, that he can do no otherwise than sin. This inherited corruption, or original sin, as a *moral* punishment, is such a quality of the nature of man, that in his natural state, he can will and do evil only. From this, it certainly follows, then, that man has no freewill. And it was, indeed, the Augustinian doctrine, that man has lost freewill, by the fall; or rather, according to Augustine, original sin, as a moral punishment, consisted especially in this, that man by nature is utterly incapable of good. The want of moral freedom, was with him the essential part of original sin. The loss of freedom, however, will hereafter

---

* The view presented in this last extract, should be steadily borne in mind, if we would not misinterpret Augustine Adam s sin is not viewed as his only, but the sin of the whole race existing in him, and each one sharing just so much of the blame as he will be punished for —Tr.

be considered, especially in regard to the weight and influence of this doctrine on the whole of Augustine's system.

The aid, which the first man had from God, and which was necessary to his perseverance in good, was lost by the fall; and its loss is a punishment of sin. De Cor et Gr. 11.

That Augustine now should consider man as already under condemnation on account of original sin, will excite no wonder. And this he indeed maintained, in many places, very earnestly According to De Pec Mer. I. 12, Adam's sin is enough to exclude men from the kingdom of God, from salvation, and eternal life, although the guilt, and consequently the condemnation, may be increased by their own sins Comp C. Jul. VI. 18. "On account of the damnable vice by which human nature is vitiated, it is condemned." De Nupt. et Conc. I 23 " They that are carnally born from Adam, contract from their first birth the infection of the old death, and will not be freed from the punishment of eternal death, unless born again in Christ by grace." Ep 217 c 5 " God created the nature of man mid way, as it were, between angels and wild beasts, so that if he, subject to his creator and true Lord, should keep his commands in devout obedience, he should pass to the society of angels, and, without the intervention of death, should attain a blessed immortality without end ; but if he should offend the Lord his God, by a proud and disobedient use of freewill, he should live like the brutes, subject to death. a slave to lust, and destined to eternal punishment after death." De Civ. Dei, XII 21. " Because Adam forsook God by freewill, he experienced the righteous sentence of God, to be condemned, together with his whole race, which, existing as yet in him, had all sinned with him. For as many of this race as are freed by the grace of God, are freed from the condemnation by which they are bound." De Corr. et Gr. 10 Hence Augustine pronounced the whole human race, in their natural state, one mass of perdition (massa perditionis), and even a condemned batch (conspersio damnata). De Pec Orig. 31 ; De Corr et Gr 7. Finally, he allowed also, that deliverance from condemnation was granted to Adam, as the church believed him to have been saved. De Nat. et Gr. 21. Christ, by his descent into hell, delivered Adam from it, as we may believe. In this, says Augustine, nearly the whole church are agreed Ep. 164. c. 3.

In order to avoid the Pelagian inference, that Augustine, by main-

taining original sin, favored Manichaeism, (according to which an
evil substance was believed to be in man, and by which God must
consequently be the author of evil, provided we hold him to be the
author of man, and yet would not, with Manes, allow an evil principle at the same time to have had a part in man's creation,) Augustine maintained, that original sin is not a substance, but a quality of
the affections (affectionalis qualitas), a vice, a languor. "Julian
speaks as if we had said, that some substance (aliquid substantiae)
was created in men by the devil. The devil tempts to evil as sin,
but does not create as it were nature   But evidently he has persuaded nature, as man is nature ; and by persuading, has corrupted
it.   For he who inflicts wounds, does not create limbs, but injures
them.   But wounds inflicted on bodies, make the limbs falter or
move feebly, but not that power by which man is just ; but the wound
which is called sin, wounds that life by which there was holy living.
—Therefore by that great sin of the first man, our nature, then changed for the worse, not only has become a sinner (peccatrix), but produces sinners.   And yet that weakness (languor), by which the
power of holy living perished, is not nature at all, but a corruption ;
just as bodily infirmity is certainly not any substance or nature, but
a vitiation" De Nupt. et Conc. II. 34. Comp. De Nat. et Gr. 54 ;
Op. Imp VI. 7   "Evil is not a substance ; for if it were a substance, it would be something good." Conf VII. 12. "But you
[Julian] without knowing what you say, object to me, that I say,
God created sin.   Withstand the Manichaean, who says, that in the
discord of the flesh and the spirit, two contrary natures of good and
evil are apparent.   For there is but one answer we can give, so that
this pest can be conquered, viz , that this discord came into our nature by the transgression of the first man ; by denying which, you
help them to conquer, and sufficiently prove yourself a false assailant and a true auxiliary of the Manichaeans " VI 6.   Hence Augustine also said (De Civ Dei, XIV. 11), that the evil is contrary to
nature, although it pertains to the nature of him whose vice it is, because it can be only in nature , and that the evil is not removed by
the removal of any superadded nature or of any part of it, but that
what had been corrupt and depraved, was healed and improved.
—Sensual lust does not remain in a substantial way (substantialiter)
after baptism, as a kind of body or spirit, but is a certain affection of
an evil quality (affectio quaedam malae qualitatis), as languor." De

Nupt. et Conc. I. 25. Comp. C. Jul. VI. 18, where Augustine calls original sin, an inborn vice, and compares it to a hereditary disease. Here also he explains himself respecting the difference between affection (affectio) and a quality of affection (affectionalis qualitas), and in such a way, that the former indicates a transitory state, and the latter an attribute. Thus, *to fear*, he calls an *affection ;* and *to be timid*, a *quality* of affection.* He adds, "an evil quality (qualitas mali) does not pass out of one substance into another, as from place to place, as though it left the place where it was and went somewhere else ; but another of the same kind is produced, by a kind of contagion, which is also wont to happen from the diseased bodies of parents to the children."—Hence, while he would not maintain that original sin is a substance, but, as it has since also been scholastically termed, an *accident*, he was fond of saying, that concupiscence *happens* to nature (accidit naturae), as we find this expression, e. g. in De Nupt et Conc I. 24 And he called original sin an accident of nature (accidens naturae),† Op. Imp. III. 189, and, as we have already seen, an evil accruing from the ancient sin (ex antiquo peccato accidens malum).

Remark. According to Augustine, there is nothing at all bad by *nature*, for all was originally created good. De Gen. ad Lit. VIII. 13. "There is no *nature of evil ;* but the loss of good has received the name of evil" De Civ. Dei, XI. 9. Here Augustine

---

* Augustine also says, in this place - "Some philosophers have termed concupiscence a vitious part of the soul, and a part of the soul is a substance, because the soul itself is a substance But I call the vice itself, by which the soul or any part of it is in this way vitiated, lust, as when all vice is cured, the whole substance is well And those philosophers also seem to me only figuratively to have called the vitiated part of the soul, lust, in which part the vice is that is called lust, just as a house is spoken of for those who are in the house "—TR

† Augustine, having once been a Manichaean, well understood their error and often guards against it, and even charges the Pelagians with running into it The Manichaeans, says he, in the passage referred to, "speak of the evil nature of the flesh, as if it were itself an evil, instead of its *having* evil; because they think vice itself a substance, not an accident of substance " Some of the zealous followers of Luther, a little after his day however, were not so guarded on this point as either the great reformer or his favorite Augustine, for they affirmed sin to be a part of our substance, and not an accident. Mat. Flacius was one of this number —TR

means only to say, that there is no *substantial* evil, but evil consists in the lack of good. This he distinguishes from the other, in c. 22. There is nothing evil by nature; but this name applies to the privation of good (privatio boni). De Fide, Spe, et Caritate, c. 11, 12. Augustine endeavors to show, that evil, universally, is not an existence in itself, but only a privation of good, as bodily disease is the absence of health. Good is properly the foundation of all things, although not without variableness and diverse degrees of change. Hence Augustine allowed, that the demons were not bad by nature, but had become so only by their defection from God. In this way, he endeavored to avoid the dualism of Manes * From this cause, we see why, on the one hand. Pelagius, without prejudice to his view of the faultless state of human nature, in its natural condition, attributed a deterioration to adult humanity, through the power of bad custom ; and on the other hand, Augustine, notwithstanding his theory of man's total corruption by the sin of Adam, could grant, that a trace of the divine image is still left, after the fall of Adam, in the rational soul of man. For nature itself, which God made, is indeed something good, according to Augustine. It is by no means ruined, as respects its substance, but only infected with corruption. "The good, by which nature exists, cannot be *destroyed*, unless herself is destroyed.—Corruption cannot consume the good, unless nature be destroyed.—If this is destroyed by corruption, then corruption itself will no longer remain ; for there is then no nature in which it can exist." Enchir. 4. Even to the most corrupt men, there still remains reason, by which they have a preeminence above the brutes. De Gen. ad Lit. IX. 9. Hence Augustine called the rational soul of man, the index of his noble origin. XI 32. " If man had lost the whole of the divine image, there would be nothing remaining of which it could be said (Ps 39 6) . Though man walketh in the image, he is vainly disquieted " Retract I. 26 He also allows, that something good still remains in human nature, because pain can be felt for the lost good ; for if there were nothing of good remaining in nature, there would be no pain for the lost good, as a punishment. " That is good which deplores the lost good ; for if there were nothing of good remaining in nature, there would be no pain for the lost

---

* The doctrine of two independent sources of created being, a good and a bad , and of two constituent parts in man, the one from God, and the other from " the principle of evil "—Tr.

good, as a punishment." De Gen. ad Lit. VIII. 14 And hence was he also induced to say of the heathen, that we know of many transactions of theirs, which deserved, not only no blame, but even praise, although, as he adds, if the design be considered, they could hardly deserve the praise of righteousness. Many of those heathen might, with the exception of their worship, be esteemed as examples of frugality, chastity, temperance, and contempt of death for their country. Not referring to the object of true and real piety, but to a vain pride of human praise and fame, they in a manner vanish and become unfruitful; and yet they afforded delight by a certain disposition of the mind. Ep. 164. c. 2 The declarations of the apostle whom he so highly revered, might easily afford the occasion of his acknowledging the legal works of the heathen. We find a remarkable passage, in this respect, in one of the earlier controversial pieces of Augustine against the Pelagians, De Spir. et Lit. c. 27, 28. After there suggesting, that the declaration in Rom. 2. 14, 15, is rather to be referred to the *converted* heathen, he thus continues . " But *if* they, who do by nature the things of the law, are *not* to be considered in the number of those whom Christ's grace justifies, but rather among those of whom, (although unholy and not really and rightly worshipping the true God), we have nevertheless read or known or hear of some acts which, according to the rule of righteousness, we not only cannot blame, but even properly and justly praise, (though, if considered in respect to their object, they will hardly be found to deserve the requisite praise or defence of righteousness), still, since the image of God in the human soul, is not so effaced, by the stain of earthly passions, that none of the extreme lineaments, as it were, remain in it, by which it may justly be said, that they, even amid the ungodliness of their lives, do or understand something of the law ; if this is what is meant by the declaration (Rom. 2: 14), that *the heathen, who have not the law,* that is, the law of God, *do by nature the things of the law,* and that such men *are a law unto themselves, and have the work of the law written in their hearts,* i. e. that, which was impressed on their hearts by the image of God when they were created, is not totally effaced ; even thus [construing the apostle], the distinction is not confounded, by which the New Testament differs from the Old, because, by the New, the law of God is written on the heart of believers, which, by the Old, was written on tables.——For, as this image of God is renewed in the mind of believers, by the New Testament, which image iniquity had

not totally obliterated, (for that remained, since the soul of man cannot but be rational), so the law of God, being not there entirely effaced by iniquity, is indeed written anew by grace.—And as some venial sins, without which this life is not led, do not bar the righteous
from eternal life ; so some good works, without which the life of the
worst man will hardly be found, do not profit the ungodly at all in
respect to eternal salvation." On Ps. lvii. he says . " this truth is
written on our hearts, by the hand of our Maker, What thou willest
not to be done to thee, do not to another. This every one knew,
before the law was given ; by which those also could be judged to
whom the law was not given " Jerome, in the epistle to Algesia
(qu. 8), expresses himself in a like manner, with the addition, that
the law written on the heart comprehends the whole.—Now, although
Augustine could not deny the praise of external rectitude to many
actions of the heathen, yet he declared even these to be sins, as
viewed in the motive or the source from which they spring, as they
come not from faith. All that is not of faith, is sin Rom. XIV. 23.
Is it sin, then—this is an objection which Julian made to him—when
a heathen clothes the naked, binds up the wounds of the infirm, or
cannot be brought by torture to false testimony ? etc. The act in
itself (the matter of the act) of clothing the naked, is no sin, replied
Augustine ; but as it comes not from faith, in this view (in respect
to its form) it is sin. The heathen performs good works in a bad
way, and a bad tree can bring forth no good fruit, etc. And virtues
which do not profit a man in gaining salvation, can be no true virtues. C. Jul. IV. 3. " What good could we do, if we did not love ?
or how do we not do good, if we love ?—Where there is no love, no
good work is reckoned, and it is never properly called a good work,
because all which does not come from faith, is sin. But faith works
by love " De Grat. Chr 26 Nay, Augustine allowed the severe,
but not illogical conclusion, that the unbeliever, who keeps the moral
law ever so strictly (as to its matter), is condemned ; but that the
believer who obeys it less, is saved. Still, however, of two believers,
he gave the preference to the one who should best fulfil the rules of
the moral law. C Duns Epp. Pel. III. 5.

CHAPTER VI.

Theory of the Pelagians on Freewill, and the opposite theory of Augustine.

With the doctrine of original sin, the doctrine of man's freewill stands in the closest connection. As the Pelagians admitted no original sin, but maintained that every man, as to his moral condition, is born in just the same state in which Adam was created, they had also to admit, that man, in his present state, has the power to do good. And this they actually taught. Among those articles of complaint presented to the synod at Carthage by Paulinus against Caelestius, are two propositions in which is substantially contained the Pelagian doctrine of man's freewill The propositions are these : "The law is just as good a means of salvation, as the gospel ;—and before the Lord's advent, there were men who were without sin." The freedom of the will is also expressly maintained by Pelagius in several passages. In his Capitula, he had said . " All men are governed by their own will, and each one is left to his own inclination." When this was presented as an objection to him, at the synod of Diospolis, he replied : " I said this concerning freewill, to which God is an assistant when choosing good ; but man himself is in fault when sinning, of freewill as it were (quasi liberi arbitrii)." De Gest. Pel. 3   In the passage already adduced from Augustine (De Pec. Orig. 13), in which he quotes some words from Pelagius' work on freewill, (which Pelagius had published after the Palestine decision, and therefore between 415 and 418, in which year Augustine wrote his book on freewill), the freewill of man is as strongly maintained, as original sin is denied. 'We are born capable of good and of evil ; and as we are created without virtue, so are we without vice,' etc. Compare the Epistle to Demetrias. " In the freedom to good and evil," says he, in c. 2. of that letter, " consists the superiority of the rational soul ; in this the honor, the dignity of our nature. Hence the best obtain praise and reward , and there would be no virtue in him that perseveres, if he had not the power of changing to evil." In c. 3, 'God has endowed man with the power of being what he will, so that he might be naturally capable both of good and evil, and

14

turn his will to either of them   He has imparted to us the capacity
of doing evil, merely that we may perform his will *by our own will.*
The very ability to do evil, is therefore a good   It makes good to
be performed, not by constraint, but voluntarily "   "That only is
good, which we never either find or lose *without our will,* the spiritual riches which thou alone canst impart to thyself   These can
only be *from thyself* and in thyself." 13, 14   "We contradict
the Lord, when we say, *It is hard , it is difficult ; we cannot ; we
are men ; we are encompassed with mortal flesh.* O blind nonsense !
O unholy audacity. We charge God with a twofold ignorance ; that
he does not seem to know what he has made, nor what he has commanded ; just as if he, forgetting the human weakness of which himself is the author, has imposed laws on man which he cannot endure " 19. Here Pelagius, in the manner of Kant, infers the *can*
from the *ought*   Still more precisely does Augustine, in his book
on the grace of Christ, describe to us the freedom of the will, as Pelagius received it   That he might not be blamed as having either
not understood Pelagius or else perverted his words, he quotes his
own language from his work on freewill   " We distinguish three
things, to *be able,* to *will,* and to *be,* (posse, velle, esse). *To be able,*
we place in nature; *to will,* in freewill ; *to be,* in the effect. The
first, *to be able,* refers peculiarly to God, who has conferred this on
his creature ; the other two, *to will* and *to be*" (i. e. to do), "must
be referred to men, because they flow from the fountain of freewill.
In the willing and the good performance, therefore, is the praise of
man ; nay, of both man and God, who has given the possibility of
the willing itself and the performance, and who always aids the possibility by the assistance of his grace   For that man is able to will
and to do good, is of God alone. The first, therefore, may exist,
though the other two do not ; but these cannot be without that   I
am therefore free to refrain from either the good volition or the action ; but by no means can I cease to have the possibility of good ;
for it is in me, even though I should wish it not to be ; nor does nature ever take her rest in this thing   Some examples may make my
meaning plainer. That we can see with our eyes, depends not on
us ; but that we see well or ill, does depend on us   And (that I may
comprise all things in general) that we *can* do, say, or think every
good thing, is of him who gave this ability, and who aids it ; but that
we actually do, or speak, or think *right,* is of ourselves ; because

we can also turn all these to evil.) Hence, (what must often be repeated on account of your perversions), when we say, that man can
be without sin, we also, by the confession of the received possibility,
praise God who has given us this ability , and there is hete no occasion of praising man, where the cause of God only is considered ;
for the discussion respects, not the willing nor the doing, but only
the thing which can be done " De Gr. Chr. c. 4. Augustine quotes
another passage from this book " We have, implanted by God,
the possibility for both, like a prolific and fruitful root, if I may so say,
which originates and produces diverse things, and which, according to
the will of the cultivator, may become brilliant with flowers of virtue,
or rough with the thorns of vice." c. 18. Comp. De Nat. et Gr. 47,
where Augustine quotes similar assertions of Pelagius from his work
On Nature, and which he endeavors to refute, though not in an appropriate manner. In Pelagius' confession of faith, it is said : " We
say that man always is able as well to sin as not to sin, by which we
always confess, that we have a freewill "

Caelestius, so far as we know, did not show himself so fully on
man's freewill, as Pelagius. But that he also received the doctrine,
may be presumed, partly because he denied original sin, and partly
because he declared in his confession of faith (De Pec. Orig. 6), that
sin is not a trespass of nature, but of will , and it was also adduced
at the synod of Diospolis, as a proposition of Caelestius, that it depends on the freewill of every one, whether to do or not to do a
thing.

Finally, how strongly Julian asserted the freedom of the will,
(which he defined as " the possibility of sinning or of not sinning"
Op. Imp. VI. 9, or in a similar way), and with what acuteness he
defended it against Augustine, may be seen from the first book of
Augustine's Imperfect Work. The law of imitation, in connection
with the acknowledged power of evil habit, was the reason why Julian would not allow that the sinner, even by his transgressions, has
lost the freedom of will. " When the Lord says, If the Son shall
make you free, ye shall be free indeed, he promises pardon to the
guilty who, by sinning, have lost, not the freedom of will, but the
consciousness of rectitude. *But freewill is as much freewill after
sins, as it was before sins.* For by its operation, it comes to pass,
that most men abandon the hidden things of disgrace, and the filth
of vices being cast away, they are adorned with the insignia of vir-

tues." Op. Imp I. 91   " We maintain, that, by the sin of man, the
state of nature is not changed, but the quality of desert; i. e that
even in the sinner, there is this nature of freewill, by which he can
cease from sin, which was in him so that he could depart from righteousness." 1. 96.

Thus the Pelagians assumed a practical or moral freedom of man,
or an ability, independent of sensuousness, to guide himself according to the laws of reason.   As man is the work of God, Pelagius allowed that he has received from God the power, as a " possibility,"
of acting one way or the other ; but he did not trouble himself with
the question that speculation meets with in reflecting on a metaphy-
sical freedom   According to the Pelagian theory, every man has
the power of willing and doing good, as well as, on the contrary, the
power of willing and doing evil.   It therefore depends on man,
whether he will he good or evil.   With the Pelagians, therefore, it
must be an abuse of freedom, when a man does evil ; for he can
certainly avoid it.   Nay, as Pelagius admitted at the synod of Diospolis, he can even again become good when he has been bad, through
his own exertion and aided by grace   In his letter to Demetrias
(c. 20), he says : " Even those who, by long habits of sin, have undermined as it were the goodness of nature, can be restored again
by repentance."   Still he held it more difficult to lay aside vices
which have once been admitted, than not to admit them at all. Ib

By this view of human freedom, the Pelagians must have come
to that conclusion, which in the sequel was so often plausibly assailed by Augustine and his followers, viz. that man *can* be without sin.
On this topic, see particularly the so called Definitions, attributed to
Caelestius, (in Augustine de Perf Just Hom.), in which the proposition, that man can be without sin, is attempted to be proved by many arguments. The following, which is said in those Definitions, is
particularly apt.   "It is to be inquired, what is sin, natural or accidental ?   If natural, it is not sin : but if it is accidental (accidens),
it may also recede (recedere) , and what may recede, may be
avoided, man may be without " De Perf. Just. Hom c. 2.   The
possibility of this, was not to be denied, so long as the idea of human
freedom was held fast.   If man has the power to will and to do good,
it is then possible that he can always will and do it.   Nothing more
than this would be maintained, at least by Pelagius, according to his
own showing. For whether any one could actually be found, who

was without sin, he did not care to contend. In his book On Nature
(Aug De Nat. et Gr. 7), he says . " We speak only of possibility.—
I again repeat it, I say, that man *can* be without sin. What say
you ?` that man can *not* be without sin ? I do not say, that man is
without sin ; and you do not say, that man is not without sin. We
are contending about *can* and *cannot*, and not about *being* and *not
being* (de posse et non posse, et non de esse et non esse contendi-
mus)." Pelagius readily granted, that great and long continued effort is requisite to a change of morals, and for every virtue to become perfected. Ep. ad Dem 27 Nor did he forget to mention the
aid of the Holy Ghost, when he exhorted Demetrias to resist the devil. c. 29 Nay, he says expressly (c. 31), that we ought not, so
long as we are in the body, to believe that we have attained to perfection ; so shall we best attain to it Not to go forward, is already
to go backward —The proposition, that man can be without sin and
keep God's commands, if he will, Pelagius acknowledged as his own,
at the synod of Diospolis. Augustine, it is true, in a letter to bishop
John of Jerusalem (Ep. 179 n 8), quotes a passage from Pelagius'
book on nature, in which he adduces Abel as an example of a man
who has not sinned ; by which he seems therefore to go beyond the
position of mere ability Comp. De Gest. Pel. 10. Furthermore, Pelagius, in his epistle to Demetrias (c 5), in order to show how great
is the goodness of nature, which taught men righteousness before
the law, adduces an Abel, a Noah, an Abraham, as men who had
done the will of God perfectly ; just as in his book on nature, he
adduces these and others, who had not only not sinned, but also lived
righteously. De Nat. et Gr. 36 But this he could say of them, and
could call them righteous and holy, without using the language in
so strong a sense as to imply, that a sinful inclination had never been found in them. In the bible too, in popular language, perfection is required of men ; and John even says Whoever is born
of God, sinneth not. To such expressions as these, the Pelagians
appealed, as we see both from Augustine's controversial writings,
and also from the first book of Jerome's dialogue against the Pelagians. Those pious men of the Old Testament, were called righteous according to the biblical use of language, against which Augustine could make no objections c. 38. And to this bible use of language, Pelagius himself referred, both in the passage of his letter to
Demetrias, and also at the council of Diospolis, in his answer to the

charge of having taught, that man can be without sin. See Aug. De
Nat. et. Gr 36.   Pelagius would always grant that, in actual experience, no one is found who is without sin   But this, according to
his definition,—as himself says (c. 42)—could not be to the purpose,
since the question does not regard what man *is*, but what he *can be*,
The reproach, cast by Augustine on the Pelagians (De Dono Persv.
5), was therefore unjust, viz. that they maintained, " that a righteous
man in this life has no sin at all."   They spoke of abstract possibility, and not of real experience.

To the Pelagian doctrine of man's freewill, the Augustinian was
diametrically opposed   According to Augustine, original sin, as a
punishment, consisted peculiarly in the inability to will and to do
good.   Consequently, the very assertion of original sin, in his sense,
was at once a denial of man's freewill   " True freedom (vera libertas)* would not have perished, if the will had remained good. But
as the will has sinned, *the hard necessity of having sin*, follows the
sinner, until the whole infirmity be healed, and so great a liberty be
received as that of a voluntary and happy necessity of living well
and sinning no more " De Perf. Just Hom 4.   And a little before :
" By the freedom of the will, it came to pass, that man should have
sin , but now, the penal vitiosity that ensued from liberty, has produced the necessity. For as the will has been subjugated by the
corruption into which it fell, freedom has been wanting to nature"
Ib   " By the greatness of the first sin, we have lost the freewill to
love God " Ep 217 c. 5.   " Man was so created with freewill, as
not to sin if he willed not to, but not so, that if he willed, he could sin
with impunity.   What wonder then, if, by transgressing, i. e. by
subverting the rectitude in which he was created, he is followed with
the punishment of not being able to do right ?" Op. Imp. VI. 12.
" There is a necessary sin, from which man has not the freedom to
refrain, which is not only sin, but the punishment of sin." VI. 59.†

---

* The word *true*, which Augustine here prefixes to freedom, but which
our author happened to omit, is essential to a right understanding of Augustine's assertion, as he does not mean to say that *all* liberty perished in the
fall. Nor does the German, in this and the next citation, quite agree with
the Latin, as given in the Antwerp edition of Augustine. Of course I feel
bound to follow the original in such cases —Tr.

† This reference and two or three that soon follow, are wrong, and I have
not succeeded in finding the passages anywhere else —Tr.

"Since that great freedom" (to be able to abstain from sin) "has been lost, the weakness remains which must be aided by greater gifts." De Cor. et Gr. 12. "The freedom to abstain from sin, has been lost as a punishment of sin." Op. Imp 1 104 Human nature sinned differently when it still had the freedom to abstain from sin, from what it does now since that freedom is lost, when it needs the aid of a liberator. That was only sin ; this is also the punishment of sin " V. 28. " By the punishment of sin, each one sins against his will (invitus)." IV. 100.

We should now have to wonder how, after the passages quoted and innumerable others in which the freedom of man is most definitely and, we might add, most revoltingly denied, the freedom of the will could still have been admitted by Augustine, if he had not himself given us the clue. It has already been remarked, that in his books on freewill, which he wrote against the Manichaeans, before the commencement of the Pelagian controversy, he defended freewill against those heretics. In the first chapter of the third book, he had asserted, that where a necessity prevails, no blame can be found ; and in the eighteenth chapter, he had further said : " Whatever may determine the will, if it cannot be resisted, is complied with without sin ; but if one can resist it, let him not comply with it and it will not be sin." Here, therefore, he makes sin dependent on freewill ; and he is here speaking only of a difficulty of doing good, which arises from the sin of Adam. Similar assertions are found in other writings of Augustine against the Manichaeans In Retract. I. 13, 15, 16, he himself quotes several passages from those writings, in which he makes sin dependent on freewill, and explains it as belonging to voluntariness ; but here he endeavors to escape the difficulty, by saying that, in those passages, he had defined sin only as *sin*, and not as being likewise the punishment of sin. Original sin is also to be called voluntary in respect to its being contracted by the wicked will of the first man, etc. Against Pelagius—who presented to him the passage quoted from the eighteenth chapter of his third book on freewill, in order thus to justify his own assertion, that man may be without sin—he knew not how to defend himself except by answering, that he had there spoken of that grace by which we are enabled to resist evil ; which answer was not wholly groundless. De Nat. et Gr. 67. Comp. Retract. I. 9.—Augustine further says (Ep. 246) ; " In all laws, warnings, rewards, punishments, etc.

there is no justice, if the will is not the cause of sin." In De Civ.
Dei, V 9, 10, written in 415, he endeavors to reconcile the freedom
of the will with the foreknowledge of God and the laws of causation.
—Augustine likewise, in his controversial writings against the Pelagians, found occasion to defend the shadowy image of a freedom
which is no longer freedom. The occasion arose from their objections and from the contests of the Adrumetian monks, which originated, at least in part, from his letter to the Romish presbyter Sixtus
(Ep. 194), who afterwards mounted the Romish chair, under the
name of Sixtus III [Augustine only said, as in his first piece against
the Pelagians, that we are not in all respects in a condition to obey
the commands of God, when not aided by God ; but that we, in order to be aided by God, must apply our own powers. " For God is
called our helper, and he only can be helped who also spontaneously undertakes something. For not as in senseless stones, or in those
in whose nature God has not created understanding and will, is our
salvation effected." De Pec. Mer. II. 5. comp. 2. In Ep. 188. c. 2,
Augustine asserts, in opposition to the principle which Pelagius had
advanced in his letter to Demetrias, that if some little should be from
man, on the score of freewill, still all is not from him. In his second
book De Nupt. et Conc. c. 3, he says, in opposition to Julian " It
is not so as you say. You are in error, or you seek to deceive
others. We do not deny freewill ; but, if the Son shall make you
free, ye shall be free indeed, saith the truth " In like manner, he
explains himself in another work, not against the Pelagians, on freewill. " The will is truly free," (says he, De Civ Dei, XIV 11),
" when it does not serve vices and sins. Such was it given by God.
And since it has been lost through its own vice, it can be restored
only by him by whom it could be given. Hence, saith the truth, If
the Son shall make you free, ye shall be free indeed " Comp. C.
Duas Epp. Pel I. 2 —" Freewill becomes the more free, in proportion as it is more healthy ; and it is the more healthy, in proportion
as it is subjected to the divine mercy and grace.—How can he be
free whom iniquity rules ?" Ep 157. c. 2. " Freewill is not destroyed by grace, but established ; because grace cures the will, so
that righteousness is freely loved " De Spir et Lit. 30 —In Ep. 217.
c. 5, he even says : " We know, that they who believe with their
heart, do this of their own freewill and choice (sua id facere voluntate ac libero arbitrio)."—In his book On Grace and Freewill, he

attempts to prove from the bible the freedom of the will, and to defend it against some of the Adrumetian monks, who were led, by his doctrine, to reject the freedom of the will in every sense, and to maintain, consecutively enough, that, at the day of judgment, God will *not* reward even adults according to their works. See Ep. 215; with which he sent this book to Valentinus and his Adrumetian monks. Nay, Augustine regarded the divine precepts themselves as a proof of freedom. " Their fulfilment would not have been commanded, if our will had nothing to do in it." De Perf. Just. Hom. 10. Also, in Ep. 175, which was written to Innocent, in 416, by Augustine and some other bishops, the remarkable assertion is found, that there is no doubt of the freedom of the will, but its power does not reach the point of refraining from sin, when not aided by grace ; and passages from the bible are there adduced in proof of freewill, as well as of grace. " Who ought to condemn or deny freewill, with which God's aid is praised ?" says Augustine, De Gest c. 3

But that the renowned bishop could not be in earnest when, in his writings against the Pelagians, he in words admits a free will, is manifest from his theory of original sin, according to which, man is so corrupted by the sin of Adam, that he can will and do only evil ; and hence the freedom of the will is lost. This last, to be sure, he will not concede, in C Duas Epp. Pel. I. 2, where he maintains, that man has not lost freewill by Adam's sin. But the freedom which Augustine allows to man, after the fall, is a freedom to evil, and therefore no longer freedom. " No man is compelled, against his will, to evil or to good," says Augustine indeed (I. 18) ; but that he *wills* the good, is there, again, a work of divine grace. The good is voluntary (voluntarium) only when God works in us the willing and the doing according to his good pleasure. De Perf. Just. 19. In this sense, Augustine attributes a greater freedom to the predestinated saints than to Adam. It is greater in them, because grace works more mightily in them. De Corr. et Gr. 12 " The will does not obtain grace through its freedom, but obtains freedom through grace " I. 8 " The weakness of freewill for doing good, human nature can repair only through the grace of Christ " Op Imp. III. 110. " By grace man comes to possess a good will, who before had a bad will " De Gr. et Lib. 15. When maintaining the freedom of the will, Augustine often hides himself behind words, because he confounds the various meanings of the word freedom, which Julian

15

very properly distinguishes (Op. Imp. I 87) ; and one can hardly repress his indignation, when he sees him playing with words on so important a question Liberty, or the ability, independently of the power of the propensities, to direct ourselves by rational laws, or, which is the same thing in this case, by the precepts of the divine law—such a liberty as Pelagius meant, and as we must adopt, according to sound ethics—Augustine directly denied, and must deny, if he would be consistent and not contradict his other positions respecting original sin and his theory of grace and predestination, which theory we shall learn hereafter. (Man, says Augustine, has only freedom for sin. De Spir. et Lit 3) The will of man is free to sin only, and not to righteousness, unless freed and aided by God.) De Nat et Gr 23 ; C Duas Epp Pel, III. 8 ; II. 5.   Man can will nothing good, if not aided by grace I 3 " Freedom is indeed lost by sin ; but it was that freedom which was in paradise, to have a perfect righteousness together with immortality.—For freewill, in the sinner, is so far *not* lost that, by it, they sin, and especially all who sin with delight and by the love of sin> Hence the Apostle says When ye were the servants of sin, ye were free from righteousness.   Behold, they are here even shown to have been by no means able to serve sin, unless by the other liberty, [the freedom from righteousness]   They are therefore free from righteousness only by the decision of liberty (arbitrio libertatis) ; and they are free from sin only by the grace of the Saviour."* Op. Imp. I. 94.   Nay, he even calls the human will the servile will of its own inclination. C. Jul. II. 8.   In these, as well as in the passages before quoted, and in others innumerable, the moral freedom of man is consequently taken completely away.   Finally, according to Augustine, it is in the power of the wicked to sin ; but that by their wickedness they do this or that, is alone in the power of God, so that in the very thing, which they do against the will of God, nothing but the will of God is accomplished. De Praedest. Sanct. 16.   The bad will alone is sin, even when the effect is wanting, i e. when it has not the power.   When the bad will receives the power to accomplish what

---

* Thus we see that Augustine held to a *happy* bondage of the will to righteousness, as well as a *servile* bondage to sin , and that the regenerated man, though still possessed of the power of sinning, has not so much freedom to *this* as the sinner has.—But we are yet to see a still further development of his views of liberty and necessity, in a future chapter —Tr

it designs, this takes place according to the sentence of God, with whom there is no unrighteousness.   For he also punishes in this way. De Spir. et Lit. 31.

CHAPTER VII.

Objections of the Pelagians against Augustine's doctrine of original sin and of freewill.

The Augustinian theory of original sin and of freewill as lost by Adam's fall, contained so much that is revolting to the moral sense of man, and was so contradictory to the demands of the moral law, that it exposed assailable points enough to the shrewdness of the Pelagians   Hence a great dialectic adroitness was requisite in Augustine, to sustain his theory in the appearance of truth

It will not be uninteresting here, to become more acquainted with some of their most acute objections.

Against the Augustinian position, that Adam's sin is propagated among all men by sensual lust in generation, the instance was adduced by the Pelagians, which has already been touched upon in connection with infant baptism.   " If baptism cleanses from that old transgression, then those who spring from two that are baptized, must be free from this sin, for they cannot transfer to their descendents what they have not themselves." De Pec Mer. III. 3.—Here Augustine remarks, (4), that even if he may not be able to refute this and other objections, still we must abide by those plain passages of scripture from which it is apparent, that no one can obtain salvation, who is not baptized; that we must explain what is obscure by these passages ; and if we are not able to do this, still we must believe it without hesitation.   The reply has already been mentioned, however, which Augustine made in order completely to cripple this objection, on which the Pelagians, according to their own assertion, placed great reliance (Since, by his theory, concupiscence itself is not removed by baptism, but only the imputation of it is annulled, he must have understood, that the person begotten through concupiscence, has the corrupt nature of his parents, the guilt of which, in him, is also to be cancelled by the new birth.] This, in conformity

with the rest of his theory, he definitely exhibits, and in its true position and just light, in Ep. 194   He further touches upon it, De Pec.
Mer. II. 27, where he says : "Regenerated parents do not corpore-
ally generate from the beginnings of what is new in them, but from
the remains of what is old "   Regenerated parents, says Augustine
(De Nupt et Conc I. 18), do not generate as sons of God, but as
children of this world. Still he often admits, what one would hardly
have expected in his case, that it is something wonderful, that the
children of baptized parents should be born with original sin, although the parents are regenerated and original sin forgiven to
them ; and he is at much pains to make this intelligible, by examples from sensible things, particularly by the example of the wild
olive tree, which springs from the seed of the good olive. Nay, he
believed, that God has made this example in nature, for the very
purpose of aiding us to believe in the possibility of the propagation
of original sin.   He explains himself extensively on this point, in
De Nupt. et Conc I. 19.   "In a wonderful manner it comes to
pass, that what is forgiven to the parents is transferred to the children ; and yet it comes to pass.   That these things invisible and
incredible to unbelievers, might have some visible example, divine
providence has given such an example in certain shrubs.   For why
should we not believe it to be appointed for this purpose, that the
wild olive should spring from the fruit of the good olive ?   May we
not believe, that in something which is created for the use of man,
the Creator provided and appointed something to serve as an example of the human race ?   It is, then, wonderful, how* those who are
by grace freed from the bond of sin, should produce children bound
by the same bond, who must be freed in the same way.   But when
would it be believed that the germ of the wild olive is concealed in
the seed of the true olive, if it were not proved by experience ?
As, then, the wild olive is produced from the seed of the wild olive,
and likewise from the seed of the good olive, although there is a
great difference between the good and the wild ; so is produced from
the flesh of a sinner and from the flesh of the just, a sinner in each

---

   * *Quemadmodum* Wiggers here translates by the German *dass*, that,
for which there is no warrant either in the meaning of the word or in its
connection   Augustine's wonder, therefore, is not so much the simple fact,
as the *philosophy, the mode,* of the fact, so that he is still more true to himself in this matter, than our author seemed to to suppose —Tr.

case, although between the sinner and the just, there is a great difference. But no one is born a sinner in act, and new in origin but
old in guilt; but a man by the Creator, a captive by the deceiver,
needing a Redeemer. But it is inquired, *how* the captivity of the progeny can be derived from parents already redeemed. And because
it cannot easily be searched out by reason, nor explained by language, it is not believed by unbelievers; just as though what we
have said of the wild and the good olive, which are alike in germ
but unlike in kind, could be easily investigated by any mind and explained in language. But this fact can be seen by him who is willing to make the experiment. It may therefore be for an example
by which that may be believed which cannot be seen " Augustine
was very fond of this example; and recurs to it again, II. 34, and
there adds " The offspring of the regenerated, as they are not produced by spiritual but sensual passion, a wild olive tree of our race,
as it were, from that good olive, receives in this way the guilt by
birth, so that they can be freed from that pest only by the new birth."
Compare with this, the passage already quoted from Ep. 194. c. 10,
and several passages in C. Jul. VI. Augustine also adduces the
wild grape vine (*lubrusca*, which springs from the seed of the good
grape vine, but is more unlike it than the wild olive to the good),
as an example how the bad may be propagated from the good. C.
Jul. VI. 7.

Another objection was presented by the Pelagians, against the
propagation of sin by concupiscence in generation, and our subjugation to the devil by birth, viz. that marriage must then be an evil;
and both that and the fruit of it, must be the work of the devil. To
repel this objection, he wrote his first book on marriage and concupiscence. In that book he attempted to show, that marriage in itself
is not an evil, but a good, and an institution of God; but that on
this account, sensual lust does not cease to be an evil, which married
people, if temperate, use only for a good object, the production of
children. " The new heretics," so begins the first chapter, " who
maintain, that children born of the flesh, need not the baptism of
Christ (*medicinam* Christi),* by which sins are healed, most invidi-
ously vociferate, that we condemn marriage and the divine work by
which God creates men from males and females, because we say,

---

* The early fathers called baptism by almost all sorts of good appellations,
as grace, salvation, regeneration, etc.—Tr.

that such as are born by such a union, contain original sin ; concerning which, the apostle says : By one man, sin hath come into
the world, etc , and because we do not deny, that they who are born
of any parents whatever, are still subject to the devil unless they are
regenerated in Christ, and rescued by his grace from the power of
darkness, and brought into the kingdom of Him who would not be
born by the same conjunction of the sexes.   Therefore, because we
say this, which is contained in the most ancient and sure rule of the
catholic faith, those asserters of a novel and perverse dogma, who
say there is nothing of sin in infants which should be washed away
by the laver of regeneration, impiously or ignorantly calumniate us,
as though we condemn marriage, and as though we call the work of
God, i. e. man who is born of marriage, the work of the devil   Nor
do they consider, that the blessing of marriage cannot be accused
on account of original sin, which is thereby transferred ; just as the
evil of adultery and fornication, cannot be excused on account of the
natural good which is thence produced.   For as sin, whether contracted by infants in this way or that, is the work of the devil; so
man, whether born in this way or that, is the work of God.   The
design of this book therefore is, to distinguish, so far as God shall
deign to aid me, between the blessing of marriage, and the evil of
carnal concupiscence, on account of which, man, who is born by it,
contracts original sin.   For if man had not previously sinned, there
would have been none of this shameful concupiscence, which is im-
pudently praised by the impudent ; but marriage there would have
been, if no one had sinned , because there would have been the
semination of children in the body of that life without this disease,
without which it cannot now take place in the body of this death."
And this design of Augustine, he executed minutely enough.   He
distinguishes what he considered as the essential good of the marriage state (bona nuptialia), from concupiscence, which he does not
assign to the essence of wedlock, but which, as an evil derived from
the fall, is to be endured and turned to good, i. e. to the production
of children, who are to be regenerated by baptism.   Among the good
things of marriage, he reckons progeny, fidelity, and a sacrament,* by
which last, marriage acquires its indissoluble character. c 17.
" The devil does not obtain power over children by what is good in

---

* The church, in the progress of accumulating ordinances, early began
to consider marriage as a sacrament.—Tr

marriage, but by the evil of sensual lust, which indeed marriage properly employs, but must nevertheless be ashamed of." 22. See also De Pec. Orig. 33, 34, 37 ; De Gen. ad Lit. IX. 7 ; and several other passages in the third and fifth books against Julian.

As might be expected, the Pelagians were at an utter remove from the Augustinian view of concupiscence They could not comprehend how Augustine could call it an evil. The sexual passion, says Julian (Op. Imp IV. 43), is implanted by God. The impulse of the members is a divine arrangement. C. Duas Epp. Pel I. 15. To this, Augustine replied, according to his system, that God so instituted these that man had not to be ashamed of them. For it was not fitting that his creature should be ashamed of the work of the Creator ; but the disobedience of the members, was given as a punishment to the first disobedient pair, of which they were ashamed when they covered their nakedness with fig-leaves, but of which they had not to be ashamed before. But nowhere is the contrasted view of both sides more definitely given, than in C. Jul. III. 21. Here Julian says · " Whoever temperately uses natural concupiscence, uses a good thing well ; he who does not observe temperance, uses a good thing badly : but he who, by the love of holy virginity, despises even the temperate use, does still better in not using a good thing ; because, in the confidence of his safety and strength, he despises remedies, that he may maintain glorious contests." Julian therefore considered concupiscence as always a good. On the contrary, Augustine says " Whoever uses carnal concupiscence temperately, uses a bad thing well ; he who is not temperate, uses a bad thing badly ; but he who, by the love of holy virginity, despises even the moderate use, does still better, in not using a bad thing : because, in the confidence of the divine aid and grace, he despises feeble remedies, that he may maintain more glorious contests." Here Augustine argues sophistically against Julian, from the term *remedy*, in order to convict him from his own reasoning. For no remedy, forsooth, can be employed against anything good, but only against an evil. But this could only prove, that the term *remedy* was ill chosen, or, at most, that Julian had attributed an undue value to entire continence ; but not that he was wrong in asserting, that concupiscence is in itself good. But Augustine is still more sophistical, in Op. Imp. IV. 53, against Julian, who would not deny concupiscence in Christ, because he had a real body.

From this, Augustine endeavored, by several arguments, to draw the consequence, that Christ, in proportion as he ruled his passions more than other men, must have been more sensual, etc   And from Julian's concession, that we must resist sensual lust and fight against it, Augustine argued, that it is an evil   " There is no conflict without an evil.   For when there is conflict, either good and evil are contending, or evil and evil; or if two good things are in conflict, the very contest itself is a great evil " C. Jul. V. 7.   " Two good things, which are both from God the father, cannot be in conflict with each other , but continence and concupiscence are in conflict," etc. IV. 13. In like manner, Augustine brought this syllogism against Julian.   No work of God, is an object of shame; but concupiscence is an object of shame ; therefore it is no work of God.   De Nupt et Conc II 9.   The minor part of the syllogism, he also endeavored to prove, from the fact, that the allowed use of concupiscence by virtuous married persons, is connected with shame. C. Duas Epp Pel. I 16. Comp. Norisii Vindiciæ Augustinianæ, p. 19, seq —Julian, on the other hand, to support his assertion that concupiscence is nothing sinful, derived an argument from the fact, that it was conferred as a gift on Abraham and Sarah, when their members had become already dead, Rom. 4 : 19, and what God confers as a gift, cannot pertain to the work of the devil.   To this, Augustine replied, that it would follow from this principle, that if God raises a lame person from the dead, even the lameness must be considered as a gift of God   Such a power of the members was restored by God, as that which the nature of this body of death, brought with itself; but not such that they could produce children without the law of the members, as was the case before the sin of Adam. C Jul III. 11.   Julian further maintained, as concupiscence, in the wide sense, was the occasion of the first sin, and was therefore found in paradise before sin, that concupiscence cannot now be in itself sinful. Op. Imp. I. 71.   To parry this consequence, Augustine said, that, by the sin of the first man, the bad will came first, and then concupiscence followed, and therefore we must regard the former as the cause of the latter.   " The sinful will preceded, by which they believed the seducing serpent, and base sensual lust followed, by which they longed for the forbidden food.   And hence, though each was sinful, the will induced the desire, and not the desire the will ; it did not precede the will, nor resist it."

Nor could the Pelagians conceive how a creature of God, as Augustine considered the infant to be, can be subject to any other authority than the authority of God, for how a person just born can be subject to the authority of the devil. On this point, Julian poured forth his derision most unsparingly. According to Augustine, said he, " men are made by God on purpose that the devil may have them in his own right." C. Jul III 9. " God and the devil have entered into a covenant, that what is born, the devil shall have ; and what is baptized, God shall have." VI. 9. In several passages, Augustine sought to defend himself against objections of this kind, and to explain how man can be a work of God, and yet can be subject to the devil. " Human nature," says he (De Nupt. et Conc. I. 23), " is not condemned for what it is in itself, which is good, because it is the work of God , but by the damnable vice by which it is corrupted. And because it is condemned, it is subjected to the damned devil. Thus, also, the devil himself is a foul spirit , and yet something good, as a spirit, but bad as being foul. For he is a spirit by nature, but foul by vice : of which two, the first is from God ; the last, from himself. He does not therefore reign over men, whether of adult or infant age, because they are men, but because they are unclean. He, therefore, who wonders that a creature of God is subject to the devil, should not wonder. For a creature of God, is subject to a creature of God, the less to the greater, as the man to the angel. Nor is it on account of nature, but vice, that the foul is subject to the foul This is his fruit from the ancient stock of impurity, which he planted in man, himself having to suffer, by the last judgment, so much the greater punishment as he is the more foul. Nevertheless, they, to whom there shall be a more tolerable punishment, are subject to him as their prince, and the author of sin · for there will be no cause of condemnation, but sin." " Although even this," says he (C. Jul. III. 9), " is more from the power of God than of the devil, that a foul progeny should be subject to a foul prince, unless renovated ; yet God does not create men in order that the devil may, in a manner, have a family ; but by that goodness, by which he causes all natures to exist, and by which he makes even the devil to subsist. If this goodness were withdrawn from things, they would forthwith become nothing. As, therefore, he does not create animals among the flocks and herds of the impious, in order to their being sacrificed to demons, although

he knew they would do this ; so does he see the human progeny subject to sin, and yet, according to the most admirable order of generations which he has arranged, he does not withhold his goodness
from sustentation." "What God makes and man begets," says he,
VI. 14, "is certainly good, in as much as it is man ; but it is not
therefore without evil, because regeneration alone frees from the
sin which generation propagates from the first and great sin."
"The devil is the corrupter, not the author of our substance. By
that which he has inflicted, he subjects to himself what he did not
create, a righteous God giving him this power ; from whose power
the devil withdraws neither himself nor what is subjected to him."
VI. 19. "The whole man, both soul and body, in respect to his
substance, belongs of right to the Creator ; but by corruption, which
is no substance, he is the property of the devil. Still he is under
the power of the Creator, under which the devil himself is also
placed" III. 46 "Men, as men, are the work of God ; but as
sinners, they are under the devil, if not rescued from him by
Christ." C. Duas Epp Pel I. 18.

The Augustinian assumption of the propagation of sin by generation, appeared to the Pelagians to stand in the closest connection
with the assumption, that the soul is also propagated by generation.
But the propagation of the soul by generation, was doubtless ques-
tionable in their view, because the soul would thus seem to be
brought down to the sphere of the corporeal world ; a consequence
which Tertullian, who first set up that hypothesis in the church, even
directly acknowledged ! (Aug. Ep 190. c. 4). Hence the remark,
that Augustine's theory of original sin leads to the *traducianism* of
the soul, must have appeared to the Pelagians as an objection to its
soundness But Augustine would not acknowledge the necessary
connection between the propagation of Adam's sin by generation,
and the propagation of the soul ; although, as we shall hereafter see,
he was much inclined to this hypothesis. That objection was made
to Augustine by Julian, in a very biting way. Op. Imp II 178
"You say," so he addresses Augustine, "that sin then passed over,
when all men, (to use your own words), *were that one*}—By such an
argument you show nothing but your own impiety ; impiety, I say,
by which you believe that souls are propagated just like bodies,
which error was formerly condemned as profane in Tertullian and
Manes ; and which is so nefarious, that, since we made the objection

to you in the letter which we sent to the east, you have endeavored to repel it by a denial, in the books you have lately addressed to Boniface, (C. Duas Epp. Pel.) For you say, *men report us as maintaining the propagation of souls, but in whose books they have read this, I know not;* just as if you would protest, that no such thing had been said by you. But that the fallacy may be disclosed by a comparison of your language, how can you say that the truly profane opinion of the propagation of souls, is not contained in your meaning, when you profess that all men were that one? For if you do not believe the soul to be contained in the seed, with what countenance can you affirm, that all men were Adam alone, since man cannot exist at all except there be both soul and body at the same time?" And as, in the work addressed to Boniface, Augustine assumes the skeptic, in regard to the origin of the soul, and says, that he adheres to the plain teaching of scripture respecting an original sin, which is to be remitted to children by the laver of the new birth, and allows the origin of the soul—a very obscure matter—to pass by, and only maintains, that every assumption concerning the origin of the soul, which stands in opposition to that plain instruction, must be false (so he also says here, it is an assertion conformable to scripture, that at the time when Adam sinned, all men were in him, or were Adam himself; but whether only in respect to the body, or in respect to both body and soul, he knows not, and is not ashamed to confess his ignorance in the matter.) Comp. C' Jul. V. 15. In other passages, too, Augustine, though so dogmatic in other points, assumes the part of the skeptic in respect to this. ("As therefore," says he (C. Jul. V 4), "both soul and flesh are alike punished, unless what is born is purified by regeneration, certainly either *both* are derived in their corrupt state from man, [traducianism], or the one is corrupted in the other, as if in a corrupt vessel, where it is placed by the secret justice of the divine law, [creationism]. But which of these is true, I would rather learn than teach, lest I should presume to teach what I do not know." In reply to Julian, he says (Op Imp. IV. 104), "Blame my hesitation as to the origin of the soul, because I do not venture to teach or to maintain what I do not know. Bring forward, on this so dark a subject, what you please, if only that sentiment remain firm and unshaken, that the death of all is the fault of that individual, and that in him all have sinned." Also, in Ep. 190, he says, that on the origin of the soul, he has many doubts; but whatever one may think respecting it, never should he bring in doubt the truth, that every descendant of Adam is under his guilt and punishment, and never can be freed from them but by the new birth in Christ In Ep. 164, c. 7, he sets it forth as doubtful, whether original sin is not propagated by the flesh, which has its origin from Adam In Ep. 166, written about the year 415, he asks Jerome for instruction respecting the origin of the soul. This assumption of the part of the skeptic, was doubtless the wisest which Augustine could adopt. For in fact, he here found himself in a difficult situation If he maintained the propagation of the soul by generation, he could scarcely escape the reproach of materialism, and if he conceded that the soul is not thus propagated, the argumentation of Pelagius hit him, which he mentions himself, in De Pec Mer III. 3, and Ep. 190, c. 6. "If the soul is not propagated, and only the flesh propagates sin, then *this* only deserves punishment For it is unrighteous that the soul just born, and not originating from the mass of Adam, should bear a sin so old and foreign; for it is by no means to be allowed, that God who forgives one's own sins, should impute a single foreign sin "

Finally, Augustine, as it was in accordance with all the rest of his system, was inclined to assume, as the peculiar seat of sin. not so much the body as the soul. " The sinning soul," says he (De Civ Dei, XIV 3), " has brought forth the corruption of the flesh " He allowed, however, that, by the mutual action of soul and body, " some incitements to vice, and even some passions proceed from the corruption of the flesh " Were the body only the seat of sin, " the devil, who has no body," might be pronounced free from sin. But, by the transgression of the first man, the body as well as the soul was corrupted. " In paradise, arrogance (elatio) took its rise indeed through the soul, and hence the propensity to transgress the command, because the serpent said, Ye shall be as gods ; but the *whole man* completed that sin. Then originated that flesh of sin, whose infirmities are healed only by the likeness of the flesh of sin " C. Jul V 4 —That the Pelagians placed sin in the soul, scarcely needs to be further remarked. Hence Jerome, in his dialogue against the Pelagians, III. 11, makes his Pelagian, Critobulus, say, " As sickness and wounds are in the body, so sin is found in the soul "

But that God punishes sin with sin, and consequently, by the punishment of sin, causes more sins to be committed, the Pelagians regarded as a position injurious to the holiness of God, as God is thus made the author of sin. Pelagius himself gives his opinion on this point, in his book on nature See Aug. De Nat. et Gr. 21, 22. Here Augustine sought to defend himself by quoting some passages from the bible, and particularly from Paul

Against the Augustinian doctrine, that, besides sin itself, the other punishments of Adam's sin have passed over to his posterity, many objections were likewise made by the Pelagians, and particularly by Julian, as may be seen from Op. Imp. VI. A few of the most striking, may here find a place.

Against Augustine's assertion, that bodily death is a consequence of Adam's sin, Julian made the acute objection, that, according to the opinion of the church, Adam was pardoned after repentance, and how then could bodily death now remain to Adam's posterity, as a punishment of his sin? To meet this objection, Augustine distinguished between the temporal and the eternal punishment. To the temporal, belongs death; and this was not removed by Adam's repentance; but in respect to eternal punishment, his repentance had the effect, that he should indeed be chastised by a long, but not an eternal punishment; for Christ, by his descent to hell, has freed Adam from hell. Op. Imp. VI 22, 30. Comp. Ep. 164.

Nor was there any lack of striking objections against the other punishments which, according to Augustine's position, come on Adam's posterity for his sin "How insane," says Julian (Op. Imp. VI. 26), "is what you assert, first, that the pain of parturition is the attendant of sin, since it is so plain, that it has more regard to the condition of the sex than to the punishment of crimes, in as much as all animals, not stained with sin, endure those pains and utter groans in parturition. Hence it can manifestly be no proof of sin, as it is found where there is no sin. Then, you bring forward another assertion, still more foolish. Woman [you say], would not suffer if she were not a partaker in the guilt; and yet there you add, But this sin for which woman suffers, is not found in the mother, but in the child. For baptized women, you say, are free from the sin, but suffer for the sins of the children they bear. According to this opinion, the transmission of sin, is not from the mother to the child, but from the child back to the parents. For if the baptized woman thus experiences pain, because iniquities are found in the child, the pro-

pagation begins to be backward, not forward. But, you will say,
she does not suffer for the sin of the child, but because she brought
sin with herself when she was born. You have said, however, that
this evil is removed from her by grace If, therefore, the pain of
parturition belongs to the sin of the mother, the removal of sin ought
to cure the pain. But if the pain, which women suffer after baptism,
cannot here be without sin, then sin is not removed from them by
grace, and the pomp of baptism becomes worthless. But if there are,
in these mysteries,* the truth and power which we believe, and you
do not fabricate, and all sin is removed, and still the pain, produced
by the difficulty of parturition, remains, the pain is manifestly an
index of nature and not of criminality " On the other hand, Augustine replied, that it is doubtful whether brutes experience the pains
of parturition. But, granting that they feel such pains, " the punishment of the image of God, then, accrues to the condition of brutes ;
but the punishment of the image of God, could not be just, if no fault
preceded." To the objection, that baptized women suffer these
pains, Augustine answered : " These pains, which we say are a punishment of sin, in a nature vitiated by transgression, thus remain after remission, in order that faith may be proved, by which we believe in a coming age when these things will not be."

This objection, derived from baptism, against the Augustinian original sin, was often repeated by Julian, and answered by Augustine
in the like way. By baptism, as Julian believed, all evil must be
removed, and hence concupiscence too. If one denied this, he would
have to admit, that there is no saving efficacy in the mysteries of

---

* Another term then frequently applied to baptism, and put in the plural,
perhaps on account of the multiplied ceremonies then added to it And baptism was probably called a *mystery*, because of the mysterious powers that
had now come to be ascribed to it, as well as from a fondness for adopting heathen appellations into the christian nomenclature, and heathen conceits to a
place among the more simple christian rites In this way, the early fathers
hoped to commend Christianity to the taste and the respect of the heathen,
who were accustomed to boast of their own splendid *mysteries*, and to deride
Christianity for its want of them —A more deplorable mistake—touching its
effects on doctrine, and practice, and the direction of the religious sensibilities, and the grand conditions of salvation—cannot easily be imagined
These effects are visible throughout the whole of the present discussion,
and may indeed be traced throughout the whole internal history of the Romish church, and of some of the protestant churches, down to the present
day.—Tr

Christ —To this, Augustine replied, that the baptized person is indeed free from all sin, but not from all evil, or as he thought it might be more clearly expressed, he is free from the imputation of all evil, but not from all evil itself. There remains still, after baptism, the corruptibility of the body, and ignorance. Such evils remain in order that faith may find scope. For if the reward were already given to faith, faith would cease, because this in its nature respects something future. It therefore endures the present evils, and confidently and patiently expects the promised good C. Jul. VI. 16, 17 ; Op Imp II. 94. Comp De Pec. Mer II 27, 31 sqq. ; and Op. Imp. II. 93, where he replies to the following objection · If bodily death is the punishment of sin, why should the baptized child die, since sin is forgiven to him by baptism ? The removal of sin must also bring the taking away of death, or else sin would produce more injury than redemption brings benefit. Why does the punishment of sin remain, when sin itself is no more ' Temporal death, replies Augustine, remains for the exercise of faith. What was the punishment of sinners before forgiveness, is the conflict and exercise of the righteous after forgiveness. Comp. Ep. 157. c. 3 ; De Civ. Dei, XIII. 4. He also remarked, in regard to concupiscence, that " this, though called sin, is not so called because it is itself sin, but because it is produced by sin ; just as writing is called the *hand* of some one, because the hand produced it But sins are what are unlawfully done, said, or thought, according to fleshly concupiscence, or ignorance, which, when transacted, hold the persons guilty, if not forgiven."[*] C Duas Epp Pel I 13.

---

[*] In this last sentence, Augustine gives us, in manner and form, his definition of sin It comes also in such a connection and accompanied by such discriminating remarks, as seem to leave no possibility of doubt as to his views of its nature, in one of the most important points of discussion at the present day, viz whether anything is really sinful in man, except his voluntary exercises Some may be surprised to find such a definition as this from one who is so continually insisting on the guilt of original sin But a careful study of this and some other passages from his pen, may show us more definitely where he placed this guilt, viz in the first act of sin which Adam committed, and in which each one of us bore a part, and not even at all in the sinful disposition or " concupiscence" which comes down from Adam to us. This concupiscence, though so often called sin by him, and regarded as truly " something bad," yet he here explains as not being really sin, but the product of sin, that is, of the first sin doubtless, for which this comes as a punishment.—For the satisfaction of those who take an interest

Finally, against the Augustinian idea, that the sweat of labor, etc. is a punishment of Adam's sin, many keen remarks were made by Julian, which Augustine, in the sixth book of his Unfinished Work,

---

in this question, I subjoin the original of the passage, together with some additional sentences which cast further light on his views of this and kindred topics —Sed haec [concupiscentia], etiamsi vocatur peccatum, non utique quia peccatum est, sed quia peccato facta est, sic vocatur, sicut scriptura manus cujusque dicitur, quod manus eam fecerit. Peccata autem sunt, quae secundum carnis concupiscentiam vel ignorantiam illicite fiunt, dicuntur, cogitantur, quae transacta etiam reos tenent, si non remittantur Et ista ipsa carnis concupiscentia in baptismo sic dimittitur, ut quamvis tracta sit a nascentibus, nihil noceat renascentibus Ex quibus tamen, si filios carnaliter gignunt, rursus trahitur, rursusque est nocitura nascentibus, nisi eadem forma renascentibus remittatur, et insit nihil obfutura vitae futurae quoniam reatus ejus generatione tractus, regeneratione dimissus est et ideo jam nun sit peccatum, sed hoc vocetur, sive quod peccato facta sit, sive quod peccandi delectatione moveatur, etsi ei vincente delectatione justitiae non consentiatur Nec propter ipsam, cujus jam reatus lavacro regenerationis absumtus est dicunt in oratione baptizati, Dimitte nobis debita nostra, sicut et nos dimittimus debitoribus nostris, sed propter peccata quae fiunt, sive in ejus consensionibus, cum ab eo quod libet vincitur quod placet, sive cum per ignorantiam malum quasi bonum placet Fiunt autem, sive operando, sive loquendo, sive, quod facillimum atque celerrimum est, cogitando —From the latter part of this remarkable passage, it still further appears, in perfect consistency with what is translated in the text, that Augustine considers the baptized as having no longer to pray for the pardon of original sin, but only for those sins which they continue daily to commit, either in thought, word, or deed In other words, nothing needs forgiveness but what consists either " in doing or speaking or thinking " That is, on this part of the great question respecting the nature of sin, Augustine was what we should now call a Hopkinsian.

The work from which the above is taken, was written as late as the year 420, eight years after Augustine had commenced the controversy, and only ten before his death, and consequently at a period when he may be supposed to have pretty thoroughly matured his own views, and settled the import of his own language, on the nature of sin, both original and actual And, moreover, that he did in fact continue, ever after, of the same opinion respecting the nature of sin, is evident from plain declarations of his in subsequent works, (some of which will hereafter be adduced), and especially from declarations found in his Unfinished Work, (e g IV 103), where he says . " There cannot be sin without will, *because it takes by the will* "

And now, if we would know in what way he would get along with this doctrine, and still hold that we are really *criminal* for original sin, our curiosity will be gratified by what soon follows in the text, in respect to our agency in the first transgression —TR

endeavored to refute at great length, (but not always to the purpose), chiefly by quotations from scripture, which he explains in his own way and which he calls the catholic way.

But the Pelagians, particularly Julian, fixed a keen eye on that side where the Augustinian theory of original sin, exposes a very naked spot, I mean, the contradiction between that theory and the righteousness of God. How Pelagius argues, from the idea of God's justice, against Augustine's doctrine of original sin, by which foreign guilt is imputed to a man, we have already seen above, while presenting his theory of the natural state of man. Augustine thus replied to him, in the spirit of his system. "Nor are those sins called foreign (aliena) in such a sense as if they did not belong at all to infants; since in Adam all sinned, as there was placed in his nature the power of producing them, and they were all as yet one with him (adhuc omnes ille unus fuerunt). But the sins are called foreign, because the persons were not yet living their own lives, but the life of one man contained whatever there was in the future offspring. *But by no means is it granted*, say they, *that God, who pardons men's own sins, imputes to them foreign sins.* He pardons, but by the spirit of regeneration, not by the flesh of generation : but he does not impute what are *now* foreign, but their own. They *were* foreign, to be sure, when they who should bear them as propagated, were not as yet , but now, by carnal generation, they are theirs to whom they have not yet been forgiven by spiritual regeneration." De Pec. Mer. III. 8 Julian reasons, in the same way as Pelagius, from the justice of God, against Augustine's original sin. If God is just, says he, he can impute no foreign sin [the sin of another] to children. But God must be just, if he is to deserve the name of a God. Justice is inseparably connected with the being of God To this, Augustine replied in the first part of the first book of his Unfinished Work In addition, however, to the remark against Julian, that original sins have become our own by the contagion of their origin, he knew of nothing to say to the purpose, but to appeal to the depth of the wisdom of God With greater appearance of truth, he thus replies to this Julian, who speaks very strongly, in another place, of the injustice of God as following from Augustine's doctrine of original sin : " Divine justice is as much more inscrutable than human justice, as it is above it ; and it differs proportionably from it. For what just man suffers a crime to be perpetrated, which it is in his

17

power not to suffer ? And yet God suffers these things, who is incomparably more just than all the just, and whose power is incomparably greater than all powers. Think of these things, and do not
compare God the judge to human judges, who is undoubtedly just,
even when he does what would seem to men unjust, and what man
would be unjust in doing." Op. Imp. III. 24. In another place,
I 57, he says to Julian " *You* rather make God unjust, as it seems
to you unjust to visit the iniquities of the fathers upon the children,
which he frequently declares by words and shows by deeds that he
does. You, I say, make God unjust ; since, when you see infants,
under the care of him, the omnipotent, pressed with a grievous yoke
of misery, you contend, that they have no sin, thus at once accusing
both God and the church   God, if they are oppressed and afflicted,
while innocent ; the church, if they are blown upon [exorcised],
while exempt from the dominion of diabolical power." [As Julian,
therefore, argued from the justice of God to the *non*-existence of
original sin, so Augustine argued, from the justice of God and the
various evils which happen to children, to the *existence* of original
sin. Without this, it would be unjust, in his view, that children
should be loaded with such misery III. 7, 68.)

Furthermore, the contradiction that lies in the idea of original sin,
—if freedom is presupposed in sin, (as is proper,) and if sin is a
wilful transgression of the divine law,—did not escape the Pelagians.
This contradiction between freedom and Augustine's original sin,
and consequently between freedom and necessity, Pelagius had in
his eye, in his book On Nature. " How can a man be guilty, before
God, of a sin which he has never known to be his ? For it is not
his, if it is necessary   Or if it is his, it is voluntary ; and if it is voluntary, it can be avoided " De Nat. et Gr. 30. " If there is no sin
without will," says Julian, according to Op Imp I. 48, " and if there
is no will without free liberty, and if there is no liberty where there
is no power of choice by reason, by what prodigy can sin be found
in infants, who have not the use of reason ? and therefore not the
power of choice, and consequently no will ; and these being irrefu-
tably conceded, therefore no will at all ?" What Augustine replied,
here and in other passages, to arguments of this sort, while still holding fast to the shadow of a freedom, is wholly inapplicable. See,
for example, IV. 93, 103.* The contradiction, however, between

---

* Still, the reader may like to judge for himself whether these passages

original sin and freedom, could properly be no objection to Augustine, since, according to his theory, as he has carried it out in the Pelagian controversy, the loss of freedom by Adam's fall, belonged to original sin and constituted an essential part of it.

The Pelagians also remarked, that there can be no natural sin, for that which is natural, cannot be denominated sin. To this, Augustine replied, but without hitting the objection itself, that there is indeed no natural sin ; but the will of nature, especially of corrupt nature, (whereby we have by nature become children of wrath,) is not adequate to refraining from sin, unless aided and amended by the grace of God through Christ. De Perf. Just. Hom 2. Julian in particular, showed, that there is no natural sin, because God is the author of nature, and he can produce nothing evil. What Augustine, who did not regard the expression, *natural sin,* as quite proper, replied to this, in accordance with his own view, may well be supposed from what has heretofore been said. Op Imp V. 63.

The reasoning of Julian, is characteristic, and not without point, which Mercator adduces in his Commonitorium, p. 115. He relates that Julian, during his abode at Rome, asked a simple Christian, What is original sin, something good, or evil ? Evil, by all means, was the answer. Upon this, he further inquired, whether God is

---

are to the point or not In the first referred to, Augustine says to Julian " Why do you not consider that there indeed is involuntary sin ? certainly in him who says, (from whatever cause he says it), *But if I do that which I would not, now I do not perform it, but sin that dwelleth in me* Why do you not consider, that there is a necessity for one to wish to live happily ? and thus, with closed eyes, oppose the one to the other, as if a will of necessity and a necessity of will, could not be ?" In the other place, Augustine says to him " You would not say, that necessity and will could not exist at the same time, if it were given you to know what you say For although there is a necessity of dying, who will deny that there may also be a will ?— Likewise he who voluntarily *commits* sin, *has* sin against his will, being willingly immodest, but unwillingly guilty , for sin surely remains against his will, though it could not take place against his will. And according to this, both are true, that there cannot be sin without will, because it takes place by the will, and there can be sin without will, because that which was done by the will, remains without the will and there is now the necessity without will, which the will produced without necessity." He then goes on to press Julian with *his* sort of necessity, resulting from the *habit of sinning ;* and succeeds somewhat better, in his argumentum ad hominem, than in some portion of the above plea.—Tr

the author and producer of this evil? Not in the least, was the reply. He then inquired, whether sin is a substance or nature; or whether it is an accident? And when the simple Christian had hesitated a while for an answer, he added ⟨Sin is by no means a substance or nature; because, if it be, it has God for its author or producer. For there is no nature which God has not made. But as it is decided that God is not the author of evil, so sin, which is manifestly an evil, is not a substance or nature. But what is no substance, we can with no justice or reason believe to pass over into a substance or nature, which man is. And hence he inferred, that it is incorrect and foolish, to believe any sin to be propagated down from Adam by generation⟩ In this spirit, was the objection of Pelagius, in his book on nature. "Before all things, I believe we must inquire, what is sin? Is it a substance at all? or a name to which there is no substance, and by which is expressed, not a thing, not an existence or bodily substance, but the performance of a bad act? I believe this is the case, and if it is so, how can that, which has no substance, weaken or change human nature?"—Finally; we have already seen how Augustine endeavored to avoid the Pelagian conclusion, that the Manichaean doctrine of a bad nature of man, follows from his theory, and that this nature could therefore have been produced only by a bad author, for Augustine explained original sin as being, not the substance of man. but an accident. See C Jul. III 8. The nature of man, as such, he regarded as good. " This is good; and God is not the author of evil. We do not complain of the nature of the soul or the body, which God has made, and which is wholly good; but we say, that it is corrupted by its own will, and cannot be healed but by the grace of God —The nature of man, is good, and may be without any evil." De Perf. Just Hom 6 " God makes the nature of men; but not the corruption by which they are evil.—He makes them as men; but not as sinners.' Op. Imp. I. 114. Comp VI. 18, 19. " The bad will is not from God. This is against nature, which is from God " De Civ. Dei, V. 9 " Corruption is so much against nature, that it cannot but injure nature." XI. 17. " No one is bad by nature, but every one that is bad, is bad by corruption " XIV 6 —On the other hand, Augustine charged on the Pelagians the consequence, (unfounded indeed,) of making God the author of sin, by believing in carnal passions before the fall, and therefore of falling into Manichaeism. Op. Imp. VI. 14.

In the quotations already made, there are likewise some very striking objections against the Augustinian doctrine of man's loss of freedom by the fall. If man has no freewill, he cannot be accountable, and it must be in the highest degree unjust in God, to punish a man for anything, the performance or the neglect of which, does not depend on himself. Hence Pelagius says, in his book on nature (Aug. De Nat et Gr. 7), " If men are thus because they cannot be different, they are not to blame." And in c. 12, he says : " Sins ought not to be visited with even the smallest punishment, provided they cannot be avoided." But all virtue ceases, and every admonition to repentence and holiness of life, is useless, and the commands of God are needless, if man has no freewill. This was very well set forth, particularly by Pelagius in his letter to Demetrias, c. 8, 19. Julian also remarked, in respect to one of Christ's admonitions to the Jews, that the whole of this species of warning, is without meaning, if man has lost freewill Op Imp I 88. This objection, Augustine could not answer at all satisfactorily , for the freewill, which he, compelled by objections of this kind, occasionally, but sophistically, admitted in words, was, as we have seen, no freewill at all ; and Julian could not refrain from ridiculing the idea, that a freewill should not be able to will what is good   The depth of the wisdom of God, as well as passages of scripture which he quoted and explained in his own way, must here often have helped him out of difficulty.

Julian also made the shrewd remark, that freewill itself could not be lost by the bad application of freewill. For the bad will is even a proof of its freedom. And how could the very capacity of its exercise, be annihilated by the commencement of its exercise ? etc. Op. Imp VI. 11.

But how revolting it was to the Pelagians, that Augustine should hold to the eternal condemnation of men on account of Adam's sin, we have already seen while on infant baptism.

These are some of the objections with which the Pelagians assailed the Augustinian theory of original sin, and against which Augustine could only defend himself with difficulty. He betook himself mostly to defence. Here and there, however, he ventured an assault on the Pelagian theory as opposed to his.

We have already seen how Augustine attacked the Pelagian principle, that concupiscence is always something good. Two other assaults on his part, may here find a place, which have already indeed, in part, been indicated, but not presented in all their consequences

He argues thus. What fault have small children committed, if no original sin be allowed, that they are born so weak and ignorant, when Adam was furnished with such great endowments? De Pec. Mer. I 36. " As original sin is denied in them, let it be answered, why such great innocence is sometimes born blind, sometimes deaf? Who can endure, (what belongs to the mind itself,) that the image of God, *enriched*, as you say, *with the dowry of innocence*, should be born idiotic, if no evil merits pass from parents to children?—But who does not know, that those vulgarly called fools, are by nature so idiotic, that the sense of brutes may almost be compared with some of them?" C. Jul. III. 4. " Whence the evil in the world, with which some of those are born, who have not yet the use of their freewill? Whence that concupiscence, the conflict between the flesh and the spirit?" etc Op Imp VI. 5. " What crime has the image of God committed, that it is encumbered with a decaying body, to the hindrance of useful knowledge, if there is no original sin?" III. 44 " And it cannot be said, that the child suffers evil in order that his virtue may be exercised, since as yet there is none of it in him." 49. " If it is not admitted, that such gross and manifest evil, with which men are born, is derived from an origin corrupted by sin, then must we adopt the Manichaean doctrine of an evil nature, by the intermingling of which, the nature of God is corrupted." V. 54. To arguments of this kind, the Pelagians might have urged much in reply. They might have adduced all with which *theodicaea*,* of later times, has defended, the holiness and justice of God, against objections of the same sort. And they might here, with greater propriety than Augustine, have appealed to *the depth of the wisdom of God*, as the question pertained, not to a hypothesis unproved, and even at war with the moral demands of reason and with revelation, but to the undeniable experience of the world of sense But we do not find that they embarked in the refutation of these objections. What Augustine adduces as Julian's opinion in this respect, is utterly insignificant VI. 27.

---

* *Theodicaea* is a term derived from Θεὸς and δικαιόω, and signifies *a vindication of God*. It is applied to that department of theology which regards the divine justice, wisdom, and power, in relation to the existence of evil J J. Wagner published a new *Theodicaea* at Bamberg in 1809 —Tr

From their own concessions, also, Augustine brought against the Pelagians the objection : If there is no original sin, what guilt has the new-born child contracted, by which it is excluded from the kingdom of heaven, according to your doctrine, if it dies before baptism ? I 136. Nothing further, however, follows from this, but the unsatisfactoriness of the Pelagian distinction between salvation and the kingdom of heaven.

Augustine also proposed this further instance to Julian, who admitted only eternal death as the punishment of sin. " If only eternal, and not also temporal death, be the punishment of sin, why does nature, which you praise as if you denied it to be corrupted, fear this ? Why does the child, just emerging from infancy, fear to die ? Why is not sense (sensus) inclined to death, just as to sleep ? Why are those so highly esteemed, who fear not death ? and why are they so rare ?—If, therefore, the fear of death is without cause, the very fear of it is a punishment But if the soul naturally fears a separation from the body, death itself is a punishment, although divine grace may turn it to a good purpose." II. 186.

As Julian defended the Pelagian explanation of freedom, as being " the possibility of good and evil," and justified the position, that virtue is not voluntary when it is necessary, and that it would have the character of necessity, if there was not the possibility of the opposite, Augustine remarked, that Julian had forgotten to think of God in this matter, whose virtue is necessary just in proportion as he cannot help willing it. V. 61.—We need not suggest how unphilosophical it was, to speak of virtue in God, of which holiness is predicated [?—Tr.]—Augustine also urged against the Pelagians the consequence, that, according to their definition, freedom must be denied to God, since there is no " possibility of evil" in him III. 120. The [glorified] saints, too, must have lost their freedom, for they also cannot sin, VI 10 ; and yet this is to be called a higher degree of freedom. De Cor et Gr. 12 , Op Imp. VI 19. To this, as well as to the foregoing objections, we find no answer, on the part of the Pelagians , which, however, would not have been difficult; but in which, the question agitated between the theists, on the one hand, and the pantheists and materialists, on the other, must have been touched upon, viz., whether, and in what sense, reason and freedom can be attributed to the Absolute.

Finally, as it respects the Pelagian position of man's being able to be without sin, in this life,—a position which, in regard to its abstract possibility, follows from the idea of freedom, and the truth of which could not therefore be denied, the moment moral freedom was allowed,—Augustine explained himself (De Pec Mer II. 6; De Spir. et Lit. 5, 35, 37), as so far allowing the possibility of man's being without sin, that the possibility is conditioned on grace and freewill, although no one is in fact found to be without sin. " We should not, with inconsiderate heat, oppose those who maintain, that man may be without sin in this life. For if we deny the possibility, we detract both from the freewill of the man who voluntarily desires this, and also from the power or mercy of God, which effects it by his aid " As Augustine regarded the good conduct of man as a " divine gift," he had to allow the possibility, that God could always afford such a gift, for with God, he added, nothing is impossible. Still he remarked (De Pec. Mer. II 20), that man must always be a sinner previously to his being able to reach such a degree of sanctification. This followed most conclusively from Augustine's supposition of a radical corruption, to which all men are subjected. But, again; he regarded freewill, which he mentions as a condition of being without sin, as an immediate effect of divine grace; by which freewill, therefore, ceases to be freewill. Consequently, Augustine agreed with the Pelagians in granting the possibility of man's being without sin ; but conformably to the spirit of his system, he differed from them in referring this ability to grace, while Pelagius and his adherents referred it to freewill. " If I also allow, that some have been or are without sin, still I maintain, that in no other way are they or have they been able to be so but by being *justified by the grace of God* through Jesus Christ our Lord, who was crucified." De Nat. et Gr 44 In respect to the virgin Mary, he was doubtful whether we ought to say that she was without sin ; but he always held it improper, and contrary to the reverence due to Jesus, to speak of the sin of Mary For we know not but grace was given her wholly to vanquish sin, who was worthy (meruit) to conceive and bear him who had no sin. 36.

CHAPTER VIII

Theory of the Pelagians on the state of man before the fall. Opposite theory of Augustine.

The Augustinian theory of original sin, first receives its full light through Augustine's doctrine of the state of man before the fall. Nay, this is inseparably connected with that. Here, then, is a fit place to introduce it, and to exhibit it in contrast with the Pelagian doctrine on the state of the first man before transgression.

How the primitive state of man was considered by both sides, may in general be anticipated. From opposite opinions of original sin, must opposite theories spontaneously shape themselves concerning the state of Adam before he sinned.

According to the Pelagian doctrine, the state of man before the fall, was the same as it is now. For as there is, by that theory, no imputation of Adam's guilt and punishment, there can, by the same theory, be nothing lost from the original state of man   The first man had therefore perception, understanding, and freedom of will, by which he could either sin or not sin. But his body was subject to disease and death, just as at present. If Pelagius himself did not expressly teach this last, yet his followers did. The words in Genesis. "In the day thou eatest thereof, thou shalt die the death," they therefore could not understand, with Augustine, of bodily death, but must have referred to spiritual death, i. e. sin; an explanation which Augustine assailed in his first work against the Pelagians.—According to their view, the primitive state of the first man, was superior only in this, that no example of sinning had yet been presented for imitation, and the first man, who came into the world as an adult, had the full use of reason at the beginning, and hence had likewise his freedom. And in this sense, the Pelagians could say, that men are not now born in the same state in which Adam was created.— Finally; in his physical and moral condition, the first man was as man now is. Even concupiscence, which Augustine held as something evil, and as the mother of all evil, but the Pelagians explained as a natural passion, was found in paradise.

18

That this was the Pelagian doctrine concerning the earliest state
of the first man, scarcely needs any further proof, since it follows
from the Pelagian view of the present structure of man's moral nature. Still the following passages may serve for further confirmation · " God, who is as just as he is good, has so made man, that he
might be free from sin if he would," said Pelagius in his book on nature See Aug De Nat et Gr 43   With this, compare the delinea-
tion of the prerogatives of human nature, in the letter of Pelagius
to Demetrias, c. 2, where no mention at all is made of a different
state of Adam before and after the fall   According to this picture,
God determined, before he created him, to make the man, whom he
designed to produce, after his own image and likeness   He designed that man should know the dignity of his nature, from his admirable dominion over the strong beasts   For God left him not naked
and helpless. He did not expose him, weak, to the various dangers.
He at least armed him most strongly within with reason and ingenu-
ity, so that he alone, by the gifts of the spirit, whereby he is superior to all other animals, knew the Creator of all things, and served
God by the same endowments that enabled him to rule the rest of
creation   Still, the Lord of righteousness designed that he should
act voluntarily, not by compulsion   Hence he left him to his own
deliberation, placing before him life and death, good and evil , and
whatever would please him, was to be given him, as God said to the
Israelites in the fifth book of Moses.   Only we should guard against
the stumbling block of the ignorant multitude, as though man were
not made truly good, because he can do evil, and is not violently
impelled by his nature to good, etc. " Freewill," says Julian, " is
as much freewill since the fall, as it was before." Op. Imp. I. 91.
Natural blessings, among which Julian reckons freewill, were " ina-
missible " VI. 19   " Both of us," says Augustine to Julian, " pronounce Adam's nature good, since we say, that it could refrain from
sinning, if it chose not to sin ; but I consider it better than you do,
since I maintain, that it also could not die, if it had refused to sin."
VI 16.   According to Julian, " man is made mortal *naturally*, and
not as a *punishment* " III 156   " Not only imperious lust, but also
oppressive fever, and all the other innumerable diseases by which
we see children suffer and die; according to your theory, would have
been found in paradise, though no one had sinned " II 236.   Still,
however, according to a passage in the letter he sent to Rome, in

which he approached the Augustinian orthodoxy as nearly as he possibly could, (as appears by a passage quoted from the same letter by Mercator, in his *Commonitorium*, Ap. p. 116), Julian admitted that Adam was created immortal, in the sense that, if he had not sinned, he would have obtained immortality by eating of the tree of life. And according to a passage in Augustine (Op. Imp. VI 30), he said that he would not contend with those who believed that Adam, if he had remained obedient, might have become immortal *by way of reward.* But his natural state is to be distinguished from the reward of obedience. And if Adam had obtained immortality, still, the native mortality would have shown itself in his posterity.

But the Pelagians might always have admitted, that Adam's sin not only injured him, but also his posterity, because it presented an example of sin for their imitation. They could also allow, without contradicting their dogma of the non-existence of original sin, that men are not now born in the same state as Adam was before transgression, since Adam, as an adult, was endowed with reason and freedom, but his posterity are born without the use of reason. In this sense, Pelagius himself condemned the proposition, at Diospolis, that "Adam's sin has injured him only, and not the human race; and that infants are in the same state in which Adam was before sin." And hence he granted, in his book on freewill, that he had condemned it in this sense, and in perfect consistency with this, is the opinion he afterwards expressed, that children are born without sin, and that nothing is found in them but what God has created. De Pec. Orig. 15. With this compare the quotations from the above-mentioned epistle of Julian, in Mercator (Common. Ap p. 115 sq.) in which Julian, in order to remove the reproach of heterodoxy from himself and his accomplices, rejected much of Pelagianism, but still adopted views on such points, different from the Augustinian. He yielded something, however, in order to conciliate Augustine, which stands in contradiction with his later and full explanations in his writings against Augustine.

Furthermore; since the Pelagians regarded concupiscence, of which Augustine had so much evil to say, as a good and natural attribute of human nature, being of use in a lawful and proper way, and indispensable to the propagation of the human race, they had therefore to admit its existence in paradise. Op. Imp. III. 212 ; VI.

16. Julian called concupiscence, when kept within its prescribed limits, " a natural and innocent affection." I. 71.

Augustine, on the other hand, had to attribute to man, in his original state, all which he lost, according to his theory, by the fall, and which was lost to the whole race by original sin. Hence Adam had a perfectly faultless and sinless nature. This faultless and sinless nature, both moral and physical, he possessed because he had not, like his descendants, been born of sinful parents. " Who does not know, that man was made sane and faultless, and furnished with free will and free power for holy living ?" De Nat. et Gr. 43. " Adam was not made like us, because, without the preceding sin of a progenitor, he was not made in the flesh of sin." De Pec Mer. I. 37.

As belonging to this original and good state, in which the first man was found, Augustine reckons the following things.

1. Adam had an intelligent and rational nature, in which Augustine places the image of God He possessed a perfect understanding, so that the wisest of his descendants cannot be at all compared with him   " Such was his power of mind and use of reason, that Adam docilely received the precept of God and the law of commandment, and might easily have kept them if he would." Ib. "As man, since the fall, is renewed in the knowledge of God after the image of him that created him, so was he also created in that knowledge itself, before he became old by sin, from which he needs again to be renewed in the same knowledge." De Gen. ad Lit. III. 20. " The image of God, impressed on the spirit of the mind, which Adam lost, we again obtain by the grace of righteousness " VI. 27. Hence he says, In the inward man, Adam was spiritual, after the image of him that created him, referring to the words of Paul, *Ye are renewed in the spirit of your mind,* etc VI. 28   " Not only the clearest reason, but also the authority of the apostle himself, teaches, that man was created in the image of God, not in the form of his body, but in respect to the rational mind " De Trin XII 7. For this, he appeals to Eph. 4 23. Col 3. 9 Comp. Conff XIII. 22, 23. —Augustine attributes to Adam " the most excellent wisdom," and regards it as a proof of the corruption of our nature, that genius and bravery are now so rare among men. Even Pythagoras considered those as the wisest who first gave names to things. But Adam did this. And if we had not known this of him, yet we might have in-

ferred his exquisite nature, from his having no corruption. The most talented of our time, regard themselves, in comparison with Adam's genius, as tortoises to birds in point of speed, etc. Op Imp V. 1. "As all was learned in paradise, which was useful to be known there, that blessed nature obtained it without labor or pain, as it was either taught by God or by nature herself." VI. 9.

2. Adam had freedom of will, so that he could sin or refrain from sinning. " But who of us says, that freewill perished from the human race, by the sin of the first man ? *Liberty*, indeed, perished by sin ; but *that liberty* which was in paradise, of having complete righteousness with immortality." C. Duas Epp. Pel. I. 2. " Adam was made with freedom to good." Op. Imp. II. 7. "The first man had not the grace to cause him never to will to be evil.—God left it to his freewill whether he would persevere in the good will." De Cor. et Gr 11. Augustine made a distinction between " being able not to sin," and " not being able to sin," (posse non peccare, and non posse peccare). 12. The first, man possessed before the fall ; the last is the portion of the saints after this life. " The first man did not receive from God the gift of perseverance in good, but perseverance or non-perseverance, was left to his freewill. For his will, which was constituted without sin, and which no passion resisted, 'had such power, that the decision of perseverance was properly left to such great goodness and such great facility of holy living." Ib. " By freewill, which then had its powers uncorrupted, the first pair undoubtedly did whatever they would, i e they obeyed the divine law, not only with no impossibility (nulla impossibilitate), but even with no difficulty." Op. Imp. VI 8. " That man had so very free a will, that he obeyed the law of God with great energy of mind." IV. 14. " Man could have refrained from sin, if he had willed not to sin." VI. 16. " It depended entirely on the liberty of the first man, to refrain from that which he inordinately desired." VI. 17. " Man was so made, that he had, of necessity, the possibility of sinning; but sin itself, only in *possibility*. But he would not have had even the possibility of sinning, if he had been of the nature of God ; for he would have been immutable, and could not have sinned. He did not therefore sin in consequence of being made out of nothing, but might have refrained from sinning " V. 60. " God is an immutable good. Man also, in respect to the nature in which God made him, is indeed a good ; but not an immutable good, like God." De

Gen. ad Lit. VIII 14. " God, the author of natures, but not of blem-
ishes, made man *right*, but when he became *voluntarily* corrupt and
was condemned, he begat the corrupt and the condemned." De Civ.
Dei, XIII. 14. Since Adam's freewill was originally adapted to good,
Augustine also said, that man was furnished by God with a good
will; for which he appealed to Ecc. 7. 29. He was disposed to obey
God, and obediently received his command. This he could fulfil
without difficulty, as long as he chose; and, when he chose, could
transgress without necessity. The good will, Augustine attributed
to the first man, in opposition to Julian, who only attributed the *possibility* of a good will to the nature of man, but the good will itself,
he ascribed to the man himself, that he might not encroach on freewill Op Imp V 61 Hence Augustine attributed a merit (meri-
tum) to man before the fall; and indeed, according to his use of
terms, a " good merit," in the good will, which was aided by grace,
and an " evil merit" in the perverted will, which forgot God. De Civ.
Dei, XIV 27

According to Augustine, therefore, man did not possess any such
perfection of will, that he could not sin at all,—for he even did sin;
—nor did the first man possess holiness and righteousness, which
have since been attributed to him, (not very philosophically, to be
sure,) as the image of God; but a moral freedom of will, by which
it was ever possible to sin, although the fulfilling of the divine command, was easy to him In a work not relating to the Pelagian controversies (De Gen ad Lit VI 27), Augustine indeed says, in quoting Paul's words—Put ye on the new man which is created according to God, in righteousness and holiness of truth—that Adam lost
this by sin But Augustine here no more takes righteousness and
holiness in the philosophical sense, than did the apostle himself—
But Augustine sought to make the possibility of sinning manifest, by
this, that man, in respect to his better part, the soul, was created out
of nothing, and therefore did not belong to the nature of God, the
immutable good. De Nupt et Conc. II. 28; Op. Imp V. 31 sqq.

3. Man needed the grace of " assistance" even before the fall,
without which, he could not have persevered in good if he would
" God had given man an assistance, without which he could not have
persevered in good if he would —He could persevere if he would,
because that aid (adjutorium) did not fail, by which he could. Without this, he could not retain the good which he might will." De Cor.

et Gr. 11. This aid, which was given to the first man, was, how-ever, different from that aid of grace, which is now afforded to the elect. Respecting this difference, Augustine thus explains himself. " Freewill was sufficient for sin , but not adequate to good, unless aided by the omnipotent good. If man had not voluntarily abandon-ed this aid, he would have been always good but he abandoned, and was abandoned. For this aid was such as he could abandon when he would, and in which he might remain if he would ; but not by which he might become what he would. This is the first grace which was given to the first Adam ; but a more powerful than this, in the second Adam For by the first aid, man might have right-eousness if he would. The second can effect more ; by which it comes to pass, that he *wills*, and so strongly wills and so ardently loves, that, by the will of the spirit, he conquers the will of the flesh, that lusts for the opposite things —But if this *aid* had been wanting to either angel or man, when they were first made, they would in-deed have fallen *without their own fault*, since nature was not made such that it could remain if it would without divine aid, because the aid would have been wanting without which they could not perse-vere "* Ib. In c. 12, Augustine distinguishes between an " aid by which a thing takes place," and an " aid without which it does not take place." The first he considers as afforded to the elect since the fall , the last, to Adam before the fall. By the first, the will it-self is produced ; by the last, the performance of good was rendered possible, if man willed it. This aid, which was afforded to the un-corrupted nature of man, Augustine compares to a light, by the help of which, sound eyes can see if they will De Nat. et Gr. 48.

According to Augustine's theory, therefore, Adam did not need,

---

* The careful reader will see, from this remarkable passage, that Augus-tine, after all, did not differ so very widely from his antagonists as has often been supposed, in respect to this one grand point, the *justice* of charging blame on beings who have never had the power to do anything but sin According to Augustine, had not the angels, and Adam, and we in Adam, had the requisite aid to stand, there could have been no fault in the fall, The difference, then, between him and the Pelagians on this point, was the simple though important circumstance, that he placed the probation of us all in Adam, where he supposed the most ample endowment for probation, while they placed the probation for each individual, in his own separate ex-istence. But neither party supposed there could be guilt where there had *never* been any power of free agency to good as well as to evil —TR.

before the fall, the grace which is *here* necessary to the elect, in order to conquer sensual passions; for these were not found in him.
As Augustine likewise expresses himself (De Cor. et Gr.), Adam
needed not the death of Christ; but he needed the grace of God, in
order to persevere in good, and steadfastly to will it. Without this
grace, as appears from the passages quoted,'Adam could not be good
by his own freewill; but he could abandon this grace by his freewill For freewill is quite competent to evil, but is not adequate to
good, if not aided by God.—Now as man needed aid, even in paradise, Augustine could say of him, that he abandoned the grace of
God by the first transgression. C. Jul. VI. 22. And to this he resorted, when he said (De Pec. Mer I 7), that the life of the soul ex-
pired in Adam by his disloyalty, which is again reanimated by the
grace of Christ, for which he appealed to Rom. 8. 10 seq.

4. In Adam, before the fall, the rational soul had a perfect dominion over sensuality, so that there was no conflict between this
and reason. The body was subject to the spirit, and the sexual impulse never moved in opposition to the will of the spirit. Nor did
the body encumber the soul. "Before transgression, the first pair
were pleasing to God, and God was pleasing to them; and although
they possessed an animal body, they felt nothing in it moving in disobedience to themselves. For such was the righteous arrangement,
that, since their soul had received the body as a servant from the
Lord, just as the soul was to obey the Lord, so the body was to obey
the soul and exhibit a becoming subserviency to that life, without any
resistance. Hence they were naked and were not ashamed. For
now, the rational soul is naturally ashamed, because in the flesh, the
right to whose servitude it received, it can no longer, (I know not
through what infirmity,) either repress or excite, at its pleasure, the
movement of the members.—This disobedience of the flesh, therefore, quae in ipso motu est, etiam si habere non permittatur effectum,
was not in the first pair, since they were naked and were not ashamed. For as yet, the rational soul, the lord of the flesh, was not
disobedient to its Lord, so as to receive, as a reciprocal punishment,
the disobedience of its servant, the flesh, with a certain sense of con-
fusion and annoyance" De Pec. Mer. II 22. "I likewise add to
the goodness of Adam's condition," says Augustine to Julian, "that
in him, the flesh did not lust against the spirit, before sin, but you
add this misery to his condition, by the discord of flesh and spirit, as

you say that such concupiscence of the flesh as there now is, would have existed in paradise, even if no one had sinned ; and that such did exist in him before he sinned." Op. Imp. VI. 16. " His nature was such, that he had no contest of the flesh and spirit in him. Such was that nature, that he contended against no vices ; not that he yielded to them, but there were none in him." 22 " He endured no contest of the flesh against himself, nor perceived anything at all of a desire which he willed not." 14. " The enjoyments of sense were such, that the highest harmony existed between the flesh and the spirit, and nothing unlawful was desired." I. 71. "Adam was tried and assailed by no conflict of himself against himself ; but enjoyed, in that place, the felicity of peace with himself." De Cor. et Gr 11 According to Augustine, the connection of the sexes would indeed have taken place in paradise ; but in such a way, that either no sensual passion would have been excited, or it would at least have been subject to the dominion of reason, and would not have risen in opposition to its dictate. C. Jul. III. 7 ; VI. 9, 14 ; Op. Imp IV. 9 ; VI. 8. " Although that command, Increase and multiply and fill the earth, can seem to have been practicable only, per concubitum maris et feminae,—still it may likewise be said, that another way might have existed, with *immortal* bodies, so that, by the mere affection of a pious love, with no concupiscence of corruption, children might have been born, and who would not have to succeed their deceased parents nor themselves to die, till the earth should be filled with immortal men ; and thus there might have been a way of being born, among such a righteous and holy people as we believe will exist after the resurrection." De Gen. ad Lit. III. 21. Comp. IX. 3 ; De Nupt. et Conc. II. 7. Before the fall, men could have propagated themselves just as well as the husbandman scatters seed from his hand on the earth. II 14. For this purpose, also, there might have been a connection without shame. II. 22. " Nor would there have been any words which would be called obscene ; but whatever might thence be said, would have been considered just as decent as when we speak of other parts of the body." De Civ Dei, XIV. 23. " In paradise, before sin, the mortal body did not encumber the soul." Op. Imp. IV. 45.

5 Man would have attained the perfection of the will, the *non posse peccare*, if he had persevered in good ; and it would thence have been as impossible for him to sin as for the good angels. " It

19

was man's own fault, that he would not persevere, as it would have
been his merit, if he had persevered ; just as the holy angels did,
who, while some fell by freewill, by just the same will stood and
merited the attainment of the due reward of this perseverance, viz.
such a perfect felicity, that it was certain they would always remain
in it.—What is freer than the freewill which *cannot* serve sin ? This
would have been the reward of obedience for man, as it was for the
holy angels.* But now, since the good merit is lost by sin, that
which would have been the reward of merit, has become a free gift
of grace, to those who become free " De Cor et Gr 11 : Op. Imp.
VI. 12   The nature of man as God made it, was therefore good ;
but the nature of the holy angels, is still better, in which there is no
possibility of their willing to sin. De Gen. ad Lit. XI. 7.

6. Before the fall, the body of man was no more liable to death
than to disease.

If Adam had not sinned, he would not have died. This is an
opinion which Augustine repeats, times without number. It is also
taught in the first canon of the synod held at Carthage in 418.   Augustine, however, distinguished, with much circumspection, between
a *greater* and a *less* immortality (immortalitas major et minor) ;
or, as he also expresses himself (De Cor. et Gr 12), between not
being able to die, and being able not to die. The first, the non posse mori, was the immortality by virtue of which the possibility of
death was utterly removed ; but the last, the posse non mori, was
that which constituted the possibility of not dying, provided one did
nothing by which he would die, although he could do it. Op Imp.
VI 30   The minor immortality, Augustine attributed to the body
of the first man before the fall   In his view, Adam was not immortal, in the sense that he could not die, but only that he would not
have died, if he had not sinned " This question is pending between you and me ; Would Adam have died whether he had sinned or not ? For who does not know, that, according to that definition by which any one is called immortal who cannot die, but mortal who can die, Adam could die, because he could sin , and that,
therefore, death was a punishment of his guilt, not a necessity of his
nature ? But according to that definition by which one is called im-

* Why has not Augustine given us the proof that the angels themselves
have such a freedom as this ? Some who *think* this doctrine true, both in
respect to man and angels, might still like to *see the proof* of it —Tr

mortal, who has it in his power not to die, who will deny, that Adam was endowed with this power ? For he who has the power never to sin, has also certainly the power never to die " Op. Imp VI 25 ; De Pec. Mer. I. 5. " Adam's nature was so formed, that he could not die if he had not willed to sin " Op. Imp. VI. 22. " Before he sinned, Adam had neither the flesh of sin, nor the likeness of the flesh of sin ; for he would not have died if he had not sinned." IV. 79. Augustine therefore called the body of the first pair, " a body in a manner immortal " They used the means of sustenance, temperately indeed, which were needful to the support of even the immortal but animal body ; and the tree of life, so that they should not die of old age, nor death steal upon them in some other way. The tree of life had therefore an occult quality, and was a means of protection against disease and death C Jul. IV. 14 ; De Pec. Mer. II 21 ; De Civ. Dei, XIII. 20 Comp. De Gen. ad Lit. III. 21 ; XI. 32 Of this they were allowed to eat before the fall, and it was first forbidden to them after the fall. Op Imp VI 30 And Adam was not afraid of death ; for it was in his power not to sin, and therefore to not die. VI. 14, 16.

The immortality major, or impossibility of dying, which is found in angels, and will be in us after the resurrection, and which is connected with the impossibility of sinning (VI 30), would have been conferred, together with the latter, as a reward on Adam, if he had persevered " Though Adam, in respect to his body, was earth, and had an animal body with which he was furnished, yet he would have been changed into a spiritual body, if he had not sinned, and would have passed into that incorruptibility without the danger of death, which is promised to believers and the holy " De Pec. Mer. I 2 ; Op. Imp. VI. 12, 39. This spiritual body would then have needed no nourishment. De Gen ad Lit. III. 3.

Before the fall, therefore, Adam's body differed from ours, as ours must necessarily die, but his had only the possibility of dying. " With us, even if we live righteously, the body will die. On account of this necessity, arising from the sin of that first man, the apostle calls our body, not mortal, but dead, because in Adam we all die." De Gen. ad Lit. VI. 26. The first man, in his original state, did not have to fear that age would oppress him, and bring on death. " It was not to be feared that the man, if he should live longer in this animal body, would be oppressed by age, and by gradually

growing old would come to die. For if God caused the clothes and
shoes of the Israelites, not to be worn out, for so many years, what
wonder is it, if obedience should be rewarded by the same power in
man, so that his animal and mortal part should be in such a state,
that he would advance in age without decay, and when God should
please, pass from mortality to immortality, without the intervention
of death ?" De Pec. Mer I 3

But Adam and Eve were free from every disease, before the fall.
This is asserted by Augustine in many passages. " When moisture
and dryness, heat and cold—are in conflict in our body, health is
impaired. And all this, like death itself, comes from the propagation of that sin Nor will any one say, that if no one had sinned,
we should have suffered these things in that felicity of paradise."
C Jul. V. 7. Comp. VI. 10, 27.

7. On the whole, according to Augustine, paradise, in which Adam
and Eve were found before the fall, was a residence of the purest
felicity, and free from all suffering and trouble. Even their very
dreams were happy, in paradise. The beasts were obedient to man.
No defect was there Trees, fruits, all things were displayed in
their greatest excellence. Here, women would have produced children, without pain , and even the beasts, in this happy abode, would
not have died, but would have left it at the approach of great age.

Hence Augustine so often speaks of the blessedness and the delights of Eden. " O, how greatly do you err [Julian] who suppose
that blessedness and those holy delights of paradise to be derived
from this corruptibility and infirmity of nature, which now exists !"
Op Imp I. 71. " Without pain or labor, Adam would have lived
forever in that paradise of joy." VI. 23. " Pain and fear were not
in that place of felicity." VI 17. " Far be it from us to believe,
that there was anything there, either internal or external, by which
either grief would wound, or labor fatigue, or shame confound, or
cold benumb, or horror assail our sensibilities." C Jul V. 5 " If
anything was learned in paradise, the knowledge of which was useful to that life, that happy nature learned it without labor or pain,
either God or nature herself being the teacher " Op Imp. VI. 9.
" If in paradise there was the vicissitude of waking and sleeping, where
there was not the evil of lusting, the dreams of the sleeping were as
happy as the life of the waking." C. Jul. V. 10. " You [Julian] believe, then, that all those evils would have existed, even in paradise,

if no one had sinned ; and you think there would have been the death
of men as well as of beasts, because you believe the mortality of
the body common to all. O miserable men ; if you would think of
the blessedness of that place with christian sense, you would not believe that beasts would there have died, just as they would not have
been fierce, but subject to man with wonderful gentleness, nor have
fed on each other, but would have lived on common aliment with
man, as saith the scripture. Or if extreme old age would finally
work their dissolution, so that human nature alone should possess
eternal life, why may we not believe, that they would be removed
from paradise, when about to die, or would go forth by a sense of
impending death, so that death might happen to no living thing in
the place of that life ? For neither could those who had sinned, have
died, if they had not gone forth, by the merit of their sin, from the
habitation of such great felicity." Op. Imp. III. 147. " In a place
of so great happiness and glory, it is not to be believed, that there
could have been, or can be, any defect of tree, or herb, or apple, or
anything, whether of fruit or flock " VI. 16. " In that felicity, there
would be no pain of parturition " De Nupt. et Conc. II. 14, 15.

In this and similar ways, was the condition of the first man before
the fall, portrayed by Augustine. Hence he called him " blessed,"
but not " fully blessed," because he had indeed the ability to not sin
and not die, but not the inability to sin and to die. To this " plenitude of blessedness," i. e to holiness and the greater immortality,
and the conciousness of them, Adam would have attained, if he had
not sinned   But he was blessed before the fall ; for he did not foresee his future lot ; and possessed the consciousness of its being in
his power to not die and become unhappy. De Cor. et Gr. 10 ;
Op. Imp VI. 14.

Now to these different views, which were taken by the Pelagians
and by Augustine, of the state of man before the fall, it may well
be supposed there was no lack of objections and inferences, on either side. Augustine remarked against Julian, that, according to his
theory, even in the happy abode of paradise, there must have been
mingled corporeal and spiritual infirmities of every sort (C. Jul. VI.
16) ; and that a multitude of natural defects must have been met

with in paradise (Op. Imp. IV. 123); and he regarded it as incompatible with the idea of a paradise, in which the most perfect enjoyment prevails, that a discord of the flesh and spirit, which is shown by concupiscence, could have existed there 19.   Even the subjugation of it, would have disturbed the perfect enjoyment, etc. (C. d. Epp Pel I 17); and man would have been unhappy in paradise, even before sin. Op. Imp. VI 14 —Julian found it, and certainly not without reason, very unphilosophical, that Augustine should discover another ground for sinning, in the first man, from that which lies in freewill itself, viz., in his being made out of nothing   " You very foolishly ask," said he to Augustine, " Whence is the bad will ? Man has sinned because he would; he has had a bad will because he has willed to have it " V 54, 60 —Augustine, in opposition to Julian, who defended the opinion, that concupiscence existed in paradise, assumed the weak position, that even then, the freewill of man was not able to prove itself efficient. " For if even then the flesh lusted against the spirit, they did not that which they would." VI. 8.

Now, as Augustine exhibited the state of man before the fall in such severe contrast with his state after the fall, and Adam's nature, according to Augustine's own exhibition, stood so high and was so distinguished, his transgression, by which so great a depravation was produced, and which deserved so great a punishment, must have been very great. For, " from his own offence, Adam begat the guilty " De Pec. Mer I 14 —Augustine could not find words to set forth the greatness of Adam's transgression   " In vain do you strive," says he to Julian, " to make the sins of his children, be they ever so great and shocking, to appear equal to the sin of Adam, or even greater.   The higher his nature stood, the deeper it fell.—The first Adam was of so distinguished a nature, because not corrupted, that his sin was as much greater than the sins of others, as he was more illustrious than others " Op. Imp. VI 22. He called Adam's transgression an " ineffable apostasy" (III 56); and a "sin much greater than we can judge of" De Nupt. et Conc. II 34; Op. Imp. VI 23. Augustine endeavors to explain the greatness of Adam's transgression, from the circumstance, that he might so easily have kept the divine command, to the transgression of which God had affixed so great a penalty, and he had no sensual passion to subdue. III. 57; II. 188; De Nat. et Gr 25, De Cor. et Gr. 12; De Civ. Dei, XIV. 12

On the contrary, the Pelagians, in conformity with their view of the present and the first state of human nature, did not find, in Adam's first transgression, the immense guilt which Augustine must have found in it in order that so severe a punishment should be grounded on it. " Who has told you," says Julian to Augustine, " how great was the sin which Adam committed ?" Here Augustine appealed to passages of scripture (Gen. 3; 19), Thou art earth, and to earth shalt thou return ; and (Rom. 8; 10), The body is dead because of sin ; and inferred from the greatness of the punishment with which God followed Adam's transgression, as well as from the righteousness of him that appointed it, how great must have been the guilt which deserved such a punishment. Op. Imp. VI. 23, 27, 33.

CHAPTER IX.

Narrative of events in the controversy, continued.

Caelestius was condemned by the synod held at Carthage in 412, his doctrine pronounced heretical, and himself excommunicated. Pelagius had before sailed for Palestine, at the close of 411. Caelestius appealed from this decision of the Carthaginian council, to the Romish bishop, Innocent I; but gave up this appeal, (Paulini libellus c. Cael in app. Ed. Ben p. 103; Merc. Com. app. p. 69 sq.), probably because he expected nothing from it, and left a country where so much evil had befallen him He went to Ephesus. Here he was fortunate enough to obtain what he had in vain sought at Carthage. He was made a presbyter. Here he lived a year

The unpretending Pelagius, who had already gone to Palestine before the Carthaginian Council, gained many friends there, by his gentle and unambitious deportment, in spreading a true and practical christianity. Among these, were John, then bishop of Jerusalem; Saint Jerome, then residing at Bethlehem; and other pious and reputable persons. Juliana, a very respectable Roman lady, with whom Pelagius had probably formed an acquaintance while at Rome, and who esteemed him as an upright man, requested him, in behalf of her daughter Demetrias, who had shortly before become

a nun, to depict the dignity of her station and excite her to strive for
the attainment of perfection. This commission he discharged in a
very worthy manner, in the Epistle to Demetrias, before quoted,
which he wrote about the year 413. For the purpose of refuting
the principles laid down in this letter, Augustine and his friend Alypius addressed a letter to Juliana, the mother of Demetrias. This
is Ep. 188. There was another letter, however, which preceded
this, but which has not come down to us. About the year 414, he
was involved in controversy with Jerome. Jerome hated Rufinus ;
and as he came to believe, that Pelagius was a disciple of the presbyter of Aquileia, he likewise became embittered against him.
Whether the vain and ambitious Jerome, who always paid homage
to only the current orthodoxy, became somewhat jealous of the
spreading fame of Pelagius, of which the latter is said to have complained (C. Jul II 10), may properly remain a question. And other
causes, which we cannot stand to develop, might have produced a
change in the views of Jerome respecting Pelagius. Enough for us,
that the matter came to a written correspondence, which was violent
on both sides.

But the quiet of the peaceful Pelagius, was particularly disturbed
by the appearance of Orosius, who arrived in Palestine, in 415, from
the extreme borders of Spain. This Orosius, a young presbyter,
was induced to leave Spain on several accounts, particularly, as it
appears, by the Priscillian controversies * He resorted to Augustine in Africa ; and wished to receive from the renowned bishop, an
explanation of the origin of the human soul. Augustine thought he
had found in him the man whom he could use for his object. He
made him acquainted with all that had been done in Africa against
Pelagius and Caelestius ; furnished him with his own writings against
the Pelagians , and sent him to Palestine to set the east also in commotion against Pelagius and his doctrine. In respect to the difficult
question on the origin of the soul, he craftily enough referred him,

---

* Priscillian taught, that the human soul is an emanation from God, and
a part of the divine substance , and for this and divers other Manichaean
and Gnostic errors, he and some of his followers were condemned and executed, by the civil power, at Treves, in 385 This was the first capital punishment for heresy, and was much complained of by many of the bishops,
though some justified it It took place a little before the conversion of Augustine , and of course he cannot be regarded as the *father* of such persecution. See Walch, Hist. der Ketz. III 387 , Mosheim, Ec. Hist I. 365 —Tr.

since the answer of it was important in respect to the doctrine of original sin—to Jerome, just as Jerome had before referred a similar question to him. And the restless zealot actually succeeded in raising an uproar at Jerusalem. In consequence of this, at the close of July, 415, an assembly of presbyters was held at Jerusalem, at which bishop John presided, and where Orosius appeared as accuser against Pelagius. Orosius, however, did not here justify the confidence which Augustine probably reposed in him. He was far inferior to Pelagius in respect to a learned education. The latter not only had a greater readiness of expression, but was also acquainted with the Greek language, of which Orosius was entirely ignorant. This must have been to the advantage of Pelagius. On the other hand, the excessive frankness of Pelagius appeared to work to his disadvantage. He who was as yet only a layman, would not acknowledge the authority of Augustine, so sacred a bishop, but asked: "Who is Augustine to me?" Upon this, Orosius, with some others, cried out: "He must be cast out of the church as a blasphemer." But this had no influence on the decision of bishop John. He knew too much good of Pelagius to condemn him on the complaint of so ignorant a man as Orosius. He consented, in the end, to transfer the investigation to Innocent, bishop of Rome, who, as a Latin bishop, could best decide this controversy, which had originated in the Latin church. It was therefore determined to send letters and an envoy to the Romish bishop, and to submit the matter to his decision. In the mean time, Pelagius was to refrain from teaching his doctrine. It may be worth remarking further, that Pelagius execrated, before the assembly, the man that would maintain, that we can be perfect in virtue without God's help. De Gest. Pel. 14. Soon after that convocation, bishop John of Jerusalem, reproached Orosius for teaching, that "man cannot be without sin, even by God's aid." This gave occasion for the apology which Orosius addressed to the bishops in Palestine, composed in 415, and entitled Liber Apologeticus de Arbitrii Libertate.

That decision, however, was not carried into effect. Two bishops, Heros and Lazarus, who were driven from Gaul and had come to Palestine, (we know not why), and who acted in connection with Orosius and the other opponents of Pelagius, repaired to Eulogius, the primate of Palestine, with charges of heresy against Pelagius. They gave him a writing, in which the heretical doctrines of Pela-

20

gius and Caelestius, were specified, and requested, that the matter should be investigated by a council   Eulogius summoned a council at Diospolis (Lydda), which was held in December of the same year, 415, and was attended by fourteen bishops belonging to Palestine, among whom were Eulogius, who presided, and John of Jerusalem.   But neither were Heros and Lazarus, the accusers of Pelagius, nor Orosius, present at this council.*   As a stout defender of his cause, Pelagius had here the eloquent and learned Anianus a pretended deacon of Celeda in Campania. Hier Ep. 143 § 2. The commendation, also, which several bishops had bestowed upon him in their letters, (he even produced one from Augustine), and which he made known to the council, may have operated in his favor De Gest. Pel. 25, 26   The accusations in the complaint of Heros and Lazarus, were read. Pelagius explained himself to the satisfaction of the synod, in regard to the errors charged against him.   The council gave him the attestation of orthodoxy ; acquitted him fully of all heterodox errors, and regarded him as a worthy communicant.

We may easily imagine the impression which the decision of this synod made on the opponents of Pelagius, and particularly on Augustine and Jerome.   The former received early intelligence of the issue of the council, by Orosius, who hastened back to Africa immediately after it was concluded   Jerome was in a rage, and called the council " a miserable synod." Augustine hit upon a clever expedient   Instead of assailing the respectability and orthodoxy of the fathers at Diospolis, he accused Pelagius of giving indefinite and false answers   " The heresy is not justified, but the man that denied the heresy," said he, in a sermon preached not long after the synod of Diospolis. T V. p 1511 ; De Pec Orig 10   Thus, though Pelagius was considered as pronounced orthodox by the council, (who moreover heard the charges against him only through a translation), yet his doctrine, instead of being approved, must rather have been condemned. De Gest Pel. 10, 11 ; Comp. Retract. II 47,

---

* Augustine says, that Heros and Lazarus were absent, as he was afterwards informed, on account of the sickness of one of them   This Augustine regards as a calamity, since the cause was thus left without an advocate, and especially as the Greek fathers did not understand Latin, in which the works of Pelagius were written, and therefore could not tell whether his explanations agreed at all with his previous writings —The name, *Heros*, is sometimes written *Hero*, and sometimes *Eros* —TR

where it is said, that he condemned the propositions read from the complaint, as being hostile to the grace of Christ. Augustine has given us (De Gest. Pel.) the charges, and also the answers and defence, together with the decision of the synod, which he had solicited and obtained from bishop John, of Jerusalem. Ep. 179, 186. Comp. De Pec. Orig. 11. For the purpose of gratifying the interest that may be felt in learning how the oriental churches thought in respect to the contested doctrines, and also what Pelagius himself allowed to be his doctrine, quotations on both these topics, from the above mentioned work, will be given in the following chapter. Whether Pelagius acted quite uprightly at Diospolis, and did not, through fear of the impending anathema, reject and condemn several positions, which at least stood in inseparable connection with his opinions,—or else received them in another and different sense from that of the synod ; and consequently, whether Augustine was in the wrong when he said, that Pelagius " had either lyingly condemned, or cunningly interpreted" (De Pec Orig. 12)—may best be left to the decision of the reader himself. A striking inconsistency (noticed by Augustine, De Gest. 17) or rather a scarcely defensible ambiguity of Pelagius, has ever remained ; viz , that he rejected the proposition ascribed to Caelestius in the tenth charge, that the grace of God is imparted according to *the merit of man*, and yet, in the answer to the eleventh charge, he allowed that God imparts all spiritual gifts to him who is *worthy to receive !*

CHAPTER X.

*Transactions at Diospolis in respect to the heresies charged on Pelagius.**

Charge I. Pelagius has said in a book [his Capitula], that no

---

* This chapter, though not marked as quotation, is really such, being extracted, as promised in the previous chapter, from different parts of Augustine's piece on the Acts of Pelagius Augustine's shrewd and ample comments on the several parts, in which he justifies the council and convicts Pelagius of duplicity, are here omitted,—perhaps because our author supposed he had elsewhere sufficiently noticed those topics If here given in

man can be without sin, unless he have a knowledge of law. This being recited, the synod said · Did you put this forth, Pelagius?

Pelagius. I indeed said it ; but not as they [the accusers] understand it. I have not said, that one cannot sin who has a knowledge of law, but the knowledge of law is a help to refrain from sinning, as it is written, He has given them the law for an aid   This being heard, the synod said : What Pelagius has uttered is not alien from the church.

Charge II. Pelagius has said in the same book, that all are governed by their own will.

Pelagius. And this I said concerning freewill, which God aids when choosing good. But when man sins, he is himself in fault, as of freewill.

The bishops. Nor is this foreign from ecclesiastical doctrine.

Charge III. Pelagius has stated in his book, that in the day of judgment, the unjust and sinners shall not be spared, but shall be burned in eternal fire.

Pelagius replied, that he said this according to the gospel, where it is said of sinners, They shall go into eternal punishment, but the righteous into life eternal. And whoever thinks otherwise, is an Origenist *

The synod therefore said, that this was not foreign from the church

Charge IV. It was objected to Pelagius, as if he wrote in his book, that evil does not come into the thoughts.

Pelagius. I have not so stated, but have said that a Christian ought to strive to commit no evil

The bishops approved

---

their connection, they would indeed place in a more glaring light the duplicity of Pelagius , but it may be hardly worth while now to adduce them for this purpose   As the charges came up, in the progress of the trial, Pelagius replied to them severally, as given in the following account which Augustine received of the trial —Tr

* Origen taught, or rather *hoped*, that wicked men and even devils would finally be purified and become subject to Christ, and thus not suffer *eternal* fire. But the bishops were at first shocked, supposing that Pelagius meant, in his book, to deny the popish doctrine of a purgatory for burning up the wood, hay, and stubble of the imperfectly righteous, whereby *they* would be *saved so as by fire* —Tr

Charge V. Pelagius has written that even the kingdom of heaven is promised in the Old Testament.

Pelagius And this it is possible to prove from scripture. But heretics deny this, to the injury of the Old Testament. But, following the authority of the scriptures, I have said it; for it is written in the prophet Daniel (7 · 18), And the saints shall receive the kingdom of the Most High.

Synod. Nor is this foreign from ecclesiastical belief.

Charge VI Pelagius has said, in the same book, that man may be without sin, if he will. And writing in a flattering way to a widow [probably Juliana, the mother of Demetrias], he has said : May piety, which has never found a place, find one in you. May justice, everywhere a stranger, find an abode in you. May truth, which no one now knows, become your inmate and friend And may the law of God, which is despised by almost all men, be alone honored by you. And again to her · O thou happy and blessed, if justice, which is believed to exist only in heaven, may be found with you alone on earth. And in another book to her, after the prayer of our Lord and Savior, teaching how saints ought to pray, he says : *He* properly lifts up his hands, *he* pours forth prayer with a good conscience, who can say, Thou, Lord, knowest how holy and innocent and clean from all offensiveness and iniquity and rapine, are the hands I stretch forth to thee; how just and pure and free from all falsehood, the lips, with which I offer to you the supplication, that thou wouldst have mercy upon me.

Pelagius. I have indeed said, that man may be without sin, and keep God's commands, if he will. For this ability God has given him. But I have not said that any one can be found, from infancy to old age, who has never sinned ; but, being converted from sin, by his own labor and God's grace he can be without sin ; still, he is not by this immutable for the future But the rest which they subjoin, is neither in my books nor have I ever said such things.

Synod. Since you deny your having written such things, will you anathematize those who hold to them ?

Pelagius. I anathematize them as fools, not as heretics ; for in fact, there is no *doctrine* there.

Synod. As Pelagius has now, with his own voice, anathematized some indefinite and foolish talk, and correctly answered, that man, by God's aid and grace, can be without sin, let him also answer to other points.

Charge VII. The principles of his disciple Caelestius, [for which he was condemned at the synod of Carthage], were charged upon Pelagius, viz. Adam was made mortal, who was to die whether he should sin or not. Adam's sin injured only himself, and not the human race. The law sends to heaven, just like the gospel. Before the advent of Christ, there were men without sin. Infants, just born, are in the same state in which Adam was before sin. Neither by the death or sin of Adam, do the whole human race die; nor by the resurrection of Christ, do the whole human race rise again.—Certain other points were also urged against Pelagius, which were sent to me from Sicily, when the catholic brethren there were troubled with such questions, which I answered sufficiently, as I think, in a book addressed to Hilary (Ep 157), who sent them to me in an epistle of his for advice. They are these. Man may be without sin, if he wills to be. Infants, although not baptized, have eternal life. Unless the rich who are baptized, renounce all, though they may have appeared to have done some good, it cannot be reckoned to them, nor will they be able to obtain the kingdom of God.—To these objections, as the acts testify,

Pelagius thus replied. As to man's ability to be without sin, I have spoken before. But as to the points whether there were men without sin before the advent of the Lord, I have said, according to the testimony of the holy scriptures, that before the coming of Christ, some lived piously and righteously. But as for the other things, even according to their own testimony, they were not uttered by me, [but by Caelestius], and I am not bound to give satisfaction for them : but yet, for the satisfaction of the holy synod, I anathematize those who thus hold, or who ever have held.

Synod. On the forementioned points, Pelagius has sufficiently and properly given satisfaction, anathematizing those things which were not his.*

Charge VIII. Pelagius has said, that the church here is without

---

* Here Augustine, and with good reason, adds "We see, therefore, and hold, that this sort of evil and most pernicious heresy was condemned, not only by Pelagius, but also by the holy bishops who presided at that trial." And he then goes on to enumerate afresh each particular error as thus charged on Caelestius and anathematized by Pelagius. If the apology of terror is to be further urged in behalf of Pelagius, it may be replied, that so genuine a reformer as some have supposed him, ought to have shown more courage, as well as more integrity.—TR

spot or wrinkle. [Augustine, however, gives this as an opinion of Caelestius. De Gest. 35].

Pelagius replied with vigilant circumspection. This was said by me ; but so, because the church is purified by baptism from every spot and wrinkle, which the Lord wills so to remain.

Synod   This is also our opinion.

Charge IX ;—from a book of Caelestius. We do more than is commanded in the law and the gospel.

Pelagius. This they adduce as ours. But it was spoken by us of virginity, according to the apostle, concerning which Paul says : I have no commandment of the Lord.

Synod. This the church also receives.

Charge X ;—also from the book of Caelestius, [against the transmission of sin]. God's grace and aid are not given for separate acts, but consist in freewill, or in law and instruction. And again ; God's grace is given according to our merits; because, if he gave it to sinners, he would appear to be unjust. And in these words, he infers: Hence even the grace of God is placed in my will, whether I am worthy or unworthy. For if we do all things by grace, when we are conquered by sin *we* are not conquered, but the grace of God, which would aid us in every way, but cannot. And again he says : If it is the grace of God, when we conquer sins, then he is in fault when we are conquered by sin, because certainly he either could not or would not guard us.

Pelagius. Whether these are the opinions of Caelestius, let those see who say they are his. I never held so ; but anathematize him who does hold so.

Synod. The holy synod receive you, while thus condemning reprobate words.*

---

* Perhaps the lover of terse logic may demand at least a specimen of Augustine's manner in this very able work On the Acts of Pelagius, as it is rather quaintly, and for a doubtful reason, entitled   The following will serve as such a specimen, while it also contains matter of some interest   It immediately follows the last sentence in the text. " Concerning all these things, certainly, both the answer of Pelagius anathematizing the same, is manifest, and the decision of the bishops condemning them, is most absolute   Whether Pelagius, or Caelestius, or both, or neither of them, or any others with them, or under their name, held these things, or yet hold them, may be doubtful or a secret   But by this decision, it is sufficiently declared, that the things are condemned, and that Pelagius would have been condemned

Charge XI;—again from the book of Caelestius. The Pelagians affirm, that every man can possess all the virtues and graces, and they take away the diversity of graces which the apostle teaches.

Pelagius. This we have said. But they maliciously and foolishly find fault with it. For we do not remove the diversity of graces;

---

at the same time, if he had not likewise condemned them   Now, certainly, after this decision, when we dispute sentiments of this sort, we dispute against a condemned heresy '

" I may even say something more cheering   Before, when Pelagius said, *By the grace of God assisting, man may be without sin,* I feared lest he would pronounce the same grace to be an ability of nature as endowed by God with freewill, as in that book which I considered his, and answered (see De Nat et Gr), and in that way would deceive his uninformed judges   But now, as he anathematizes those who say that God's grace and aid are not afforded for single acts but consist in freewill or in law and instruction, it appears sufficiently evident, that he calls *that* grace which is preached in the church of Christ, and which is afforded by the ministration of the Holy Spirit, in order to our being aided to our separate acts , and whence also we always implore timely aid, lest we be led into temptation   Nor do I now fear lest perhaps, when he said, *One cannot be without sin unless he have a knowledge of law,* and so explained it *as to place the aid to refraining from sin, in a knowledge of law,* he meant that same knowledge of law to be understood as being the grace of God. For behold, he anathematizes those who think this '   Behold, he would have neither the nature of freewill, nor law and instruction, to be understood as grace, by which we are aided in individual acts '   What then remains, unless that he understands that which the apostle says is given by the ministration of the Holy Ghost ? concerning which the Lord says   Think not how or what ye shall speak, for it shall be given in that same hour what ye shall speak , for it is not ye that speak, but the Spirit of your Father that speaketh in you   Nor is it to be feared lest perhaps, when he said, *all are governed by their own will,* and explained, that *he said this of freewill, which God aids in choosing good,* he spoke of aid by the nature of freewill and by a knowledge of law   For when he justly anathematizes those who say, *The grace and aid of God are not given for single acts, but consist in freewill or in law and instruction,* certainly God's grace and aid *are* given for single acts,—and according to this, we are governed by God in single acts , nor is it in vain that we say in prayer, Direct my ways according to thy word, that no iniquity may have dominion over me "

Passages of the like stringent logic, abound in this work of Augustine , and the whole is fitted to show us the sad plight in which Pelagius must have appeared to the Latin church, while in the grasp of the powerful bishop, after the affair at Diospolis   We cease to wonder that the *man* was crushed by his antagonist, think as we may of his cause.—TR.

but we say, that God gives all the graces to him who is worthy to receive them, as he gave to the apostle Paul.

Synod. And consequently you have believed in the opinion of the church respecting the gift of the graces which are contained in the holy apostle.

When some of the bishops now murmured, and said, that Pelagius would maintain, that man could be perfect without God's aid, bishop John opposed this, and quoted, besides other passages, 1 Cor. 15 10. Rom. 9: 16. Ps. 127 · 1. But they not being convinced, and still continuing to murmur, Pelagius said : I also believe. Anathema to him who says, that man can attain to all the virtues, without God's aid.

Charge XII ;—from the book of Caelestius. 1. Those cannot be called the sons of God, who have not become in every respect free from sin. 2. Forgetfulness and ignorance are not matters of sin, as they do not take place according to the will, but of necessity. 3. There is no freewill, if it needs God's aid ; since every one has it in his own will either to do or not to do a thing. 4 Our victory is not from God's aid, but from freewill. This he is said to have maintained in these words · The victory is ours, because we have taken up arms by our own will ; as, on the other hand, it is ours when we are conquered, because, of our own will, we scorned to be armed. 5. He adduces the passage from the apostle Peter : We are partakers of the divine nature ; and is said to have made this syllogism · If the soul cannot be without sin, then God is the subject of sin, since the soul, which is a part of him, is guilty of sin. 6. Pardon is granted to the penitent, not according to the grace and compassion of God, but according to the merits and labor of those who through penitence are worthy of compassion.

Synod. What says the monk Pelagius, here present, to these points which have been read ? For this the holy synod reprobates, and the holy catholic church.

Pelagius. Again I say, that even according to their own testimony, these things are not mine ; for which, as I said, I owe no satisfaction. What I have confessed to be mine, I affirm to be right. But what I have said are not mine, I reprobate according to the judgment of the holy church, and pronounce anathema on every one who contravenes and contradicts the doctrines of the holy catholic church. For I believe in the trinity of one substance, and all

21

things according to the doctrine of the holy catholic church : and if any believes things foreign from her, let him be anathema.

Synod. Now, as satisfaction has been given us respecting the accusations against the monk Pelagius, here present, who indeed agrees in pious doctrines, and anathematizes what are contrary to the faith of the church, we acknowledge him to belong to the ecclesiastical and catholic communion.

CHAPTER XI.

Narrative of events continued.

Thus was Pelagius formally acquitted and pronounced orthodox by fourteen oriental bishops. This must have been as flattering to Pelagius as it was disagreeable to his opponents. He was loud in his joy on this occasion. Nay, he did not omit to inform Augustine himself of what had happened at Diospolis, in an account which he sent him of his defence De Gest. Pel. prooem, and 32, 33.*

Augustine's reputation was now at stake. He had declared against the Pelagian doctrine , and the author of it, a layman, (who had moreover trod so close on the heel of episcopal pride, by presuming to say, " Who is Augustine to me ?"), was now pronounced fully orthodox by an oriental council of fourteen dignified bishops. This might produce disastrous consequences, especially as the party of the Pelagians grew stronger. Augustine therefore set all in commotion to prevent this. At two provincial councils in 416, the Pelagian doctrine was declared one which ought to be rejected, and the

---

* This account differs in but two or three points from the acts of the synod, which Augustine afterwards received, and which have been given in the previous chapter Augustine is careful to tell us the chief points of difference , and also to say, that he did not dare to publish the facts merely on the authority of Pelagius, before receiving the acts of the synod, lest Pelagius should deny the genuineness of his own letter Pelagius, in his account, omitted entirely his renunciation of the doctrines of Caelestius, contained in the seventh charge, and his anathema on all who ever held them And Augustine tauntingly inquires, whether he had not ink, and space, and time enough, just to state that fact ' Pelagius also added to his anathema at the close of his reply to the last charge, " a like anathema upon those who had falsely accused and calumniated him '" These were the only important discrepances, according to Augustine.—TR

council held at Carthage in 412, was approved   And no pains were
spared to win the Romish bishop Innocent ; from an apprehension,
perhaps not wholly groundless, that he might even confirm the decision of the fathers at Diospolis   In addition to this, Augustine
wrote, about this time, to bishop John of Jerusalem, by whom Pelagius was much loved (Ep. 179), warning him of the poison of the
Pelagian heresy. It is worthy of remark, that Augustine, even in
this letter, speaks of Pelagius with esteem, and calls him "our
brother."

Of the two synods just mentioned, the first was held at Carthage,
in 416, at which Aurelius presided   This is the second Carthaginian council on the Pelagian controversy. It consisted of sixty-eight
bishops. Augustine, who did not belong to the Carthaginian or
proconsular province, was not one of them.   At this synod, it was
resolved, that Pelagius and Caelestius should be put under anathema,
if they should not most explicitly condemn the errors charged upon
them   Bishop Innocent was, at the same time, informed of the
whole case, with all the preceding circumstances.   For the fathers
sent him a synodical letter, and appended to it both the acts of this
synod and of the one before held at Carthage, together with the letter of Heros and Lazarus, which Orosius had brought   The acts
of this second synod are lost ; but the synodical letter to Innocent,
has come down to our time.   It is found not only in the Mansic Collection of Councils (IV. p 321), but also among Augustine's letters,
Ep. 175. But it is very remarkable, that the African bishops, who
were confessedly so jealous of their rights, should express themselves
to the Romish bishop, in this letter, in the following manner.   "We
have considered, Rev brother, that this act ought to be communicated to your holy excellency, in order that the authority of the
apostolical seat may also be added to the decision of our mediocri-
ty." Finally, two errors in doctrine were charged, in that letter,
against Pelagius and Caelestius   One was, that they taught that
man is in a state, by his own power, to live right and keep the commands of God, by which they showed themselves the opponents of
divine grace : the other, that they denied that children are freed
from corruption and obtain eternal salvation by baptism, inasmuch
as they promised eternal life also to those *not* baptized. In the synodical letter, however, with much circumspection, and probably
not without an eye on the acquittal of Pelagius at Diospolis, the

anathema was held as necessary only in general for those who
taught these errors, and not for Pelagius and Caelestius themselves,
for they, forsooth, had possibly reformed.

The second of these synods, was held the same year at Mila, (anciently Milevis), in Numidia. 'About sixty bishops of this province,
were present, among whom was Augustine   The fathers acceded
to the resolutions of the Carthaginian synod, only we find no proof
of anything being said at Mila in respect to condemning the two alleged heretics, if they should not retract the doctrines referred to
The canons of this synod are lost ; for what are presented as such,
in the collections of canons, are selected from other synodical acts.
See Fuchs Bibli. der Kirch Th. 3 S. 346. The fathers assembled
at Mila, also sent a letter to the Romish bishop, in which they entreated him to set himself in opposition to the Pelagian errors. This
letter has reached us, as well as that of the Carthaginian council,
and is among Augustine's letters. Ep. 176.

Besides this, in order by every possible means to win Innocent, a
confidential letter was sent, at this time, by Augustine and four other
African bishops, to the Romish bishop, in which they made every
effort to show, that the African doctrine was orthodox, and that no
injustice was done to Pelagius and Caelestius   This private letter
is also preserved and is among Augustine's letters Ep. 177. In
this, the Romish bishop was requested either to have Pelagius come
to Rome and to examine him personally,' or else to do this by writing.   In connection with this, they placed distinctly before him their
orthodox doctrine of grace, and bid him beware of the ambiguity of
the word *grace*, behind which Pelagius hid himself.   They also added Augustine's book on nature and grace, together with the work of
Pelagius which had occasioned it.   In the latter, in order to save Innocent the trouble of reading the whole, they marked the passages
in which Pelagius, in their opinion, had expressed himself hereti-
cally   Besides this, they added a letter to Pelagius, composed by
one of their number, probably Augustine himself, with the request,
that Innocent would be pleased to send him that letter, that it might
thus have the greater effect.

From this step, which Augustine and his adherents took, and in
which Augustine was doubtless the man who directed the whole affair, it is manifest, that passion already mingled in the strife. This
step must unquestionably have been a costly one to the ambitious

Augustine and the other proud African bishops.   Hitherto, the African church had in every way set themselves in opposition to the pretensions of the Romish bishop to the primacy.   What they now did, however ambiguously they expressed themselves, (they did not ask the *decision* of Innocent but his accession to their party,) must have appeared as homage to the authority of the Romish bishop.   In order still more to flatter his pride, even a bishop, Julius by name, was sent to him with that letter.

This step was devised so craftily and executed with so much skill, that it could not fail of its object.   The aspiring Innocent, to whom it must have been very gratifying, did not let slip this fine opportunity for making his authority valid.   He regarded the step in a light in which the Africans would not have looked at it.   He answered with an arrogance and a pride which would not have been endured in another case.   In his replies (August. Epp. 181, 182, 183) to those three letters, of Jan. 417, he set himself up as the one to whom alone belonged the decision of this matter.   He commended the deference with which they had applied to the apostolic chair, and said, that he had investigated the case.   He confirmed their doctrine and their decision against the Pelagians.   By the authority of apostolical power, he excommunicated Pelagius, Caelestius, and all who obstinately defended their doctrine, until they should reform.   And he expressed himself, in relation to the Pelagian theory of infant baptism, almost in the words of Augustine   Innocent remarked further, that it was not necessary to summon Pelagius to appear in person, since, if he thought he had not deserved the condemnation of the Romish chair, he must hasten to him and seek his acquittal.—But Pelagianism is no more fairly set forth and condemned in the letters of the Africans, than, (as might be expected,) in the answers of the Romish bishop.   As we shall see in the sequel, Pelagius had never maintained the proposition, assailed in these letters, that man needs no grace, and therefore the inference could not be imputed to him, that prayer to God for aid against sin, is superfluous.   The Pelagians had never taught what was here charged upon them, that the baptism of children does not aid in their salvation, since, as we have seen, they maintained, on the contrary, that children obtain the kingdom of heaven by baptism.*—Thus, therefore, were the pre-

---

* Still they could enjoy an inferior salvation out of the kingdom of heaven, *without baptism.*—Tr.

tended doctrines of Pelagius, and likewise their advocates, declared and condemned as heterodox, by the Romish chair.

The answer of Innocent excited the most lively joy among the African bishops ;—so greatly did party zeal outweigh their pride. It was universally proclaimed abroad. Augustine could not refrain from even saying in the pulpit, that by two councils, and *by the rescript of the apostolical chair*, the matter is settled Serm 131. § 10

But on the twelfth of March, 417, Innocent died His successor was Zosimus Caelestius, (who had recently betaken himself to Constantinople, when driven from Ephesus on account of the unpleasant affair with bishop Atticus,) now hastened to Rome, and presented an appeal to Zosimus, (or rather renewed the previous one), and also presented a written defence, containing his confession of faith, in which he directly denied the transmission of sin, and spoke of the contested question as one that did not belong to the faith. Zosimus received him kindly, and without troubling himself about his predecessor's having already decided the controversy, commenced the investigation anew. For this purpose, a convocation of the clergy was summoned at Rome ; and the expressions of the man, who cunningly enough declared his willingness to submit all to the decision of the apostolical chair, were found orthodox. No decision concerning his orthodoxy, however, was at this time pronounced. The same year, 417, Zosimus wrote a letter to Aurelius and all the African bishops, informing them of what had been done , declared the propositions presented by Caelestius, perfectly orthodox, and the accusers of Pelagius, (Heros and Lazarus, to whom he was opposed for other reasons,) deposed and excommunicated ; censured the Africans gently for their conduct in this affair ; and demanded of them, if they had anything further to object to the orthodoxy of Caelestius, either to appear at Rome, within two months, or else to be quiet. Finally, Zosimus added, that he had reminded Caelestius and the priests that were present, that such subtle questions and foolish disputes arose from a childish love of novelty, etc. This is very remarkable, as we may hence conclude, that the doctrine of original sin and of its remission by infant baptism, which Caelestius explicitly rejected in his confession of faith, did not yet belong to the Romish system of doctrine *   The letter is found in Mansi, IV. 350 ; and in Aug Opp XII. 122

---

* If this doctrine had not yet been acknowledged as a constituent part of

During this time, a letter and a confession of faith arrived at Rome from Pelagius. Probably he had been informed, at Jerusalem, of the step taken against him in Africa, and what this had also occasioned at Rome. In order to justify himself, he wrote to Innocent; placed before him his creed; and added the request, that he would either teach him a better one, and show in what his errors consisted, (as he would gladly receive instruction from him who possessed the faith and the chair of Peter,) or else would pronounce him orthodox. This prayer was supported, in a separate letter, by Praylus, the bishop of Jerusalem and successor to John. Both letters reached Rome after the death of Innocent and the accession of Zosimus to the Romish chair These occasioned the calling of a new convocation at Rome (by which the creed of Pelagius was also approved), and a second letter of Zosimus to the African bishops, which was probably written only a few days after the first. Pelagius's confession of faith extends to all christian doctrines, beginning with the Trinity and going to the resurrection of the dead. It then touches very briefly on some of the contested doctrines; upon which, however, it is far too indefinite.

The second letter of Zosimus to the Africans, as well as the other, was first made known, from the Vatican library, by Baronius, and is contained in Mansi, IV 353, and in Aug. Opp. XII. 124. In this, the Romish bishop first mentions its occasion, and asserts, that Pelagius had fully justified himself, and that it could no longer be a subject of doubt, that both Pelagius and Caelestius were orthodox men, who had been calumniated before the Africans by those base men, Heros and Lazarus * And he remarked, not without bitterness, that it did not become the episcopal dignity and wisdom, to make up their decision on the representations of such vain calumniators; and that it should now be a real joy to them, to acknowledge those, who had been erroneously condemned, as men who had never been separated from the church nor from catholic doctrine. To this letter, he annexed copies of the writings which Pelagius had sent him.

---

the Romish creed, it had certainly been extensively held by the fathers from as early a period as that of Origen, who tells us that infants were baptized for original sin —Tr.

* In this letter, it is asserted, that Lazarus had long been " a diabolical calumniator" of the innocent while in Gaul, and guilty of enormous cruelty, by which he became odious and had to flee, and that Heros was like him.—Tr

Both of these letters of Zosimus to the Africans, which were probably sent at the same time, were delivered by one Basiliscus, a sub-deacon, to Aurelius, the bishop of Carthage. Conceive of the sensation which this must have excited through all Africa ! What was the object of Zosimus in all this, whether he meant to win a still greater triumph than his predecessor had gained, by a still deeper subjugation of the Africans to the Romish chair, or whether he intended to mortify the Africans who had so often scorned the decisions of the Romish bishops—cannot be determined. But whichever it might be, it was a failure. The pride of the Africans was offended, and they had spirit enough to set themselves in opposition to Zosimus. Scarcely had Aurelius received these letters, when he forthwith summoned a council at Carthage, which was held in November of this year, 417, consisting of 214 bishops. At this synod, (of which. according to the language of Prosper in his *Carmine de Ingratis*, " Aurelius was the president and Augustine the ruling spirit,") their former decisions and those of Innocent, against the Pelagians, were confirmed. To the decrees of this synod, was added, by the Africans of the council, a letter to Zosimus, (to whom another letter had already gone,) in which they find fault with his decision about the orthodoxy of the Pelagians, and request him to institute a new investigation with Caelestius. " We have decided," say they in this letter, according to a fragment preserved by Prosper, (Contra Collatorem, c. 5. Ap. p. 176), " that the sentence pronounced by the venerable bishop Innocent, from the seat of the most blessed Apostle Peter, against Pelagius and Caelestius, remains in force until they, by the most unequivocal confession, acknowledge that we are aided by the grace of God through Jesus Christ our Lord, not only to know righteousness, but also to practise it in each act, so that without it (grace) we are not able to have, think, say, or do anything truly pious " Paulinus, also, the accuser of Caelestius, who had been requested by the abovementioned Basiliscus, Nov. 2, 417, to appear at the court of Zosimus and prosecute his complaint against Caelestius, did not appear, but justified himself, in a notification, sent to Zosimus, dated Nov. 8, on the ground, that the case had already been decided in his favor by the Romish chair This notification which was first made known by Baronius, is found in Mansi, p. 381, and in Ap. Ben. Ed. p. 102.

This opposition of the Africans, however, would hardly have inclined Zosimus to change his conduct towards the alleged heretics, had not two circumstances conspired to compel him to it. The first was an insurrection of the opponents of Pelagius at Rome, at the head of whom a monk, called Constantius, appeared to stand,* who, very likely, made their displeasure at the conduct of Zosimus in this matter, to be heard aloud, and which probably led to a violent scene. De Pec. Orig. 8, 21 ; Prosp in Chron. ad annum, 418 ; Sacrum Rescriptum, Ap. p. 105. The second circumstance, and perhaps the most important was this, that the emperor Honorius declared against Pelagius and his adherents, and in favor of the Africans, whom political considerations might incline him to favor.

Zosimus shifted his part in the scene. In his answer, which followed the letters before mentioned to Aurelius and the rest of the bishops who had met at Carthage, (Mansi, IV. 366. Ap. 104), dated March 21, 418, after some proud assertions respecting his dignity, he says, that it was not his intention directly to acquit Caelestius, but only to leave the matter undecided, till everything pertaining to it should be investigated. He added, with perhaps not an unintentional obscurity, that after receiving their letters, he had left all in the same condition in which it had long been. In this he seemed to point to the transactions under his predecessor Innocent, by whom the Pelagians had been condemned.

The emperors Honorius and Theodosius gave a *rescript* (sacrum rescriptum, Ap. 105) which of course implied an application, and indeed, as is highly probable for many reasons, an application of the African bishops.† The rescript was given at Ravenna, April 30,

---

* This Constantius is probably the one of whom it is said, by the author of the *Praedestinatus*, that "a certain Constantius, an expounder, undertook against Pelagius and Caelestius without scripture" Mansi, IV 384.—To this case at Rome, the reproach of Julian seems to refer, that the catholics had excited disquiet at Rome Op. Imp III 35

† It is doubtful whether this act of the emperors was originally called a *rescript*, i e. an order given in answer to some written application, or merely a *decree* It is found in Ap. Aug Opp. XII. 153, where it is called *Constitutio* instead of *Rescriptum ;* and reasons are given why it should *not* be called a rescript. Nor is it called a rescript in the Magdeburg Centuries, where it was first published Still it is called Sacrum Rescriptum in Ap Aug. Opp. X. 70, where reasons are given why it *should* be so entitled. But the question is certainly too doubtful to serve as the basis of an inference, that the Africans solicited this persecuting edict from the emperors, though it may have been the fact —Tr

22

418, and was directed to Palladius, a praetorian praefect of Italy.
In this rescript, which is drawn up in a pompous style, it is said, that
Pelagius and Caelestius had been guilty of falling into many heretical errors and of artfully spreading them   For example, they had
taught, that death was produced at the same time with man, and was
included by God in the plan of creation, and is not a consequence of
sin but an irrevocable ordinance, and hence it would have befallen
us even if we had not sinned; and that the sin of Adam does not
pass over to his posterity; and that, according to information, the
poison of this heresy had spread to Rome and other places, and was
disturbing the peace of the church   " Therefore," continues the
decree, " your illustrious authority is to know, that we have decided
by law, that Caelestius and Pelagius, the first heads of this execra-
ble dogma, being banished from the city, whatever other persons
may anywhere be found as followers of this sacrilege, or again ut-
tering anything of the condemned perverseness, being caught by
any one, they are to be brought before a competent judge.   Any
one, whether clergyman or layman, is to have the power of accusing
and prosecuting, without any limitation, such as he may find abandoning the common light of opinion and introducing the darkness of
novel disputation, and thus fighting against apostolic instruction and
the clear, certain, and gospel doctrine, with the sly subtlety of a rude
sect, obscuring the resplendent faith of truth by dark and intricate
discussion.   These, therefore, wherever found conferring on this
so nefarious a wickedness, we command to be seized by any persons,
and brought to a public hearing, there to be promiscuously accused
by all "   If proved guilty, they were to be sent into exile   And
this decree was directed to be published throughout the whole em-
pire, that no one might plead ignorance of the law, if found transgressing.—This rescript occasioned also an edict (Ap. 106; Aug
Opp. XII. 159), in the name of Palladius and two other praetorian
praefects, Monaxius praef. praet of the East, and Agricola praef.
praet. of Gaul, in which the rescript was made public for universal
observance   But in addition to exile, the confiscation of goods,
which is not mentioned in the rescript, is also expressly introduced
as a punishment of the Pelagians.   That many were thus induced
to abandon the Pelagian party, may well be supposed. Possidii Vita
Aug c. 18.

These were the first steps taken by the state against the Pelagians.

But still the Africans did not think enough had been done for the suppression of the Pelagian heresy. Hence they ordered what is called a plenary council, i. e one to which all the African bishops were summoned, or a general synod ; and at this, also, the principles of the Pelagians were condemned. It commenced May 1, 418, at Carthage, and more than two hundred bishops were present. Aurelius of Carthage and Donatianus of Telepte presided But here, again, Augustine was the ruling spirit. The first nine canons of the synod, were levelled against the Pelagian heresy. Ap. 106; Aug. Opp. XII. 133   The ninth canon, which Walch quotes in his history of heresies (Th. IV. s. 637), is erroneously placed here, as Fuchs rightly remarks in Bib Kirch. Th. 3. s. 378.   On the other hand, the third canon, (" It is likewise decreed, that if any has said," etc) which is wanting in some manuscripts and collections, is certainly genuine. It is wholly in the spirit of Augustine and the Africans. Augustine alludes to it in his work on the soul and its origin (II 12), and Photius quotes it in his Bibliotheca Cod. 53.

These canons, which contain several positions against the Pelagian theory of grace, of which only an occasional notice has yet been taken, are important enough to merit a literal translation in this place.

CHAPTER XII.

Canons established against the Pelagians by the General Synod (plenario concilio) of the African bishops, held at Carthage in 418.

I. Whoever says, that the first man Adam was made mortal, so that whether he should sin or not, he would die as to the body, i. e. depart from the body, not by desert of sin, but by a necessity of nature, let him be anathema.

II. Whoever denies that children just born are to be baptized, or says, that they are baptized for the remission of sins but derive nothing of original sin from Adam which is to be expiated by the laver of regeneration, from which it follows that, in them, the form of baptism for the remission of sins, is to be understood, not as true, but false, let him be anathema.   For what the apostle says, By one man

sin entered into the world, and death by sin, and so death hath passed to all men, (in quo) in whom all have sinned, is to be understood
in no other way but as the catholic church, everywhere diffused, has
always understood it.   For according to this rule of faith, even little
children, who have not yet been capable of committing any sin in
themselves, are thus truly baptized for the remission of sins, that
what they have derived by generation may be cleansed by regeneration.

III. If any one says, that because the Lord has said, In my Father's
house are many mansions, it is to be understood, that there is a place
in the kingdom of heaven, or a place anywhere at all, in which children are happy who leave this word without baptism, (without which
they cannot enter the kingdom of heaven, which is eternal life,) let
him be anathema   For since the Lord has said, Whoever is not
born again of water and the spirit, cannot enter into the kingdom of
God, what orthodox man can doubt, that he who does not deserve
to be a joint heir with Christ, has his part with the devil ?   He that
does not stand on the right hand, will doubtless be on the left.

IV. Whoever shall say, that the grace of God, by which we are
justified through Jesus Christ our Lord, avails only to the remission
of sins already committed, and is not also an aid against their commission, let him be anathema

V. Whoever shall say, that the same grace of God through Jesus
Christ our Lord, assists us in avoiding sin merely in this, that by it
there is revealed and opened to us a knowledge of commands, whereby we may know what we ought to seek and what to avoid, but by
which nothing is afforded whereby, when we know what to do, we
may also be able and delight to do it, let him be anathema.   For
since the apostle says, Knowledge puffeth up, but charity edifieth, it
is very impious for us to believe, that we have the grace of Christ
for that which puffeth up, but have it not for that which edifieth ;
since to know what we ought to do and to delight to do it, are both
the gift of God, so that, by charity edifying, knowledge may be unable to puff up.   And as it is written of God, He teacheth man
knowledge , so is it likewise written, Love is from God.

VI. Whoever shall say, that the grace of justification is given to
us, so that we through grace may the more easily do what we are
commanded to do through freewill, as though, if grace were not given, we could fulfil the divine commands even without it, though not

easily, let him be anathema. For the Lord was speaking of the fruits of commandments, when he said, not, Without me ye do *with more difficulty*; but, Without me ye can do *nothing*.

VII. Whoever thinks that what the apostle John says, If we say we have no sin, we deceive ourselves, and the truth is not in us, is to be received as if he were to say, It does not become us on the score of *humility*, not that of *truth*, to say, We have no sin, let him be anathema. For the apostle goes on to say, But if we confess our sins, he is faithful and just who forgiveth our sins and cleanseth us from all iniquity. Where it sufficiently appears, that this is not only said humbly but also truly. For the apostle could have said, If we say we have no sin, we *exalt* ourselves, and *humility* is not in us He sufficiently shows, that whoever says he has no sin, speaks not the truth but falsehood.

VIII. Whoever says, that in the Lord's prayer, saints say, *Forgive us our debts*, not as though they said it for themselves, for this petition is not now necessary for them, but for others among their people who are sinners, and therefore each one of the saints does not say, Forgive *me my* debts, but, Forgive *us our debts*; so that the just is understood to ask this for others rather than for himself, let him be anathema. For the apostle James was holy and just when he said, In many things, *we all offend* For why was it added, *all*, unless that this sentiment might agree with the Psalm, where it is said, Enter not into judgment with *thy servant*, for in thy sight, *no one living* shall be justified? And in the prayer of the most wise Solomon, it is said, There is *not a man* that sinneth not, and in the book of Job, He marketh in the hand of *every man*, that *every man* may know his infirmity. Hence even the holy and righteous Daniel, when in prayer he says, in the plural, *We* have sinned, *we* have done iniquity, etc.—lest it should be supposed, when he truly and humbly confesses these things, that he said them, (as some now think,) not of his own, but rather of his people's sins,—afterwards said, When *I was praying and confessing my sins* and the sins of my people to the Lord our God He would not say, *our sins*; but mentioned the sins of his people and his own, because, as a prophet, he foresaw there would be those who so badly understand.

IX. Whoever will have those words of the Lord's prayer, *Forgive us our debts*, to be so spoken by saints as if they were not humbly and truly said, let him be anathema. For who would endure one praying and lying, not to men, but to God himself; who, with his lips, says, he wishes to be forgiven, and in his heart, says, he has no debts to be forgiven![*]

Such are the canons established against the Pelagians at this " plenary council " On close examination, we see it follows from them, and particularly from the seventh, eighth and ninth canons, that even those were condemned who maintained, that there were men who, by God's aid, had led a life free from sin. Augustine himself, in his earliest writings against the Pelagians, (De Pec. Mer. II 6, De Spir. et Lit. 1), had granted, nay even defended the position (taken in the abstract, as the Pelagians took it), that, by God's grace, man *can* be without sin. And though he did not himself believe, that any one *is* without sin in this life (De Pec. Mer. II. 7), still he did not regard this as a dangerous opinion, provided only that one does not believe we can attain it by our own power. De Spir. et Lit 2, De Nat. et Gr. 60. " I know this is the opinion of some," (viz. that there have been, or are, men without sin) ; " whose opinion in this matter, I dare not censure, though I cannot defend it." De Perf. Just. Hom 21. In the letter of the five bishops to Innocent, as well as in several of the early pieces of Augustine, this position was left doubtful, or at least pronounced a sufferable error (tolerabiliter in eo quisque falliter) Even Ambrose had held to it, in a certain sense And in his book On the Acts of Pelagius, c. 30, written soon after, Augustine numbers this question, both in the abstract and in the concrete, among those which are not to be denied as though already decided in opposition to the heretics, but to be kindly discussed among the catholics. But, after this synod, (in C d. Epp. Pel. IV. c 10), he represents this opinion as a dangerous and detestable error He does not, however, here present it in the abstract sense in which the Pelagians really held it, but as if they maintained that there were and had been righteous men who, in this life, had no sin. And from this time onward, as appears from C. Jul. IV. 3, he could not endure the doctrine of man's ability to be without sin. Finally, he referred

---

[*] These canons were probably adopted by the unanimous voice of the synod, as the first of them commences thus—" It pleased *all* the bishops who were in the sacred synod," etc —Tr

the "ability to be without sin," not to concupiscence which, as he had always maintained, remains continually in man, but to our *consent* to this concupiscence. II. 10.

[The "*inability* to be without sin," our author should have said As the passage to which he refers, is a striking proof that Augustine continued to regard nothing as really criminal in us but the *voluntary acts* of the mind, I shall here give it at some length.—After quoting from Ambrose, Augustine thus continues · " For how is sin dead, when it works many things in us while we struggle against it ? Many what ? unless they be those foolish and noxious things, which plunge those that yield to them in destruction and perdition ; to endure, by all means, and not to comply with which, is the contest, is the conflict, is the battle. The battle of what ? unless of good and evil, not of nature against nature, but of nature against the vice, now dead, but yet to be buried, i. e. entirely cured ? How, then, do we say, that this sin is dead by baptism, as this man [Ambrose] also says, and how do we confess that it abides in our members and, while we struggle against it, produces many desires, which we resist by not consenting, as he also confesses ; unless that it is dead in respect to that guilt by which it held us, and rebels, though dead, till cured by the perfection of sepulture ? Although now it is not called sin in the sense of making us guilty, but because it was produced by the guilt of the first man, and because by rebelling it strives to draw us into guilt, if the grace of God through Jesus Christ our Saviour do not so aid us, that even dead sin should not so rebel as, by conquering, to revive and reign. Laboring in this war as long as human life is a trial on earth, it is not on this account that we are not without it, viz., that this, which in this sense is called sin, warring against the law of the mind, works in the members, even while we do not consent to it in unlawful things ; (for, as far as respects us, we should always be without sin, until the evil were cured, if we were never to consent to evil) ; but in whatever things, by its rebelling, we are still, though not fatally, yet venially conquered, in these we contract that for which we are daily to say, Forgive us our debts. Sicut conjuges quando modum generationi necessarium, causa solius voluptatis, excedunt ; sicut continentes quando in talibus cogitationibus cum aliqua delectatione remorantur, non quidem decernentes flagitium, sed intentionem mentis, non sicut oportet, ne illo incidat, inde avertentes, aut si incideret inde rapientes. Respecting this law of sin, which law is, in another sense (alio modo), even called sin, which law wars against the law of the mind, and concerning which the blessed Ambrose has said many things, testify the saints Cyprian, Hilary, Gregory, and very many others." C. Jul. II. 9, 10.

From the passage thus given at length, as well as from many others, it is plain, that Augustine considers the sin of which the baptized are guilty, as consisting *wholly* in their consent to the feelings and acts prompted by the evil, but not in itself morally culpable, propensity which they inherit from Adam, and which still remains in them for their trial while on earth. And, at least so far as this passage is concerned, it ought to be said, that Augustine refers the *fact* of our not being without sin, rather than our *inability* to be without it, to our compliance with the bad propensity.—Tr.]

It may perhaps be worth remarking further, that the doctrine of the entire want of freewill, is here (in the sixth canon) only very softly expressed, and not in the severe Augustinian way.

It was only after this synod, as some have remarked, that Augustine treated the Pelagians as complete heretics, and applied this name to them, which he had scruples about applying to them in his sermon at Carthage in 413   But he could now do it, as the anathema had been pronounced upon them by a general synod.

The Pelagian theory of grace, at least the theory which the Africans ascribed to their opponents, was consequently condemned by the Carthaginian synod.   It is therefore now time to present the Pelagian doctrine of grace, together with the opposite theory of Augustine.

CHAPTER XIII.

Theory of Pelagius and his followers respecting grace. Opposite theory of Augustine.

Pelagius had not, at first, fully explained himself respecting grace; and he had no occasion for doing it, while his orthodoxy on the point, was not called in question. In his letter to Demetrias, he had spoken of the aid of God's spirit, or of divine grace, in general, and, (as Augustine afterwards asserted), in an ambiguous generality But even this keen eyed bishop had found nothing *heretical* in these expressions, though something contradictory. De Gr. Chr. 37, 40 He, however, made occasional remarks, in his book on nature, respecting the nature of grace, which were perhaps partly caused by the offence that some had possibly taken at his opinions on the uncorrupted nature of man. De Gest 10. He was also sufficiently incited to speak of grace when treating of the nature of man, as we find Augustine, in his earliest works against the Pelagians, referring to some expressions of theirs respecting this subject But Pelagius must soon have found a more urgent occasion for speaking of grace, as his opposers charged on himself and Caelestius the consequence that, according to their theory of the freedom of the will and of man's ability for good, they could admit of no grace at all; nay, they even attributed to Pelagius the rejection of grace, in their sense, as a position peculiar to him The first was done, for instance, at the synod of Carthage, in 416 ; and the last, among other things, at the synod of Diospolis.

Pelagius therefore explained himself more definitely respecting grace, particularly in his book on freewill, now lost, which was written after the synod at Diospolis, and from which Augustine gives extracts in his book on the grace of Christ By the manner of this explanation, he seemed to frustrate the object of his opponents to make him a heretic in this particular also; but by it, he *seemed* also to contradict his own positions on freewill and the uncorrupted state of man. In his third book Pelagius says, among other things: " The ability of nature" (i e. freewill, which, as we have before

23

seen, according to Pelagius, was a gift of God), " God *always* aids
by the help of his grace.—God aids us by his doctrine and revelation, while he opens the eyes of our heart; while he shows us the
future, that we may not be engrossed with the present; while he
discloses the snares of the devil; while he illuminates us by the multi-
form and ineffable gift of heavenly grace.—Does he who says this,
appear to you to deny grace? or does he appear to confess both divine grace and the freewill of man?" De Gr. Chr. 4, 7. Even the
willing of good, is also there explained as an effect produced by
God. 10

[The passage here referred to, is worth quoting, in order to show
more fully both the sentiments and the manner of Pelagius. " In
another place, to be sure," says Augustine, " after he had been long
asserting, that a good will is produced in us, not by God's aid, but
from our own selves, he brings up against himself the question from
the apostle, and says How stands that assertion of the apostle—*It
is God that worketh in us both to will and to do?* Then, that he
might, as it were, dissolve the opposition which he saw to be so vehemently contrary to his dogma, he went on to say . *He operates in
us to will what is good, to will what is holy, while, by the greatness
of future glory and the promise of rewards, he rouses us, who are
devoted to earthly desires, and delighting like dumb beasts in the
present; while, by the revelation of wisdom, he rouses our stupid will
to the longing desire for God; and while he commends to us all that
is good.* What is plainer than that he calls the grace by which God
works in us to will and to do what is good, nothing else but law and
instruction?" This last assertion, Augustine goes on to establish by
examining the several parts of what he had thus quoted from Pelagius. In the course of his criticism on the passage, he says, that by
grace there is not only *suasion* but *persuasion* to all that is good (non
solum suadetur omne quod bonum est, verum et persuadetur). Pelagius had only said *suadetur*. This vital distinction, the crafty are
apt to confound; and the undiscriminating, just as apt to overlook.
Pelagius did not intend unequivocally to assert anything like what is
meant by the work of the Holy Spirit on the *heart* of man.—TR]

In a letter to Innocent soon after this time, (towards the beginning
of 417,) Pelagius says · " Behold, before your blessedness, this epistle clears me, in which we directly and simply say, that we have
entire freewill to sin and not to sin, which, in all good works, is al-

ways assisted by divine aid.—Let them read the letter which we wrote to that holy man, bishop Paulinus, nearly twelve years ago, which perhaps in three hundred lines supports nothing else but the grace and aid of God, and that we can do nothing at all of good without God. Let them also read the one we wrote to the sacred virgin of Christ, Demetrias, in the east, and they will find us so praising the nature of man, as that we may always add the aid of God's grace.—Let them likewise read my recent tract which we were lately compelled to put forth on freewill, and they will see how unjustly they glory in defaming us for the denial of grace, who, through nearly the whole text of that work, perfectly and entirely confess both freewill and grace." De Gr. Chr. 31, 35, 37, 41. In his confession of faith, Pelagius says. "We so profess freewill, that we maintain the standing need of God's help."

But how do these assertions of Pelagius agree with his preceding opinions on man's ability for good, and the uncorruptedness of his nature? The contradiction vanishes as soon as we consider the different sense in which Pelagius used the word grace, which is entirely wide of the Augustinian use of it Such a difference could not possibly escape the acuteness of the bishop of Hippo, who found in it an *intentional* ambiguity. And in fact, one needs only to read two lines from the work of Pelagius on freewill, according to the fragments which Augustine has preserved, in order to convince him, how different was the Pelagian from the Augustinian grace For how could Augustine say, with Pelagius, "Our being able to do, say, think all good, is the work of him that has given us this ability, and that aids this ability, but that we do, or speak, or think *well*, is ours, because we are also able to turn all these to evil." 4.

Pelagius comprehended under grace : 1. The power of doing good (possibilitas boni), and therefore especially freewill itself. "We distinguish three things," says he, in the passage above cited on freewill, "the ability, the willing, and the being (the posse, velle, and esse). The ability we place in nature , the willing, in the will, the *being*, in the effect The first, i. e. the ability, pertains properly to God, who has conferred it on his creature ; the other two, the willing and the being, are to be referred to man, as they descend from the fountain of the will. Hence in the intention and in the good act, is the praise of man ; nay, both of man and of God, who gave the ability for the intention itself and for the act, and who al-

ways aids the ability itself by the help of his grace But that man
is *able* to will and to do, is of God alone." But in his book on nature, Pelagius had already explained himself as meaning by the
grace of God, that our nature has received by creation the ability to
abstain from sin, since it is endowed with freewill. De Gest. 10. He
therefore used the term grace in this sense, when he conceded in
that piece, that man could be without sin only by grace. De Nat. et
Gr 10, 45, sqq. It is not easy to render the sense of the following
passage intelligible in a translation · " Quia non peccare nostrum
est, possumus peccare et non peccare. Quia vero posse non peccare, nostrum non est ; et si voluerimus non posse non peccare, non
possumus non posse non peccare." 49 * " The possibility of not sinning, is not so much in the power of the will, as in the necessity of
nature. Whatever is placed in the necessity of nature, pertains undoubtedly to the author of nature, that is, to God. How, then, can
that be considered as spoken of as without the grace of God, which
is demonstrated to pertain peculiarly to God ?" 51. De Gest. 23.
And in this sense, to be sure, he could make grace the requisite for
all moral perfection, without infringing on his theory of the good
state of human nature For freedom is indeed indispensable to
every good action, and hence to the good deportment of man generally. And again, it is a power which we do not possess from ourselves, but have derived from God, who made us rational men.—
And hence it is not falsely said, in the letter of the Carthaginian
synod to Innocent (Ep 175) " Pelagius and Caelestius maintain,
that the grace of God must be placed in his having so constituted
and endowed the nature of man, that it can fulfil the law of God
by its own will "

* Augustine himself complains, that Pelagius " said this crookedly and
rather obscurely ," and undertakes to straighten it Its translation, as the
mere English reader may like to know, is this As refraining from sin
depends on ourselves, we can sin, and we can refrain from sinning. But as
the *ability* to refrain does not depend on us, we cannot be unable to refrain,
even if we wished to be so ' Why this passage, if once understood, could
not easily be translated into German, I know not The radical idea is as
distinct as it is important to the full development of this view of human
agency But why Pelagius should choose to envelop it in the obscurity of
so many negatives, and then chase it away into the abstraction of an endless
series of infinitives, we can hardly conjecture With some reason surely
might the persecuting emperor complain of his dark disquisitions '—TR.

2 Under the term grace, Pelagius included the revelation, the law, and the example of Christ, by which the practice of virtue is made easier for man. In this sense, Pelagius said (De Lib Arbitrio, in Augustine's De Gr. Chr. 10); "God works in us to will what is good, to will what is holy, while, by the greatness of future glory and the promise of future rewards, he rouses us, who are devoted to earthly desires and delighting like dumb beasts in the present; while, by the revelation of wisdom, he rouses our stupid will to a longing desire for God; and while he commends to us all that is good" In Ep. 175, before cited, it is said: "Pelagius and Caelestius maintain, that even the law belongs to the grace of God, because God," (according to the Septuagint translation of Is. 8 20), "has given it to man as a help" To this point belongs also what Pelagius said in the ninth chapter of his letter to Demetrias: "If even before the law, and long before the coming of our Lord and Savior, some are said to have lived holy and righteous lives, how much more is it to be believed, that we can do this, since the illustration afforded by his advent, as we are now instructed by the grace of Christ (instructi, or according to Augustine's quotation of this passage, De Gr Christi 38, instaurati, restored), and are regenerated into the better man ; and being reconciled and purified by his blood, and incited by his example to the perfection of righteousness, we ought to be better men than they who were before the law ; better also than they who were under the law, according to the declaration of the apostle, Sin shall no longer reign over you, for ye are not under the law, but under grace." Here Pelagius manifestly refers grace to the teaching and example of Christ. When, in the sequel he speaks of the good of grace (bono gratiae), he comprehends under it, the instructions of scripture. In the treatise De Spir. et Lit. 2, Augustine says, in reference to the Pelagians : "They are most vehemently and strenuously to be resisted, who suppose that, by the mere power of the human will, without God's grace, they can either perfect righteousness, or attain to it by protracted effort. And when they begin to be pressed with the question, How they presume to assert this as taking place without divine aid, they check themselves, nor dare to utter the word, because they see how impious and intolerable it is. But they say, that these things do not take place without divine aid, inasmuch as God has both created man with freewill and, *by giving precepts, teaches him how he ought to live ; and in*

this, certainly, he aids, as he removes ignorance by instruction, so that man may know what he ought to avoid and what to seek in his actions; and thus by freewill, which is naturally implanted, entering the way that is pointed out, and by living continently, and justly, and piously, he deserves to attain the blessed and eternal life." Grace, in this sense, Pelagius regarded as necessary in order to be without sin. "No man is without sin, who has not attained the knowledge of law." De Gest Pel. 1.

In his commentaries on 2 Cor. 3. 3, Pelagius distinguishes the law from grace. Here he comprehends under law, the Mosaic law; and under grace, the immediate and the mediate instruction of Jesus. In his commentary on 1 Cor. 12. 11, in a still more specific sense, he comprehends under grace the individual miraculous gifts of which the apostle speaks; and on 2 Cor 3: 5, the immediate aid of God, which was afforded to the apostle.

3. As already appears from the quotations, Pelagius comprehended likewise under grace, the forgiveness of sins and future salvation. The Pelagian heresy maintains, that the grace of God consists in our being so made as to be able, by our own will, to abstain from sin, and in God's giving us the help of his law and his commands, and *in his pardoning the previous sins of those who return to him.* In these particulars alone is the grace of God to be placed, and not in the aid to particular acts For man can be without sin and fulfil God's command, if he will. De Gest. 35. In his commentary on Rom. 5· 6, Pelagius remarks: "The apostle designs to show, that Christ died for the ungodly in order to commend his grace by the contemplation of beneficence." "He confesses," says Augustine, (De Nat et Gr. 18), " that sins already committed must be divinely expiated, and that prayer must be made to God in order to merit pardon (propter veniam promerendam) · for his much praised power of nature and the will of man, as himself confesses, cannot undo what is already done. In this necessity, therefore, nothing is left but for him to pray for pardon." And even in respect to grace in this sense, according to the complaint at Diospolis, Caelestius, in the spirit of the Pelagian theory, would have something meritorious, on man's part, to precede his becoming a participant of the grace. " Pardon is not granted to the penitent [merely] according to the grace and mercy of God, but according to the merits and labor of those who have become worthy of mercy by repentance." De Gest. 18.

According to Augustine, this was the single grace in which the Pelagians admitted nothing meritorious on the part of man. " The Pelagians affirm the grace by which sins are forgiven to man, to be the *only* grace imparted not according to our merit. But that which is imparted in the end, viz : *eternal life*, is rendered to our preceding merits." De Gr. et Lib. Arb. 6. According to the spirit of their system, the Pelagians must certainly have made future salvation to depend on man's conduct, and therefore thus far on his merit ; and just as certainly must repentance have been with them a condition of the forgiveness of sins , and therefore in grace, even in this sense, there must have been something of merit on the part of the man to whom it should be imparted, if we would be strictly definite in our ideas and not contend about words Its necessity also, for every one who had sinned, could not have been doubted, according to the Pelagian system

Baptism, also, by which one receives the forgiveness of sins and the benefits of Christianity in general and of the kingdom of heaven in particular, was regarded by the Pelagians as a grace, and so called by way of eminence. See what has preceded on infant baptism. In this sense, the Pelagians could always say, " We hold the grace of Christ to be necessary for all children and adults." C. d. Epp. Pel. I. 22.

4. Pelagius also used *grace* for *gracious influences*, i. e. for God's supernatural influences on the Christian, by which his understanding is enlightened and the practice of virtue is rendered easy to him. To this relate the words already quoted from the work in favor of freewill. " God aids us, in as much as he enlightens us by the manifold and *unspeakable* gift of heavenly grace." In his commentary on the declaration of the apostle (2 Cor. 3: 2), *For ye are the epistle of Christ*, he gives this explanation to the words : " It is manifest to all, that ye have believed on Christ through our doctrine, the Holy Ghost confirming the power."

Julian also expressed himself respecting grace, in the like manner with Pelagius. For example, he speaks of a grace of God by which the burden of the charge of sins is removed from us. Op. Imp. II. 227 He also admits, that divine grace aids men in ways innumerable. III 106. Among these, he reckons " the giving of precepts, blessing, sanctification, restraint, incitement, and illumination, (praecipere, benedicere, sanctificare, coercere, provocare, illuminare)," and refers these to the doctrines as well as to the mysteries. The passage which Augustine has preserved (I. 94, 95), is especially characteristic, and deserves to be quoted here. " We therefore acknowledge a manifold grace of Christ. Its first gift is, that we are made out of nothing. The second, that we excel living things in the gift of sense; and sentient beings, by reason, which is impressed on the mind, that the image of the Creator may be taught; to the dignity of which, pertains equally the freedom of will that is bestowed. We reckon as proofs of the benefits of grace, the blessings with which it does not cease to distinguish us   Grace sent the law as an aid. It is owing to its office, that the light of reason, which is made dull by evil examples and the practice of vices, excites by various instruction and cherishes by its invitation. It is therefore owing to the plenitude of this grace, i. e. of the divine benevolence, which gave origin to things, that the Word became flesh and dwelt among us   For as God required from his image a return of love, he openly showed to the uttermost with what inestimable love he had dealt towards us, in order that we might, though late, return love for love to him who, commending his love towards us, spared not his own son, but gave him up for us ; promising that if we would, after that, obey his will, he would make us fellow heirs with his only begotten son.—This grace, therefore, which not only forgives sins in baptism, but, with this benefit of pardon, also carries forward and adopts and consecrates ; this grace, I say, changes the merit of the guilty, but does not originate freewill, which we receive at the very time of our creation, but which we use when we attain the power of discerning between good and evil. Thus we do not deny, that innumerable kinds of divine aid, assist the good will ; but not in such a manner, by any of these kinds of aid, that either a liberty of the will, which had before been destroyed, is again produced, or, liberty being excluded, a necessity of either good or evil, can be supposed to rest on any one. But all aid cooperates with freewill."

Here also belongs the passage which Augustine adduces (C d Epp. Pel. I 18) from the letter ascribed to Julian, and which, in the main, is certainly genuine   " We maintain, that man is the work of God, and by his power is no more compelled to good than to evil, but that he does good or evil of his own will ; but in a good work, he is always aided by the grace of God ; in a bad, he is urged on by the suggestions of the devil."

Julian, therefore, as well as Pelagius, admitted the supernatural influences of grace. They are included among " the innumerable kinds of divine aid" which Julian expressly allows. This Pelagian theory of gracious influences, however, is distinguished from the Augustinian in several essential points.

(a) According to the Pelagian theory, the operation of grace must be referred, as it would seem, immediately to the understanding of man. The expression, *illuminates* (dum nos multiformi et ineffabili dono gratiae coelestis *illuminat*, De Gr. Chr. 7), as well as the phrase, " to open the eyes of our heart" (ib.), leads to this conclusion. But besides this, Pelagius expressly mentions " doctrine and revelation" as the means which divine grace employs. In his letter to Demetrias (31), Pelagius also used the expression " illumination," respecting the reading of the scriptures.—It did not escape the penetration of Augustine, that Pelagius adopted merely such a gracious influence on the understanding of man. " But whatever Pelagius in his four books on freewill appears to say for that grace, by which we are so aided as to shun evil and do good, he so says it as in no way to avoid the ambiguity of words which he can so explain to his disciples, that they will believe in no aid of grace by which the ability of nature is assisted, except by the law and doctrine , so that our very prayers, as he most openly affirms in his writings, he believes are to be presented for no other purpose but that doctrine may be opened to us by divine revelation, and not that the mind of man may be aided in order to accomplish, in love and action, what it has already learned should be done " De Gr. Chr. 41. " But we may believe, that whatever little aid Pelagius admits, he places in this, that knowledge is added to us, by the revealing spirit, through instruction (per doctrinam), which we either could not have had or could have had with difficulty through nature " 40. Hence Augustine also says (Haer. 88) : " God, according to the principle of the Pelagians, operates only through his law and doctrine, that we should learn what we ought to do and what to hope for, but not also, by the gift of his spirit, that we should practise what we have learned as duty. And on this account they profess, that knowledge is given us by God, by which ignorance is removed ; but they deny that love is given us, by which we are to live piously." This influence of grace on the understanding was, however, transferred to the will of man, because, by the clearer knowledge of good, a greater inclination is produced

24

to practise it ; and hence Julian could always say, without abandoning the theory of Pelagius, that the will of man is aided by divine help in ways innumerable.

(b) The Pelagians utterly denied *the necessity* of gracious influences for the performance of good. They only facilitated the practice of it. Pelagius says, in his letter to Demetrias (29), " James shows how we should resist the devil, by submission to God and by doing his will, that we may also merit divine grace, and the *more easily* resist the evil spirit by the help of the Holy Ghost." He might here, indeed, be thinking only of the moral influence of instruction ; but that Pelagius would not limit the facilitation of the practice of good by grace, to the indirect teaching of the divine spirit through the word, may be seen from a passage quoted by Augustine himself (De Gr Chr. 7), from the work of Pelagius on freewill. " Here the dullest of men suppose we do injury to divine grace, because we say, it by no means works holiness in us without our will ; just as if God had commanded his grace to do something, and not that he affords the aid of his grace to those whom he has commanded, in order that what men are commanded to do by freewill, they may the more easily accomplish by grace. *Which grace we confess to be in God's aid, and not, as you suppose, merely in the law.*" Here " God's aid," which is set in opposition to the law, would have had no meaning at all, if Pelagius had not intended, by it, a supernatural influence of God upon men * Hence, in reference to this passage, it is said, in the letter of Augustine and Alypius to Paulinus . " He appears to believe, that one must concede a *superfluous* help of grace, so that, even if the help is not granted, we have still a strong and firm freewill for resisting sin." Ep. 186 c. 10. And Augustine is perfectly right in concluding (C. d. Epp. Pel. II. 8), that man can therefore do good, even without grace, " although with more difficulty." Comp. De Gr Chr. 26 sqq " The Pelagians are

---

* Augustine, in his remarks on the passage above quoted, says, that if Pelagius did not confine grace to the *law* merely, yet he " placed it in law and instruction ," as appeared from what Pelagius immediately added about God's aiding us by revelation, by opening the eyes of our heart, showing the wiles of the devil, etc This sequel of the passage has been before quoted, as the reader may recollect Both Pelagius and Augustine may possibly have meant *supernatural* instruction, just as our author here understands the passage from Pelagius. Still it does not seem at all clear, that Pelagius meant to say, that even all the *pious* are thus illuminated —Tr.

so hostile to divine grace, that they believe man can practise all the divine commands without it. Finally, Pelagius was blamed by the brethren for attributing nothing to the aid of God's grace. According to their censure, he did not set grace before freewill, but, with infidel cunning, behind it, because he said, it is afforded to men in order that, through grace, they may *the more easily* perform what they are commanded to do through freewill. By his saying that they can more *easily*, he meant it to be understood, that men can always fulfil the divine commands without divine grace, though with greater difficulty. But that grace of God, without which we can do nothing, consists, according to their position, only in freewill, which our nature has received from him, without any preceding merit.". Aug. Haer. 88 In reference to gracious influences as not being necessary to the performance of good, Caelestius could say, (as quoted by Jerome in his letter to Ctesiphon, Ap. p 75): "That will is in vain, which needs any other help. But God has given me a freewill, which would not be free, unless I could do what I would;" or, as he expressed himself in his Capitula (De Gest 18): "The will is not free, if it needs God's help, because it depends on each one's own will, to do or not to do a thing." To this easier attainment of perfection through grace, is to be referred what Augustine quotes from Julian's writings (C. Jul. IV. 3) : "When man is divinely aided, he is aided in order to attain perfection. Man is incited to anything laudable, by the impulse of his own generous heart." Comp. Op. Imp. II. 198, where Augustine says · "To those inquiring of you, why Christ died, provided nature or the law makes men just, you answer, In order that this may be done more easily ; as if it *might* be done, though with more difficulty, either by nature or by the law " Here, at least in part, the supernatural influences of grace are intended, which, according to the Pelagian view, are a consequence of Christ's merits, and are imparted to none but Christians.

That Pelagius did not consider gracious influences indispensably necessary to the practice of good, appears from his ascribing real virtue to heathens. "The good of nature is so general among all, that it sometimes shows and manifests itself even among heathen men, who are without any worship at all of [the true] God. For how many philosophers, as we have heard, read, and ourselves have seen, have been chaste, patient, modest, generous, temperate, kind,

despising both the honor and the wealth of the world, and not less
the lovers of righteousness than of knowledge ! Whence, then, in
men who are far from God, is that which pleases God ? whence, in
them, anything good, unless from the good of nature ? And, as we
see what I have mentioned, either all in one, or severally in different
individuals, and as nature is the same in all, so they show, by their
mutual example, that all can be in all, which is found either all in
all, or each in individuals If now even men without God [without
the aid of God] show how they are made by God, then think what
Christians can do, whose nature and life are improved through Christ,
and who are also aided by the help of divine grace." Pel. Ep. ad
Dem. 3. Comp. Aug. De Gr. Chr 31. With this, Julian also agrees.
According to him, the origin of all virtues, lies in the rational soul
of man, from which proceed the cardinal virtues of " prudence,
justice, temperance, and fortitude." C. Jul IV. 3. How wide Augustine is from this view, and, by his other principles, how wide he
must be, we have already seen.

(c) In close connection with this, stands the principle, that gracious influence is not given for each individual good act. For if
grace is not universally necessary for the performance of good, it
certainly cannot be needed for the practice of each individual act,
but many may be performed without it. Nay, grace may even be
confined to those good acts, the performance of which is difficult for
the natural powers of the man.

Pelagius, it is true, at the synod of Diospolis, would not acknowledge as his, the proposition, that " God's grace and aid are not
given for single acts," but pronounced anathema on him who received it. It may be that Pelagius, at that council, rejected an old and
freer opinion. But it is more probable, that he hid himself behind
the manifold meaning of the word *grace*, and comprehended under
it freewill ; in which sense, Jerome, in his first dialogue against the
Pelagians, makes Critobulus, who sustained the part of a Pelagian,
assert the aid of grace for each individual act. Under *aid*, he might
comprehend the law and instruction of Christ. In a like sense, he
said, in his letter to Innocent, " Freewill is always aided by divine
help in all good works." De Gr Chr 31 He could also, in a conference with Pinianus, Albina, and Melania, even say, " Anathema
be to him who thinks or says, that the grace of God, by which Christ
came into the world to save sinners, is not necessary, not only every

hour (per singulas horas) or every moment, but also in *every act* of
ours ; and let those go to eternal punishments, who strive to remove
this doctrine " 2.   For here he certainly did not think of including,
under the term grace, any supernatural operation of grace, any supplying of ability (subministratio virtutis), in the sense of Augustine ,
but, as Augustine remarks, either the remission of sins, or the example of Christ.   Pelagius could not regard any supernatural influence
of grace, as necessary to the performance of each individual good
act, because he did not even hold it necessary to the performance of
good in general.   It is therefore ever the Pelagian position, that " the
grace and aid of God are not given for single acts," even when grace
is taken for supernatural influence ; and Caelestius, as this position
was adduced as his, in the tenth charge at the synod of Diospolis,
only spoke out more freely, what Pelagius might be loth to say in
plain words.

(d) Pelagius, in his admission of gracious influences, also differed
from Augustine by supposing something meritorious on the part of
man in the case.   The aid of grace, said Pelagius, is bestowed only
on those who rightly apply their powers   He did not, therefore, allow grace to precede freewill, but this to precede that.   True, at the
synod of Diospolis, he even condemned the position, that " the grace
of God is given according to our merits."   But here, again, he took
the term *grace* in a different sense from that in which Augustine
used it ; and, indeed, as even his own disciples acknowledged, for
freewill itself; in which gracious gift, to be sure, no mention could
be made of a merit on the part of man.   That Pelagius, as well as
Caelestius, made the supernatural influences of grace dependent on
the preceding merits of man, we see from several of his own expressions.   To this point pertains what he says of such as are not
Christians, in his oft-mentioned letter to Innocent, according to the
fragments in Aug. De Gr Chr 31.   " The power of freewill, we
affirm to be in all men, Christians, Jews, and gentiles.   Freewill is
in all equally ; but in Christians only is it aided by grace.   In the
others, the goodness in which it was constituted (conditionis bonum),
is naked and defenceless   But in these who pertain to Christ, it is
fortified by Christ's aid.   *Those* are to be judged and condemned,
because, when they have freewill, by which they might come to the
faith and merit God's grace, they abuse the liberty granted them.
But *these* are to be rewarded, who, by rightly using freewill, *merit*

(merentur) *the grace of the Lord*, and keep his commandments."
Pelagius does not, indeed, here declare definitely what he comprehends under grace ; but the connection shows, that he is speaking
of the grace which is given to Christians. Now, as he admitted gracious influences, but regarded them as benefits peculiar to Christianity, (which is not to be overlooked), and as he universally placed
the grace of Christ in connection with the merit of man, so, according to his view, those influences must likewise be imparted only according to man's merit. For what is meant of the genus, must also
be meant of the species.—But Pelagius had also said before, in his
letter to Demetrias (c. 29), that, by keeping God's commands, one
can *merit* divine grace, by which he will the more easily resist the
evil spirit And we have already seen, that the divine grace spoken
of, must also be referred to supernatural gracious influences, according to Pelagius's own explanation.

Here it may, indeed, be objected that the verb *to merit* (mereri)
was used by the fathers and theological writers of that time, for *obtain, successfully to seek* (nancisci, feliciter consequi) ; and that
therefore it may have this meaning here. But such a meaning
would be entirely opposed to the connection in which the word
stands Pelagius had also said directly, at the synod of Diospolis,
(see charge 11) " God gives all spiritual gifts to him who *is worthy
to receive* (donare Deum ei, qui fuerit dignus accipere, omnes gra-
tias)."—Julian thought in the like way. " When man is divinely
aided, he is aided for the purpose of attaining perfection.—The nature of man is good, which deserves the aid of such grace " C. Jul.
IV. 3 Concerning this " merit" on the part of man, the Pelagians
explained themselves still more precisely, as, according to Augustine's account (De Gr. et Lib Arb 14), they would not have " the
merit of good deeds," but " the merit of good will," to precede
grace. " For they say, although it [grace] is not given according
to the merit of good works, because by it (per ipsam) we perform
good works, yet it is given according to the merit of good will (secundum merita bonae voluntatis) , because, say they, the good will of
the person *asking*, precedes, and this is preceded by the good will
of him *believing*, so that the grace of God in *hearing* follows according to these merits."—It was, therefore, with no injustice, adduced by Augustine as a Pelagian opinion, that grace, (in the Augustinian sense), is bestowed according to man's merit—an opinion

which was an abomination to him, and against which he constantly protested with the utmost emphasis. He goes into a minute confutation of this position, in Ep. 194, from which the following remarkable words may here have a place. "Although, therefore, they [the Pelagians] are hostile and bitter against this grace, yet Pelagius, at the ecclesiastical tribunal in Palestine, (for he could not otherwise escape with impunity), anathematized those that say that the grace of God is given according to merit. But even in their subsequent discussions, nothing else is found but that, to merit is awarded the same grace which, in the apostolic epistle to the Romans, is spoken of in the highest commendation in order that its praise might thence, as from the head of the world, be spread through the whole earth ‧ for it is that by which the ungodly is justified, i. e. becomes righteous, who was before ungodly. And so no merits precede in order to the reception of this grace ; for not grace but punishment is due to the merits of the ungodly. Nor would this be grace, if it were not given gratuitously but awarded as due. But when they are asked, what grace Pelagius supposed to be given without any preceding merits, when he condemned those who say that the grace of God is given according to our merits, they say, that human nature itself, in which we are made, is grace without any preceding merits. For before we existed, we could not merit anything in order to our existence. This fallacy is spurned from the hearts of Christians. For the apostle does not commend at all that grace by which we are created men, but by which we are justified when we were already bad men. For this is the grace by Jesus Christ our Lord. For Christ did not die for non-entities, that they might be made men ; but for sinners, that they might be justified " Ep 194, c. 3. " You would have it, that in the will of man, the striving for holiness, without God's aid, precedes, which striving God is to aid according to merit, not from grace." C Jul. IV. 3. " In Rom 10: 3, Paul says : They, being ignorant of God's righteousness and seeking to establish their own righteousness, have not submitted themselves to the righteousness of God. And this is just what you do ; for you wish to set up your own righteousness, which God is to reward with grace according to merit ; nor would you have grace precede, which should cause you to possess righteousness." Op. Imp. I 141 To this meritoriousness on the part of man, is also to be referred what Augustine says (C. d. Epp. Pel. II. 8) : " For they would have it, that the *desire* of

good commences in man *from man himself*, in order that the grace
for performing may follow the merit of this beginning; if indeed
they hold to at least this" It was certainly not the intention of Julian to deny the necessity of grace to merely the *beginning* of a
good work and to hold it as indispensable to the *completion*, as Vossius assumes, in his work (p 669) already quoted, and as this and
other passages (I. 19) from Augustine, would lead us to suppose.*
For how could so philosophical a mind as Julian's be so inconsistent
and so contradict his own theory of the freedom of the will and of
the uncorrupted nature of man? Julian undoubtedly intended
nothing more than this, that for the attainment of the grace by
which good would be *more easily* performed, the merit of man, in
earnestly willing good, and his consequent good purpose and the application of his own power to its performance, are demanded; and
this merit must therefore precede that grace. The nature of man
is good, said Julian; and it merits the aid of such grace. And in a
passage preserved from Julian's writings by Beda (Ap. 118), he
says, that the help of the Holy Ghost is imparted when " our desires
and merits precede."

(e) The Pelagian theory of gracious influences, must also have
differed from the Augustinian, in denying them to be irresistible, and
defending the free exercise of man's own power. A grace which
man cannot resist, they called "fate under the name of grace." In
the Pelagian letter which Augustine refutes in his second book
against the two letters of the Pelagians, it is said, (c 5) · " Under the
name of grace, they [Augustine and his adherents] maintain fate
when they say, that unless God inspires the desire of good, even of
imperfect good, into unwilling and resisting man, he can neither turn

---

* The *connection* of the passage above quoted, shows still more clearly
than is indicated by the last clause in it, that Augustine was himself suspi-
cious that the Pelagians of whom he was then speaking, did not in fact
mean to depart from their master, Pelagius, and to assert any real dependence on divine influence for the *completion* of good any more than for its
commencement Still, he did not know but this might be their meaning in
a passage from their letters, on which he was commenting. " *Perhaps,*
therefore," adds Augustine, " they in this way reserve a place for grace, as
they may think that, without it, man can have a desire of good, (though a
good incomplete, boni imperfecti) , but that he not only cannot *more easily,*
but cannot *at all,* complete the good, without grace " And then he goes on
to refute this new and possible notion of theirs —Tr.

away from evil nor lay hold on good.—We acknowledge baptism to be necessary for every age, and that grace aids the good purpose of every one, but not that it implants the love of virtue in him while resisting, for there is no accepting of persons with God." Against this objection, as if Augustine's grace were fate or a respect of persons, Augustine defended himself at length, in the sequel. "The dullest of men," says Pelagius, "suppose we do injury to divine grace, because we say it by *no means works sanctification* in us *without our will*, as if God commanded his grace to do something, and did not even afford the aid of his grace to those whom he commands." Pelagius De Lib. Arb. in Aug. De Gr. Chr. 7.

In these various senses in which Pelagius and his disciples used the word *grace*, if the different meanings are not distinguished, they will seem, in particular expressions, to contradict their doctrine of original sin and of freewill But by thus distinguishing, there is not only no contradiction, but the latter become all the more lucid.

The Pelagian theory of grace, then, may be reduced more precisely even than was done by the Pelagians and by Augustine, to the following propositions.

1. Freewill is a gracious gift of God, by which man is in a condition to do good from his own power, without special divine aid. This, according to a later technical expression, may be called " creating grace (gratia creans)." Grace in the wider sense.

2. This gracious gift, all men possess, Christians, Jews, and heathen But that man may the more easily perform good, he gave him the law, by which knowledge is more easily gained, and the reasons why he should do thus and not otherwise, become the more manifest to him. For this purpose, he gave him the instructions and example of Jesus, and for this he aids Christians further by supernatural influence. This is " illuminating grace ;" and in reference merely to *supernatural* influence, " cooperating grace ;" grace in the *more* restricted and the *most* restricted sense.

3. He, to whom this grace is imparted, can do more than they who do not receive it. By it, he more easily reaches a higher step than he would have reached by his own power. On this account, the Christian can attain a higher degree of moral perfection, than one who is not a Christian.*

---

* Our author uses the term *Christian* here in distinction only to the terms

25

4. The supernatural influence of gracious operations, however, is imparted only to him who merits it by the faithful application of his own power.

5. The supernatural operations of grace, do not relate immediately to the *will* of man, but to his understanding. This becomes enlightened by those operations; and thus also the will is *indirectly* inclined to do what the understanding has perceived as good.

6. These gracious operations do not put forth their influence in an irresistible manner, (this would be *determinism*); but the man can resist them. There is therefore no " irresistible grace."

7 It is also grace, that God remits to the sinner the punishment of his past transgressions. And so is baptism to be called grace, by which Christians become partakers of the benefits of Christianity and a higher salvation.

This Pelagian theory of grace, will now appear still plainer by the opposite Augustinian theory, in which we shall everywhere see the reverse of Pelagianism.

Augustine's theory of Grace.

As Pelagius and his disciples were led to their theory of grace by their idea of freewill and the uncorrupted state of man after the fall, so Augustine, by admitting a radical corruption of human nature, through which man's freewill is lost and he can will and do nothing but evil, would naturally be brought to a theory of grace conformable to this doctrine. And so indeed we find the fact. By the fall, man lost all freedom of will. Thereupon, original sin followed as a punishment, and was transferred as a punishment to all posterity, so that all men are under the curse and the righteous judgment of condemnation. Consequently, grace must do all, if man is to be freed from this punishment, and is to will and do good

Augustine could have no objection, indeed, to the Pelagians using the word grace in the wider sense. Himself admitted various operations of God's grace, in as much as the scriptures speak of a manifold grace. 1 Pet. 4 10; Op Imp II. 120 And it was not to be denied, that man's existing as a living, sentient, and rational being, may be termed grace. Ep. 177 c 7 And according to Augustine,

---

Jew, heathen, etc The parts of this proposition are not very congruous, if indeed they are all exactly expressive of the Pelagian view.—Tr

it was entirely right and agreeable to his system, as will more fully appear in the sequel, that the pardon of sin and eternal salvation, should be considered as the grace of God. "Grace aids in both ways, as it pardons the evil we have done and helps us to turn from evil and do good." Op Imp II. 227. "Without the grace of Christ, no one is freed from the condemnation which he has either derived from him in whom we have all sinned, or has since added by his own trespasses." De Perf Just. Hom. 19. Comp. De Gen. ad Lit IX. 18, where he explains himself, in a most remarkable manner, concerning the relation between *providence* and that grace by which the sinner is saved. He there says, that "God has *in himself* the hidden causes of *certain* acts, which he has not implanted in the things he has made; and these causes he puts in operation, not in that work of providence by which he makes natures to exist, but in that by which he manages as he will the natures that he constituted as he chose. And *there* is the grace by which sinners are saved. For as it respects nature, depraved by its own bad will, it has of itself no return, except by God's grace, whereby it is aided and restored. Nor need men despair on account of that declaration, Prov. 2. 19, None who walk in it, shall return. For it was spoken of the burden of their iniquity, so that whoever returns, should attribute his return, not to himself, but to the grace of God, not of works, lest there should be boasting. Eph. 2: 9. Therefore the apostle speaks (Eph 3. 9) of the mystery of this grace as *hidden*, (not in this world, in which are hidden the causal reasons of all things which arise naturally, as Levi was hid in the loins of Abraham), but in God, who created all things," etc.* "If our good life is nothing else but the

---

* The topic here thus summarily despatched, is one of deep interest to reflecting minds; the theme of much discussion, and the starting point of a radical division, both among divines and philosophers. Has God, by creation, endowed matter and mind with certain powers, which now really exist and *act* in them? Or, on the contrary, is all creation, instead of really possessing any powers of action, merely clothed with *susceptibilities* of impression, motion, feeling, etc, from the *immediate* hand of God? And if created minds and things *do* possess active powers, what *are* those powers? and where is their *limit?* These are questions lying at the foundation of the whole discussion respecting divine and human agency, and precisely on the manner in which Augustine would answer such questions, depended the whole superstructure of his theory.

What more, then, had so thinking a man as Augustine to say on these

grace of God, without doubt eternal life, which is given as the *reward* of this good life, is *also* God's grace, and is itself given gratuitously,

---

points, in addition to the hints implied in the last extract? A few sentences immediately preceding that extract, will sufficiently inform us. " The whole of this most common course of nature, has certain natural laws of its own, according to which even the spirit of life, which is a creature, has certain appetites of its own, limited in a certain way, which even the *bad will* cannot exceed   And the elements of this corporeal world, have *their* definite power and quality, what each one can or cannot do, and what can or cannot be done respecting each   From these, the origin as it were of things (primordiis rerum), all things which are generated, take, each in its time, their rise and growth, and the limits and variations of their respective kinds. Hence it comes to pass, that pulse is not produced from wheat, nor wheat from pulse, nor man from brute, nor brute from man   But in addition to this natural motion and course of things, the power of the Creator keeps with itself the ability to do, respecting all these, something different from what their quasi seminales rationes (kind of seminal qualities) have   It is therefore a *different mode* of things, by which this plant germinates thus, and that thus , this age is prolific, and that is not , a man can speak, and a brute cannot   The qualities (rationes)'of these and the like modes, are not only in God, but are even *implanted and concreated* by him in created things   But that wood, cut from the earth, dry, polished, without any root, without earth or water, should suddenly flourish and bear fruit,—that an ass should speak, and whatever there is of this kind, he gave indeed to the natures he created, that these things might take place from them ,—but he gave it in a different way, so that they should not have these things in the natural movement, but in that by which they were so created that their nature should be more amply (amplius) subject to a mightier will   God, therefore, has in himself the hidden causes of certain acts," etc as quoted in the text   And among *these* acts, for which God has indeed given an original *susceptibility*, but not a power of production, Augustine would rank the regeneration of a fallen human soul   According to Augustine, (as might be more fully shown by extending these extracts), God " implanted and concreated, in all created things,' certain powers, subject indeed completely to his own control, but still really *active* in themselves , while, with an eye on what himself would further do, in a *miraculous* way, with some of them, he at the same time made them capable of having certain things done *with* or *in* them, by his own immediate power, which they have no implanted power at all of doing themselves. Thus the dry rod of Aaron, was such that it could be made to germinate, and a dumb ass such as to be made to speak , and the human soul such that, when fallen, it could *be* regenerated, though destitute of all power of self-renovation.

Such was Augustine's philosophy, touching these profound depths of ontology ;—by a peculiar turn, indeed, making the soul of fallen man but a

because that to which it is awarded, is given gratuitously.—So that this which is awarded, is only grace for grace," etc. De Gr. et Lib. Arb. 8; Comp. C. Jul. IV. 3. And Augustine had no objection to make to the declaration of Paul, By grace are ye saved; where Pelagius, however, would always be thinking of something meritorious on the part of men, which consisted in the application of their powers to the performance of good. Ep. 194. c. 3. Eternal life was with him at once a reward and grace; or, as will hereafter appear, the good works of men were the effects of grace; properly grace for grace. De Gr. et Lib. Arb. 8, 9. He further agreed with Pelagius in this, that baptism is a grace; nay, with him, this must have been the more so, the greater his idea of its effects. "They [children] are regenerated in Christ by grace." Ep. 217. c 5. It was previously, however, a common mode of speech, in the ancient African church, emphatically to call baptism, *grace*. By this mode of speech, one is reminded of Cyprian's book On the Grace of God. Augustine also used such language, when he inquired of Ambrose, what he should particularly read in the bible in order properly to prepare himself for receiving *the divine grace*. Conff. IX. 5. The law was also with him, in a certain sense, an aid of grace. Ep. 157. c. 2. "The letter [of the law] is an aid to the elect, because by commands and not by help, it admonishes the weak to flee to the spirit of grace." Op. Imp. I. 94.—But Augustine could no longer speak of freewill as a gracious gift of God, for with him it was a lost good. And besides, he believed, that, according to the scripture use of language, and especially that of Paul, *grace* must be used in respect to the supernatural operations of God's spirit on men. Ep. 177. c. 8; De Praed. Sanct. 5. This he considered as grace in the appropriate sense. C. d. Epp. Pel. IV. 5. He also called it "spiritual grace." De Pec. Mer. I 10 Nay, Augustine even distinguished between grace before the fall, and grace after the fall. But the precise point of difference in which Pelagianism varied from Augustinism, and must vary, lay in the different ideas which Pelagius and

dry stick, in regard to renovation,—and yet heaven-wide of the popular and sweeping theory that makes the common laws of nature to be only *the modes of God's immediate agency* on things And equally far was his philosophy from making the common laws of mind, the *mere* modes of God's *immediate* agency.—Some explanation of this matter, seemed needful to a more just and easy comprehension of what is yet to follow.—Tr.

Augustine had of grace, as a supernatural operation of God upon men in their present state   Such a point of variance is indicated by Augustine himself (De Gr. Chr. 30), where he shows the difference of views on both sides.   " The grace by which we are justified, i e. by which the love of God is poured forth into our hearts by the Holy Ghost, which is given to us, I have never found from Pelagius and Caelestius in their writings, so far as I have been able to read; and yet this must be acknowledged "   With Augustine, it was a communication of power (subministratio virtus) for avoiding sin (2); a " communication of the spirit, and hidden compassion" (Ep 177. c. 7), a " hidden inspiration of God." Ep. 217. c. 6.   In this connection, he used the expression, " infused spirit of grace" (De Spir. et Lit. 36), like the idiom, Christ confers love by *breathing into*. He calls it the " inspiration of faith and of the fear of God" (Ep. 194 c 6); " inspiration of love by the Holy Ghost." De Gr. Chr. 39.   This grace must precede, before the grace of the remission of sins can follow.   " We acknowledge," says he to Julian, (Op Imp. I. 140), " grace without merit, which not only remits sins to man, but produces righteousness in human nature by the Holy Ghost " " The grace of God through Jesus Christ our Lord, is to be understood, (by which alone men are freed from evil, and without which they perform absolutely nothing good, whether in thinking, willing, loving, or doing), not only that, by its indication, they may know what is to be done, but also, by its aid, may with love perform what they know.   For, this inspiration of good will and of action, the apostle implored for those to whom he said, But we pray God, that ye may do no evil,—but that ye may do what is good." De Cor. et Gr 2.   He defines this grace, in opposition to Pelagianism, as " an aid for doing well, added to nature and to instruction, by the inspiration of the most burning and luminous charity." De Gr. Chr. 35.

Often and gladly, and sometimes with a charm of ravishing eloquence, (because here his religious heart spoke out,) are depicted, by Augustine, this work of Deity in men, and its mysteriousness. But the most remarkable of all, is a passage in which he at the same time declares the relation of the gracious operations of God in respect to the relation of the Three Persons in the work.   " For," says Augustine, " if every one that has heard and learned of the Father, comes [to the Son], certainly every one who does not come, has not heard of the Father nor learned ; for if he had heard and learned, he would come. For no one has heard and learned, and not come; but every one, as saith the Word, who hath heard and learned, cometh. Widely removed from the senses of the flesh, is this school in which the Father is heard and teaches, in order that men should come to the Son. There is also the Son himself; for he is his word, by which he thus teaches. Nor does he do this with the ear of the flesh, but of·the heart. At the same time, there is also the Spirit of the Father and of the Son. For neither does he not teach, nor teach separately for we have learned, that the works of the Trinity, are inseparable.—But this is especially attributed to the Father, because the Only Begotten is begotten by him, and from him proceeds the Holy Ghost.—We see many come to the Son, because we see many believe on Christ; but where and how they heard and have learned this from the Father, we see not Doubtless this grace is secret; but that it is grace, who should doubt?" De Praed. Sanct 8.

Concerning this grace, Augustine taught the following things:

1. Faith, as well in respect to its beginning as its progress and its completion, is a work of the preceding grace;—that faith which he regarded is the source of all good acts, and which has as its consequence the love without which nothing good can be done, and with which nothing bad can be done.

This is universally maintained by Augustine in his writings against the Pelagians. Earlier, he had had the semi-pelagian view on this point. In De Praed. Sanct. 3, and De Dono Persev 20, Augustine grants, that at a former period, he was himself in error, and held faith in God, or the assent which we give to the preaching of the gospel, not as a gift from him, but as something which we ourselves produce, by which we obtain God's grace to live devoutly and righteously; but that he had been taught something better, especially by the words of Paul, 1 Cor. 4 7; But what hast thou that thou hast not received? But if thou hast received it, why dost thou boast, as if thou hadst not received it? After the beginning of his episcopate, as his first book to Simplicianus shows, he learned to see, that even the *beginning* of faith, is a gift of God.—During the contests with the Pelagians, Augustine fully professed this opinion: "Although faith obtains the grace for doing well, yet certainly by no faith have we deserved to *have* faith itself; but in giving us that by which we obey the Lord, *his compassion precedes us.*" De Gest. 14.

" Faith is not possessed by all who hear the Lord, through the scriptures, promising the kingdom of heaven ; and all are not persuaded who are counselled to come unto him.—But who *do* possess faith, and *who* are persuaded to come to him, he has himself sufficiently shown, where he says, No one cometh unto me except the Father that hath sent me, draw him." De Gr Chr. 10. " The law says truly, Whosoever keepeth my commandments shall live by them. But in order to his keeping them and living by them, it is not the law, which commands it, that is necessary, but the faith which obtains this." C. d. Epp. Pel. IV. 5. That faith is a work of grace, he endeavors to prove at length from scripture, in his book De Gr. et Lib. Arb. 7. 14 —" God works in a wonderful manner in our hearts, in order that we should believe." De Praed. Sanct. 2. " Faith, begun and completed, is a gift of God " 9. " Faith, both in its progress and in its beginning, is a work of grace." 11. Comp. Ep 194. c. 3, 4, where it is also shown, that even prayer is an effect of faith, and therefore also of grace. In reference to this letter, Augustine says, in one of the following letters (Ep. 214), " I have proved in this letter, by passages of scripture, that our good works as well as our devout prayers and right faith, could in no wise be in us, if we did not receive this from him of whom the apostle James says · Every good gift and every perfect gift is from above, and cometh down from the Father of Lights "

Since therefore Augustine considered faith as an effect of grace, he must likewise have considered salvation, a consequence of faith, to be a gift of grace.

But we should be cautious of transferring the Lutheran doctrine of faith, to the Augustinian theory. This was unknown to him as well as to his whole age. Faith with him was the holding as true the phenomena in the life of Jesus This needs no proof, since the whole of his writings declare it See especially De Fide et Operibus composed about the year 413, and found ed. Ben. P. VI. A principal proof passage is also found in his work De Pec. Orig. 24. " Christian truth," says he, " does not doubt, that *without faith in the incarnation, death, and resurrection of Christ*, even the ancient saints, could not, in order to their being righteous, be purified from sins and justified through God's grace. Even *their* hearts were purified by *the same faith in the Mediator*, and love was poured into them." Comp. De Spir. et Lit. 31.—In C. d. Epp. Pel. III. 5, Augustine

says, that " the catholic faith" does not distinguish the righteous from
the unrighteous by the law of works, but by the law of faith itself;
and that whoever does not hold the right and " catholic faith," passes
from this life into perdition   Faith (fides, πιστις) was therefore with
him exclusively the *historical* belief.   The passages which are commonly adduced for a more limited and definite idea, afford, when
more closely examined, no other sense *

It was not easy to treat of faith without also mentioning justification.   This, however, was only done incidentally , and this doctrine
no more than that of faith, (as might indeed be expected from the
state of the controversy), became a subject of minute examination.
Nevertheless, thus much is certain, that Augustine believed justification to be obtained through faith, since grace justifies only through
faith. De Spir. et Lit. 13, 29.

But it may not be unimportant, on account of several passages
already quoted and others yet to be quoted from the writings of Augustine, here just to remark, that he did not admit this doctrine in
the more limited sense of the Lutheran system.   For although he
sometimes took it, with the Pelagians, for the forgiveness of sins,
yet he also, at the same time, regarded it in the sense of *making
just.*   Consequently he included sanctification under it.   In opposition to Julian, who had explained justification (Rom 5: 1) as " the
pardon of sins," he says, " God justifies the ungodly person not
merely by pardoning the evil he commits, but also by imparting love,
that he may turn from evil and do good through the Holy Ghost."
Op. Imp II. 165 Comp. C Jul. II. 8.   " God justifies the wicked,"
says he to him.   " By Jesus Christ, he spiritually heals the sick or
resuscitates the dead." De Nat et-Gr. 26.   By *justified*, he therefore
meant as much as *rendered just ;* from an ungodly, one is made a
righteous person De Spir. et Lit. 26.   " We are justified by the
grace of God, that is we are caused to be just (justi efficimur)."
Retract. II 33.

The Pelagians also took the expression *justification* for *making
just*, and called God the author of our justification.   But they referred this, as appears from the exhibition already made of their system,
at least in part, to the natural effect of the law, of which God is the

* Not, however, that *all* correct historical belief is saving faith   No man
was ever farther from such a view than Augustine, as I shall soon endeavor
to show —Tr.

26

author (De Spir. et Lit. 8); while Augustine on the contrary, referred the sanctification of man only to the power of gracious influence. He refers the justification of believers (De Pec. Mer. I 10), to " the secret communication and inspiration of spiritual grace ;" and the act of justifying as performed, to the outpouring of the love of God into our hearts by the Holy Ghost De Gr. Chr. 30.

Faith therefore—to return to the point from which we have digressed—was with Augustine the effect of God's preceding grace. But as he took this in the historical sense, and as with him " to believe" was the same as " to believe what is spoken to be true" (De Spir. et Lit 31), or, as he elsewhere expressly signified, " to think with assent" (De Praed Sanct 2), therefore, also,

2 He must have admitted a supernatural influence of grace on the understanding or the intellect of man Whether he thought of this connection, cannot be determined, but it may well be doubted, as he does not appear to have obtained clear views of the nature of the faith which he adopted, and he did not make it an object of close investigation Enough, that he everywhere joyfully allowed and taught, that the supernatural influence of grace was needful to obtaining the true knowledge of good. " The grace of Christ produces internally our illumination and justification," said he De Pec. Mer. I. 9 " *To come to the knowledge of good, which was hidden,* is the grace of God " II. 17. The certain knowledge of right conduct, is sometimes wanting even to saints, in order that they may see, that the light by which their darkness is illuminated, comes not from themselves, but from him II 19 " No man can know what ought to be done, unless God give it him " Ep 188 Still more clearly does he explain himself (Ep 214) to the Adrumetian monks. "If it could take place through freewill, without the aid of divine grace, that we should understand and be wise, it would not be said to God, Grant me understanding, that I may learn thy commands," etc.

Augustine, however, did not confine the influence of grace to the supernatural illumination of the understanding, but adopted a supernatural and immediate effect of it on the *will* of man. He taught, that,

3. By preceding grace, not only is the understanding enlightened, but the *good will* is also first produced in man · *by its supernatural and immediate inward operation, man first obtains the power to will*

good. The goodwill itself, with him, was nothing else but love; which love, as we have seen, he explained as a consequence of faith, and "which we have from God and not from ourselves, as that scripture testifies which says. Love is from God, and every one that loveth is born of God and knoweth God." De Gr et Chr. 21. He held this love as the necessary condition and mother of all good. 26.

[But if Augustine thus held to holy love as absolutely essential to the first good act in man, and the mother of *all* good, how could he, at the same time, hold to an act of *holy faith* as *preceding* this love, and as obtaining from God the gift of love? If such is our author's meaning, it is of importance to inquire a little more minutely into Augustine's views respecting the grand question of faith and love, and how man comes to the first exercise of these graces. And this inquiry is here rendered the more needful by the suggestion above made in respect to Augustine's ignorance of the nature of that faith to which he held, and his not having made it an object of close investigation.

How far Augustine was in fact ignorant of the nature of *faith*, and especially of the relations between faith and love, and also what he believed concerning them, will be shown in the most sure and speedy manner by suffering him to speak for himself. The reader will soon see whether he regarded *any* faith as holy which does not itself imply love; or any faith, which is *not* thus holy, as the condition of obtaining love.

In his treatise On Faith and Works (14), he thus proceeds in an argument on his general subject: "When, therefore, the apostle said, that he concluded a man is justified by faith without works of law, he did not do this in order that precepts and works of righteousness should be despised in consequence of faith professed, but that every one may know that he can be justified by faith, though works of law have not preceded.—Since, therefore, this opinion" (that faith dissolves the obligation to good works) "had then arisen, other apostolical epistles, those of Peter, John, James, and Jude, in a special manner direct the attention against it and urgently maintain, that faith without works profits nothing; just as even Paul himself has defined, not *any kind whatever of faith* by which one may believe in God, but *that saving and plainly evangelical faith, the works of which proceed from love:* And faith, he says, which works by love. Hence that faith which seems to some sufficient for salvation, he thus asserts to profit nothing, when he says . Though I have all faith, so that I could remove mountains, but have not love, I am nothing. But where believing love operates, there is doubtless right living "

The following passage is designed to show, that grace must precede both faith and prayer " If we inquire for the desert of mercy, we find it not, for there is none —For if we say, that *faith* precedes, in which there should be the desert of grace, what merit had the man *before* faith, in order to his receiving faith ? —If we say the merit of *prayer* precedes, that he may obtain the gift of grace,— even prayer itself is found among the gifts of grace. For, says the teacher of the gentiles, we know not what to pray for as we ought, but the spirit itself intercedeth for us with groanings that cannot be uttered. But what is his interceding, except that he causes *us* to intercede ? For, to intercede with groans, is a most certain indication of one in need. But we are to believe the Holy Ghost in need of nothing. But he is thus said to intercede, because he makes *us* intercede, and inspires us with the affection of interceding and groaning : like what is said in the gospel, It is not ye that speak, but the Spirit of your Father that speaketh in you. For neither does this take place respecting us as though we did nothing. The aid of the Holy Spirit, therefore, is so expressed, that he may be said to do what he causes us to do." Ep. 194. c. 4.

In regard to the nature and effects of a merely *historical faith,* the following are still more specific. " This faith, which works by love, is the faith which distinguishes those who trust in God, from *foul demons ,* for they, the apostle James says, *believe* and tremble, but they do not perform good works. Therefore they have not *this* faith by which the just man lives, i. e. which works by love " De Gr. et Lib. Arb. 7. The next passage is the one in which Augustine speaks expressly of faith as a belief of historic facts, and will be found to possess a twofold interest   " Now attend to that which I have proposed to discuss, viz , whether faith is in our power ?—that faith by which we believe God, or believe in God,—as Abraham believed, and it was counted to him for righteousness.—See, now, whether any one believes if he is unwilling (si noluerit) ? or does not believe if he *is* willing (si voluerit) ? If this is absurd, then truly faith is in our power ; for what is it to believe, unless to consent that what is said is true? and consent certainly belongs to one willing.—Since, therefore faith is in our power, as every one believes when he will, and when he believes, he believes while willing (volens credit), we should inquire, or rather should recollect, *what* faith the apostle would commend so earnestly? for it is not good to believe every sort of thing.—No doubt, that faith is commended by the apostle by which we believe in God. But there is still a further distinction to be made. For they who are under the law, moved by the fear of punishment, strive to work a righteousness of their own, and hence do not work the righteousness of God.—They, therefore believe; for if they did not believe at all, they certainly would not fear the punishment of the law. But this faith the apostle does not commend. —That fear therefore is servile, and so, although it believes in the Lord, it does not *delight in righteousness*, but fears damnation. But the children cry *Abba Father*," etc. De Spir. et Lit 31, 32.

Here is surely no lack of discrimination between an *affectionate, confiding* faith, and that which is merely speculative, or which is servile.—Nor does love here follow as a *consequence* of this faith, but enters into its living essence.—Still it is true, that Augustine frequently speaks of *love*, or the good will, as being obtained from God in consequence of the *faith* with which it is sought. And he even speaks in the following strain of faith as *meriting* something. " We cannot deny, nay, we most gratefully confess, that faith merits the grace of performing good works. And we wish those brethren of ours who boast so much of their good works, *had this* faith, by which they would obtain *the love* that alone performs works truly good." But it may be questioned whether Augustine really designed to teach anything more than what has before been stated of his belief, viz, that God rewards grace by grace—to the prayer of him that exercises something of " that spirit of faith," of which he often speaks, God will give more grace, by which he will perform good works. —Augustine, however, it must be confessed, has not always spoken with that precision on this matter, which would sufficiently guard each separate passage from a different interpretation. And it may furthermore be true, that he considered faith as taking the precedence of love in the order of *nature* though not of *time*, so that while true faith never exists without love, it may yet be the *foundation* of love; and in this sense, love be its consequence

And now, in view of what has here and elsewhere been adduced,

what shall we say of Augustine's ignorance and want of attention to
the nature of that faith which he professed ? The amount of the
facts appears to me to be simply this, that so far as the above topics
are concerned, Augustine had come to a very clear view of the nature and relations of saving faith ; while at the same time his views,
like those of the fathers in general, were indefinite and unsettled on
the nature and relations of faith touching many of those grand points
which first came up in earnest debate in the time of Luther. Nor
can we expect to find any doctrine well settled in the views of men,
and the language respecting it definite, till it has been long and warmly debated. Augustine discussed, to very good purpose for himself
as well as subsequent ages, the connection between faith and love,
and the doctrine of faith too in some of its more immediate relations
to the repenting sinner—his *free* pardon, through faith, of all sins
then past, for instance—while the need and reception of an equally
free pardon of *subsequent* sins in the believer, was at best but more
dimly and transiently seen. And I may just add, that it was in consequence of this dimness that the floodgates were left wide open to
errors and papal impositions,—such as the merits of holy faith itself
and of repentance in those who have once believed—and then, pe-
nances, and purgatory, and popish pardons, all for doing away the
sins committed after baptism —A pity truly would it be if the Lutheran, or any other church of the Reformation, had not better views
of faith, in many of its relations, than are to be found in *any* period
of the church from the time of the apostles down to that grand era
of its more ample discussion by Luther and the Reformers. This
early and lasting defect in doctrinal knowledge, is nearly if not quite
the saddest, in its results, of any ever found in the christian church

Still Augustine should have the full credit of all he did see in regard to this grand doctrine. Nor in fact did those founders of the
Lutheran church consider Augustine at all so ignorant of their dar-
ling doctrine of faith as Dr W. seems to suppose him. They continually adduce his authority in support of their positions, and especially on some of the chief points now just considered   Take, for
instance, the following sentence from their grand " standard," the
Augsburg Confession, Art. 20.   In support of the view of faith
there given, they say : " Augustine in speaking of the word faith,
admonishes the reader that in scripture this word does not signify
mere knowledge, such as wicked men possess, but that confidence

or trust by which alarmed sinners are comforted and lifted up."—
We now return to our author.—Tr.]

As here is a grand distinction between Augustinism and Pelagianism, Augustine is very particular in the discrimination of this doctrine, that the good will of man is originated by the immediate and
supernatural influence of divine grace. Some of the most important passages ought not here to be passed by.

"We say, that the human will is so aided by God to the practice
of righteousness that, besides his being created as man, with the free
exercise of will, and besides instruction by which he is directed how
to live, he receives the Holy Spirit, by which there is produced in
his mind the enjoyment and love of that supreme and incommunica-
ble good which is God, even now while as yet he walks by faith and
not by sight ; so that by this pledge as it were of a free gift, he burns
to cleave fast to the Creator, and longs to arrive at the participation
of that true light, that it may be well with him from the Author of
his being.   For freewill avails nothing except to sin, if the way of
truth is concealed ; and when that which is to be done and how it is
to be attempted, begins not to be hid, unless it also delights and is
loved, it is not done ; it is not begun, there is no holy living.   But
that it may be loved, the love of God is shed abroad in our hearts,
not by freewill which arises from ourselves, but by the Holy Ghost
which is given unto us." De Spir et Lit. 3.   Without the life-giving
spirit, the instruction of law is a dead letter. 4.   "This is the righteousness which God not only teaches by the precept of law, but also
gives by the gift of the spirit."   "But we wish him [Pelagius] at
length to confess that grace by which the greatness of future glory
is not only promised but is also believed in and hoped for ; and by
which wisdom is not merely revealed, but also loved ; and which is
not only suasive, but also persuasive to that which is good." De Gr.
Chr. 10.   "By this grace, it comes to pass, not only that we know
what we ought to do, but that we *do what we know ;* not only that
we believe what is to be loved, but also that we *love what we believe.*
If this grace is to be called instruction (doctrina), let it be called so
in such a sense that God may be regarded as *infusing it more deeply and internally with an ineffable sweetness,* not only by those who
plant and water externally, but also by himself who secretly gives
his increase, so that he not only shows the truth but also imparts

love." 12, 13   After speaking of God's turning the heart of the
Assyrian king in the time of Esther, he says, " Let them therefore
read and understand, let them examine and confess, that, not by law,
and instruction from without, but by an internal and secret, a wonderful and ineffable power, God produces in the hearts of men, not
only true revelations, but also good volitions (bonas voluntates)." 24.
" Not only has God given our ability (posse nostrum) and aids it,
but he also works in us to will and to do.   Not as though we do not
will and do not do ; but because, without his aid, we neither will nor
do anything *good*." 25.   ' And what the law commands, is not performed unless by *his* aiding, inspiring and giving, who commands ;
to whom the church prays that believers may persevere and advance
and be perfected, and to whom she also prays that unbelievers may
begin to believe " Op Imp. VI. 41.   " But when good is performed
through fear of punishment and not from love of righteousness, the
good is not rightly performed, nor is that done in the heart which
appears to be done in the act, as the man would prefer not to do it,
if he could with impunity.   Therefore the blessing of sweetness
(benedictio dulcedinis, Ps. 21 3), is God's grace, by which it comes
to pass in us, that we are delighted and we desire, that is, we love
what is commanded us ; in which, if God does not precede us, not
only is it not done, but it is not begun by us " C. d Epp. Pel II. 9.
" For how is there a good purpose of man, without the Lord's first
having compassion on him, since it is the good will itself which is
prepared by the Lord ?—But in all which any one does according
to God, his compassion precedes him " IV 6 Comp. Ep. 177 c. 7 ;
217. c. 6.   In the last passage, it is said, that the good will is prepared by grace. " Grace precedes man's will, and does not follow
it, that is, it is not given to us because we will it, but by it God
causes us to will " 5.   " No human merit precedes God's grace ;
but grace itself deserves to be increased, so that, being increased, it
may deserve to be perfected, *the will accompanying and not leading ;
following like a servant, and not going before.*" Ep. 186. c. 3. " If
grace does not precede and produce the will, but only cooperates
with the will already existing, how could the apostle's declaration be
true, God worketh in you to will?" Op Imp. I. 95.   " The pious
will indeed obtain a reward according to the merit of their good will ;
but the good will itself, they have obtained by the grace of God."
Ep. 215.   " By the grace of God, it comes to pass that the man has

a good will, who before had a bad will   By this it comes to pass also, that the will already good, is increased and becomes great, so that it can fulfil God's commands," etc. De Gr. et Lib. Arb. 15. " When the man is aided by God, he is not only aided in order to obtain perfection, but, as the apostle says, he that hath *begun* the good carrieth it on to perfection " C Jul. IV. 3   " In the elect, the will is prepared by the Lord " De Praed. Sanct. 5.   " Grace takes the lead in man, so that he loves God ; by which love, he performs good." Op. Imp II. 131.

This is the *preceding grace* (gratia praeveniens) of Augustine, which, as we have already seen, he also referred to faith, in opposition to the *cooperating* grace of the Pelagians ; or the *operating* grace (gratia operans) of Augustine   For preceding grace, he also employed the expression *antecedent* grace (gratia antecedens). Ep. 217. c 7.*

4 Grace—so the bishop of Hippo further taught—is the necessary condition *to the performance* of each good act, and is afforded *for each individual good act in particular.*

Augustine compares God's grace to a light. De Pec. Mer II. 5. As the bodily eye cannot see without light, so God, who is the light of the inner man, aids our spirit to perform good, not after our own righteousness, but his.   Hence even the regenerate (perfectissime justificatus) needs, in order to a holy life, the continual and divine aid of the eternal light of righteousness, as Augustine expresses himself. De Nat. et Gr 26.   " Whatever is not of faith, is sin ; and faith works by love.   And according to this, every one, (who desires truly to confess the grace of God, by which the love of God is shed abroad in our hearts by the Holy Ghost which is given unto us), so confesses as not in the least to doubt that *without it there can be nothing good as pertaining to piety and true righteousness.*" De Gr. Chr 26.   " The grace or aid of God is afforded *for every individual act,—and we are swayed (regimur) by God, when we do right.*" De Gest. Pel. 14   That God's grace is given for separate acts, is also denoted by Augustine as being a catholic doctrine, in his letter to Vitalis. Ep 217.   " God does much good in man which man does

---

* The term *preventing* grace is still sometimes used, in theological works, in the sense of *preceding ;* but as that sense is now obsolete and ambiguous, I have chosen to employ the word *preceding,* though some would doubtless prefer to see the same time-hallowed phrase, *preventing grace* —Tr

not do ; but man does nothing which God does not cause him to do.
For if without him we can do nothing, we can in fact no more begin
than we can accomplish without him   In reference to beginning, it
is said, His compassion will precede me ; and in reference to accomplishing, His compassion will follow me " C. d. Epp. Pel. II. 9.
" The will of man is aided to every good act and word, and to every
good thought, by the grace of God " II. 5.   " The soul lives from
God, when it lives well ; for it cannot live well, if God does not
work in it what is good." De Civ. Dei, XIII. 2.   " It is true, that we
act when we do act ; but he [God] causes us to act by affording
most efficacious strength to the will " De Gr. et Lib. Arb. 16.

[Augustine was far enough from denying that our actions and volitions are really our own, in distinction from our being passive instruments by which the divine spirit acts   Nor did he place the
main difficulty with fallen man, in our not being able to do right if
we *will*.   Hear what he has to say on this topic in the chapter just
referred to.   " The Pelagians think they know some great thing,
when they say, *God would not command what he knew could not be
done by man.*   Who does not know this ?   But he commands some
things which we cannot do, whereby we know what we ought to ask
of him.   For it is faith which obtains by prayer what the law commands.—For true it is, that we keep the commandments if we will
(si volumus) , but as the will is prepared of the Lord, we must seek
of him that we may will as much as is sufficient in order to our doing by volition (ut volendo faciamus).   Certain it is, that we will,
when we do will , but he causes us to will good, of whom it is said,
It is God that worketh in you to will and to do.   Certain it is, that
we *do* when we do, etc.—Whoever therefore *wills to do God's command* and cannot, *has already the good will*, but it is as yet small
and weak ; but he will be able when he shall have it great and strong.
For when the martyrs performed those great commands, they performed them certainly by a great will, that is, by great love." De
Gr. et Lib. Arb. 16, 17.

Here, again, we see, that " the good will" is the same as holy
love.   We see also, that whoever wills *at all* to keep God's commands, has already this love in some degree   Of course Augustine
did not suppose saving faith, by which we pray for the good will, to
commence before love in the order of time ; but by this love, this

" spirit of faith," in a small degree, we can obtain of God a larger
degree for the performance of any good works—just as was stated
while on the nature of faith. See also in that connection a further
illustration of Augustine's views respecting our ability to *do if we
will* or *believe if we will.* The great difficulty, in his view, is further back—to gain the will *to believe*, or *to do* —Still, one would
like to know from Augustine *how* it is, that he does not consider God
as commanding what he knows we cannot do, nor even properly
pray for, before he gives us this love in *any* degree, i. e. before regeneration. Perhaps he has left nothing to pour light on this obscure
spot in his theory, and by which he can be defended from the charge
of inconsistency

Since writing the above, I have met with the following passage
which amply confirms the view I have given of his theory in respect
to the simultaneous commencement of faith and love, and also of
our entire impotence even to pray for the gift of love, until God gives
at least a little love,—though it affords us no clue to the sense in
which he would suppose God does not command what he knows we
cannot do " Whatever a man thinks he does well, if it is done
without love, it is by no means done well. These commands of love,
therefore, would in vain be given to men, not having the free decision of will But as they are given in both the old and new law,—
whence to men is the love of God and of their neighbor, unless from
God himself? For if not from God, but from men, the Pelagians
have conquered ; but if from God, we have conquered the Pelagians.
Let, then, the apostle John sit as judge between us, and say to us,
Beloved, let us love one another. When, at these words of John,
they begin to erect themselves and to say, How is this commanded
to us, unless we have power of ourselves to love one another' the
same John immediately continues, confounding them and saying,
Because love is of God. It is *not* therefore of ourselves, but of God
Why, then, is it said, Let us love one another, *because love is of
God*, unless that freewill is admonished to seek the gift of God ?
Which freewill, indeed, would be admonished entirely without its
fruit, unless it first received something of love, in order to seek the
addition of what should be needful to its fulfilling what was commanded " De Gr. et Lib Arb. 18. In what sense, then, (if in any
at all), could Augustine say, that God commands an impenitent
sinner to love him ? or even to pray aright for *grace* to love him ?

and yet, that God does not command what he knows the sinner cannot do ?—His supposed change of views, is here, perhaps, the more
rational conclusion.—Tr.]

"And *victorious* love sometimes fails for a good work even in
saints, in order that they may see that it comes from God " De Pec.
Mer. II. 19. " No one, except by the grace of Christ, can have the free
exercise of will for doing the good which he wills, or for not doing
the evil which he hates. Not as though his will were dragged to
good, as it is dragged like a captive to evil; but as freed from captivity, it is led by the freeborn sweetness of love, not by the servile
bitterness of fear." Op Imp III 112   The grace of Christ over-
comes the frailty of the flesh, which here still remains for conflict.
By the pledge of the spirit, we obtain strength to strive and to conquer. II. 137, 140.

Repentance also, (which Augustine did not confine to sorrow at
baptism, but which he considered as a satisfaction for sins by way of
punishment received), he explained as a gift of grace, although done
by the will of man Op Imp IV. 126. See Munscher's Handbuch
der Dogmengesch. B. IV. § 127. [As an explanation and a proof
of the rather startling assertion in the above parenthesis, we may
take the following sentence from one of Augustine's sermons. " It
is not enough to reform the morals and abandon evil deeds, unless
satisfaction be also made to God for what has been committed, by
the grief of penitence, by the groan of humility, by the sacrifice of
a contrite heart, with alms cooperating." Sermo 351, Opp. V. p.
1362.—Tr.]

Therefore the willing, as well as the ability and the performance,
Augustine regarded as the supernatural effect of grace. Compare
the fifth canon of the Carthaginian council, in the twelfth chapter,
and the letter mentioned, in the eleventh chapter, as sent to Zosimus
by the Africans of that council.—" If Pelagius agrees with us, that
not only the ability in man, but also the will and the performance,
are aided by God, so that without this aid we will and do nothing
right,—and that it is by the grace of God, through Jesus Christ our
Lord, in which he makes us righteous by his righteousness and not
ours, so that this is truly our righteousness which comes from him,
no controversy, as I believe, will remain between us, in respect to
the aid of God's grace." De Gr. Chr. 47. " That we should will,

therefore, God works without us; but when we will, and so will as
to do, God cooperates with us. Still, without him either working in
us to will, or working with us when we will, we can avail nothing to
good works of piety." De Gr. et Lib. Arb. 17.

Augustine therefore distinguished grace operating from grace cooperating (coopeians). The first he referred to the willing; the
last to the doing For the first, he adduced Phil. 2 13; for the last,
Rom. 8: 28. "The Holy Ghost helps our weakness and cooperates
to our health." De Nat. et Gr. 60 Cooperating grace, Augustine
also called accompanying grace (consequens), because it works
jointly with the will already produced by antecedent grace C d.
Epp. Pel. VI. 6. And he called it subsequent (subsequens) grace,
because it follows the good will which is produced by preceding
grace "Subsequent grace, indeed, aids the good purpose of man;
but it would not itself exist, if grace did not precede." II. 10

This aid of God to each individual good act of man, Jerome also
maintains clearly enough, in his dialogues against the Pelagians In
his third dialogue, he makes his Atticus say · "By this long discussion, it is shown, that the Lord aids and helps, in individual acts, by
his grace, by which he has given us freewill."

5. In bestowing grace, God has no respect to the worthiness of
man—nay, according to Augustine's theory, man can have no worthiness at all—but God here acts after his own freewill. By what
reasons of propriety he is influenced, it is not for us to decide.

"The Holy Spirit bloweth where it listeth, and follows not merits
but itself produces merit For God's grace can by no means exist,
if it is not in every way gratuitous." De Pec Orig 24 "What is
the merit of man before grace, by which grace is awarded to him,
since mere grace produces all our good desert in us, and God, when
he crowns our merit, crowns nothing but his own gift?" Ep. 194,
c. 5. "Even the very name of grace and import of it, are taken
away, if it is not imparted gratuitously, and he *who is worthy* receives it—And has not the apostle so described grace as to show,
that it is so called because it is given gratuitously? Rom. 11 6;
4: 4.—Grace, therefore, is given to the unworthy, as debt is paid to
the deserving. But he, who has given to the unworthy what they
did not have, causes them to have what he will reward them for as
worthy." De Gest. 14 "It belongs to faith, to believe in Christ.
And no one can come to him, that is, believe in him, unless it is

given unto him. No one, therefore, can have a righteous will, un-less, *without any preceding merits*, he receives true, that is, gratui-tous grace from above." C. d Epp Pel I. 3. "We do not unjustly pronounce anathema on the Pelagians, who are so hostile to grace, as to maintain, that it is not bestowed gratuitously, but according to merit, so that grace is no more grace ; and who attribute so much to freewill as to maintain that, by the right use of it, man merits grace ; whereas it is by grace that he is first able rightly to use free-will, which grace is not imparted according to desert, but is given by the free mercy of God." I. 24. "But what avails it to them that, by the praises of freewill, they even maintain, that grace aids the good purpose of every one ? This might, without scruple, be re-ceived as spoken in a catholic way, if they did not place merit in the good purpose, to which merit the reward is rendered according to debt, and not according to grace. But they should see and acknow-ledge, that even the good purpose, which accompanying grace aids, could not be in man, if grace did not precede." IV. 6 "Good works follow grace, and do not precede it ; for grace causes us to do them ; and we do not set up our own righteousness, but the righ-teousness of God is in us, that is, the righteousness which he gives " Op. Imp. I. 141. "Grace, which makes good men out of bad, is not debt." I. 133. Not only no " good deserts," but even " bad de-serts," precede grace De Gr. et Lib. Arb. 14 " Grace is not given according to the merits of the recipients, but according to the good pleasure of his will, that he who boasts should not boast of himself, but of the Lord " De Dono. Pers 12. " To those to whom grace is given, it is given by the gratuitous mercy of God." Ep 217, c. 5. " What has the apostle here taught us, (Rom 9 14, 15), unless that it pertains, not to the merits of men, but to the mercy of God, that any one, from that mass of the first man to which death is due, is freed ; and thus there is no unrighteousness with God ; for he is not unjust, either in remitting or in exacting what is due. And where punishment might be justly inflicted, pardon (indulgentia) is grace. And hence it still more evidently appears, how great is the benefit to him who is freed from deserved punishment and gratuitously justi-fied, while another, equally guilty, is punished without the unrigh-teousness of him that punishes " Ep. 186, c. 6. " Why God aids this man, and not that , one more, another less; one in this way, another in that ; he knows the righteous but hidden reasons ; and in

this consists the sovereignty of his power." De Pec. Mer. II. 5.
"God could also incline the will of the evil to good. Why then has
he not done it? Because he has not chosen to. Why he has not
chosen to, rests with him" De Gen. ad Lit. XI. 10 "Why this
man believes, and that does not, when both hear the same things, and
if a miracle is wrought before their eyes, both see the same, this is
a depth of the wisdom and knowledge of God whose judgments are
inscrutable, and with whom there is no unrighteousness when he has
mercy on whom he will, and hardens whom he will; nor are those
judgments unjust because they are hidden." Ep. 194, c. 3.

6. This aid of grace is *irresistible*, and is afforded to man notwithstanding his resistance.

"The hearing of the divine call, is produced by divine grace itself, in him who before resisted; and then the love of virtue is
kindled in him when he no longer resists." C. d. Epp. Pel. IV, 6.
"This grace, which is secretly imparted to human hearts, by divine
bounty, is rejected by no hard heart. For it is indeed given for the
very purpose that the previous hardness of the heart may be removed. When, therefore, the Father is internally heard and teaches,
in order that men should come to the Son, he takes away the stony
heart and gives the heart of flesh." De Praed. Sanct. 8. Divine
grace operates on the will of man in a manner not to be avoided
nor resisted (indeclinabiliter et insuperabiliter). "The strongest
man [Adam] God left to do what he would; but for the weak, he
has provided that they should, by his gift, most invincibly will what
is good, and most invincibly refuse to desert it." De Cor. et Gr. 12.
"It is not to be doubted, that human wills cannot resist God's
will" 14.

[This passage does not relate so much to *gracious* influence, as
to that by which God sways the hearts of men in general, in the
course of his providence. The whole sentence reads thus: "It is
not therefore to be doubted, that human wills cannot resist God's
will, that *he* should not do what he will, who has done whatsoever he
would in heaven and on earth, and who has even done (fecit) those
things which are future; since indeed concerning the very wills of
men, he does what he will and when he will." Augustine then goes
on to illustrate his meaning by the cases of Saul and of David[1] whom
God placed successively on the throne by moving the hearts of the

people to prefer them. "And how did he move them? Did he bind them by any corporeal bands? He acted internally, held their hearts, moved their hearts, and drew them by the wills which he produced in them. If, therefore, when the Lord wills to establish kings on the earth, he has the wills of men more in his power than themselves have their own wills, who else causes the salutary chastisement to take place, and the correction in the chastised heart, that it may be established in the celestial kingdom?"—Nor is it merely in respect to things lawful, that Augustine supposes God to move the hearts of men in general   He also moves them to sinful acts, in some sense, as Augustine occasionally affirms in pretty strong terms. After quoting the passage of scripture respecting the Lord's stirring up the spirit of the Philistines and of the Arabians to devastate the land of Judah, Augustine says : " It is here shown, that God excites enemies to devastate those lands which he judges worthy of such punishment   But did the Philistines and Arabians come to devastate the land of Judea, without their own will? or did they so come by their will as that it is falsely written, that the Lord stirred up their spirit to do this? Nay, each is true —The Lord stirred up their spirit; and yet they came of their own accord   For the Omnipotent produces in the hearts of men even the motion of their will, that he may do by them what he wills to do by them " And after adducing a variety of other like facts from scripture, he says · " By these and other testimonies of the divine annunciations, all of which it would be tedious to recount, it is sufficiently manifest, as I think, that God works in the hearts of men to incline their wills to whatever he pleases, whether to good on the ground of his mercy, or to evil on the ground of their deserts, according to his own judgment, which is sometimes manifest and sometimes concealed, but yet always just " De Gr. et Lib. Arb. 21.   Still, Augustine elsewhere makes a most important distinction between the manner in which God acts on the hearts of men in the two cases.   " Nor does God harden by imparting wickedness (impertiendo malitiam), but by not imparting mercy." Ep 194, c. 3.   We are not, however, to suppose, that he held to a mere *negation* of influence of all kinds; at least he did not so believe when writing the last passage but one, for he there adds, that "if God is able, whether by angels either good or bad, or in any other way, to operate even *in the hearts of the wicked*, on account of their deserts, (whose wickedness he has not himself pro-

duced, but it was either originally derived from Adam or increased
by their own will), what wonder is it if he, who changes hearts themselves from bad to good, works in those hearts of the elect, *their*
good?"—Tr.]

But it was only in the sequel of the controversy that the Augustinian theory of grace was so far perfected, that its author adopted
an irresistibleness of grace, an impartation of it to men notwithstanding their resistance. We need only recollect the passage already
quoted, on the doctrine of freewill, from Augustine's first work
against the Pelagians. De Pec. Mer. II. 5. How could the sentiment there assumed, that he only is aided by God, who spontaneously undertakes something, because God does not work our cure in
us as in senseless stones, or as in those in whose nature reason and
will are not implanted—how could this sentiment, I say, be brought
into unison with the doctrine of irresistible grace? "The consenting to the calling of God or the dissenting from it," which Augustine attributed to man's own will (De Spir et Lit. 34), could
hardly agree with irresistible grace. He here speaks like a semi-
pelagian, and still earlier, in his writings against the Manichaeans,
as we have already seen, he explains himself almost like Pelagius,
in respect to freedom. Augustine's convictions, in this particular,
may therefore be divided into three periods The first, when he defended freewill against the Manichaeans. Here he must have conceived of the relation of freedom to grace, in the Pelagian way,
however more highly he then thought of the influence of grace
The second, when he came forward in his first productions against
the Pelagians. Here, however severely he expressed himself respecting the loss of freedom, he regarded the relation of freedom to
grace, in the semi-pelagian way; for he could not otherwise have
ascribed to the will itself the power of receiving or of resisting
grace. The last, after his system had reached its full result in the
progress of the controversy with the Pelagians. Now he adopted
"irresistible grace."

This position, that grace is imparted to man notwithstanding his
resistance, is also entirely in the spirit of the Augustinian system.
For if man is so corrupt by nature that he can will only evil, this
bad will must first struggle in opposition before grace can transform
it to a good will. And as soon as the predestination theory was to

be defended, an irresistible grace was to be assumed. Both doctrines, therefore, Augustine placed in connection, in the passage quoted from De Praed Sanct. 8.

He could not, however, endure it, when his opponents, particularly Julian, reproached him with teaching, that man is *compelled* to will good. If he is compelled, he does not will, said Augustine. Op. Imp I. 101. But still the bishop of Hippo could not deny that, according to his system, the willing of good is produced by grace, in opposition to the will of the man, and that therefore the man is actually compelled, in this case, to will good. For "the grace of God makes one, *not* willing, to *be* willing" Ill. 122. But there is no *contradiction* in this doctrine in itself. According to Augustine's view, the effect of grace consists in this, that the bad will ceases and a good will comes in its place Between the compulsion and the good will, there is therefore only an apparent contradiction, since the compulsion *precedes*, and the good will follows as an effect.

7. To this was further added, (according to the canons of the general synod at Carthage, already quoted), the position that even those to whom gracious influences are imparted, are not without sin ; so that they, too, have still always occasion to pray, Forgive us our sins. Concupiscence remains in them, which, according to Augustine, although not imputed to the converted, is always something evil. And he did not pronounce them free from the sins of ignorance, inadvertency, and weakness. De Cor et Gr. 12 He therefore distinguished between a greater and a less righteousness (justitia major and justitia minor) That perfect righteousness by which we love God with the whole heart, and our neighbors as ourselves, will be gained only in the future life. But this imperfect righteousness by which he lives who is justified by faith, and does not (willfully) sin, is to be gained in this life. De Spir et Lit. 36. Some "venial sins, without which this life is not passed, do not exclude the righteous from eternal life." 38. But the elect commit no deadly sins. Among deadly sins, Augustine comprehended those sins by which one would abandon faith till death. De Cor et Gr. 12 The most perfect love is found in no man while on earth, and hence there are none just upon earth. Ep. 167. c. 4. But on the question, why grace still suffers sin in the elect, he answered, that this is done for their discipline, that they may not become proud. De Pec. Mer II 17.

CHAPTER XIV.

Objections of the Pelagians against Augustine's doctrine of grace.

In the conflict with the Pelagians on the doctrine of grace, Augustine acted rather by way of defence than of assault. And certainly his theory on this subject, however consequent upon and closely connected with his other anthropological doctrines, had so much to shock the moral feelings of man and oppose a just view of the moral attributes of God, that a greater expense of talent was actually requisite for its successful defence. And when Augustine acted the assailant, he chiefly employed passages of scripture for refuting the Pelagians, of which we shall speak in the sequel. But when thus acting, it cannot be denied that Augustine did not fully present the Pelagian positions. The Pelagians, as we have seen, actually admitted supernatural gracious influences. But this, Augustine very often forgets, and argues against them as if they really denied gracious influences altogether. Proofs enough are at hand, in his book On the Grace of Christ, and his Imperfect Work. Wholly inapplicable was the objection of Augustine (De Nat. et Gr. 18, 55), that prayer or supplication for divine aid to man, must be superfluous, according to Pelagius' supposition of ability to do through natural aid, and to will through freewill. The benefit of prayer could be shown much more obviously by a Pelagian, than Augustine could do it according to his system; and just as Pelagius therefore commended prayer to Demetrias, as a means of growth in goodness. Ep. ad Dem. c. 26.

Of the objections which the Pelagians brought against the Augustinian theory of grace—some of which are very acute, and not easily to be refuted—the following are the most important.

1. Augustinian grace totally destroys freewill. For those to whom grace is not imparted, are impelled to sin, against their will, " by a necessity of their flesh." Op. Imp. I. 94 ; Comp C. d. Epp. Pel I 2, 3, Aug. Ep. 194. This could strictly be no objection for Augustine, since, by his theory, freewill no longer existed. As often, however, as the objection was made against him, that by his theory there was no place for freewill, he endeavored, sophistically

enough indeed, to extricate himself by saying, that certainly a freewill always remains, but it is a freewill to evil.   Right well did Caelestius remark, in this respect, (according to Jerome's epistle to Ctesiphon) ; *That* will is annihilated which needs the power of another.
Either I use the power which is given me, and so freewill is preserved ; or if I need the power of another, the freedom of will in
me is destroyed.   In his letter to Hilary (Ep 157. c. 2), written in
414, Augustine says. "Freewill is not destroyed when it is aided,
but it is aided when it is *not* destroyed."   This answer would have
been altogether to the purpose, if only, according to his theory, this
had not been all, and freewill had still only *done* something.

2. Augustinian grace is nothing but "fate under the name of
grace ;" and " a respect of persons" is attributed to God, when, in
precisely the same case, his mercy comes on some, and his wrath
remains on others.   To this, Augustine replied   "Those who believe in fate, contend that not only acts and events, but even our
very wills depend on the position of the stars, or what they call con-
stellations, at the time when each one is conceived or born.   But the
grace of God not only surpasses all stars and all heavens, but also
all angels.   The asserters of fate, furthermore, attribute to fate
both all the good and all the bad things of men.   But in the evil
things of men, God follows their deserts with deserved retribution,
while he bestows the good through unmerited grace, from his compassionate will ; doing both, not by the temporary conjunction of the
stars, but by the eternal and deep counsel of his severity and his
goodness.   We, therefore, see that neither pertains to fate.   If you
here answer, that this very benevolence of God, which does not follow merit, but confers unmerited good from gratuitous goodness,
ought rather to be called fate, although the apostle calls it grace,
saying, By grace are ye saved through faith, and that not of yourselves but it is the gift of God ; not of works, lest any one should
boast , do you not consider, do you not perceive, that *fate* is not asserted by *us* under the name of *grace*, but rather *divine grace* is called by *you* by the name of *fate* ?" C. d. Epp. Pel. II. 6. Comp. C.
Jul. IV. 8.

In respect to the objection, that this theory of grace implies a respect of persons with God, Augustine thus defends himself · " It is
rightly called an accepting of persons, when he who judges, abandoning the merits of the case which he judges, decides for one

against the other because he finds something in the person which is worthy of honor or of compassion. But if a man has two debtors, and he chooses to forgive the debt to one and to exact it of the other, he gives to whom he will, but defrauds no one. Nor is it to be called an accepting of persons, since there is no injustice." C. d. Epp. Pel. II. 7. Here he appeals to Mat. xx, where the lord of the vineyard gave to those who had labored but one hour, as much as to those who had labored the whole day, and who could not be pronounced unjust on account of his goodness, since he, who labored the whole day, received as much as his due, and was not robbed of his merited reward by the goodness shown to others. "It is by a righteous decision of God, that grace is not given to those to whom it is not given." Ep. 217. c. 5.

Augustine also endeavored to show, that the Pelagians made God an "accepter of persons·"—for, in order to keep clear of an "accepting of persons" with God, and to admit of no fate, they supposed some merit on the part of man, in the bestowment of grace, by their peculiar theory on infant baptism, with which they connected a participation in the kingdom of heaven (Ep. 194. c. 7) ; and that, according to them, children, who have no merit, are baptized through *fate*, and admitted to the kingdom of heaven by fate ! C. Jul IV. 8.

3. In close connection with this, stands another objection : It is unjust, in one and the same bad case, that one should be freed and another punished. To this he replies. "It is, then, doubtless just, that both should be punished. Who would deny this? Let us therefore thank the Savior, while we do not see inflicted on ourselves what we know, by the condemnation of those like us, to be also due to us. For if every man were freed, what is justly due to sin, would remain hid ; but if no one, what grace would bestow [would remain hid]. Let us therefore, on this most difficult question, rather use the words of the apostle (Rom. 9: 22), God, willing to show his wrath and make his power known, endured with much long suffering the vessels which are prepared for destruction, and that he might make known the riches of his glory in the vessels of mercy. To him, the thing formed cannot say, Why hast thou made me thus? since he has power of the same mass to make one vessel to honor, and another to dishonor. For since that whole mass is justly condemned, justice awards the merited reproach ; and grace confers the undeserved honor, not by the prerogative of merit, not by the necessity of

fate, not by the chance of fortune, but by the depth of the riches of
the wisdom and knowledge of God; which the apostle does not dis-
close, but admires as concealed, exclaiming, O the depth of the
riches —For the whole mass is justly condemned as guilty of sin;
*nor does God harden by imparting wickedness, but by not imparting
mercy.*" Ep 194 c 2, 3   Comp De Cor. et Gr. 10; De Praed.
Sanct 8.

4. " Men who are not willing to live honestly and faithfully, will
exculpate themselves, saying, What have we done who have lived
wrong, in as much as we have not received the grace by which we
could have lived right ?" Ep 194. c. 6.—This objection was in fact
irrefutable, and showed the practical evil of Augustinian grace, in a
very striking attitude.   Among other things, Augustine attempted to
destroy its force, in this way : " They who live wrong, cannot truly
say, that they do no evil. For if they do nothing evil, they live
right; but if they live wrong, they live wrong from what belongs to
themselves (de suo), either what they derived originally or what
they have also added   But if they are vessels of wrath which are
prepared for destruction, which is awarded as due to them, let them
impute this to themselves, because they are made of that mass which
God has condemned justly and according to desert for the sin of the
one in whom all have sinned.   But if they are vessels of mercy, to
whom, though formed of the same mass, he has not willed to award
the punishment due, let them not inflate themselves, but glorify him
who has shown them unmerited mercy ; and if they regard anything
otherwise, God shall also reveal even this to them " Ib   To this he
subjoins the answer of Paul to a similar objection · Why doth he
yet find fault ? etc , (Rom 9 19 sqq) and then proceeds in the following manner   " In the meantime, let it be enough for the Christian, which still lives by faith and does not yet discern what is perfect, but knows in part, to know or believe that God frees no one except by gratuitous mercy through our Lord Jesus Christ, and con-
demns no one except by the most impartial justice (aequissima veritate), by our same Lord Jesus Christ. But why he frees or does
not free this person rather than that, let him search who can search
so profound a depth of judgments ; yet let him beware of the abyss
For is there iniquity with God ? God forbid. But his judgments
are inscrutable and his ways past finding out.—All who would exculpate themselves in vices and iniquities, are therefore most justly

punished, since those who are freed, are freed only through grace.
For if there were here any just excuse, not grace but justice would
free them.   But since nothing but grace frees, it finds nothing just
in him whom it frees ; not the will, not the act, not even the excuse
itself ; for if this excuse were just, whoever uses it would be acquitted by merit, not by grace.   For we know that even some of those
are absolved by the grace of Christ, who say, Why doth he yet find
fault ? for who resisteth his will ?   But if this excuse is just, they
are not acquitted by free grace, but by the justness of the excuse.
But if it is grace by which they are freed, certainly this excuse is
not just.   For it is then true grace by which a man is freed, if retribution is not taken according to the debt of justice.   Nothing therefore takes place in those who say, *Why doth he yet find fault ? for
who resisteth his will ?* except what is read in the book of Solomon,
*The folly of a man perverteth his way ; but he casteth the blame upon
God in his heart* " Ib.

Augustine endeavored further to show, that the present corrupt
nature of man, is to be ascribed to the will itself, since man has voluntarily sinned, and by the wrong use of freewill, sin has passed
over to the posterity who were contained in the first man.   God
therefore does not produce unrighteousness, but punishes it.—Here
Augustine's reasoning is perfectly just, according to his premises ,
but how much may be urged in opposition to these assumptions, has
already been shown, while on the doctrine of original sin.

In the like very striking manner, was the argument also carried
on, in the cloister at Adrumetum, against Augustinian grace   Why
is it proclaimed and commanded to us, said they, that we should
turn from evil and do good, if *we* do not do this, but God works in
us the willing and the doing ?   On that ground, our superiors may
only prescribe for us what we should do and pray for us that we
may do it, but not punish nor blame us, if we do not do it   How
can that be reckoned to me which I have not received from him by
whom alone such and so great a gift can be bestowed ?   Could I
give to myself the love towards God and my neighbor, and I were
not to do it, or had I slighted it when given, I should be justly punished ; but now I am blameless, since the will itself is prepared by
the Lord.

To refute this reasoning, Augustine wrote his book On Rebuke
and Grace (De Correptione et Gratia).   What he presents in that

work, is indeed by no means satisfactory; still, as might be expected from his acuteness, much which he there says, is not without plausibility In that book, Augustine teaches that, (although it is the grace of God by which alone men are freed from evil and without which they do nothing good, since grace not only shows what they have to do, but also inspires the good will and the voluntary execution), still the punishment of bad men, who have not received this grace, is no more unjust, as they are bad by their own will, than it is useless, as it may impel to goodness; though it cannot be denied, that it is only by the grace of God that it profits. Perseverance in good, is truly in fact a great gift of God; still he who, without having received this gift, relapses by his own will into sins, is not only liable to punishment, but, if he persevere in evil till death, incurs eternal damnation Why one receives this gift, and another not, is inscrutable.   But, as it is not known who belong to the number of the elect, and who not, a serious rebuke is to be applied to all sinners for their reformation, that they may not themselves go to perdition, or ruin others To the predestinated, the rebuke (correptio) is "a salutary medicine; to the reprobate, a penal torment" God can indeed reform any one, without his being reproved by men for his sins. In whom this takes place, and why in this and not in another, God only knows; and not the clay but only the potter should venture to decide concerning it. Rebuke, therefore, is not done away by grace, nor is grace denied by rebuke.—Finally, in a letter which he sent to the Adrumetian monks (Ep. 215), with his book on grace and freewill, Augustine himself warned them of the moral abuse which might so easily be made of his doctrine of grace, and which actually was made in the cloister at Adrumetum. "Nor should you so defend grace that, relying as it were upon it, you may delight in evil works; which may the grace of God itself avert from you.—He will be found ungrateful to grace itself, who chooses to live in sin in consequence of grace, by which we die unto sin."—Thus he endeavored, feebly enough indeed, to guard against the consequences which might be practically injurious.

[Whether Augustine's efforts in so good an attempt, were or were not too feeble for the defence of the position he had assumed, it is but an act of justice to the departed champion to show a little more fully what his efforts were. Nor will a more extended extract be devoid of some incidental and important interest on a connected topic, as we shall thereby see that Augustine had even a greater abhorrence of *antinomonism* than he had of Pelagianism itself. After telling these monks, at considerable length, that the scriptures represent it as much *worse* to turn to the *left* hand than to the right, from the middle course of truth and righteousness, he thus proceeds to show them what he believes to be the left and what the right, and what the middle and safe way, in this matter "Wherefore dearly beloved, whoever says, My will is sufficient to me for the performance of good works, departs to the right hand But again; they, who suppose a holy life is to be relinquished when they hear God's grace so preached as to be believed and understood *itself* to change men's wills from bad to good, and itself also to guard the wills it has formed, and who therefore say, Let us do evil that good may come, depart to the *left* Hence he (the Holy Spirit) saith unto you, Decline neither to the right hand nor to the left; that is, *you should not so defend freewill as to attribute to it good works without the grace of God; nor should you so defend grace that, relying as it were upon it, you may delight in evil works;* which may the grace of God avert from you For, presenting the words of such men, the Apostle says, What shall we then say? shall we continue in sin that grace may abound? And to these words of erratic men, who do not understand the grace of God, he answers, as he ought, saying, *God forbid. For if we are dead to sin, how shall we live in it?* Nothing could be more briefly or better said. For what more profitable does the grace of God confer upon us, in this present malignant age, than that we die to sin? And according to this, he will be found ungrateful to grace itself, who chooses to live in sin in consequence of grace, by which we die unto sin But may he who is rich in mercy grant unto you both to think sanely and progressively to continue in a good purpose to the end."—This it must be confessed, is very *sane* doctrine on the most important bearing of the whole subject;—whether it fully meets the *objection*, as brought against Augustine's peculiar views or not. Our author, as shown, supposes it does not —Tr]

5. As an objection to the necessity of grace for the performance of good works, the Pelagians brought up against Augustine the many virtues of the heathen. These, merely through the power of innate freedom, were often merciful, discreet, chaste, temperate C. Jul IV.

29

3.—But as Augustine excluded the heathen from grace, he could attribute to them no good deeds, as already remarked   What the Pelagians adduced as instances, he of course directly denied.   With him, the alleged virtues of the heathen, were even sins in form, because not springing from faith.   Generally he distinguished more acutely and correctly than Julian himself, between the matter and the form of an act.   The distinction which Julian made between the man who does well fruitfully and the one who does well barrenly (steriliter), according to which the first refers his actions to things eternal, and the last to things temporal, was not deeply founded ; and Augustine was wholly right, when he said, " It cannot be true that we should be *barrenly* good ; but we are *not* good in whatever we are barren "—Augustine further remarked, that if men can attain to true virtue without faith in Christ, then Christ has died in vain   The good works which unbelievers perform (as to the matter), are not their own but God's, who employs the evil in a good way ; but the sins are theirs with which they do good in a *bad* way, etc   Augustine also found no reason why the Pelagians then, according to their view, would not allow the righteous heathen to share the salvation of Christians, but excluded them from the kingdom of heaven   Comp. De Civ. Dei, V 19, 20 ; XIX. 25 , Ep 144   In the latter passage, he calls the change of Polemon from intemperance to temperance, a " gift of God."

But while Augustine's system was consistent with itself, as he developed it in the Pelagian controversy, and his theory of grace peculiarly so, yet he was inconsistent and must be, as soon as he came to speak of *moral* obligation, and to establish the *ought* (debere), seeing he had denied the ability to man from his own power. So prayer was and must be according to Augustine's theory, an effect of divine grace, as he shows clearly enough, among other things in Ep 194, c. 4 And yet he says (Op. Imp III. 107), " Adults, when they hear or read, that every one shall receive according to the things which he has done by the body, *ought* (debent) not to trust in the power of their own will, but rather to pray that such a will may be prepared for them by the Lord that they may not enter into temptation "   This objection of inconsistency, is also applicable to Augustine's assertion, that divine grace is obtained " by seeking and doing" (Ep. 157 c 2), since, according to the Augustinian theory, nothing at all, in this respect, depends on the conduct of man. The system presented by Augustine, was therefore as consistent as he was himself, for he did not always abide by it in the application ;—a lapse which happens with all theories that stand in contradiction to the moral nature of man !

[Had Augustine said, in the passage last cited, that an *impenitent sinner* is first to obtain grace " by seeking and doing," the objection of inconsistency would have been more manifest. But he is here answering the question proposed to him, whether " man can be without sin, and easily keep God's commands if he will ;" and seems rather to be speaking of one already converted " The love of God," says he, " is diffused in our hearts, not by ourselves, nor by the power of our own will, but by the Holy Spirit that is given unto us. And thus freewill avails to good works, if it is divinely aided, which takes place by humbly seeking and doing." And this is in perfect accordance with the doctrine, already exhibited, in respect to God's answering the prayers of his people, and his giving grace for grace—more grace for the right improvement of some grace.—Tr.]

Remark. The grace which Augustine allowed the elect Christians to receive, he also allowed to ancient saints (antiquis justis) ; that is, to the elect among the worshippers of the true God, as well before as after the law, or as he expressed it, as well before the law as during the time of the Old Testament Hence he could maintain, respecting them, that they had performed good works under the aid of grace And this aid was the necessary condition for them, as they could obtain the pardon of sins only though faith in Christ. This is amply set forth in the passage already quoted from De Pec Orig 24 sq.—But the Pelagians thought differently of this matter, in compliance with their system. They maintained, that men had lived right easily, first by nature, then under the law, and finally under grace. " The Creator was first known by the guidance of reason, and it was written on the heart how man should live, not by the law of the letter, but of nature. But when, after the depravation of morals, nature, now discolored (jam decolor), was no longer adequate, the law was added to it, by which, in like manner as by the illumination of

the moon, it was again restored to its ancient lustre by the removal
of its rust.   But after a habit of sinning, too great for the law to heal,
had gained the mastery, Christ appeared, and came not by his disciples, but by himself, as a physician, to relieve the desperate disease."
Lib. cit. c. 26.   Against this Augustine was full of zeal, and sought
to prove from the bible, that the grace of the Mediator extended to
the ancient saints, and that, through this grace, they believed on the
then future incarnation of Christ.—Comp. C. d. Epp. Pel. III. 4,
where he says of the ancient saints, that they were Christians in reality, though not in name, that they had received the same grace
through the Holy Ghost, and that he was to them not only an aid to
virtue—which even the Pelagians conceded in reference to the laws
given by Moses and the revelation of the Old Testament—but also
a bestower of virtue.   The Holy Spirit produced the good disposi-
tions in them, IV 7.—Pelagius agreed with Augustine in allowing,
that the saints of the Old Testament partook of the salvation of
Christians, which the synod of Diospolis (charge 5) had declared as
an orthodox position.   Augustine was only stumbled, that they
should have lived righteously and should have shared in salvation,
without the aid of grace (in his sense) and without faith in the Mediator, who shed his blood for the pardon of sins. I 21 Op Imp. II 188.
According to Augustine, as may further be remarked, the faith of the
ancients in Jesus, remained concealed in their time, and was first
revealed afterwards. Ep 177 c. 12.

[The passage on which this last remark is founded, is as follows.
"But I believe it escapes Pelagius, that the faith of Christ, which afterwards came into revelation, was a secret (in occulto) in the times
of our fathers; through which faith, nevertheless, even they were
freed by the grace of God, whosoever, in all periods of the human
race, have been able to be freed, by the secret though not culpable
decision of God "—This seems strongly to resemble one of War-
burton's startling positions in his Divine Legation of Moses—that
the patriarchs and prophets did not promulgate all they knew of divine truth.—Tr.]

CHAPTER XV.

Further account of the Events.

The doctrine of Pelagius on infant baptism, original sin, and grace, was condemned in the plenary council at Carthage, by the nine canons already adduced ; and instead of it, the Augustinian doctrine, so far as yet presented, was pronounced orthodox.   The decrees of this council were communicated by them to Zosimus, who, about this time, held a new convocation, in order to bring Caelestius, by a fresh examination, to a confession of his opinions.   But Caelestius avoided it by quitting Rome.   And now the general decision was made by the Romish bishop, by which Pelagius and Caelestius were excommunicated, unless they would renounce their errors, submit to penance, and accede to the African resolutions

Zosimus, now·finding himself once brought to espouse the African orthodoxy, forthwith sought his own honor in forcing it on the whole christian world—in impressing as it were the stamp of sound faith upon Augustine's system, from the fact of declaring himself in its favor.   This was accomplished principally by his famous Epistola Tractoria, only some fragments of which have reached us, and which he sent to all the bishops of the East and the West, before the middle of the year 418.   In this letter, the errors of Pelagius and Caelestius were mentioned, and the condemnation of both of them was declared.   Every bishop was to subscribe this letter, by which tumult enough would be produced   It might be expected the majority would be brought to favor it.   Some there were, however, so high-minded as to resign their stations rather than condemn the men whom they believed to be innocent.   Those who would not subscribe, bishop Julian of Eclanum and seventeen other bishops, were deposed and banished from Italy, in consequence of the imperial mandate and the priestly decrees.

The African bishops, in a letter addressed to Zosimus, extolled him for the purity of doctrine contained in his circular letter.   Prosper contra Coll. c. 5. Caelest. Ep ad Galliarum Episcopos c. 8. p. 109, 133.   To the Romish presbyter Sixtus also, (whom report had

represented as a Pelagian, but who, after Zosimus changed his part,
had declared his anti-pelagian opinion to the Africans), Augustine
signified his most hearty joy at the news, and encouraged him to
take care that those who publicly spread the Pelagian error, should
be punished " with salutary severity," etc. Ep 191, written towards
the end of the year 418

But the impression made on the deposed bishops, by the conduct
of Zosimus, may be imagined.   Julian accused him of prevarication.
C. Jul I 4.   He, as well as those who shared a like fortune, spoke
with bitterness of the whole procedure of Zosimus, in this affair, and
left nothing untried in order to induce the emperor Honorius to cause
a new investigation of the matter.   In a letter to bishop Rufus of
Thessalonica, they sought to interest the oriental church in their behalf. They blamed the stupidity and cowardice of the Romish clergy
for having again taken up the former sentence in respect to the Pelagian doctrine.   They called Augustine's doctrine Manichaeism,
because he made human nature utterly bad ; and his grace, *fate.*
They called upon Rufus in particular, to oppose the Manichaeans
To this period, also, belong two letters from Julian to Zosimus, on
the contested doctrines Op. Imp I 18   From one of them, Mercator quotes several passages, (Ap. p 115, 116), in which Julian
endeavors to approach Augustinism as much as possible, but frequently connects a Pelagian sense with Augustinian words   About
this time, was also composed, and sent to Rome, the first letter refuted in Augustine's first book Against the Two Epistles of the Pelagians.   This letter was ascribed to Julian as the author, but was
not acknowledged by him, perhaps because of some falsifications.
Op. Imp. I 18.   So of the work called Libellus Fidei, which proceeded, if not from Julian, yet from bishops inclined to Pelagianism,
who sought to justify themselves, to their metropolitan, respecting
their doctrine and their refusal to subscribe that letter. Ap. p 110 sqq
The deposed bishops desired especially to have their cause investigated by a general council.   They complained bitterly, that they
were not allowed to defend it before learned judges, but were abused
by the noisy and inexperienced multitude , and that their opponents
employed the temporal arm while they abandoned the help of reason. But in vain. Comes Valerius,* a distinguished disciple of

* *Comes* was a title of office, civil or military, applied by Augustine to
this man—probably about equivalent to Colonel of the body guard, in the

Augustine and opposer of Pelagius, knew how to frustrate all their endeavors, and to procure the victory for Augustine. Augustine himself was crafty enough to represent it as implying a doubt in the ancient catholic faith, if the temporal authorities would still allow the Pelagians time and place for the investigation. They ought to be prohibited by force. De Nupt. et Conc. I 12 , Op. Imp l. 10.* Julian also reproached the bishops with party spirit, who had condemned Pelagianism at the synod. They hated the cause before they had understood it. C. Jul. Ill. l.

To this was added still another step, on the part of the state, to extirpate, not only Pelagianism, but with it also, the Pelagians themselves. The first imperial rescript of the emperor Honorius to Palladius, by which Pelagius and Caelestius, as well as their disciples, were to be punished by exile and confiscation of goods, could reach none but declared Pelagians. Many, inclined to Pelagianism, might conceal themselves. But on the ninth of June, 419, appeared a letter of both the emperors, Honorius and Theodosius II, to Aurelius, the bishop of Carthage, in which, not only was the earlier order repeated, and the Pelagians threatened with the assigned punishment, but this penal law, with the unchristian spirit of persecution, was extended to those who should fail to send away or to inform against the secret Pelagians. In this letter, it was made the duty of Aurelius, in particular, to see to it, that all the African bishops, under him, should subscribe the condemnation of Pelagius and Caelestius, and to give them to understand, that every one, who would not subscribe, should lose his episcopal office, be hunted from the towns, and forever excommunicated. Some of the African bishops not present

---

time of the emperors To him Augustine addressed his work De Nupt. et Conc , and there calls him " his dear son"—doubtless in the spiritual sense. —Tr.

* The first of these references is a mistake, as the passage has no relation to the subject Probably it should be c 2, where Augustine assigns the following as one reason for addressing this work to the Comes, Valerius " Because these profane novelties, which we have resisted by discussion, you have effectually resisted by power ' The other passage referred to will also show, that Augustine was in favor of temporal coercion " Far be it from the rulers of an earthly republic, to doubt of the ancient catholic faith, and on this account to afford time and place of examination to its assailants, and not rather, being certain and established in it, to impose the discipline of coercion upon such enemies of it as you [Julian] are "—Tr

at the Carthaginian council, who tolerated Pelagianism, may have
given the occasion for this.   At least it is said, in this "epistle imperial," that the episcopal authority of Aurelius must interfere " to
correct the pertinacity of certain bishops who either promote their
wicked discussions by tacit consent or do not destroy them by public assault "   Finally, Honorius declared expressly, in the same letter, that he followed, in that rescript, the decision of Aurelius (and
consequently of the other African bishops too), according to which
they had been condemned by all in respect to the errors specified
According to some subscriptions, this letter was also sent to Augustine.

Aurelius did not loiter in executing the commission conferred on
him.   By the first of August, 419, he issued a letter to all the bishops of the Byzacine and Arzugitane province, acquainting them with
the imperial order, and requiring them all to sign that condemnation,
whether they had been present at the Carthaginian synod and had
consequently there signed it already, or had been hindered from being present.   As may well be supposed, such a letter did not fail of
its anticipated effect

This letter, as well as the imperial order, of which Aurelius added
a copy, this early and grievous memorial of spiritual domination and
the compulsion of conscience, are still extant, and were first brought
to light by the Magdeburg Centuriators *   They are printed in the
Appendix, p 109   The " imperial epistle," however, is not perfect
It will be found perfect among the Augustinian epistles. Ep. 201.

But freedom of thought would not be suppressed by the law of the
state   Even the history of the present controversy proves this.
Not long after the severe edict referred to, a mandate to the city pre-
fect, became necessary, from the emperor Constantius, whom Honorius had received as a co-regent   From this mandate, it appears,
that the Pelagian doctrines had again occasioned trouble at Rome,
and it was supposed, at the imperial court, that Caelestius might be
lurking in Rome and occasioning those commotions.   In this law,
(which was likewise first brought to light by the Magd. Centuriators,
and which is printed in their appendix, p 126), it is said   Since the
Pelagian errors are continually spreading and the discord thence

* The authors of the Magdeburg Centuries, a masterly work on ecclesiastical history, by several of the early Reformers residing in and near the
city of Magdeburg —Tr

arising produces commotion among the people, it is deemed necessary to renew the former penal law against the Pelagians. Valusianus should therefore search out those who discard divine grace (qui Dei invident pietati), and remove them from the city and the region a hundred miles around it. Particularly should the agitator Caelestius be removed from the city —To this is also added a threat to Valusianus, should he be negligent in executing this command. Upon this followed the advertisement of Valusianus, which may be seen in the appendix at a 'O. As Caelestius, the disturber of the church and the state, could not be discovered, (hence his stay at Rome could not be improbable), orders were issued against him as against one absent He was therefore to be forever banished from the city; and a like punishment to fall on any one who harbored him.

That Augustine, however, had the chief hand in these persecutions of the Pelagians, that he was the most active in producing them, is confirmed by all, both friends and foes. Of the former, we need only read Prosper, in his " Poem on the Ungrateful." Ap. p. 68. Hence Julian also calls him, " The head and cause of all these evils." Op. Imp. II. 104.* He employed especially the aid of his Alypius,

---

* This passage seems not at all to refer to the point of Augustine's *intentionally* exciting persecution, if indeed it refers specifically to persecution, at all Julian says to Augustine " But your opinion will not avail so much with the wise, since you are the head and cause of these evils, and would withdraw yourself from the conflict, by placing the apostle in it, and think he ought to be assailed instead of you, by whom as our teacher and chief, we are especially armed against you," etc To this Augustine replies " You throw out, among other things, that I am *the head and cause of these evils*, as though I were the first to believe or discuss original sin You think, forsooth, your readers so ignorant as not to know how many and how renowned are the doctors of the church before us, who have so understood and explained the words of the apostle, as the whole catholic church, from its very beginning, understands or believes If these words of the doctors are evil, as you do not scruple to say, how, I pray you, am I the head and cause of these evils, unless as you are the head of those calumnies which you more rabidly heap on me ? For if you would consider, with a sane brain, the miseries of human life, from the first weeping of infants to the last groans of the dying, you would indeed see, that neither I nor you, but Adam himself was the head and cause of these evils."—Our author seems less cautious and less impartial when treating of the *character* of Augustine, than when presenting his doctrines Still, Augustine no doubt had some hand in these persecutions, as shown from passages before adduced —Tr.

who was now bishop of Tagaste, and whom Julian hence called "the 'slave of Augustine's sins" I. 7. This man, in the year 421, brought over the four books of Augustine, C d. Epp Pel, to bishop Boniface, who, after the death of Zosimus, (which occurred Dec. 26, 418), had succeeded to the Romish chair, and who opposed the Pelagian doctrine with all his might. He also brought the second book De Nupt. et Conc , to Comes Valerius. That Alypius here employed bribery, in order to gain the temporal authorities and incline them to the African orthodoxy, Julian asserts in several passages, and reproaches the catholic party generally with intrigue of various kinds, (e. g Op. Imp. I. 42, 74) ; which accusation Augustine contradicts.

In this later period of the bishop of Hippo's life, when Pelagius himself had long been off the stage, occurred the further development of his system, which formed, as it were, its keystone—the development, I mean, of his predestination theory, and of the connected doctrine of the limitation of Christ's redemption. These doctrines stood in the closest connection with his other doctrines, and especially with his theory of grace as being irresistible and having no respect to man's merit , and therefore as a consecutive reasoner, he was inclined to adopt all the consequences that flow from this theory.

But here it should by no means be said, that during the contest with the Pelagians, Augustine *first* set up his predestination theory, because he saw that consistency led him to it. The impartial examiner of Augustinism, will readily allow, that one of our most acute theologians has judged quite right, in his famous dissertation on the doctrine of election, in affirming that this doctrine did not first come to Augustine in and from the contest, and that it was not an excessive zeal against Pelagius, that first led him to this view. But the matter, strictly considered, is thus.

At first, Augustine, with all the rest of the fathers, admitted only a *conditional* predestination. In his books on freewill, he taught a foreknowledge of God, which had no determining influence on the conduct of men; a foreknowledge, therefore, which was no predestination, in his sense, and which therefore pre-supposed no irresistible grace. In his Exposition of certain Propositions from the Epistle to the Romans, composed about the year 394, he taught (prop. 60), in plain language, a predestination founded on prescience ; and

he confessed his error in Retract. I. 23.   But when he afterwards
gave a wider range to the doctrine of grace and even regarded the
commencement of faith as an effect of grace, he began to teach an
absolute predestination.   Hence, in the first book to Simplicianus
(De Div. Quest. Opp. T. VI.), which he composed soon after the
beginning of his episcopate, in the year 397, and consequently *long
before the Pelagian contests, we find the predestination theory set
forth, in its essential principles, together with the doctrine of the
commencement of faith through the grace of God.*   After this, he
did not always remain consistent with himself.   Nay, he even could
not deny (De Praedest. Sanct. c 9), that in " the question on the
time of the christian religion" (Ep. 102) he referred the preaching
of salvation to Christ's foreknowledge as to who would believe and
who would not.*   We also meet with expressions which cannot
be brought to harmonise with the mode in which Augustine had
formed the doctrine of absolute predestination.   Thus, according to
De Trin IV. 13, the smallest number remain with the devil, and the
greater part flee to the Savior.   But according to the predestination
theory, only a small number in proportion to those that are lost, are
predestined by God to salvation.†

   In his writings which were composed during the Pelagian contests, Augustine speaks in the *dogmatic,* but not often in the *polemic*
manner, respecting foreordination   In his first piece against the
Pelagians, (De Pec. Mer. e. g. II. 29), he speaks of the " predestinated;" as also in his homilies on John's Gospel, (e. g. tract. 45)
written about the year 416, he represents predestination as a matter
decided   And in the work written soon after (De Gest. Pel. c. 3),
he said, " God forbid that they who are called according to the design, whom he foreknew and foreordained to be like the image of his
son, should so lose their love as to perish   For, this the vessels of
wrath suffer, which are prepared for destruction, by whose damnation itself he makes manifest the riches of his glory towards the vessels of his mercy   To them therefore happens what is written
God hath given them up to their own hearts' lusts ; but not to the

---

* Here, however, Augustine himself shows expressly and fully, that there
was no inconsistency in his representations, as it was but saying in effect,
that Christ preached his gospel where he knew his elect to be.—TR

† The comparative number of the saved, however, is no essential part of
the theory.—TR

predestinated, whom the spirit of God rules," etc. But that this doctrine had as yet no polemic interest, we see from the fact that, in
the canons of the synod, nothing was decreed respecting it. In the
canons against the Pelagians, at the general council at Carthage,
418, no more mention was made of predestination than of the consequence of redemption.

It was in his tract " On Rebuke and Grace," written about the
year 427, that Augustine first presented the predestination theory,
in its extent and its connection with his other doctrines. He says
himself (De Dono Perseverantiae c 21), that he did not before so
plainly and fully present it   The occasion of this more extended
presentation, was the inference urged against him, that by his theory
of free grace, no one could be punished for not keeping God's commands. Retract. II. 67   The position, also, which he set up against
the Pelagians, that in imparting grace, God is not guided by the conduct of men, must have strengthened him in his view of predestination, because this contained precisely the opposite of the Pelagian
opinion, that God is guided by man's desert, in the bestowment of
grace.   To defend his doctrine of predestination against objections
of the semi-pelagians, of whom some traces had already become
visible, he wrote, somewhat later, his books On the Predestination of
Saints, and On the Gift of Perseverance.   The three books mentioned, in which Augustine developed his theory of predestination in
its entire consistency, are therefore the main sources for this doctrine,
which must now be presented in contrast with the Pelagian theory.

How perfectly convinced Augustine finally was of this doctrine,
and how completely he had interwoven it with his whole manner of
thinking, we see from De Dono Persv c 19. " This I know," he
there says, " that no man can dispute but from error, against this
predestination, which we defend according to holy scripture."   The
terms *praedestinare* and *praedestinatio*, he found however in the Vulgate, and borrowed them from it

CHAPTER XVI.

*Augustine's theory of predestination.   Pelagian view of fore-
ordination.*

In harmony with the rest of his anthropological system, Augustine taught the following in respect to predestination.

1. By Adam's sin the whole human race became a corrupt mass
(perditionis massa), and justly subject to eternal damnation, so that
no one can blame God's righteous decision, if none are saved from
perdition. But few, in comparison with those that are lost, (though
many in themselves), are freed, by the grace of God, from the righteous condemnation. The rest are left to the deserved punishment.

" That whole mass would have received the reward of a righteous
damnation, if the potter, not only just but also merciful, did not form
some vessels to honor by grace, not by debt ; while he aids infants,
of whom no merit can be named, and aids adults that they may be
able to have some merits." Ep. 190, c. 3 " The dominion of death
has so far prevailed over men, that the deserved punishment would
drive all headlong into a second death likewise, of which there is no
end, if the undeserved grace of God did not deliver them from it."
De Civ. Dei, XIV. 1. " But why faith," (the condition of salvation),
" is not given to all, need not move the faithful, who believes that by
one all came into a condemnation, doubtless the most just ; so that
there would be no just complaining of God, though no one should be
freed. Hence it appears that the grace of God is great, as very
many are freed and behold, in those who are not freed, what would
be due to themselves, so that he that glories, should not glory in his
own merits, (which he sees to be equalled in the damned), but in the
Lord." De Praed. Sanct 8. " Of that corrupt mass which sprung
from the first Adam, no one can be freed but he who has received
the gift through the grace of the Savior " De Cor, et Gr. 7. " Because by freewill Adam deserted God, he received the righteous sentence of God, that he should be condemned, together with his whole
race, which, being as yet all placed in him, had sinned with him.
For as many of this stock as are freed, are certainly freed from con-

demnation by which they were then held bound. Hence if even
no one were freed, no one would justly blame God's righteous decision   That *a few, therefore, (in comparison with those that perish,
though in their own number many), are freed,* is of grace, is gratuitous, thanks are to be rendered for it, lest any one should be exalted as it were on account of his own merits, but that every mouth
may be stopped, and he that glorieth may glory in the Lord." 10.

2. Deliverance from just condemnation, is the consequence of
election or predestination to salvation   This took place before the
creation of the world, from free grace, without any respect to the
moral character of man.

Augustine consequently admitted an eternal, unconditional decree of God   According to him, no mention could be made of merit,
since all men by nature, according to his assumption, are a mass of
corruption throughout, and the power to good is wanting in them all.
But grace, with him, was irresistible.

" Not by merit, (for the whole mass was condemned as it were
in the vitiated root), but *by grace, God elected a definite number* "
De Civ. Dei, XIV 26   " He works all in the elect, who has made
them vessels of mercy, who also *chose them in his son, before the
creation of the world, by the election of grace,*—not by their preceding merits, for grace is all their merit." De Cor. et Gr. 7.   " Not
because we have believed, but that we *might* believe, has God elected us , and not because we have believed, but that we might believe,
are we called." De Praed Sanct. 19.   " This is election, that God
has chosen whom he would, in Christ, before the creation of the
world, that they should be holy and unspotted before him, as he predestinated them to the adoption of children." De Dono Persv. 18.
" In order that we might receive love with which *to love,* we were
loved, while as yet we had it not.   This says the Apostle John very
clearly, Not that we loved God, but because he first loved us." De
Gr. Chr. 26.

Augustine also incidentally remarked before, in his first work
against the Pelagians, that God's grace and Spirit, which bloweth
where it listeth, passes by no kind of natural endowment And for the
purpose of illustrating the wonderful calling of God, he adduces the
example of one born almost as destitute of sense as the brutes, who,
he says, " was still so much of a Christian that, although with wonderful fatuity he patiently bore all his own injuries, yet the injury of

Christ's name or of religion in himself, with which he was imbued, he was so unable to endure as not to refrain from stoning those dear to him, when he heard them blaspheming in order to provoke him, nor in this cause did he spare even his masters. Such therefore, I think, were predestinated and created, in order that those who can may understand, that God's grace and spirit [*perhaps* the same as gracious spirit], which bloweth where it listeth, does not, on this account, pass by any kind of mind, in the children of mercy; and likewise that it does pass by every kind of mind (omne ingenii genus) in the children of hell, that he that glorieth may glory in the Lord." De Pec. Mer. I. 22

Remark. Augustine presented the relation of predestination to grace in such a way as to make the latter the effect of the former. It need not be suggested, that he here takes grace in his own sense, i. e. for supernatural gracious influence. Grace with him was the actual impartation itself, which was foreordained by predestination. " Between grace and predestination, there is only this difference, that predestination is the preparation of grace, while grace is the conferment itself. And thus what the apostle says, *Not of works, lest any one should be exalted, for we are his workmanship, created in Christ Jesus in good works*, is grace; but what follows, viz, *Which God before prepared that we should walk in them*, is predestination; which predestination cannot be without prescience; but prescience may be without predestination. For by predestination, God foreknew those things which himself would do. But he is able to foreknow what he does not do, as all sins.—God's predestination, which is in good (quæ in bono est), as I said, is the preparation of grace; but grace is the effect of predestination itself." De Praed. Sanct. 10 Here we see how Augustine thought of the separation of predestination from prescience. Predestination with him was *that kind of divine prescience which relates to what God does himself.* He did not therefore consider every part of God's foreknowledge as predeterminate, because he still held fast at least the idea of man's original freedom. " In his foreknowledge (which cannot be deceived and changed) to arrange his future works, this exactly and nothing else is it, to predestine (prædestinare)." De Dono Persev. 17. " This and nothing else is the predestination of the saints, viz. the foreknowledge and the preparation of the benefits of God, by which most certainly are freed all who *are* freed." 14.

3. God employs means to effect the salvation of the elect. They receive baptism. Opportunity is afforded them to hear the gospel. When they hear it, they believe. They persevere in faith, which is active through love, to the end. And if at any time they swerve, they are reformed by rebuke. Nay, even their swerving is directed to their best good. They are justified by the blood of the Mediator, freed from the power of darkness, and brought into the kingdom of Christ.

"For those therefore, who are separated from that original condemnation, by this free gift of divine grace, the hearing of the gospel will doubtless be provided ; and when they hear, they believe ; and they persevere to the end in faith which works by love. And if at any time they deviate, being reproved they are reformed ; and some of them, though not reproved by men, return to the path they left ; and a few having received the grace [baptism], at whatever age, are removed by speedy death from the dangers of this life." De Cor et Gr. 7. "For such as love God, he works all things for good ; so absolutely all, that if any of them deviate and wander, he causes even this to work for their good, as they return the more humble and wise." 9 " To the number of the saints predestinated,— the mercy of their Savior abides—alike when converted, when in conflict, or when crowned." 13. "The children of perdition, God punishes in wrath ; but the children of grace, he punishes in grace, for whom the Lord loveth he chasteneth, and scourgeth every son whom he receiveth" De Pec Mer II. 16. And thus too, according to Augustine, as shown by the preceding passages, the children predestinated to salvation, receive baptism before they die, while others die without it. "When the Father is internally heard and teaches that men should come to the Son, he takes away the stony heart and gives the heart of flesh.—For so he makes sons and the vessels of mercy which he has prepared unto glory " De Præd. Sanct. 8. " Men are not elected on account of their merit, but through the grace of the Mediator , that is, *they are freely justified through the blood of the second Adam.*" De Cor. et Gr. 7. " God's mercy precedes man, that he may be freed from the evils which he has done, and which he would do if not ruled by God's grace, and which he would eternally suffer if not delivered from the power of darkness and translated into the kingdom of the Son of God's love." 13. Hence Augustine called the elect also, " Elect to rule with Christ, elect to obtain the kingdom of Christ." 7.

4. Election is certain and unchangeable, because it is made without any condition. Hence no one is missing from that definite and happy number; no one of them is lost. And hence no one who has wandered from the path of goodness, dies before he returns to it, for he is so committed to Christ, that he shall not be lost, but have eternal life.

"The number of those who are predestinated to the kingdom of God, is so certain, that not one shall be either added to them or taken from them.—The number of the saints predestinated by the grace of God to the kingdom of God, by perseverance given them to the end, shall there be brought *entire* (integer), and there, now most secure and happy, shall be kept without end" De Cor. et Gr. 13. "There are sons of God who do not yet belong to us, but they already belong to God; of whom the evangelist John says, that Jesus was about to die—that he might gather together in one the dispersed sons of God; who were surely to believe by the preaching of the gospel, and yet before it was done, were already immutably enrolled as sons of God, in their Father's book of remembrance.— These therefore are understood to be given to Christ, who were ordained to eternal life. They are the predestinated and called according to the purpose, of whom no one is lost And accordingly no one of them ends this life, changed from good to evil; for he is so ordained and therefore given to Christ, that he shall not perish but have eternal life.—Whoever therefore, in God's most provident arrangement, are foreknown, called, justified, and glorified, are already God's children, and can by no means perish, although, I do not say not yet born again, but not yet born at all. These truly come to Christ, because they so come as he has said, All that the Father hath given me shall come to me" 9. "If any one of those predestinated and foreknown, perishes, God is deceived, but no one of them perishes, for God is not deceived. If any one of them perishes, God is conquered by human depravity, but no one of them perishes, for God is conquered by nothing. — The faith of these, which works by love, either never fails at all, or if there are some whom it fails, it is revived again before life is finished, and the iniquity, which intervened, being blotted out, perseverance to the end is reckoned (deputatur) But those who shall not persevere, and shall so fall from christian faith and conversation, that the end of this life shall find them such, beyond a doubt are not to be reckoned in

31

the number of the elect, even for the time in which they lived well and piously * For they were not separated from that mass of perdition by God's foreknowledge and predestination, and therefore not called according to the purpose, and consequently not elected " 7. Hence,

5. Perseverance is a special gift to the elect, which is afforded to to all the elect and to none but the elect.

" They who are called according to the purpose, persevere in the love of God to the end · and those who deviate for a time, return, that they may bring to the end what they began in good." De Cor. et Gr 9. " Those who, having heard the gospel, and being changed for the better, have not received perseverance,—have not been selected from that mass which is evidently condemned." 7 " Nor need it move us, that God does not give that perseverance to some of his sons. God forbid that it should be so, if they were of those elected and called according to the purpose and who are truly the sons of the promise —If they had been, they would have a true and not a false righteousness †—But the Apostle, when showing what it is to be called according to the purpose, presently adds For whom he foreknew and predestinated conformable to the image (predestinavit conformes imaginis) of his son, that he might be the first born among many brethren But whom he predestinated, them he also called, i. e. according to the purpose," etc 9 " He, therefore, makes them persevere in good, who makes them good But those who fall and perish, were not in the number of the predestinated. To the elect, are given both the ability and the will to persevere, by the free conferment of divine grace " 12 " It is necessary that this should remain a secret" (as to what individuals belong to the elect and shall persevere to the end), " so that no one may be elated, but that all, even those who run well, may fear, while it is a secret as to what ones will reach the mark On account of the benefit of this secret,

---

* Augustine maintained, in the work from which this passage is taken, that some who are truly righteous for a time, fall away and perish, but they never belonged to the elect See c 9 —Tr

† Here our author has committed quite a mistake, in not quoting the connection of this sentence, which is as follows. " *Not* that they feigned righteousness, but that they did not *persevere* in it For the Evangelist does not say, If they had been of us, they would have held (tenuissent) a true and not a feigned righteousness, but he says, If they had been of us, they would doubtless have continued with us "—The dash, it will be recollected, generally denotes a chasm in the citation —Tr

therefore, it is to be believed, that some of the sons of perdition, not
having received the gift of persevering to the end, begin to live in
the faith which works by love, and live for a while devoutly and righteously, and afterwards fall : but they are not taken from this life before this happens." 13. "It is on account of the benefit of this fear,
in order that after we are regenerated and have begun to live piously, we may still not think ourselves safe, that some who will not persevere are, by the permission or foreknowledge and arrangement of
God, mingled with those who shall persevere By their fall, he
moves us, with fear and trembling, to walk the right way, till we
pass from this life to another, where pride is no longer to be sub-
dued, and seductions and temptations are no longer to be encountered." Ep. 194 c. 4 * Compare the whole of the first part of the
book On the Gift of Perseverance, in which Augustine endeavors to
prove, that perseverance in Christ to the end, is a gift of God without reference to the merits of those who receive it

It appears, at the same time, from the passages adduced, that in
respect to the elect, Augustine held to a " vocation according to the
purpose " Vocation he considered twofold , one general, which
extends to all to whom the gospel is preached ; and one, particular,
which is afforded only to the elect Hence he says, " All who are
called, are not of course chosen " De Cor. et Gr. 7 He presents
his opinion with peculiar clearness, in the following passage : " God
calls his many predestinated sons, that he may make them members
of his predestinated and only begotten Son, not with the vocation by
which *they* were called who would not come to the marriage feast ;
for with that vocation, even the Jews were called, to whom Christ
crucified is a stumbling block ; and also the heathen, to whom the
Crucified is foolishness But he calls the predestinated by that vocation which the apostle designated, saying, that he preached Christ,
the power of God and the wisdom of God, to the called, both Jews
and Greeks. For he says, *To the called*, in order to show that the
others were not the called ; knowing that there is a kind of definite
call (quandam certam vocationem) of those who are called according to the purpose, whom He foreknew and predestinated to be like
the image of his Son." De Praed Sanct 16.

* I give this reference, though wrong, as I find it in Wiggers, and am
compelled to translate the passage from his version, as I have not found the
original.—Tr

Finally ; as Augustine distinguished between "being able not to sin," and "not being able to sin," and between "being able not to die," and "not being able to die;" so he made a distinction between "being able not to desert good," and "not being able to desert good." The ability to persevere, was found in Adam in paradise, who had freewill. The inability to apostatize, is now, since freewill is lost, a gift of grace for the elect. A complete assurance of participation in this grace, the full persuasion that one can never fall, is however first found in the blessed in the future life. De Cor. et Gr. 11, 12, 13.

6. The final reason of the salvation of man, then, lies simply in the will of God. If God willed that all men should be saved, all would be saved ; for no will of man withstands God's will to save.

"Why then does he not teach all so that they come to Christ ?— Because he has mercy on whom he will, and pardons whom he will " De Praed. Sanct 8. "Grace frees from the condemnation of the whole mass those whom it does free ;" which means nothing else but that God frees whom he pleases to free Op. Imp. I. 127. "When, by chastisement, men either come into the path of righteousness or return to it, who works salvation in their hearts but that God who gives the increase, whoever may plant or water, and whoever may labor in the fields or the vineyards ? whose will to save, no freewill of men resists. For to will or to refuse, is so in the power of him that wills or refuses, as not to impede the divine will nor surpass its power. For even in the case of those who do what he does not will, he does what he will —And even respecting the very wills of men, he does what he will, when he will " De Cor. et Gr. 14. "By his merciful goodness, God leads some to repentance, while, by his righteous judgment, he does not lead others to it. For he has the power to lead and draw, as the Lord himself says, No man cometh unto me unless the Father that hath sent me, draw him." C. Jul V 4. "Two children are born If you ask what they deserve, both belong to the mass of perdition But why does the mother bring one to the grace [to baptism], and suffocate the other in her sleep ? Can you tell me what the one merited which was brought to baptism, and what offence the other had committed, whom the mother suffocated in her sleep ? Neither has deserved any good. But the potter has power of the same mass to make one vessel to honor, and another to dishonor." Sermo 26, de Verb. Ap. c. 12, preached against the Pelagian heresy.

In a work not against the Pelagians, Augustine says incidentally that, by receiving a large number of men to heaven, God would supply the chasm occasioned by the loss of the fallen angels. Enchir. c. 29.

7 Since the final reason of the salvation of man, lies in the will of God, he, to whom salvation is not imparted, is not saved because God did not extend the decree of salvation to him   There is, however, only *one* unconditional decree, and this refers to the elect, not to the reprobate. The final reason of *damnation*, therefore, does not lie in the absolute will of God, but in Adam's sin or original sin Whoever is damned, is not damned because God willed his damnation, but because Adam sinned, and the sin of Adam, as a merited punishment, came upon all men, for by this also come even their own sins By Adam's sin, the whole human race became an object of God's deserved abhorrence ; and hence in his righteousness he must condemn them. In his goodness, he determined to save a few by grace. The *deserved* ruin comes on all the rest. But why he frees this man from the condemned mass, but not that, and consequently displays his goodness in this, and his justice in that, this question belongs to the unsearchable counsels of God, as does also the question, why God does not afford perseverance to those whom he causes to live in a christian way for a length of time

As Augustine taught, that all men would be saved if God willed it, so he could not deny, that many would not be saved because the almighty divine will has not willed their salvation   Hence he says, in reference to children who die before baptism . " Many are not saved, not because themselves do not will, but because God does not will it " Ep. 197 c 6. But this always means only so many as the decree of election does not reach   That Augustine considered those who will not be saved, as damned on account of Adam's sin, in which the whole race have participated, may be seen from the passages now to be adduced for Augustine's opinions just stated.

" Grace frees, from the damnation of the whole mass, those whom it does free, which you are heretics for denying. But respecting the merit of origin, all are in condemnation from one ; but in respect to grace, which is not given by merit, whoever are freed from this condemnation, are called vessels of mercy ; but on those who are not freed, the wrath of God *abides*, coming from the just judgment of God ; which procedure is not to be complained of because inscruta-

ble. And they are furthermore called *vessels* of wrath, because
God also uses them for a good purpose, that he may make known
the riches of his glory in the vessels of mercy. For what is exacted
of others, God being the judge, is forgiven to them by his mercy
Which unsearchable ways of the Lord, if thou wouldst esteem culpable, hear, O man, who art thou that repliest against God?" Op.
Imp I 127. "But well might it appear unjust, that they become
vessels of wrath for perdition, if this whole mass from Adam, were
not condemned   That they therefore become vessels of wrath even
from birth, pertains to deserved punishment. But that by being
born again, they become vessels of mercy, pertains to unmerited
grace."* So Augustine expressed himself, about the year 418, in
a letter to Optatus. Ep. 190. c. 3   "To whom grace is not imparted, to them it is not imparted through the just judgment of God."
Ep. 217 c. 5. "They who do not belong to that definite and most
happy number—either lie under the sin which they originally contracted by generation, and go hence with that hereditary debt, which
is not forgiven through regeneration, or they also add others by freewill ᐧ a will, I say, *free*, but not *freed ;* free of righteousness, but the
slave of sin (peccati servum), by which they are hurried along
through diverse noxious passions, some more, others less ; but all are
evil, and according to this diversity are to be sentenced to different
punishments ᐧ or they receive the grace of God, but endure only for
a time, and do not persevere. They desert and are deserted. For
they are abandoned to freewill by the just and secret decision of
God, not having received the gift of perseverance." De Cor. et Gr. 13.
"But why God frees this one rather than that, is his unsearchable
judgments and his incomprehensible ways. And here too it is better that we hear or say, O man, who art thou that repliest against
God?" De Praed Sanct 8   "If I am here asked why God has not
given perseverance to those to whom he has given the love by which
to live in a christian way (Christianè), I reply, I do not know.—Inscrutable are his judgments and unsearchable his ways" De Cor et
Gr. 8.

---

* The following will show what Augustine understood by the phrase, *ves-*
sels of wrath   "*Man that is born of a woman,* as it is written in the book of
Job, *is of short life and full of irascibility* (iracundiae). He is a vessel *of the*
thing of which he is full   Hence they are called vessels of wrath (irae) "
Ep 190 ᴄ 3.—Tʀ

This is the hard predestination theory of Augustine, shocking to the moral feeling of every unbiassed mind. Augustine therefore admitted all those consequences which flow from the decree of election ; that those whom God has not predestinated to salvation, cannot possibly be saved, from which it then follows, that those whom he has predestinated to it, *must* at all events be saved ; that many men may have truly reformed, and yet were damned, because God did not find it good to have them persevere in good , that the others, to whom the cross of Christ is foolishness, would have come to Christ, if the Father had taught them, in order that they might come to him ;—nay, he assiduously sets forth these consequences, in his books On the Predestination of the Saints, and On the Gift of Perseverance, as if he intended, by the frequent repetition, to harden himself against their shockingness *

He proceeded, however, more philosophically than Calvin and Beza, in this respect, that he did not extend the eternal decree to damnation also. According to him, as has been shown, those who are damned are not damned because God from eternity decreed their damnation, but because they sinned in Adam. So the justice of God could still be defended, at least in appearance. All men might even have been saved, if Adam had not sinned How we all shared in Adam's sin, it may indeed be difficult enough to explain ; but the punishment for this participation, cannot be unjust, for there is no unrighteousness with God. But why God frees one from eternal perdition, and not another ; why God affords this unmerited grace to one, and not to another ; nay, what is still more inscrutable, why he causes one of two pious persons to persevere, and not the other,—on these questions, we cannot venture to dispute with God "One is taken and another is left, because great is God's grace and true is God's justice." Op. Imp I. 39 This was the view which Augustine held fast and very acutely defended against his opponents

Passages are indeed found in Augustine's writings, in which, (induced by declarations of the Bible, particularly of the Old Testament, which he explained in the severest sense of the words, with-

* In view of the hard points in Augustine's system, which our author has here grouped together and placed in at least a sufficiently forbidding aspect, we are led to see, among other things, the value of the more modern distinction between *natural* and *moral* inability.—TR

out regard to the occasion and object of the particular writers, and
therefore often falsely), he supposed it necessary to admit, that God
so operates on the hearts of men, that they are led to wickedness as
a punishment. But it must here be considered, as one part of the
thing, that, according to Augustine, the very withholding of divine
aid, leads to evil, for without it, man can do nothing good (C d.
Epp. Pel I 18) ; and as another part, that Augustine considered it
as a punishment annexed by God to sin, that man is led by one sin
to another still greater, where Julian admitted barely a divine permission C. Jul. V. 3. In relation to this, he said, to the Adrumetian monks, "When you read in the scriptures of truth, that men
are seduced by God, or their hearts hardened or made dull, do not
doubt that their evil merits precede, so that they justly suffer these
things" De Gr. et Lib. Arb 21   We should recollect this, when
Augustine hazards the expression, respecting the traitor Judas, that
he had been chosen " in judgment to the shedding of the blood of
Christ" De Cor. et Gr 7.—Besides, he referred this only to a particular act, and by no means intended to assert with it an " absolute
decree of reprobation." And when, in the homilies on John's gospel, (e. g. tract. 48), the expression occurs, " predestinated to eternal death," and (in De Pec Mer. II 17), " predestinated to be
damned," and when furthermore (De An. et ejus Orig. IV. 11),
Augustine speaks of those whom God has foreordained to eternal
death, and in other places, of those whom he has predestinated to
righteous punishment, he meant not an absolute and unconditional,
but a *conditional* predestination   For since, by his theory, the reason for condemning lies not in the unconditional will of God, but in
original sin, there might perhaps be in God a foreknowledge that the
condemnation would follow ; or, (if one would employ the human
expression respecting God), a decree of condemnation induced by
his foreknowledge, but not of foreordination to it   He himself says
(De Perf. Just. Hom. 13), that God's prescience has decided concerning those destined to perdition   And, as he says in his fifty-
third homily, God does not compel any one to sin by his foreknowing the future sins of men ; or, as he expresses himself (De Civ.
Dei, V. 10), man does not sin in consequence of God's foreknowing
that he will sin   And in the passage quoted from his fourth book on
the soul, he pronounces God, in respect to those destined to eternal
death, "the most righteous awarder of punishment;" just as he

says (De Pec. Mer. II. 17), that the reason why grace does not aid some, lies in themselves and not in God, because they are appointed to perdition " for the iniquity of pride."

In Ep. 190. c. 3, Augustine explains himself on the following questions, among others, viz , why should any be born, except those whom God has designed for salvation ? and why does he call only these, in the present life, and not the others on whom the deserved punishment falls ? God thereby shows his goodness, which would remain hid if no one received the righteous punishment; and he also shows his power, because he uses the wicked in a proper way. In this sense, Augustine calls God " the disposer of the wicked (peccatorum ordinatorem)." Conff. l. 10. Their wickedness, too, is for the discipline and warning of the good, etc And an incomparably greater multitude (incomparabili multitudine plures) are lost, that it may be shown, by the multitudes of the reprobate, how lightly God esteems even so great a number of the most righteously condemned. " God does not create one of them unadvisedly and without design, nor is he ignorant of the good to be effected by them ; for good is thus effected by his creating human nature in them and adorning by them the order of the present world." C. Jul. V. 4. " Even the patience of God towards the sons of perdition, is not in vain nor fruitless ; for it is necessary in order to profit those whom God selects from the mass of perdition, not by human merit, but by divine grace ; since they give thanks either because they are separated from them, or, while by God's arrangement they are born of those who *are* to perish, *they* are not to perish." Op Imp IV 131. " God shows the freed what he bestows on them, not merely by themselves but also by those who are not freed. For each one then sees himself delivered from evils, not by merited but by gratuitous goodness, when he is freed from the society of those men with whom he might justly have shared a common punishment. Why, then, should not God create those whom he foreknew would sin ? since in them and by them he might show both what their guilt deserves and what is conferred by his grace ; nor, under him as creator and disposer, would the perverse disorder of the delinquents, pervert the right order of things." De Civ. Dei, XIV. 26. " Those who have chosen the part of iniquity and have corrupted their commendable nature by a culpable will, ought by no means not to have been created, on account of their being foreknown. For even they have their place, which

32

they fill to the benefit of the saints. For God needs not the righteousness of any virtuous man whatever ; how much less the iniquity
of the perverse," etc [Reference omitted]. Comp Ep 156. c. 7.

[It may be well to add, in this connection, the following. " Sinners, both angels and men, do nothing by which the great works of
the Lord are impeded   For he who providentially and omnipotently
distributes to each his own, knows how rightly to use not only the
good but even the evil.   And consequently why should not God,
rightly using the evil angel, (now so condemned and hardened for
the desert of the first bad affection, that he would never afterwards
have a good volition), permit the first man, who had been created
righteous, i. e with a good will, to be tempted by him ?—When,
therefore, God was not ignorant of his future fall, why should he not
permit him to be tempted by the malignity of the envious angel ?
by no means indeed uncertain that he would be conquered, but nevertheless foreknowing that this same devil would be conquered by
his seed, aided by his grace, with greater glory of the saints. It
was so done that nothing future should be hid from God, nor that he
should compel any one to sin by his foreknowing ; and he would
show, by the consequent experience, to the angelic and human creation, the difference between confiding to his tuition, and to their
own presumption. For who would dare to believe or say, that it
was not in the power of God that neither angel nor man should
fall ?   But he preferred not to take it out of their power ; and thus
to show both how much evil their pride, and how much good his
grace, would effect." De Civ Dei, XIV. 27.   According to this passage. did not Augustine consider both the divine purpose and the divine agency as extending to all sin just as truly as to holiness ?
though the agency is not exerted in the same way , nor does the
purpose find its *ultimate* object either in the sin or in its punishment —Tr.]

Finally, Augustine would have his predestination theory treated
with proper caution, in public discourses   One should not say to
the unversed multitude, " Whether you run or sleep, you will only
be what the Infallible has foreseen you will be "   Instead of that,
he should express himself thus ·   " So run that ye may obtain ; and
that you may yourselves know by your running, that you were so
foreknown that you would run right."   Instead of saying, " The rest
of you, who remain in the love of sin, have not yet arisen because

the aid of compassionate grace has not yet raised you," one can well and properly express himself thus; "If any of you still remain in the love of damnable sins, embrace the most salutary discipline. But when you have done this, do not boast as if it were by your works, or glory as if you had not received it; for it is God that worketh in you both to will and to do of his own good pleasure," etc De Dono Persv. 22 —Thus, by a mitigating presentation, would Augustine veil what is revolting in his theory of predestination— what he felt himself; and its offensiveness to every man whose head and heart have not been corrupted by the school, was to be removed.

As yet the question has not been presented, whether Augustine was a sublapsarian or a supralapsarian. He is commonly considered as a sublapsarian. But the question itself in its import, belongs to a later theory, which was unknown to Augustine; and hence we are in danger of not rightly apprehending his meaning, if we regard him either as a sublapsarian or a supralapsarian Augustine would have been sufficiently shy of adopting the sublapsarian opinion, which the synod of Dort professed two hundred years ago, according to which God first determined *after* the fall of Adam, to save some of the fallen. A philosophical mind, like Augustine, could not maintain anything so. By this doctrine, the condition of time is transferred to God, and besides this, a change in his will is admitted. For by this doctrine, a decree is supposed to have been made at the creation of the world, to save all men, which was afterwards changed. We might rather call Augustine a supralapsarian, in as much as he held, that God had decreed from eternity the salvation of some, and consequently before the fall of Adam Only we must be cautious of attributing to him the supralapsarian opinion of *Calvin*, who referred the unconditional decree of God, formed before the fall, even to the reprobate, and by which therefore, if this doctrine is to be consistently pursued further, God is made the author of Adam's transgression.

[But what, after all, is the difference which our author, or Augustine, or any one else, would make between an unconditional decree to suffer satan to make what was foreknown as a fatal temptation to Adam, and an unconditional decree extending to Adam's sin itself? To decree the *certain means*, and that too with the *design* that the end should take place, is probably all which Augustine or even Calvin ever meant by a decree in any case, when regarded in distinction from a precept of God. If more was meant, it should be shown *what* more.—Tʀ]

That Pelagius himself came forth against Augustine's predestination doctrine, cannot be maintained ; for, as already mentioned, Pelagius had left the stage long before Augustine had fully developed this theory of his. But that Pelagius *thought* differently on the subject, might be presumed from his view of man even if he had not declared himself on the point in his exposition of the epistle to the Romans.

According to Pelagius, foreordination to salvation or to damnation, is founded on prescience. Consequently he did not admit an " absolute predestination," but in every respect a " conditional predestination." God designed those for salvation who, as he foreknew, would believe in him and keep his commands , and reprobated those who, as he foreknew, would remain in sin. Thus, on Rom. 9 15, where God " said to Moses, I will have mercy on whom I have had mercy, and I will show mercy on whom I will have mercy," Pelagius remarks ; " This in the true sense, is understood thus . I will have mercy on him whom I have *foreknown* to be able to merit mercy, as I have already had mercy on him " On verse 10, he remarks : " Jacob and Esau, who were born of Rebecca at the same birth, were with God separated *by the merit of faith*, before they were born —Those among the gentiles whom he *foreknew* as future believers, he chose ; and those of Israel as unbelievers, he rejected." On verse 12 ; " God's *prescience* does not pre-judge sinners, should they be willing to be converted, for he says by Ezekiel, If I say to the sinner, thou shalt surely die, and if he being converted shall work righteousness, he shall surely live, he shall not die In the book of Genesis, it is said, Two nations and two peoples (populi) are in thy womb, and people (populus) shall surpass people, and the greater shall serve the less   The prophecy, therefore, is not concerning those who are Jacob and Esau according to the flesh, but concerning those who were to be good or evil by works, and, by the works themselves, to have the hatred of God, or to obtain his mercy " On Rom 11: 2 ; " He has not rejected the people whom he *foreknew* as afterwards to believe."   Verse 5 ; " The election of grace, is faith ; as works are the election of the law. But what election, where there is no diversity of merits ?"   " On Rom. 8· 29,

30, Pelagius remarks, among other things · " To predestinate is the same as to foreknow. Vocation collects the willing, not the unwilling."

Augustine also presents the Pelagian opinion on predestination, in the like way. " God foreknew, says the Pelagian, who would be holy and spotless by the decision of freewill, and therefore he chose them before the foundation of the world, in that prescience by which he foreknew that they would be such. Therefore he elected, says he, those whom he foreknew as afterwards to be holy and immaculate, predestinating them as sons before they existed. He certainly did not make them such, nor foresee that he should make them, but that they would be such.—The Pelagians suppose, that, having received the commandments, forthwith by freewill we become holy and spotless in his sight, in love ; which because God foreknew as to be, they say he chose and predestinated us in Christ before the foundation of the world." De Praed. Sanct. 18, 19. In Ep. 194, c. 8, Augustine remarks, that the Pelagians, when the argument of the Apostle (Rom 9: 10 sqq) is presented to them in proof of (Augustinian) free grace, explain the words, " Jacob have I loved, and Esau have I hated," thus ; " God hated one of those not yet born, and loved the other, because he foresaw their future works." Comp. C. d. Epp. Pel. II. 7.

Julian also in particular, (whose arguments against Augustine's doctrines of original sin and grace, must be objections against his theory of predestination), adopted this in the Pelagian sense. " The comparison of God with a potter, who, of the same lump, makes one vessel to honor and another to dishonor, ought not to be mentioned by you [Augustine] at all, because, as consistently explained by us, it is entirely against you ; for when some are said to be made to honor and others to dishonor, the opinion of the catholics is aided, by which *a different end of the vessels is announced according to the diversity of human will*" Op Imp. I. 126.

Remark. The author of the *Hypognosticon*, objects indeed to he Pelagians that, since they allow a predestination in the case of the Apostles, they ought to allow it in all who serve God in a proper way. " We should admit a predestination, not merely as you are wont to say, in the case of the apostles, but also in the patriarchs, prophets, martyrs, and confessors, and in all the saints and worthy servants of God." Lib. VI. at the end, app. p. 50. But when the

Pelagians admit, in respect to the apostles, a predestination to spread christianity and to preach its doctrines, they say nothing of a predestination to salvation, nothing of an absolute decree   Such a predestination they could admit; for this stood in no connection with God's unconditional decree ; and besides, it did not at all exclude a regard to the foreseen worthiness of the apostles for this calling.

CHAPTER XVII.

Augustine's doctrine on the extent of redemption.   The Pelagian doctrine.

Of Augustine's doctrine of redemption, we can here speak no further than as it stands in close connection with his theory of predestination.   And this connection concerns the extent of redemption. As, by the predestination theory, only a definite number of elect would obtain salvation, Christ's redemption could extend only to those whom God had destined to salvation.   For the rest, his death even, as well as his whole incarnation, had no object   Christ therefore died and rose again only for the elect.   Consequently, by his theory of predestination, Augustine was led to a peculiar view of the extent of redemption, which, however, was only touched upon incidentally by him, and never developed with the particularity with which he exhibited the rest of his doctrines against the Pelagians.

According to Augustine, therefore, redemption was not universal. God sent his Son into the world, not to redeem the whole sinful race of man, but only the elect   " By this mediator, God showed, that *those* whom he redeemed by his blood, he makes, from being evil, to be eternally good." De Cor. et Gr 11   The following passage is peculiarly clear, and is taken from the first book " on adulterous marriages," c 15, a work written about the year 419, and not directed against the Pelagians.   " Every one that has been redeemed by the blood of Christ, is a man ; though not every one that is a man, has been redeemed by the blood of Christ "   Hence the words in John 10 26, ye believe not because ye are not of my sheep, according to Hom. 48. on John's gospel, mean as much as this, Ye believe not, because ye are not bought for eternal life by my blood. "No one perishes of those for whom Christ died." Ep. 169, c. 1.—Nay, according to his theory, Augustine would have no mediator between God and the whole human race, but only a mediator between God and the elect "Christ redeemed the sinners who were to be justified (justificandos peccatores)." De Trin IV 13. The bestowment of grace on the elect, as is already clear from Augustine's doctrine of grace, was connected with the redemption of Jesus. See Munscher's Handbuch, Th. IV § 118 Salvation could be obtained only by faith on Christ. Hence faith in the mediation supposed the appearance of the mediator himself. Only according to Augustine's idea, the elect were not predestined because Christ had redeemed them, but they were redeemed because God had predestinated them.

Against Augustine's limitation view of redemption, just presented, which is clear as the sun from the passages adduced, some doubtful expressions of his, and therefore proving nothing, may indeed be adduced; and especially one passage, which seems, at first view, to declare a directly contrary doctrine, viz , the universality of the work of redemption. This passage is found in De Cor. et Gr. 15. He there says, " Who has more loved the weak, than he who became weak *for all* and was crucified *for all* ?" It would now be very remarkable for Augustine to have presented so contradictory a view, in this little book in which, as appears from so many passages already quoted, he so definitely and emphatically maintained the limitation. But the connection fully shows, that Augustine would by no means here maintain the universality of redemption. He is here calling to admonition and reproof, because we cannot know who is predestinated, and adduces as a reason for the call, the example of Christ. He had become man and endured the death of the cross for all, viz., those whom the Father would free from the misery of sin.—To understand the passage as referring to the efficacy of the redeeming death as *sufficient* for *all* men, if they were to have been redeemed, would not accord with the spirit of Augustine. To him, as well as to his whole age, the speculation respecting the *power* of Christ's atoning death, was foreign.

Finally, the consequences of redemption, according to Augustine, extend both to the soul by freeing it from sin and its punishment, and also to the body, by the resurrection to felicity. De Trin. IV. 3.

By no means, however, did Augustine confine the work of redemption to the atoning death of Christ. In his first book De Pec. Mer. Augustine says, that He in whom all are made alive, has presented himself as an example to his imitators. The object of Christ's incarnation, he regarded as twofold, as he rhetorically shows in Serm De Tempore, 118. Christ as man must suffer for us, to free us from the chains of sin, and consequently from the power of the devil. De Lib Arb. III 10. The other object was, not merely, by the aid of his doctrine and grace, to redeem us from imperfections and vices, but also by his example to inflame us with a zeal for holiness.—Against the genuineness of this discourse, doubts have indeed been raised by the critics But the thoughts adduced are certainly Augustinian, since, in other passages innumerable, Augustine not only admits but very minutely shows, that the teaching and example of Christ are given for our compliance and imitation, and that we are brought by the first to the knowledge of the truth. Comp De Trin. IV. and Munscher, loc. cit. According to his theory of grace and predestination, however, Augustine must always have limited the doctrine and example of Christ to those to whom divine grace affords the will and the power to obey and imitate Op Imp IV. 87.

We do not find that Pelagius opposed Augustine's assumption of the atoning death of Christ for the elect. But conformably to the rest of his system, his view of the bearing of redemption, must have been entirely different from the Augustinian. True, he did not deny the atoning effect of the death of Jesus, as some have unjustly reproached him with doing; but he admitted, that the death of Christ is actually the cause why God may pardon all who have sinned All *sinners* are pardoned by God simply for Christ's sake, are freed merely on his account from the guilt and punishment of their sins. In his exposition of Romans (e. g. 5 5 sqq.), Pelagius teaches expressly, that Christ died for sinners; that God forgives our sins on account of Christ's death; and that his death is necessary for us. But since, according to him, men are able to live without sin and to practise virtue by their own power, so all men are not sinners ; and hence the atoning virtue of the death of Jesus, is imparted to those only who have actually sinned And now, that the Pelagians could maintain concerning children, whom they considered innocent, that " for them the blood was not shed which, as we read, was shed for the remission of sins,"—an opinion which the fathers at the synod of Carthage attributed to them in their letter to Innocent (Ep. 175), is manifest of itself.

And Augustine himself allows (C Jul. VI. 4), that the atoning power of Christ's death was conceded by the Pelagians. He there says to Julian, " You say, that Christ died also for sinners. I say, he died *only* for sinners " According to him, the Pelagians themselves ascribed still a further power to Christ's death besides that of atoning ; while Augustine confined it to this. That is also manifest from Julian's allowing, that Christ died for children. C. Jul. III. 25. Nor did they any more confine Christ's work of redemption to his atoning death, than Augustine did. According to the Pelagian view, the mission of Jesus, and consequently his death too, were by no means superfluous to the men who needed no atonement. By his teaching and example, they might be led to higher virtue and perfection, just as all Christians attain through Christ a higher felicity, (the salvation of Christians), and the supernatural influences of grace, as we have already seen while on the doctrine of baptism and grace. In that relation, therefore, very great stress was laid by the Pelagians on the *teaching* and *example* of Christ. C. Jul V. 15. The design of Jesus in his appearing, was also to excite us, by his doctrine and example, to more perfect holiness of life. Consequently those who had no occasion for the virtue of Christ's atonement, might still receive this salutary effect of the redemption of Jesus, as a means of incitement to higher virtue and perfection. In this view, the words of Pelagius himself are especially worthy of notice, which have already been quoted in another connection. " If before the law, as we have said, and long before the advent of our Lord and Savior, some are reported to have lived righteously and holily, how much more must we admit, that we can do this since the phenomenon of his advent, as we are instructed by the grace of Christ and are regenerated into better men [i. e. by baptism], as we are reconciled and cleansed by his blood, and *are impelled by his example to a more perfect righteousness*, and ought to be better than they who were before the law, and better than they who were under the law, since the apostle says, Sin shall no longer have dominion over you, for ye are not under the law, but under grace." Ep. ad Dem. 9. From the third book of Pelagius on freewill, Augustine quotes the words, " Christ impels us to more perfect holiness by the imitation of himself, and subdues the habit of vice by the example of virtues." De

33

Gr. Chr. 39. Finally, Julian says, according to Beda's quotation (Ap. p. 120), Christ assumed human nature in order to give the most perfect example of virtue.

Of a vicarious satisfaction, in the judicial sense, as the Lutheran system receives it, the Pelagians no more thought than did Augustine.

Thus much on Augustinian predestination and the doctrine closely connected with it, of the limit of redemption, which may be regarded as a corollary from the former when contemplated on this side ; —and thus much on the Pelagian views which differ from them

As predestination was not specifically a matter of dispute between Augustine and the Pelagians, the latter adduced no particular reasons against it   What he says, in his book On the Gift of Perseverance, against the objection urged by the Massilians, that the benefit of preaching is removed by the predestination doctrine, belongs to the history of semi-pelagianism.   Only it may be allowable here to adduce what Augustine likewise remarks in that tract (c. 22) against the Massilians, in respect to the objection, that the doctrine leads to despair.   " Ought it to be feared, that man would despair of himself, when it is shown, that he has to place his hope on God, but that he should not despair, when he, most proud and wretched, places it in himself ?"

By the close connection, however, of the Augustinian system, all the objections made by the Pelagians against the other anthropological doctrines of the renowned father, must at the same time be objections against his theory of predestination.   Particularly does this hold true of the objections against Augustinian grace, which, by the close connection of this doctrine with predestination, are just so many objections against the latter.

But here one objection against it must not be passed by, which appeared very weighty to Augustine himself, because his whole anthropological system was shaken, the moment it could not be answered   In his tract De Cor. et Gr. he sought to answer it   Whether Augustine raised this objection to himself, or whether it was made by others, is not sufficiently clear.   Enough, that it was as follows (c. 10 sqq) :

If those are justly punished by God who do not persevere, although they have not received from God the gift of perseverance, without which no one perseveres, and have not received it, moreover, *because* they have not been separated, by the free gift of divine grace, from the condemned mass, then was Adam blameless, (of whom this cannot be said), because he did not yet belong to that condemned mass which originated from his sin, and who nevertheless cannot have received perseverance from God, for he did not persevere in good.

Augustine took much pains to refute this acute objection. For if he did not refute it, then Adam's transgression could not be imputed to himself. Of course, original sin vanished ; and with it, the foundation on which the whole of Augustinism rested. In the mean time, this refutation must come forth of itself from his view of the original state of Adam, and which view he was first led by this objection more exactly to develop.

Augustine remarked, that the case was entirely different with Adam and angels, from that of fallen man. In the former, God designed to show what freewill is able to do, not while he should leave it without his grace, but while he placed the employment of grace in their freewill : but in the latter, what grace through Christ can effect on the one hand, and on the other, what justice can do. The benefit of grace through Christ, appears in the elect, whom he irresistibly impels to good by this greater and mightier grace. The decision of justice is shown in the reprobate, to whom God does not afford his saving grace, in order that he may show in them what the whole corrupt mass have deserved. Here Augustine amply sets forth the distinction already mentioned between that " aid without which nothing is effected," and that " aid by which something is effected." The first, " that aid without which nothing is done," was afforded to Adam and the angels ; for without it, they could not have persevered in good, even if they had willed it. Perseverance and non-perseverance were left to their freewill, and the grace was given by which they might have had righteousness if they had willed it ; but the use of it God had left to their freewill. The last, " that grace by which something is effected," is given to the elect, by which they could not be otherwise than persevering. Such a grace is given them, not only that they might have righteousness if they would, but that they should also will it, i. e. such grace is afforded as does not depend on their freewill but subjects their freewill to itself. The reason of this difference, Augustine derived from the originally good

state and the subsequent corruption of the human will. While
Adam's will was incorrupt and no desire withstood it, the decision to
persevere was justly left to such goodness and facility for living
right. But since that great freedom is now lost as the punishment
of sin, and the will lies a captive under the yoke of reigning lust,
help is afforded to its weakness, that it may be irresistibly and invincibly impelled by divine grace. God therefore left it to the strongest [Adam] to do what he would ; the weak he so aided that, by his
gift, they should invincibly will the good, and by this aid invincibly
refuse to abandon it.

A still further reason for this difference, but which depends on the
preceding, Augustine here just notices. God designed utterly to
eradicate the pride of human presumption, that no flesh might glory
before him   Man could indeed possess merits ; but he had lost
them ; and lost them by the very means by which he might have
had them, i e by freewill   Hence there only remains for those
who are to be delivered, the grace of the Deliverer   In words, Augustine allowed merits to the elect, i. e. the merits of grace, not of
freewill.   They are imparted to them by that grace which subjects
the will to itself.   But Adam might have had merits, as the holy angels also might have, not of grace, but of freewill, because these
merits arose from freewill, which was aided indeed by grace, but
only so far as to have the power conferred, but not the very doing
and the will itself.

It was on these principles, that Augustine now replied to the objection derived from the fall of Adam against his doctrine of predestination.   Adam fell by his own fault, because he had received from
God that aid " without which nothing is done," without which he
could not persevere and by which he could persevere in good if he
would. If he had not received this, he would have fallen without
his own fault at all.   But those who now do not persevere, are not
without fault, although they have not received from God that aid
without which they cannot persevere, because it is a punishment of
sin, that such aid fails them —But Adam did not receive that aid by
which anything is done (adjutorium quo aliquid fit), in order that
God might be able to show the greatness of his grace and his almighty goodness in the elect.*

* By comparing this condensed view with the extended development that
Augustine has given in the work referred to, the reader will find it perfectly

That there are many gratuitous suppositions in this reasoning of Augustine, is evident; yet he could hardly sustain his system in any other way; and it amply proves his acuteness, that, after once assuming that position, he could defend himself, in so adroit a manner, against all attacks

We now proceed further with the historical narration.

CHAPTER XVIII.

Final adoption of the Augustinian system for all christendom, by the third general council at Ephesus, 431.

By Augustine's zealous exertions, by the violence of the temporal magistracy, by the concurrence of the Romish bishops, and, what must not be wholly overlooked, by a certain disinclination of that period to the improvement of christian ethics, to which Pelagianism manifestly tended, the Augustinian system, about the year 424, was pretty generally received, in public, among the *Latin* church, though many might still find themselves in heart inclined to Pelagianism. During the pontificate of Caelestine, who succeeded Boniface in the holy chair in the year 422, Caelestius appeared once more at Rome and demanded a hearing, in the year 424, or somewhat later. But he was banished from all Italy. Prosper c. Coll. c. 21, Ap. p. 195. There was still also, here and there, a public manifestation. Even in Africa, commotions arose among the monks of Adrumetum, respecting freewill and grace, about the year 426, which caused Augustine to write his books De Gr. et Lib Arb. and De Cor. et Gr. The disturbances which arose at Marseilles, must be noticed in the history of semi-pelagianism.

---

just Indeed much of it is almost a literal translation of diverse phrases there employed by Augustine

From this, as well as from other works of Augustine, it is manifest that he did not suppose that man could be blamed for *commencing* a course of sin, provided he had not at least a *theoretical* ability for holiness ,—nearly if not exactly such an ability as many now ascribe to all sinners—an ability which God upholds, or an *aid*, on which guilt is predicable, *because* holiness is thus rendered *possible ;* but yet an ability by which no good is actually effected without God's *special* grace.—Tr

Nevertheless, the Augustinian doctrine, about the year 424, was the orthodox doctrine in the Latin church.

But it was otherwise in the east Men did not generally seem to have that interest, in the east, for the anthropological part of divinity, which was felt in the west. They contended rather about the relation of the Logos to the Father, and about the two natures in Christ; in short, they busied themselves in speculative questions in theology proper, instead of giving themselves much trouble about man's corruption, freewill, grace, predestination, and thus about anthropological doctrines. Even the *Greek* fathers of the fifth century, a Socrates, a Sozomen, a Theodoret, say not a syllable on the Pelagian controversies Most of the oriental bishops remained neutral, because they felt no interest in the controversy.

Those, however, who declared for either party, declared rather for Pelagius, who in general had many friends in the east. The reasons of their doing this, lay not merely in the fact, that there is so much of the hard and repulsive in Augustine's opinions, and that the uncorrupted moral sense is more in accordance with the doctrine of Pelagius, but also in other relations which it is not difficult to discover. The principles of Pelagius accord better with the opinions of the Greek fathers, than do those of Augustine, which were entirely foreign to the Greek church. And then the orientals would not suffer the African orthodoxy to be imposed upon them, and their opinions to be modeled according to Augustine, with whom they had no connection. The political separation of the east from the west, after the death of Theodosius the Great, also caused the religious controversies of the west to be confined more to the latter; and of the east to the former. Finally, the circumstance that monkery flourished more in the east than in the west, contributed somewhat, perhaps, to a greater approbation of the opinions of the monk Pelagius, than of those of the bishop Augustine, who, though he brought the monkish life into repute in Africa, still looked down with prelatical pride on the monks as laymen Enough, that all the means which Augustine applied to win the east, were ineffectual.

[In addition, however, to the causes just mentioned as inclining the oriental bishops to favor the Pelagians, the influence of Origen and most of the other teachers in the theological school at Alexandria, is of too much importance to pass unnoticed. The general bearing of their doctrines, or, to state the fact more precisely, the main bearing of what they had to say on these anthropological doctrines, was such as to prepare the minds of their pupils and their readers, to reject any system which would even *seem* to countenance the doctrine of heathen *fatality*, or to infringe on man's perfect freedom and accountability. Almost all their efforts on such topics, for two hundred years, were directed to the demolition of such views of fatal necessity and human impotency, with which the heathen world has always been filled. Hence they were led, if not themselves to over-estimate, yet most excessively to *over-preach* man's ability to repent and keep the divine law. And thus, in process of time, (as must ever be the case), the way was prepared for lightly esteeming the almost forgotten doctrines of man's dependence and God's prerogatives. This, however natural, was one of the worst mistakes of the Greek fathers —The Latin ecclesiastical writers came later upon the stage, when (as well as where) there was probably less occasion for bending their chief energies in opposition to heathen fate —Tr.]

Not long after the synod of Carthage in 412, at which Pelagius was first condemned, Augustine sent Paul Orosius, as we have already related, into the east, in order, in union with Jerome, who was then living in a cloister at Bethlehem, to instigate the orientals against Pelagius, who was then gone to Palestine. But Jerome, no more than Orosius, could accomplish this. At the convocation which bishop John of Jerusalem held there in 415, the bishop could not be induced to declare Pelagius a heretic. He would decide the matter by the Bible , but Orosius wished it to be decided according to the Carthaginian synod of 412, and the Augustinian orthodoxy ; to which John could not bring himself. Consequently there was merely an appeal to Rome But this did not suit Orosius. He therefore sought to work upon the metropolitan, Eulogius of Caesarea, by two expelled Gallic bishops, Heros and Lazarus, who were then staying at Jerusalem. Eulogius also held a synod with fourteen bishops, at the close of this year, 415, at Diospolis. But here Pelagius was even declared orthodox. Jerome could now do nothing further than to call this " a miserable synod ;" and the Africans, nothing else but again to condemn Pelagius That Pelagius should afterwards be condemned by a synod at Antioch, at which bishop Theodotus presided, is very improbable, although Marius Mercator, from whom we have an account, but a very imperfect one, of this matter (Ap. p.

72), appeals to a letter, as though in his hands, of Theodotus to the
Romish bishop At least it is remarkable, that neither Augustine
nor any other writer has said a syllable of so important a fact.   According to the account of this same Mercator, Pelagius was also driven
from Jerusalem in consequence of that condemnation ; concerning
which he affirms that he had also in his hands a letter to the Romish
bishop from bishop Praylus of Jerusalem, who had, however, before
declared himself in favor of Pelagius.—Furthermore, Jerome,
(whose letter to Ctesiphon had been refuted by the occidental deacon Anianus), had the mortification of seeing his dialogue against
the Pelagians refuted by an oriental bishop, the renowned Theodore
of Mopseusta in Cilicia.   According to some fragments of his
work, (which was drawn up in five books, and which fragments are
given by Marius Mercator, Op. T. I, and reprinted in the second
part of Valla's edition of Jerome), he agrees with Pelagius, that the
death of the body is no consequence of Adam's sin, but maintains,
that death is the natural way chosen by God to immortality, in which
Adam only preceded us.   This was altogether remarkable, as by
this opinion he would have differed entirely from the orthodox
church —Still even Theodore, after Julian's removal from Cilicia,
pronounced condemnation upon him.

Jerome died, Sept. 30, 420 , and now all seemed lost for Augustinism in the east. Augustine himself appeared now willing to confine his efforts to the west. Unexpectedly, however, a circumstance
occurred, by which Augustine's system received the most valuable
sanction for the east.

Some bishops who were inclined to Pelagianism and who had not
subscribed the epistola tractoria, Julian, Florus, Orontius. and Fabius, had come to Constantinople, about the year 429, where Nestorius had shortly before been partriarch, and they had applied to the
emperor Honorius the younger. Although Atticus, a predecessor of Nestorius, had removed them from Constantinople in 424,
yet Nestorius found no reason for regarding them as heretics, and
therefore had doubts as to excommunicating them. Yet Nestorius
himself was so far from agreeing fully with the Pelagians that on the
contrary, soon after the arrival of those bishops, he defended the doctrine of original sin, in several discourses against the Pelagians   In
the perplexity in which Nestorius found himself with them, and induced perhaps also by the desire of an opportunity to justify himself to the

Romish bishop respecting the suspicion of heterodoxy on the doctrine of the person of Christ, into which Cyril had brought him with Caelestine, he applied to the latter, in several letters, two of which are still extant, and inquired of him the circumstances of his affair with the alleged heretics. Both letters have come to us in a Latin translation and are found, as well as Caelestine's answer, in Mansi IV. 1021 sqq ; and in an abridged form, in the appendix, p. 129 sq. In the first letter, he says : "Julian, indeed, and Florus and Orontius and Fabius, declaring themselves bishops of the western parts, have often approached the most pious and celebrated emperor and bemoaned their case, as orthodox persons suffering persecution in orthodox times," etc. In the other, he says , " Often have I written to your blessedness respecting Julian," etc. Further on, come the remarkable words, " The examination of a pious sect, as you know, Most Rev. Sir, is no trivial thing, nor small is the investigation of those who do this."*—The busy Marius Mercator, in the meantime, without the interposition of Nestorius, had so managed, that Julian and his friends were banished from the city by the imperial mandate.

Caelestine's answer, dated Aug. 11, 430, was not such as Nestorius might have expected. It was written with a bitterness which Nestorius by no means deserved Caelestine gave him to understand his surprise, that he should receive heretics who had already been condemned, and whom his predecessor Atticus had treated as condemned ; that he who declared himself so orthodox on the doctrine of original sin, should hold intercourse with heretics who denied original sin This could not take place without the suspicion of his not thinking altogether differently from them The greatest part of his letter, however, was occupied with the contest in which Nestorius was involved with the metropolitan Cyril of Alexandria, respecting the relation of Christ's divine nature to the human, on which Caelestine had been consulted by Cyril himself, and in respect to which he had declared himself unconditionally in favor of Cyril

This circumstance, as well as several other reasons, shows a combination between the Alexandrian and Romish bishops, in the highest

---

* I am not sure that I give the true sense of this insulated passage, as the words admit of a very different rendering. " Non est, O venerandissime, sicut nosti, res vilis discussio piae sectae, nec parva est probatio eorum qui hoc agunt." Wiggers offers no translation —Tr.

degree probable.   Many traces of their alliance, are elsewhere found in ecclesiastical history.   As Cyril wished to ruin Nestorius, the concurrence of the occidentals, and particularly of the Romish bishop, whom he might justly regard as the representative of the western church, was of the utmost importance to him.   Most probably he now came to an agreement with Caelestine, that himself would take care that the Pelagian system should be condemned in the east, as soon as he would declare against the opinion of Nestorius respecting the doctrine of the person of Christ and condemn it in his synods.   This appears evident from all that occurred at the general council at Ephesus, 431, as well as from the measures which Caelestine took for the condemnation of Nestorianism.   In the council at Ephesus no more than in the whole contest between Cyril and Nestorius, did the discussion concern the Pelagian doctrine. Although Pelagius was ranked in the same class with Nestorius, yet he had nothing in common with him.   The adherents of Caelestius or Pelagius, as well as Nestorius, were condemned ; and the clergy who thought with Caelestius, were deposed. See the doings of the fifth session, and the first and fourth canons of the seventh, at full length in Mansi, Part I. and abridged, in the appendix, p. 135.   Besides this, we see the connection in which Caelestine stood to Cyril, not only from the letter which he sent to Cyril with his delegates to the council—for the Romish bishop had now become too eminent to appear in person at a general council—but also from the insinuations which Cyril made to Caelestine to the prejudice of Nestorius, one consequence of which was the accusation of heresy against Nestorius, which Caelestine had already published previously to the council, 430 ; as also from the secret instructions which Caelestine gave his delegates, to adhere closely to Cyril ; and from many other circumstances. All this is more minutely treated of in the history of the Nestorian controversies. See Walch in the fifth part of his history of heresies —At the close of the letter in which the synod inform Caelestine of what took place, we read this remarkable assertion " After the records of the negociations were read in the holy synod, respecting the deposition ($\varkappa \alpha \vartheta \alpha i \varrho \varepsilon \sigma \varepsilon \iota$) of the unholy Pelagians and Caelestians, Caelestius, Pelagius, Julian, Persidius, Marcellinus, Orontius, and those of the like sentiments, we also believed, that what has been decided by your holiness respecting them, must remain in force, and we all agree with you in declaring them deposed ($\varkappa \alpha \vartheta \eta$-

ρημένους)." Mansı, p. 1337. The terms, καθαίρεσει and καθηρημένους, are not here sufficiently precise, as they at least cannot refer to Pelagius, who was never a clergyman.

Thus Augustinism consequently became the orthodox belief for the whole christian world, by the decision of the universal council at Ephesus, or, properly, of Cyril and Caelestine—for we know that the orientals had no part in the matter. By the zeal of Augustine and a favorable concurrence of several circumstances, this was effected in twenty years It is remarkable enough, that the fall of Nestorius should be decreed in consequence of Pelagianism! Pope Caelestine, in his answer to the synod, March 15, 432, did not neglect to confirm their decrees, and particularly those against the Caelestians; and in a separate letter, he reminded Maximian, the successor of Nestorius, that all who adhered to the Caelestian error, " should be driven from all human society." Ap. p. 135.

Augustine's faith therefore ought now to have been received by the whole christian world. Whether this actually took place, and what further happened, the second period will show.*

As we have now endeavored to exhibit the historical facts in this controversy, as well as the several Augustinian and Pelagian doctrines, in the *pragmatic* manner (pragmatisch), it may facilitate the review of the reader, to collect, in one brief view, the main points of Augustinism and Pelagianism.

Remark.—In order to find a point of union between Pelagianism and Nestorianism, the Pelagians have at one time been accused of the Nestorian error, and at another, Nestorius has been accused of Pelagianism. Both accusations are groundless. How little of a Nestorian Pelagius was, may be seen most plainly from his confession of faith. An objection against the Pelagians in this respect, was never made by Augustine. At least he seems to concede their orthodoxy on the doctrine of the Trinity itself. Ep. 188. When Augustine charged on the Pelagians the consequence that, by their theory of grace as founded on merit, the man Jesus must have deserved, by the goodness of his will, to be the only begotten Son of God, he made this objection to them in order to show the incorrectness of their doctrine by the parodox it afforded How far Augustine was from ascribing this opinion to the Pelagians, may be seen, among

---

* The period of *semi-pelagianism*, of which our author treats in an additional volume.—Tʀ

other passages, from De Cor et Gr. c. 11, where he even says, that no man is so blind in the faith as to set up such a proposition.

It may, however, be readily admitted, that individual Pelagians were likewise Nestorians, or differed from the subsequent orthodoxy respecting the person of Christ. This was true particularly of Leporius. Still he did not do this as a Pelagian; and in this respect the connection between Pelagianism and Nestorianism must be totally denied   And nothing even of this kind, was maintained by Pelagius, Caelestius, and Julian, the proper representatives of Pelagianism. See Walch's History of Heresies, Part IV p. 816, 817.

Nestorius, too, we may venture to regard as no Pelagian in the proper sense, though he, as also all the orientals, might differ from the Augustinian theory, on many points.

CHAPTER XIX.

View of the Augustinian and Pelagian systems, in their main features.

I. Infant Baptism.

Aug.—The baptism of infants as well as of adults, is for the forgiveness of sin. Children have, indeed, committed no actual sins, yet, by original sin, they are under the power of the devil, from which they are freed by baptism. Hence christian children who die before baptism, no more escape positive punishment in the future life, than do all who are not Christians

Pel—The baptism of children takes place, in order to their receiving the benefits of Christianity, and particularly to procure for them the salvation of Christians   Even without baptism, they may obtain salvation in general (salus); but baptism is the necessary condition to the salvation of Christians, or the kingdom of heaven. But by no means is the forgiveness of original sin the object of baptism.

II. Original Sin.

Aug.—By Adam's sin, in whom all men jointly sinned together, sin and the other positive punishments of Adam's sin, came into the world. By it, human nature has been both physically and morally corrupted. Every man brings into the world with him a nature already so corrupt, that he can do nothing but sin The propagation of this quality of his nature, is by concupiscence.

Pel.—By his transgression, Adam injured only himself, not his posterity. In respect to his moral nature, every man is born in precisely the same condition in which Adam was created. There is therefore no original sin.

III. Freewill.

Aug.—By Adam's transgression, the freedom of the human will has been entirely lost. In his present corrupt state, man can will and do only evil.

Pel.—Man's will is free. Every man has the power to will and to do good, as well as the opposite. Hence it depends on himself, whether he will be good or evil

IV Grace.

Aug.—If, nevertheless, man, in his present state, wills and does good, it is merely the work of grace. It is an inward, secret, and wonderful operation of God upon man. It is a preceding as well as an accompanying work. By preceding grace, man attains faith, by which he comes to an insight of good, and by which power is given him to will the good. He needs cooperating grace for the performance of every individual good act. As man can do nothing without grace, so he can do nothing against it. It is irresistible. And as man by nature has no merit at all, no respect at all can be had to man's moral disposition, in imparting grace, but God acts according to his own freewill.

Pel.—Although by freewill, which is a gift of God, man has the capacity of willing and doing good, without God's special aid, yet, for the *easier* performance of it, God revealed the law ; for the easier performance, the instruction and example of Christ aid him ; and for the easier performance, even the supernatural operations of grace are imparted to him. Grace, in the most limited sense (gracious influence), is given to those only who deserve it by the faithful employment of their own powers. But man can resist it.

V. Predestination and Redemption.

Aug.—From eternity, God made a free and unconditional decree to save a few from the mass that was corrupted and subjected to damnation. To those whom he predestinated to this salvation, he gives the requisite means for the purpose. But on the rest, who do not belong to this small number of the elect, the merited ruin falls. Christ came into the world and died for the elect only.

Pel.—God's decree of election and reprobation, is founded on prescience. Those, of whom God foresaw that they would keep his commands, he predestinated to salvation ; the others to damnation. —Christ's redemption is general. But those only need his atoning death, which have actually sinned   *All*, however, by his instruction and example, may be led to higher perfection and virtue.

These were the grand principles in the systems of Augustine and the Pelagians. We cannot but perceive the great consistency of each system. If one doctrine is adopted, all the doctrines must be adopted ; for they stand in indissoluble connection   In Augustine's system, the doctrine of original sin is to be regarded as peculiarly the central point, from which his doctrines of grace and predestination necessarily spring. Predestination forms as it were the keystone of the structure, from which the theory of redemption may be regarded as a corollary.—The doctrine of Pelagius, too, is distinguished for its consistency,—or, as I have not undesignedly expressed it, the *Pelagian* doctrine, since several opinions, which incontrovertibly lie in the grand principles of Pelagius, cannot be historically exhibited as announced by him, though Caelestius and other Pelagians expressly acknowledged them.

As man is not by nature corrupt, but finds himself in the same state in which Adam was created, he needs no special grace in order to be saved   It is not, however, inconsistent with this, that he may thereby obtain a higher degree of morality, and consequently a higher degree of felicity.

By this system, redemption must be general, and acquire a more comprehensive import than it could have according to Augustine's assumption, which always confined it to the elect few. And even these, according to Augustine's view, not the bare example and doctrine of Jesus could ever induce to good, if the irresistible inworking of divine grace was not added for each individual act

Predestination, according to the doctrine of Pelagius, acquired a better import, as not casting the holiness and justice of God into the shade, and also not impairing the freedom of man. By predestination founded on foreknowledge, it depends on man, how he shall act; and God can by no means be charged with injustice, when he suffers the consequences of transgression to fall on him who does not act according to the moral law.

If we justly acknowledge the consistency of the Augustinian system, particularly as it is displayed and developed in the later anti-pelagian works, yet we cannot thereby maintain the consistency of *Augustine himself.* He sometimes departed, as we have seen, from his own principles, as set forth in his theory, when applying them to practice. So strove his just moral sense to lead to life again, where an austere theory of the school stood in contradiction to it.

But the question now arises, how Augustine and Pelagius endeavored to *prove* their opinions, or what were the grounds on which they relied. By the consistency of each system, the question turns mainly on the reasons by which each justified the main position on which his other opinions rested, or from which they could be derived as consequences. And these positions were, with Augustine, the doctrine of *original sin;* and with Pelagius, that of *the uncorrupted state of human nature.*

[We may, however, with perhaps equal propriety, affirm the doctrine of *gracious influences* to lie at the foundation of each system. For if not the first in the order of philosophical speculation when reasoning from cause to effect, yet it is first when reasoning from effect to cause. And in all probability, it is the first, in the order of time, that is established in a large majority of minds, and the one from which they are respectively led to their conclusions on the other kindred topics. Thus one man first becomes convinced, from the bible or from self-inspection and effort, that he is dependent on the direct agency of God for a change of heart and for the work of righteousness, and is hence prepared to adopt strong views of original depravity; while another comes to a different conclusion in respect to *his* moral dependence, and is thence led to adopt different views of man's native state. And surely the doctrine of gracious influences, or man's *need* of them, is the more immediately practical point. It is here that the two systems are found in the most frequent and severe collision, and put themselves forth in the most tangible results, both in the style of preaching and the modes of religious action.—Tr.]

The reasons which each employed, were partly philosophical and partly derived from the bible. On the latter, and particularly on Paul's epistle to the Romans, Augustine chiefly relied to prove the main position of his whole system, the doctrine of original sin

---

CHAPTER XX.

Augustine's reasons for his theory.

When we here speak of the scripture passages on which Augustine based his theory, it will of course be understood, that all the passages cannot be examined which he occasionally adduced for his several opinions, but only the chief texts to which he very often recurred in his way.

The main scripture proof of original sin, Augustine found in the epistle to the Romans, and he must have found the more of it, the less he was of an exegetical scholar and the less he knew of the original language of the New Testament.

Romans 5: 12, he used as the chief passage. He took it in the Latin translation "By one man, sin entered into the world, and death by sin, and so hath passed through unto all men, *in whom all have sinned* (et ita in omnes homines pertransivit, in quo omnes peccaverunt)." In this he believed he found the most complete proof for his original sin, propagating itself by generation. De Pec. Mer. I. 8 sqq. In c. 9, it is said, among other things, "He, in whom all die, besides being an example to those who voluntarily transgress the Lord's commands, infected in himself, with the occult plague of his carnal concupiscence, all who come from his stock. Hence entirely, and from no other cause, does the apostle say, By one man," etc. Augustine understood the one man to be Adam, and the death, bodily death. Before the verb *passed through* (pertransivit), he supplied *sin and death*, because he could not think of punishment without crime. Op. Imp. II. 63. The phrase *in whom* (in quo, *ἐφ' ᾧ*), which he chose to refer to Adam, he took literally, and supposed by it, that we all existed in Adam, and therefore sinned together with him. C. d. Epp. Pel. IV. 4. " By the evil will of that individual," says Augustine in quoting that passage from Paul, " all men sinned in him, as all were that one, from whom every individual has consequently derived original sin to himself" De Nupt. et Conc. II. 5. " In that one all have sinned, as all died in him. For those who were to be many in themselves out of him, were then one in him. That sin, therefore, would be his only, if no one had proceeded from him. But now no one is free from his fault, in whom was the common nature." Ep. 186. c. 6. According to the second canon of the general council at Carthage, 418, the Augustinian explanation of that passage of Paul, was even declared the orthodox explanation, by which explanation it contained a proof of original sin.

From the comparison, also, which Paul instituted in the following verses, between the consequences of Adam's sin and Christ's merits, Augustine argued in support of his original sin, the guilt of the Adamitic sin (reus peccati Adamitici). " Death reigned from Adam to Moses, even in those who had not sinned after the similitude of Adam's transgression " These words Augustine explained thus : The imputation of Adam's sin concerned those too who had not sinned, like Adam, by their own will, and transgressed a command of God. Or he would even understand it thus, (which explanation he declares, in another place, to be still better) : The imputation of Adam's sin concerns also those before the law, who had not sinned, " because there was in their members the likeness of Adam's transgression ;"—so that the words, *in the likeness of Adam's transgression*, contained the reason why death has reigned even over those who were not sinners, i e. even those who had not intentionally sinned. *Transgression* (praevaricatio) he took, as did Julian, for violation of law, and regarded it as one " species of sin ," so that sin (peccatum) indicates the *genus*, and transgression (praevaricatio), one species of sin.

This *transgression*, in addition to original sin, must first have occurred *after* the Mosaic law. For this view, he appealed to Rom. 4: 15: " Where there is no law, there is no *transgression*." Op. Imp. II. 217, 218. Comp. 185. Consequently, a *transgression* was indeed committed by Adam, (who violated, not a written command,

35

but one given immediately by God), and by those who lived after
the Mosaic law, but not by those who lived between Adam and
Moses

The variation of many Latin and some Greek manuscripts, which,
without the negative read, *who sinned*, caused Augustine no difficulty. For even then, the passage contained for him a good proof
of the imputation of Adam's sin. He explained it thus : " Who
sinned in him, that they should be created like him, as men from
man, so sinners from a sinner, those who were to die from one who
was to die, those condemned from one condemned."

And these other assertions of the apostle, too, " For the offence
of one many are dead , judgment by one to condemnation ; for
one's offence death reigned by one ; by one's offence unto all men
to condemnation,"—these, to Augustine, were illustrious proof-texts
from which to educe his original sin, to which all men are subject
and by which all deserve damnation. De Pec. Mer. I 11 sqq. Ep.
157. c 3

Also the words in Gen. 2: 17, In the day ye eat of it, (i e of the
tree of knowledge of good and evil), ye shall die the death, which
he referred (De Civ. Dei, XIII. 12) as well to temporal as to spiritual and eternal death, contained in his view a proof that the necessity for temporal death for men entered when Adam sinned, and on
this account he was excluded from the tree of life Op Imp. VI **30.**
God could not say to the sinner, " Earth thou art and to earth shalt
thou go," if he would have died as to the body without transgression. I. 68 : VI. 23, 27. Also from Rom. 8 10, " The body is
dead because of sin, and the spirit is life because of righteousness,"
Augustine inferred that bodily death is a consequence of Adam's
sin, which God annexed as a punishment. De Pec Mer. I 4. He
however allows (Retract I. 26), that he earlier understood this passage wrong, and afterwards discovered, that the body is called dead,
" because it now has a necessity of dying which it had not before
sin " With this he compares 1 Cor. 15. 21, 22. " By one man
death, and by one man the resurrection of the dead. As in Adam
all die, so in Christ shall all be made alive," and other declarations
of the apostle pertaining to this topic. Ep 157 c. 3.

For the pains of parturition as a punishment of Adam's sin, he refers to Gen. 3: 16. " Multiplying I will multiply thy sorrows ;" and
this he explains as meaning, " I will cause them to be many."
Op Imp. VI 25, 26

Further, in support of his theory of original sin and of the moral freedom of the will as lost by Adam's fall and of evil passions remaining to be resisted after repentance, Augustine adduces Rom 7· 14—25. To Paul as speaking in the name of himself and the saints who contended against fleshly lusts, he refers the whole passage, and particularly the words, " I am carnal, sold under sin—for I know that in me, that is in my flesh, dwelleth no good —I see another law in my members, warring against the law of my mind and leading me captive under the law of sin which is in my members.—O wretched man, who shall deliver me from the body of this death." Still here, too, Augustine does not deny, that he once misunderstood this passage and referred it to impenitent men, of whom and of himself in his impenitent state, Paul thus expressed himself C Jul VI 23; Ep. 157. c. 3; Retract. I. 26; II. 1. The words, *body of this death*, he also refers to the necessity of death, which is a punishment of Adam's sin, a disease which we contract at our generation. De Gen ad Lit. IX 10.

The objection which might be brought against the justice of his representation of the entire destitution of good in man, from the words, " To will is present with me, but how to perform what is good, I find not," he endeavored to avoid by indeed a rather forced interpretation of his *To perform good*, he explained, *to be free from all lusts* " Perfect good" he considered as consisting in there being no evil desire at all, but " imperfect good," in our not following an existing evil desire. But the willing was an effect of preceding grace. Op. Imp. VI 9. According to this exposition, then, Paul said : " I am not indeed subject to base desire, but the base desire itself is not extinguished." The declaration in verse 15, " What I do, I know not," Augustine explained by, " What I do, I approve not, consent not to." De Nupt. et Conc. I. 29 ; C d. Epp. Pel l. 10, 11.—From the words " Wretched man I," he argued against the Pelagians, that before Adam's sin, there was no concupiscence. Op. Imp. VI. 14.

The passage in Eph 2 3, " We were by nature children of wrath even as others," could not but be very welcome to him Punishment must presuppose guilt ; and whence could this be by nature, if it came not from Adam ? With this passage, he connected many parallel passages, even from the Old Testament apocrypha, from which to prove that we are all subject to the wrath of God through

Adam's sin. " Of this wrath, says the prophet Jeremiah, Cursed be the day in which I was born Of this wrath, said the holy Job, Perish the day in which I was born. Of this wrath, said he again (c. xiv), For man born of a woman, is of short life and full of irasci-bility Like a flower of the grass, he doth fall; and like a shadow he fleeth and shall not stand. Hast thou not also caused his care, and made him to enter into judgment in thy sight ? For who shall be pure from filth ? not even one, though his life on earth be but of one day. Of this wrath, says the book of Ecclesiasticus, All flesh wax-eth old like a garment; for it is the decision from of old (testamen-tum a saeculo), thou shalt die the death. And it likewise says, The commencement of sin is from the woman, and on account of her, we all die. And in another place : Great occupation is created for every man and a heavy yoke upon the sons of Adam, from the day of exit from their mother's belly to the day of burial in the mother of all. Of this wrath Ecclesiastes says, Vanity of vanities, and all things are vanity. What abundance to man in all his labor in which he labors under the sun ? Of this wrath is the apostolical declara-tion, Every creature is subject to vanity.—From this wrath of God, no one is freed if he is not reconciled to God by the Mediator. Hence even the Mediator himself says," (properly, however, John the Baptist), " He that believeth not the Son, shall not have life, but the wrath of God abideth on him —Of this the Apostle speaks when he says, When we were yet sinners, Christ died for us ; much more, being justified now by his blood, we shall be safe from wrath by him," etc. C. Jul. VI 24 Besides those already quoted, he ad-duced as proof passages for original sin (De Nupt et Conc. II. 29), Ex. 20. 5; Ps. 51. 7; 144. 4, 39 6 ; Zech 3. 4, (De Pec. Mer. II. 3), Ps. 143 2, " No one living shall be justified in thy sight "—Au-gustine even found a proof for original sin in the children of the So-domites being consumed with the parents, and in God's sometimes commanding the destruction of children with their parents. Op. Imp VI. 23 ; IV. 128.

As proof of the corrupt state of man's nature being propagated *by generation*, Augustine employed a passage from the Book of Wisdom, (12: 10, 11), the authority of which he defended against the objections of the Massaliens. " For if the seed itself is not cor-rupted, why is it said, in the Book of Wisdom, Not being ignorant that their nation is vile, and their wickedness natural, and that their thought could not be changed forever; for their seed was cursed from the beginning?" De Nupt et Conc. II. 8   Here, as well as in Op. Imp. III. 11; IV. 129, he refers the expressions *natural wickedness and seed cursed from the beginning*, to man's nature being corrupted by Adam's sin and propagated by generation

Also circumcision under the Old Testament, which Augustine regarded as a sacrament which baptism supplied the place of in the New Testament, was a proof to him of original sin   "To perish from his people," in Gen. 17. 14, he understood of eternal damnation.   Such a punishment should not have been affixed to the neglect of circumcision on the eighth day, if human nature had not been corrupt. De Pec. Orig. 30. Comp c. Jul VI 7; Op. Imp. II. 201.

That man's freewill was lost by Adam's sin, Augustine endeavored to prove from John 8. 36, "If the Son shall make you free, then ye shall be free indeed.   How can Julian attribute to freewill the power of living right, since the sons of men do not live right, unless they become the sons of God?" Op Imp. I 94.   Near this, he refers to Rom. 6. 20 sq ·   "When ye were the servants of sin, ye were free from righteousness   What fruit therefore had ye then in those things of which ye are now ashamed? For the end of those things is death.   But now, freed from sin, but made the servants of God, ye have your fruit in sanctification, and the end eternal life."   And also, John 1 12, "As many as received him, to them gave he power to become the sons of God"   Here he indulged the remark, destructive of all freewill, "In a good man, nothing can be free, if the Redeemer does not make it free.   A bad man, on the contrary, possesses freewill for evil."   Augustine also inferred the want of freewill from the words of Paul, Rom 7. 15, 19, "I do not what I will, but what I hate I do.   I do not the good which I will, but the evil which I will not, that I do." Op. Imp. I. 91.   To Augustine, who knew not how to enter into the language and spirit of the ancient world, Old Testament passages, in which all the intentions and acts of men are referred immediately to God, must have contained the total annihilation of human freedom. De Gr. et Lib. Arb. 20.

That concupiscence is evil, Augustine sought to prove, in opposition to Julian, from 1 John 2: 16, where it is said, "The concupiscence of the flesh is not from the Father." Op. Imp. IV. 69.

So much for the *scripture* proofs which Augustine used for the purpose of establishing from the bible his theory of original sin and the loss of freewill by the fall. But he also called experience to his help in proving both the moral and physical ruin of man. " Why is the nature of mortals more inclined to sin, if original sin has done nothing?" Op. Imp. V. 48. " When you (Julian) say, that no sin is to be imputed to infants, you make God unjust, who has imposed a heavy yoke upon them from the day of exit from the mother's belly. Which if the scriptures had not said, yet who is so blind in mind as not to see, that the misery of the human race begins with the weepings of infancy?" II 119 " Your God, therefore, by so many and so great evils which children suffer, will lose either justice or omnipotence or the very care of human affairs." I. 49.

And to the philosophic mind, Augustine also endeavored to make intelligible the possibility of the propagation of Adam's sin to his posterity; and this partly by allowing original sin to be propagated by concupiscence, and partly by assuming, that we all existed in Adam, or as he also expressed himself, in allusion to Heb. 7: 10, all were in the loins of Adam. Of concupiscence, we have already spoken minutely. Respecting the view of an existence of the whole human race in Adam, (in which Augustine was perhaps confirmed by the assumption of the *realists* of the universal idea, " human nature"), a few of the weightier passages from his writings, deserve here to be quoted.

[It has been urged that, in philosophy, Augustine belonged to the school of the *realists*, who held " that all abstract conceptions have something in actual existence which corresponds to them,"—that he derived such views from the Platonic writers, of whom he had been so fond,—and that this system of philosophy had a material effect in leading him to the notion of the whole human race, or the whole of" human nature," as existing in Adam, in a generic way, or according to the " universal idea" of man See Ch. Spec. IV. 291.—Tr.]

" In Adam all have sinned, as all were that one man " De Pec. Mer. I 10 " Those are not condemned who have not sinned, since that sin has passed from one to all, in which *one* all have sinned in common, previously to the personal sins of each one as an individual." Ep. 194, c. 6. " In respect to the origin of the seed from which all were to spring, all were in that individual, and all these were *he*, none of whom as yet existed individually. Agreea-

bly to this seminal origin, Levi is also said to have been in the loins
of his father Abraham —When in respect to his substance, he did not
yet exist, still, as respects the relation of seed, it is not falsely nor
idly said, that he was there and was tithed," etc. Op. Imp. IV. 104.
" In respect to seed, all were in the loins of Adam when he was condemned, and hence he was not condemned without them." V. 12.
We all, who were to spring from Adam by fleshly lust, were in the
loins of Adam. Hence Augustine also said that, " by right of semination and germination," Adam's sin is ours. 1. 48. " What is done in
each one by the force of habit, (which some of the learned have said
is according to nature), is done by the penal force of that highest
and greatest sin of the first man, in all who were in his loins and
were to spring from his concupiscence, seeing the human race are
propagated." V 59. " When that pair received the divine sentence of condemnation, the whole human race were in the first man,
which by the woman were to pass into posterity ; and what the man
became, not in consequence of his creation but of his sin and punishment, *that* he begat, so far as the origin of sin and death is concerned." De Civ. Dei, XIII. 3. " We were all in that one, as we
were all that one who fell into sin by the woman, who was made
from him before sin. Not as yet was the form created and distributed to us singly, in which we were individually to live ; but the nature was now seminal, from which we were to be propagated. This
being now vitiated on account of sin and bound by the chain of death
and justly condemned, man of a different condition was not to be
born of man. And accordingly, from the bad use of freewill, has
arisen the series of this calamity, which, by a connection of miseries,
is leading the human race from a depraved origin, as from a corrupt root, to the destruction of the second death, which has no end
except for those only who are freed by the grace of God." XIII. 14.
" What else is every earthly man, as to his origin, but Adam ? "
Retract. 1. 15.

How unsatisfactory, however, is the assumption of our sinning in
Adam, how absurd to admit a sin before there was a will, or to admit a will before the person existed to possess it, was most strikingly
shown by Julian. Op. Imp. IV 104.

On the supposition that we all existed in Adam, the philosophical
question could not be overlooked respecting the origin and propagation of the soul How Augustine, being here perplexed by the ob-

jections of the Pelagians, preferred to assume the part of an inquirer, and not to declare himself dogmatically, as at other times he was so ready to do, we have already seen in Chap. VII. But to which hypothesis Augustine *inclined*, and must incline, according to the spirit of his system, must here be shown somewhat more particularly.

The soul either exists before its union with the body (preexistentism), or it is created by God at the same time with the body (creationism or coexistentism), or it springs from physical generation (traducianism, evolution system). These are the three principal hypotheses on the origin of the soul, each of which had its advocates and its opponents before and at the time of Augustine.

That the soul exists before its union with the body, was a notion commonly attributed by the fathers to Origen. Augustine could not possibly have relished it; and it must also have been generally offensive to the orthodoxy of that time, because presented as the opinion of Origen * In his book on freewill (III 20, 21), Augustine does not indeed directly reject the opinion of the soul's existing somewhere before its connection with the body, but leaves the truth of it undecided. Comp. Ep. 143; 166. c. 3; De Gen ad Lit VI 9. But in Ep. 217 c. 5, he represents the rejection of preexistentism as a principle of the catholic church In Ep 190. c 1, he declares against the opinion that the human soul comes into this corruptible body as a punishment for a bad life already led · "For the apostle says (Rom. 9 11), while speaking of the twins of Rebecca, that they, not yet born, had neither done good nor evil." This opinion of the body as a prison for the soul on account of transgressions committed before their union, Augustine also rejects in Ep. 164 c. 7; 166. c 9.

As, then, he rejected the preexistence of the soul, he could not have regarded it as a part of Deity. "We do not believe it to be a part but a creature of God." Ep. 190. c 1; Ad Orosium contra Priscillianistas et Originistas, c. 2, 4; De Civ Dei, X 31; De Gen. ad Lit. VII. 1.

The creation of the soul at the same time with the body (creation-

---

* Origen supposes all created spirits to have existed and to have fallen, more or less, in a previous state, and to be now in diverse degrees of just and salutary punishment, according to their several degrees of guilt, from the worst devil to the least erring human or angelic spirit; and on this principle, he accounts for all the diversity we find in the condition of men —TR

ism), he with Jerome was shy of admitting, as then the condemnation of infants dying before baptism, and having committed no sin, seemed to him unjust, and he became embarrassed with his original sin His language to Oceanus (Ep. 180 § 2), is remarkable "It is justly asked, (provided it is true that a new soul is created out of nothing for each child that is born), how such an innumerable multitude of infant souls, which God knows will leave the body without baptism before the years of understanding, and before they can comprehend or do anything just or unjust, should righteously be consigned to damnation, by him with whom there is no unrighteousness. On this point, *it is not necessary to say more, since you know what I would, or rather what I would not say. What I have said, I think to be enough to a wise man.*"* In Ep. 166, Augustine sets forth minutely and strongly the difficulties that lie in creationism, particularly in regard to original sin, which he considered as immovable. Why are so many thousand infant souls lost, that die without the indulgence of baptism ? Whence, in the case of the death of the newborn infant, has the soul brought on itself the guilt by which it is eternally damned ? — "Where, whence, or when have the souls of infants begun to have the desert of damnation, if they are new, unless you would make God, (or else a nature which God has not created), either the author of their sins or of the damnation of the innocent ?" Ep. 190. c. 4. Comp. De Gen. ad Lit. X., which was written long before the commencement of the Pelagian controversies.

To the traducianism of the soul, (which was admitted by Tertullian and, according to Jerome's account, Ep 126, by most of the oriental bishops), Augustine did not indeed directly subscribe, because he could not escape the difficulties that beset it, especially in regard to materialism Ep. 190. c 4. But how strongly he was inclined to this, may be seen from the words already quoted from his epistle to Oceanus And certainly the Augustinian original sin can be more easily comprehended, if we allow nothing in man but what has sprung from the seed of Adam, than if, with the creationists, we suppose the soul created by God out of nothing at the time when it is clothed with the body. How could Adam's guilt be imputed to the soul, if it in no manner originated from Adam, but was newly

---

* Augustine, however, begs his correspondent to let him know it, if he has learned anything further by which this question can be solved.—TR.

created by God in each instance ?   Indeed, by his theory of the propagation of sin by generation (peccatum ex traduce), and by which
he would consequently regard *physical* generation as a moral evil,
Augustine could scarcely think at all of the propagation of the soul
otherwise than by generation.   He allowed, as above shown, the
poison of sin to be communicated through sensual lust in coition.
But surely the poison of sin could not be communicated, in any con-
ceivable way, to the body, but only to the soul.   Hence he says (De
Anima et ejus Origine, I 13), " We ask, why the soul is condemned
to receive original sin, if the soul is not derived from that one soul
which sinned in the first father of the human race ?"   In this sense,
he declared before, (De Gen ad Lit X 23) I should regard the
reasons for both opinions (creationism and traducianism), as equal,
if infant baptism did not give the preponderance to the opinion, that
souls are begotten by the parents. Comp 11   He however allows
that the propagation of souls by generation, cannot be proved from
the bible De Pec Mer. III 10 ; De An et ejus Orig. I 18 , Ep
1.4.   But he also shows (Ep. 19`), that creationism can no more
be proved from the bible ; and particularly in opposition to Vincentius Victor (De An et ej. Orig. 1), he shows that the passages of
the bible which the latter had adduced against the propagation of
the soul by generation, do not prove the point.

Finally Augustine everywhere maintained the immateriality of
the soul, in the strongest terms, together with its immortality   Nay,
he even wrote four books On the Soul and its Origin, in which he
assailed the materialism of the soul which Victor defended.   In this
work, he established its incorporeal nature , respecting which he
explains himself, in order to avoid all logomachy, in the second
chapter of Ep. 166   If one would call that a body which exists by
itself, or is a substance, or would confine the idea of the incorporeal
to the immutable, then he conceded that the soul is to be denominated a body.   But he denied to the soul all those attributes which pertain to bodies in the visible world   The soul has its own peculiar
nature, which is constituted of a substance more noble than the elements of the mass of the world.   It cannot be truly conceived of
under the idea of corporeal images which we receive by the senses ;
but can only be understood through the mind and felt through the
life.

Whether, however, the immateriality of the soul, as Augustine

conceived of it, was anything but a more refined materialism, is a
question which cannot be directly answered in the negative. For,
(to adduce only one passage, from Ep. 190 4), he doubted " utrum
semen animae sua quadam occulta et invisibili via seorsum ex patre
currat in matrem cum fit conceptus in femina " This seems to lead
to a " spiritual substance" which afterwards had so many defenders
among the scholastics—an idea of a spirituality which, however refined, always savored of materialism! Besides, that an idea of a
spiritual substance (materia spiritualis), as Augustine called it, was
not strange to him, may be seen from De Gen. ad Lit. VII 6 sq.,
where he shows its difficulty.

By the assumption therefore of the propagation of original sin by
sensual lust and of an existence of the whole human race in Adam,
Augustine endeavored to render the *possibility* of the propagation
of his original sin, comprehensible to the philosophic mind. He
also found an example in experience, as bodily diseases are propagated from parents to children, and it may be said of the latter that
they are *recompensed* with these diseases " If any one," says Augustine, " brings the gout upon himself by intemperance and transmits
the same to his children, as often happens, is it not properly said that
this vice passes into them from the parent? and that they also did
this in the parent (ipsos quoque hoc in parente fecisse)? because
when he did it [i e contracted the gout by intemperance], they
were in him and so they and he were as yet one They therefore
did it, not by action as individual men, but as already acting semin-
ally (fecerunt ergo, non actione hominum, sed ratione jam semi-
num). That, therefore, which is occasionally found in diseases of
the body, took place in that ancient and great sin of the one progenitor, by which human nature was corrupted. This He knew to have
been done who said, (by the clearest declaration, which you strive to
obscure), By one man sin entered into the world," etc. Op. Imp.
II. 177 —Augustine also thought it not improbable that the sins of
ancestors *universally* are imputed to their descendants. Enchir. c.
46, 47.

[On so startling a topic as the one brought to view in the last quotation, and still more strongly in the last remark of our author, the
reader may well demand a further citation of Augustine's own language. And this I shall give a little more fully than is needful barely

for this topic, as additional light will thus be reflected on some other questions, and also on Augustine's general mode of thinking.

In the passage last referred to, he says : " In that one sin, (which has entered the world by one man and passed into all men, and on account of which infants are baptized), *many* sins may be understood, if this one be divided as it were into its several members. For there is also pride there, because man delighted rather in his own authority than that of God ; and impiety (sacrilegium), because he did not believe God , and homicide, because he plunged himself into death ; and spiritual fornication, because the integrity of the human mind was corrupted by serpentine suasion ; and theft, because the forbidden food was taken ; and avarice, because he sought more than ought to satisfy him ; and whatever else may be found, on diligent consideration, in this one offence   And it is not without probability said (non improbabiliter dicitur), that children are also liable (obligari) for the sins, not only of the first pair, *but also of those from whom they are born*. For, that divine sentence, *I will visit the sins of the parents upon the children*, certainly holds them before they begin by regeneration to belong to the New Testament : which Testament was predicted when it was said by Ezekiel, that the children should not receive the sins of their fathers, nor should there be any longer that parable in Israel, The fathers have eaten sour grapes, etc.   For each one is regenerated in order that he may be absolved from whatever of sin is born with him   But sins which are afterwards committed by wrong doing, *may be healed by repentance*, just as we also see to take place after baptism.   And accordingly regeneration was instituted only because generation is vicious ; and that so far, that one even born in lawful wedlock, could say, In iniquities was I conceived and in sins did my mother nourish me in the womb   Nor did he say, In iniquity or sin, though this also might be truly said ; but he preferred to say, In iniquities and sins.   Because in that one which has passed into all men, and is so great that by it human nature is changed and converted to the necessity of death, are found, as shown above, many sins.   And *other sins of parents*, though they cannot thus change nature, yet *bind the children in guilt*, unless free grace and divine compassion relieve them.   But respecting the sins of the other parents, the progenitors from Adam down to one's own immediate father, it may not improperly be debated, whether the child is implicated in the evil acts and multiplied original faults of *all*, so that each one is the worse in proportion as he is the later ; or that, in respect to the sins of their parents, God threatens posterity to the third and fourth generation, because, *by the moderation of his compassion*, he does not further extend his anger in respect to the faults of progenitors, lest those on whom the grace of regeneration is not conferred, should be pressed with too heavy a load in their own eternal damnation, if they were compelled to contract, by way of origin (originaliter), the sins of *all* their preceding parents from the commencement of the human race, and to suffer the *punishment due for them* Whether, on so great a subject, anything else can or cannot be found, by a more diligent reading and scrutiny of the scriptures, I dare not hastily affirm !''

And here, indeed, we might well suppose the good father, consecutive and undaunted as he generally was, must be brought to the solemn and fearful pause in which this extract leaves him —There are also other grounds of hesitation in addition to this frightful accumulation of guilt and woe   For this consecutive reasoner would here have to reflect on the principle upon which alone he considered us justly liable at all for Adam's first offence, namely, that we acted in him, and therefore the guilt is truly ours. No " *foreign* sins" are imputed, was his steady and indignant reply to that perpetual objection to imputation.   Of course, then, if we are to bear the sins of our immediate ancestors, it must be, in his view, on the ground of our existing in them and sinning with them, just as we existed in Adam and shared in his first transgression   And so in fact he did view the case as appears from his declaration in respect to inheriting the gout, etc.   And if this is true of our more immediate ancestors, those of the last three or four generations, it is equally true of the whole line from Adam to us   How, then, could God pardon *any* portion of this mass of our transgression, without a compliance in the individual with any of the *conditions* of pardon ? And again ; if he could remit some sins because the mass was so great, why not all, so far as principle is concerned ?—and thus we be absolved from the guilt of even the original sin itself.

This was one hard and complicated difficulty involved in the fearful premises   But there would be found yet another. For if we have really been sinning in our ancestors, from generation to generation, we must have been sinning, not merely in one, but in many persons at the same time. For, as a man has two parents, four grand-parents, eight great-grand-parents, etc., the time was when each one of us was at the same instant in a great many places and committing sins in the persons of a great many individuals. How strange a view must this have presented to Augustine of that doctrine of the traducianism of the soul, which has before been noticed as meeting with at least some favorable regard from him;—the soul in its descent from Adam, divided into so many parts—and these all to meet again, at the proper time and in their own destined body, to constitute " *the individual*" person and to " live their own life !"

Nor was this all which might well hold Augustine in check, at such a stage in the theory then before his mind. The fearful matter which he more distinctly notices, is the *amount* of sin and woe thus resting, if *all* unremitted, on a single soul Fearful thought ! For, as Augustine himself had doubtless eight great-grand-parents, so, tracing back his pedigree for only thirty generations or one thousand years, according to this law of geometrical progression, he would find, theoretically, a single generation of his own ancestors amounting to no less than 1,099,958,224, and himself accumulating all the sin which they were committing from day to day. *Theoretically*, I say, his progenitors *might* amount to that number, if so many progenitors were then on earth Suppose him, however, to make all due allowance for the actual deviations from this law of geometrical progression in the case (and from the fact that so many never lived at one time)—but, on the other hand, to carry back the series to the time of the building of Babel—and might he not well fear he should find about the whole weight of that tower of guilt, resting on himself!

Nor is this all. For what would rest on him, would likewise press, with all its force, on every other descendant of those impious builders,—increased, too, by all the other sins that would thus come on each one from his whole line of ancestry

And again, one would have, as he turned his eye on his own posterity, to regard every sin that himself committed, as virtually committed by each one that should ever descend from him—millions upon millions as they might become—and his own repentance could not stop the descending tide !

All this might indeed be regarded by Augustine as showing the frightful nature of sin—or rather of that " *law* of sin and death" which his theory assumed. But still no one can wonder that he should here pause and tremble, and finally leave the question without daring positively to affirm that each impenitent sinner will actually have to bear forever the concentrated guilt of all the millions of his progenitors. Nevertheless Augustine appears to have had no doubt that this whole guilt actually belongs to each, and that it will be through the mere mercy of God if each one does not have to suffer to the full extent.

But while such appears to have been the view of Augustine on this fearful topic, as is sufficiently manifest from the passages already cited and a few others which might be adduced, still it is a topic on which he by no means delighted to dwell, and which he but rarely mentions. Perhaps he did not, in this connection, extend his contemplations on the law of consanguinity so as to see how, on his theory, a single individual might be the child of a whole nation, and thus concentrate in himself all the guilt which that nation had committed some ages back ,—and again, how he might become in turn the father of that nation, some ages forward, and thus pour the whole tide of his collected guilt into its future millions :—or, how baneful would be the intermarriage of a single foreigner, thus diffusing the guilt of his whole race through another whole race —or how, (if it is the duty of men to prevent instead of increasing even those sins which possibly God in his compassion may not punish), it would become a duty of the highest order to restrict intermarriages to the nearest possible kindred, and thus brutalize mankind —or, finally, how it would, if universally adopted, even extinguish our race by the force it would lend to the doctrine of universal celibacy.

However much Augustine would favor the celibacy of the clergy, and of a portion of the rest of the human race for monks and nuns, he would be horror-struck at the thought that marriage itself should cease and man become extinct in the world. And equally revolting to his mind would be the thought that our race should be continued only as the " seed of evil doers." But why would not his doctrine of the propagation of sin, especially on this great scale, make it virtually the greatest possible crime against God, for one knowingly and intentionally to be the means of adding another human being to the long line of his sinful race and thus, by this very addition, to double as it were the whole amount of sin which himself had either committed or inherited. If sin is really an evil at all, aside from the punishment that it actually brings, or in other words, if it really de-

serves any punishment, and if it is only the *mercy* of God which
spares the impenitent from any part of the accumulation, it must certainly be a sin in us thus to multiply its amount.   And this, too, is
in exact accordance with Augustine's own principle as clearly stated
in a passage before cited, where he attempts to show that God's justice is different from human justice and that it is right in God not to
prevent sin; though wrong in us not to prevent it when we have the
power.

The consideration here adduced is entirely distinct from that sin
of sensual concupiscence, of which Augustine says so much: and
coming in addition to that sin, what wonder is it that celibacy should
increase under the auspices of such a twofold doctrine in its favor?
and, on the other hand, what wonder that an age of celibacy should
be peculiarly favorable to the spread of such doctrine?—though the
spirit of monkery was adverse to the assumption of human impotency
to virtue.

I have suggested above, that Augustine might consider his view of
this boundless increase of sin, as showing the frightful nature of sin
itself, or rather of that supposed law by which sin multiplies and
pours itself through our race   And truly it is a shocking view.   But
a topic so deeply practical cannot be dismissed without one further
inquiry   What is the precise influence of such a view on him who
cherishes it? Is he in fact thus brought to regard sin as *morally* a
more odious and bitter thing? and really more *deserving* of punishment? Or, while overwhelmed with the magnitude and complication
of its baneful workings, and his attention diverted and absorbed in the
attempt to comprehend this strange and mysterious mode of *ante-
natal* sinning, does not his perception of the very nature of sin as a
moral evil, become obscure and wavering? and consequently feeble
as to its appropriate office, that of heartfelt conviction and evangelical
repentance?   And while he may still perhaps say truly, that he has a
deeper and more dismaying view of sin as an inconceivably *great*
evil, has he either so just or so salutary a view of its moral turpitude?
And has he so proper or even so strong a view of the need of a Savior in order to its pardon? or of the necessity of those *conditions*
of pardon which God has propounded?   And—one question more—
was it not from this very source, that such a man as Augustine himself, and in this same connection, was led to think it possible that
God should pass by infinitely the greater number of a reprobate's

ante-natal sins, without those conditions of faith and repentance, and consequently, in his view, without any reference to the merits of Christ?

But the mind of Augustine, as above noticed, seemed instinctively to recoil from the full contemplation and positive avowal of all the consequences which his theory involved. And it was doubtless well, so far as the effect on himself was concerned, that it did so recoil. But the view he did take and the consequences which he distinctly avowed, were enough to make him shudder; and enough, likewise, to make one of the grand pillars, in another part of his system, to totter. For, though consistent and courageous as he so generally was, he was here led, at least for the moment, to relax his grasp on the fundamental position he had so often avowed, that God can suffer no sin at all to go unpunished, except on the conditions propounded in the gospel.

But still was there not possibly a more excellent way? and might not a little more of this same excellent courage and honesty, have found that way? just as enough of these good qualities might timely arrest the schemes of a virtual bankrupt. For, how much better would it have been, had he contemplated the whole subject fully; and then, instead of wavering on *this* point, had abandoned, as no longer tenable, the theory from which such consequences flow—the theory of moral guilt as propagated by generation and of our existing and sinning in our ancestors. He might still have held firmly to our connection with Adam in such a way that, in consequence of his fall, we become sinners, and are even born with a *propensity* to sin.

My apology for the length of this presentation of Augustine's views, is the relative importance of the topic and the chasm which would otherwise be left in the history. Nothing can ultimately be gained to the cause of sound doctrine, by suffering any part of its history to lie in obscurity; and the least of all can be hoped by closing our eyes to the real difficulties into which its best but still imperfect advocates have fallen.

It will be noticed, as we now proceed with our author, that the comparison implied in the first sentence of the next paragraph, refers only to the view which himself had given of the topics here under discussion —Tr.]

But there was still a much more difficult point in Augustine's theory of original sin. The moral as well as the physical punishment of Adam's sin, was a naturally *necessary* consequence of it. The kind of transgression did not involve in itself such a moral and physical deterioration of the whole race, but each was a positive punishment which God appointed for Adam and all his posterity; a *curse* inflicted by him upon all men, and by which they all came under the power of the devil.

To this view a sound philosophy cannot possibly subscribe. It seems to contain a manifest impeachment of the holiness and justice of God. For the transgression of a single individual, that the whole human race, even if supposed to exist in Adam, should be given up, to the dominion of the devil and thus the whole mass doomed to moral and physical corruption, is in fact something in the highest degree shocking to the moral sense of man! But here even, Augustine sought an escape for the philosophical mind, though in a most unsatisfactory way.

Of the seduction of Eve by the devil—for with all his christian cotemporaries, he regarded the serpent as the devil—he gave a one-sided view, such as had already been adopted by many of the earlier fathers By the seduction of Eve, the devil was supposed to have acquired a *right* to man by which he was subjected to his dominion. This acquired right of satan's, God, if he would not be unjust, could not impair. He could not rescue them by force from his dominion, which brought so great a calamity upon them It was only through Christ's suffering for men, that the perfect right of the devil was cancelled; and only by his death could the men destined to salvation be delivered from the devil's dominion, without doing injustice to the devil.

Hence, in the pieces against the Pelagians, once and again is mention made of the *rightful* power of the devil over men in their natural state, e. g. the passage already quoted in c V. from De Nupt. et Conc I 23. The devil was even the author of Adam's sin. Op. Imp IV. 120 But nowhere is Augustine's view of this "acquired right" of the devil over men, more plainly declared than in his earlier work on freewill (III. 10), although mingled with many ideas which were differently represented by him during the Pelagian disputes.

It is there said among other things . " There are two sources of sin, one in spontaneous thought, the other in the persuasion of another.—Each is voluntary ; for as one does not sin unwillingly (invitus) from his own thought, so when he consents to one tempting him, he does not consent except by volition. Still it is more grievous to sin, not only by one's own thought with no enticer, but even to persuade another to sin through envy and deceit, than to be led to sin by another's enticement The justice of an avenging God, is therefore preserved in both sins. For even this is decided by the scrutiny of equity, that man should not be denied to the power of the devil himself, who had subjected him to himself by enticement For it was unjust that he should not rule over him whom he had taken. Nor can it possibly be that the perfect justice of the supreme and true God, which extends everywhere, should cease from superintending the ruin of sinners. And yet, as man had sinned less than the devil, this very circumstance has been useful to him in recovering salvation, that he was consigned to the prince of this world—the prince of all sinners, and the king of death as respects the mortality of the flesh, [as this would check and humble him].—For who so much needs mercy as the wretched ? And who so unworthy of it as the *proud* sufferer ? And the word of God, the only begotten Son of God, being clothed with humanity, subjugated to man even the devil himself, whom he always had and will have under his laws ; wresting nothing from him by violent domination, but overcoming him by the law of righteousness. So that, as the woman was deceived and the man overthrown through the woman, the devil, while his power remained, by a malicious love of injuring, indeed, but yet by the most perfect right, punished the whole progeny of Adam as sinning according to the laws of death, until he slew the Just One in whom he could show nothing worthy of death, not only as he was slain without any crime, but as he was born without lust. To this lust he had subjugated those he had taken ; so that whoever was thence born, he should retain, as the fruit of his own tree, by a corrupt desire of having, indeed, but by no unjust right of possession. Most justly therefore was he compelled to surrender those who believe in him whom he most unrighteously slew —But those whom he persuades to persevere in unbelief, he will justly have with him as companions in perpetual damnation. Thus it comes to pass, that man is not rescued from the devil by force, nor did he take him by force but by persuasion : and he who is justly more humbled that he should serve him to whom he consented in evil, is justly freed by him to whom he consents in good ; for the one has sinned less in consenting than the other in persuading to evil."

In a later work, finished during the Pelagian controversy, (De Trin. XIII. 13 sq.) Augustine maintains at large, that the devil had to be vanquished by way of right and not by power, because he rightfully held those in chains whom, as guilty of sin, he had involved in the condition of death. He there quotes, as proofs that the elect are freed by Christ from the power of the devil, several passages of scripture, as Col 1· 13, " Who delivered us from the power (potestate) of darkness," etc. Comp. De Nupt. et Conc. I. 20 ; De Trin. IV. 13, where it is said, " The devil possessed man, whom he had seduced with his consent, by a complete right (integro jure)."

As Augustine had now proved his chief doctrine of original sin, he needed no particular proofs for his other doctrines, for they were necessary consequences from that one established principle   The necessity of infant baptism " for the remission of sins," appeared plain from the universality of original sin,* because, in consequence of the imputation, salvation could not otherwise be imparted to children.   Without this baptism, they, like all who are not Christians, must be eternally damned   As man was by nature totally corrupt and subject to punishment, he must first be freed from the guilt and punishment of sin,—and this, baptism was to effect.   Hence, in order to prove that infants, dying before baptism, are eternally damned, Augustine employed those passages of scripture which he was accustomed to quote as proofs of original sin. Ep 157. c. 3

As man by nature is so ruined through Adam's sin, that he cannot but sin, and has therefore no freewill, he must be renewed by the irresistible influence of God's spirit, if he is ever to be saved. The bestowment of this influence must again be founded on an unconditional predestination on God's part, as nothing at all can be said of merit in so corrupt a race of men, and hence no moral reason can be discovered why one should be saved and another condemned. And on this account, Christ's redemption cannot be universal but must extend only to the elect.

---

* Our author does not here mean that Augustine attempted to prove infant baptism itself from original sin, for this was not the fact   But he argued that the reason *why* they are baptized is found in the fact of their possessing original sin.   The point is, not simply that they were baptized, but baptized " for the *remission of sins* "

Still, however, Augustine did seek to confirm his other doctrines by particular proofs, by which in turn the main doctrine of original sin received fresh support.

In order to prove that unbaptized children will be eternally punished, Augustine appealed to Mark, 16. 16, He that believeth not shall be damned. The want of faith is here assigned as the reason of condemnation. Unbaptized children cannot believe, but the baptized believe " by the hearts and mouths of those who present them." C Jul. VI. 3. For children therefore to believe, is the same as to be baptized ; and not to believe, the same as not to be baptized. De Pec. Mer. I. 27.

From Rom. 6. 3, Whoever of us have been baptized in Christ (in Christo), have been baptized in his death, he endeavored to show that the pardon of original sin is the object of infant baptism. The universality of the expression *whoever*, allowed of no exception for children. " To be baptized in the death of Christ," he explained by " to die to sin " And the sin of children, he regarded as original sin, since they could commit none of their own C. Jul VI. 3. In confirmation of his theory of infant baptism, he appealed further to the universality of Christ's declaration, John 3 5, Unless one is born of water and the Spirit, he cannot enter into the kingdom of God. Also from the passages where it is said that Christ died for sinners, that one died for all, and especially from 2 Cor 5· 14, Because one died for all, therefore all were dead, and he died for all—he endeavored to prove, together with its universality, the pardon of original sin as the object of infant baptism. VI. 4.

Against the Pelagian view of a difference between salvation or eternal life, and the kingdom of heaven, of which the former is to be awarded to unbaptized children, Augustine made several scripture declarations available. To these belong the passages, John 3: 16, God so loved the world as to give his only begotten Son, that every one who believeth on him should not perish, but should have *eternal life* (De Pec. Mer. I. 33) ; Titus 3: 5, He hath *saved* us by the laver of regeneration (I 18) ; John 3 36, He that believeth not the Son, shall not have *life*, but the wrath of God abideth on him (III. 2) ; 1 John 5: 12, He that hath the son, *hath life* ; and he that hath not the son, *hath not life* (I. 27). Here he remarked ; " Children will not only not have the kingdom of heaven, but not even *life*, provided they have not the Son, whom they cannot have without his baptism." Here, from the connection in which the eucharist at his time stood with infant baptism, Augustine could likewise use the passages in which life is attributed to the supper as an effect, against the Pelagian doctrine respecting the object of infant baptism. Thus he quoted (De Pec. Mer III 4) John 6: 53, Unless men eat his flesh, they will not have life. The first words he explained as meaning, "Unless they shall become partakers of the body of Christ. Does he not plainly declare," continued he, "that infants not only cannot enter the kingdom of God, but cannot even have eternal life, without the body of Christ? to be incorporated with which, they must be imbued with the sacrament of baptism"

The doctrine of the damnation of unbaptized christian children, in his view thus biblically established, now presented to Augustine a new and grand argument in support of his doctrine of original sin "For what cause, with what justice, are children, if they believe not, condemned, provided they have no original sin in them?" C Jul. VI. 3. And why are the gifts of grace, which are needful to salvation, denied to some children, if they have no original sin? Op Imp. I. 53 Also in the customs of the church, of exorcism and afflation at baptism, Augustine found a proof of original sin and of the dominion of the devil over the unbaptized. A principal passage in this respect, is De Nupt. et Conc II, 29. Julian had complained, that his doctrine of original sin was Manichaeism Augustine answered, that the rites of baptism, exorcism, and the blowing out of unclean spirits, were older than Manichaeism, so that the very mysteries of baptism proved that those children only were brought into the kingdom of Christ who were delivered from the dominion of darkness. To what purpose is exorcism in the case of the child who is to be baptized, (it is said, De Pec Mer I. 34), if he is not enthralled in the family of the devil? God himself would be greatly offended, provided his own innocent image, not subject to the power of the devil, were exorcised and blown upon Op. Imp. IV. 120. Julian accused, therefore, the catholic church of a treasonable offence against God. III 299 Comp. 142, 144; De Pec. Orig. 40; Ep. 194 c. 10

In like manner the " renunciation" was a proof to Augustine of original sin. "If the child to be baptized is to renounce sin, say, *what sin?*" Op Imp. II. 224; De Pec. Orig. 40

The eucharist, connected with baptism, also afforded him such a

proof. "Why is the blood, shed for the remission of sins, given to
the child to drink, that he may have life, if he is subject to death by
no hereditary sin?" Op. Imp II 30.

In order further to confirm his theory of grace by particular
proofs from the Bible, Augustine employed those passages of the
Old and New Testaments in which all the good purposes and acts of
man, as well as faith, are referred immediately to God as their author. Thus, besides those already quoted, he cited (Ep. 215), Prov.
4. 27, according to the Septuagint, He shall make thy courses
straight, he shall conduct thy journeyings in peace, (De Praed.
Sanct. 11), Ezek. 36. 37, I will cause you to do, Rom. 8: 14, As
many as are led by the spirit of God, they are the sons of God;
1 Cor. 12: 11, All these things worketh one and the same spirit, de-
viding severally to each one as he will, on which Augustine remarked, that in all this the apostle meant faith;—(Lib Cit c 8), Ezek.
11: 19, I will take away the stony heart and give the heart of flesh;
(Op. Imp II 157; C. d. Epp. Pel. I. 18), Phil. 2· 13, It is God
that worketh in you both to will and to do according to his own good
pleasure; (De Dono Persev. 20), Baruch 2. 31, I will give them a
heart for knowing me, and hearing ears; (De Haeres. 88), John 6:
65, No one cometh unto me unless it be given him of my Father;
15: 5, Without me ye can do nothing; (ib. and Ep. 188), Rom. 5:
5, The love of God is shed abroad in our hearts by the Holy Ghost
that is given unto us; (Ep. 176), Luke 22 32, I have prayed for
thee that thy faith fail not; (Ep. 188), Matt. 19: 11, All do not receive this saying, but they to whom it is given; Rom. 12· 3, God
imparteth to each the measure of faith; (De Dono Persev. 13),
2 Cor. 3: 5, We are not able to think anything as of ourselves, but our
sufficiency is of God; (Ep. 217), Ps 37: 23, The steps of man are
directed by the Lord, and he shall will his way; (Ep. 194), I Cor.
7: 25, I have obtained mercy to be faithful; Matt. 10: 20, It is not
ye that speak, but the spirit of your Father that speaketh in you;
Gal. 4· 6, Because ye are sons, God hath sent the spirit of his son
into your hearts, crying, Abba, Father; (C d. Epp. Pel. IV. 6), Jer.
32: 40, 41, I will give my fear into their heart, that they may not
depart from me, and I will visit them that I may make them good;
(De Gest. Pel. 14), 1 Cor. 15 10, By the grace of God, I am what
I am; (De Gr. et Lib. Arb. 8), Eph. 2: 10, We are his workmanship, created in Christ Jesus in good works which God hath prepared

that we should walk in them; Ps. 51: 12, Create in me a clean
heart, O God; (C. d. Epp. Pel. I. 3), Phil 1· 29, To you it is given,
for Christ's sake, not only to believe on him, but also to suffer for
him, Eph. 6: 23, Peace to the brethren, and love from God the
Father and the Lord Jesus Christ; John 6· 44, No one can come to
me except the Father which hath sent me, draw him, (Op. Imp III.
107), Matt. 26. 41, Pray that ye enter not into temptation; (Ep.
179), 2 Cor. 13 7, We beseech God that ye may do no evil; (De
Praed. Sanct. 2), Rom. 11: 35, Who hath first given to him and it
shall be recompensed to him? for of him and through him and in
him are all things; (C. Jul. V 4), 2 Tim. 2· 25, 26, Lest God
should perhaps give them repentance to the knowing of the truth and
they should escape from the snares of the devil.

For his " preceding grace," Augustine further quoted particularly
1 John 4: 19. "Grace precedes man, in order that he may love
God, and by this love perform good works. This the apostle John
shows most clearly when he says, We love because he first loved
us" Also Prov 8 35, according to the Septuagint, The will is prepared by the Lord Op Imp. L 131, 134, 141.—Against the Pelagian
reference of the immediate effect of divine grace only to the understanding of man, Augustine cited (Haer. 88) 1 Cor. 8. 1, Knowledge
puffeth up but charity edifieth: and remarked, that the Pelagians held
knowledge, which without love puffeth up, as a gift of God, but love
itself they would not so regard.

Augustine also adduces the example of children who receive baptism, as a proof that grace is not imparted according to the merit of
works nor according to the merit of the will. Ep. 217. c. 5 The
free bestowment of grace is shown especially and incontrovertibly in
children, many of whom, when they even resist with weeping, receive nevertheless the grace of baptism, and that though born of unbelievers; while others on the contrary, even children of believers,
do not receive it. De Gr. et Lib. Arb. 22. That the conversion of
man depends not on his will but on the supernatural grace of God,
for this Augustine, in the same epistle, appealed to the prayer of the
church for the conversion of unbelievers and her thanksgiving for
their conversion. Perseverance to the end, he regarded as a grace
of God, because the end of this life depends not on us but on God,
and hence God can take any one away the sooner, that he may not
change the evil of his mind, etc. (Ib.). Believers, he further says, dai-

ly pray the Lord's prayer, and particularly, *Hallowed be thy name*, which however has already been done by the laver of regeneration. They *thereby* confess, as well as in the thanksgiving, that perseverance is a gift of the Lord. De Cor. et Gr. 6 ; De Dono Persev. 2.

The eternal, unconditional decree, Augustine thought he found as clear as the sun in the ninth chapter of Romans. "He hath mercy on whom he will, and whom he will he hardeneth. Willing to show wrath and demonstrate his power, he bore with much patience the vessels of wrath which were prepared for perdition, and that he might make known the riches of his glory in the vessels of mercy which he prepared for glory." Passages of this kind, which, according to his custom, Augustine took in the strongest sense and without regard to the occasion and object of the apostle, (e. g. De Praed Sanct. 8), must now indeed have put the unconditional decree beyond all doubt with him, and Augustine hardly needed to connect with it still other passages from the Old and New Testament, where it is said, for example, I the Lord have seduced that prophet, I have hardened Pharaoh, I will have compassion on whom I will have compassion, and I will show mercy to whom I will be compassionate. The expression " to harden sinners," Augustine explains (De Diver. Quaest ad Simp. lib. I. n 15), entirely according to his own theory, that God will not have mercy on them. God adds nothing to the man by which he becomes worse. he only does not afford him that by which to become better. Thus the Tyrians and Sidonians would have believed, if they had seen the noble miracles of Christ. It would however have profited them nothing, as they were not predestinated by him whose judgments are unfathomable and whose ways are unsearchable De Dono Persev 14.—But he laid special stress also on Eph. 1· 4 sq., (De Praed. Sanct. 18), where it is said, He chose us in Christ before the foundation of the world, that we should be holy and immaculate in his sight in love, predestinating us to the adoption of sons by Jesus Christ for himself, according to the good pleasure of his will. As proofs of predestination, he adduced the children that are saved, as well as Jesus in respect to his human nature. 12—15. By no preceding merits have they deserved to have a preference before those who are damned ; and whereby has the man Jesus deserved that he should be received into a unity of person by the Word coeternal with the Father, and become the only begotten son of God ?

But in order to destroy the force of the instance which might be adduced against the Augustinian limitation of redemption to the elect, from the words of Paul, 1 Tim 2 4, God would have all men to be saved and come to the knowledge of the truth, Augustine availed himself of a peculiar interpretation of those words   They were to mean as much as this, All who are saved are saved only by the will of God Ep 217. c. 6 ; Enchirid 103   "For God causes us to will " De Cor. et Gr. 15.   In like manner he interpreted the words of Christ, Every one that hath heard and learned of the Father, cometh unto me   No one comes to Christ in any other way. but as he has learned it of the Father   In a like sense we say of a teacher of languages who is the only one in a city, he instructed all ; not that all learn, but that no one learns otherwise than by him De Praed Sanct. 8 ; De Pec Mer I 28 —He proposes still another explanation of those passages of Paul, De Cor et Gr. 14 ; Enchir. 103   By " all men," may be understood the elect, because all kinds of men are included among them, rich and poor, superior and inferior, learned and ignorant.   In like manner Christ said to the pharisees, Ye tithe every herb.   " Every herb" is here the same as every kind of herb Op Imp IV. 124

To justify his forced construction of the apostle's words, as himself perhaps felt it to be, Augustine remarked against Julian (C. Jul. IV. 8), " If God wills that all men should be saved and come to the knowledge of the truth, but they do not come because they themselves will not, why do not the many thousand infants, who die without baptism, come into the kingdom of God, where the knowledge of the truth is certain ?"

And as Augustine's philosophy contributed much to the formation of his theological system generally, and on its foundations he sought for confirmation of his supernatural doctrines, so is this also especially the case in his predestination theory and the limited view of redemption as connected with it   The doctrine, for instance, of the almighty will of God, he conceived of rather in the physical than the moral aspect   What God wills, takes place—so Augustine philosophized—must take place, because his will is an almighty will. Had God willed that all men should be saved, then all men must have been saved.   Hence, (in his Enchiridion, l. c. composed about the year 421, and therefore in the midst of the Pelagian dispute), he presents for adoption his explanation of 1 Tim. 2 4, " if we would

not be compelled to believe the Almighty God to have willed something to take place and it is not done." We see therefore how greatly philosophical speculation on the relation of God's will to man's
conduct, confirmed Augustine in his theory of predestination.

But that Christ's death is to be regarded *only* as an atonement,
and consequently only for the benefit of sinners, he endeavored to
prove from 2 Cor. 5: 14, already quoted in another relation. " The
apostle says, One died for all, therefore all were dead ; and thereby
shows, that he could have died only for the dead. For he proves
that all are dead because one died for all. Now, because the cor-
poreally dead cannot here be meant, it follows that no Christian can
doubt or deny, that all for whom Christ died, are dead in sin." C.
Jul. VI. 4.

But Augustine also reasoned backwards sometimes, as we have
already seen on the doctrine of infant baptism, from the truth of the
consequence to the truth of the supposition on which it is founded.
" Where is the freedom of those who need divine grace to free them
from the bondage in which they are subjected to the dominion of
sin ?" From redemption he inferred the corruption and incapacity
of the natural man for good. De Pec. Mer. I. 18, 26.

CHAPTER XXI

Proofs of the Pelagians for their Theory

Augustine found the principal scripture proofs for his theory of
original sin, in the epistle to the Romans   Pelagius knew how to
explain these passages so that his theory would be confirmed by
them.

In the noted passage, Rom. 5: 12, he took θάνατος death, not with
Augustine for bodily death, but for spiritual, or the moral ruin which
came into the world by the example and imitation of Adam's sin.
Sin, and moral death with sin, came into the world by Adam, for
Adam gave the first example or form, as Pelagius expressed himself, of sin, which did not there exist before him. So moral corruption came upon all, with the exception of a few righteous, because

all sinned after the example of Adam. The phrase, *in whom* (in quo) all have sinned, he explained thus, " *In as much as* (in eo quod) all have sinned, they sin *by Adam's example.*" See his commentary on Rom v. The sense of the whole passage, therefore, according to Pelagius, was the following. As by one man sin has come into the world, and moral ruin with sin, so moral corruption has come to all, *because* all have sinned after Adam's example. By the Pelagian explanation, therefore, there was no proof at all for the Augustinian original sin, in this passage, but it means only thus much, that by Adam, sin and moral corruption came into the world, because he sinned first. " By imitation," not " by propagation," have sin and its consequences come upon the human race. De Pec. Mer I. 9 sq. De Nat. et Gr. 9; Sermo 294 n. 15

In a like spirit, Pelagius commented on the comparison which the Apostle instituted, in the following verses, between the consequences of Adam's sin and Christ's merits See his Commentary. The declaration, " death reigned—even over those who had not sinned after the similitude of Adam's transgression," he, without making use of the variation above mentioned as so favorable to him, explained thus : Moral corruption reigned over those also who have not, like Adam, broken a command of God, but the natural law. On the words, " who is the image of the future one," (of which he as well as Augustine attempted several explanations), he remarked " As the first Adam, who transgressed God's command, is an example for those who would transgress God's law, so is Christ, who fulfilled the will of the Father, an example for those who desire to imitate him "— Pelagius also knew how to explain away original sin from the rest of the chapter He supposed Adam only to have given the pattern of sin by which those died who followed his example But this does not mean that they suffered *temporal* death, for this befalls the righteous as well as sinners ; but they suffered morally But Christ by his grace justifies many, in as much as he freely forgives sin, and has given an example of righteousness By baptism Christians become partakers of Christ's kingdom, without having merited it. This with him was " the abundance of righteousness," the partakers of which were to reign through Jesus Christ. On the words, " by one offence on all men unto condemnation," he took the term *all*, for *many*, in consequence of the antithesis " by the righteousness of one on all men unto justification of life ;" because if the term *all* were to be taken in the strongest sense, " no one would be left for further punishment," etc. Pelagius also argued from the words, " if by the offence of one many were dead, much more the grace of God and the gift by the grace of one man Jesus Christ, hath abounded unto many," that if Adam's sin has injured those who are not sinners, then Christ's righteousness must also benefit unbelievers, because, according to the Apostle's declaration, more are delivered by one than before perished by one De Pec. Mer. III. 2 ; Aug. Sermo 294. c. 17 ; Mer. in Com. p. 70, 71 This argument, however, Augustine would not admit. " It cannot be positively asserted," replied Augustine, " that Adam's sin has injured those who have not sinned, since scripture says, " in whom all have sinned." Nor are those sins said to be foreign, as though they did not at all belong to children , since all then sinned in Adam, when as yet they were that one, as there was placed in his nature that power by which he could beget them. But the sins are called foreign, because the persons were not yet living their own lives, but the life of that one man contained whatever there was in the future race." De Pec. Mer. III. 7.

That Pelagius explained the words in Genesis, " in the day thou eatest thou shalt die the death," of spiritual death only, or the death of the soul, might be supposed, even if we had not the testimony of Augustine for it, De Pec. Mer 1. 2, 4. The words of Paul, Rom. 8· 10, " If Christ is in you, the body is dead because of sin," he explained, If ye imitate Christ, sensuality does not resist you, which is as it were dead. The passage, 1 Cor. 15 21, " By man death, and by man the resurrection of the dead," Pelagius thus explained : As death came into the world by Adam because he died first, so the resurrection by Christ, because he has risen first. As the former is the pattern of those that die, so is the latter of the resurrection. Or it may be thus explained, adds he The words, " by man is the resurrection of the dead," may be referred to the hope of the resurrection, and hence understood thus . As in Adam we are mortal, so in Christ we become immortal

Further ; Pelagius sought to prove, from Rom 7 8, " Without law sin was dead," the absurdity of an original sin which is imputed to us. " If when there is no law, sin is dead, they are insane who maintain that sin comes to us from Adam by propagation. Paul says, sin is dead, because it does not live in infants who are without law,

i. e. it is committed with impunity. For when the infant maligns its parents, it seems indeed to be sin, but it is not a living but a dead sin. Although the lad sins, yet the sin in him is dead, because he is not subject to law." Comment. in Ep. ad Rom. In verses 14—25, he considers Paul as not speaking of himself but in the person of one that finds himself under the law and in whom the habit of sensual desires reigns   For God's grace through Jesus Christ makes free from this, and Paul was already a partaker of this grace when he wrote the passage   By *grace*, he finally here understood no supernatural influences, but the instructions of Christ. " For what Moses and the law before him, did not teach, that Jesus Christ our Lord taught, namely to despise the world and subjugate vices." Compare the passage quoted by Augustine, (De Gr Chr 39), from the third book of Pelagius on freewill. " In the person of a single man," it is here said " the apostle designates the people as still sinning under the old law, who, he says, were to be freed from this evil of custom by Christ, who first forgives all sins through baptism to those who believe on him, and then excites them to perfect holiness by the imitation of himself, and conquers the habit of vices by the example of virtues."*

On Eph. 2 3, Pelagius refers the phrase " we were by nature children of wrath," to " the custom of paternal tradition," so that all appeared to be born to condemnation. Com. in Ep. ad Eph.

In this manner, Pelagius knew how, by his exegesis, to dispose of the sin propagated from Adam by generation, and to argue against it. Augustine's chief proofs for his original sin, were thus directly

---

* In the sentence preceding what is here quoted, Pelagius asserts that *all the orthodox* then considered that noted passage in Romans vii, as depicting the struggle in the breast of an *awakened* but very *wicked* man ,—a fact of some interest in the history of its exegesis   Addressing his antagonist, Pelagius says, ' For this which you would understand of the *apostle*, all orthodox men (ecclesiastici viii) affirm him to have spoken in the person of a *sinner* as yet under the law, who is held by the excessive practice of vices as by a sort of necessity ; and though with the will he would seek good, yet by habit (usu) he is precipitated into evil ''   And such, too, was Augustine's early view of the passage, as is apparent from what has before been said Whether the more modern interpretation of it is right or wrong, it has probably been owing more to the authority of Augustine than to that of any other ancient writer, that this interpretation has gained so general a prevalence —Tr.

weakened or rendered entirely useless. But Julian especially showed great acuteness in assailing the Augustinian theory of original sin, both with exegetical and philosophical weapons, as may be seen by the quotations in Op. Imp., from Julian's work against Augustine

The whole second book of that work is occupied in explaining the grand passage, Rom. 5· 12 sqq , in which Julian at least weakens all Augustine's conclusions, and endeavors to show, that the question here respected the example of sin, which extends, not to all posterity, but only to sinners by imitation. By θάνατος death, Julian also understood, not bodily death, but the death which was threatened to sinners, eternal death. *In quo, ἐφ' ᾧ*, he explained by *propter quod*, or *quia, on account of which, because,* just as this expression is elsewhere used in the bible. *All* here stands for *many,* as in innumerable places in the bible. Op Imp II 173—175; C Jul VI 24.

Julian remarks, among other things, (Op Imp II 56 sqq.), that if the passage, As by one man, etc , were to refer to the propagation of sin by generation, it must have said, as by *two* persons For *one* person can indeed present an example for imitation, but is not enough for propagation

To this Augustine replied · Eve to be sure sinned first, and by her we all die ; but precisely because the apostle would not mean imitation but generation, he has said, sin came into the world by *one* man For the man commences generation Again ; the apostle may have said, By *one* man, because it is written, Twain become one flesh ; and this was especially by coition, whereby posterity are propagated, etc. Augustine further remarked (De Nupt. et Conc. II. 27), that if the apostle had meant imitation. he would not have said " by one man," but " by the devil " For it is written, (Sap. 2: 25), " They who are of his party imitate him." But he has said, " by one man," in order to teach that original sin passes to all by generation. It was never said of the devil, " in him they have sinned." Sermo 294 c. 15

Julian proceeds : It is not said that *sin* has come to all, but *death*, namely, spiritual death, which is ordained by divine justice as the punishment for sin ; and this punishment follows, " not the seed of the bodies, but the corruption of morals." But the death extends to all men, because *one* form of the sentence comprehends all transgressors in subsequent time ; yet neither holy men nor the innocent suffer this death, but they only who imitate the transgression The transgression was indeed not natural, but yet it was one form of sin ; and though it does not injure infants, it accuses imitators. This judicial death has spread further, *because* all have sinned, though by freewill. By the word *all*, is not meant the whole human race, but a multitude, after the manner of the scriptures Op. Imp. II. 63 sqq.

Augustine replied · It appears doubtful, in the passage quoted, whether it was said of sin, or of death, or of both, that they passed upon all men. But the case itself shows what is to be understood. For if sin has not passed to all men, then every man would not be born with the law of sin which is to be found in his members. And if death had not passed to all, then all men would not die.

Julian suggests, that by Augustine's explanation of Paul's words, " And not as by one that sinned, is the gift ; for judgment is from one to condemnation, but grace is of many offences to justification," and by his view of original sin, the apostle is made to contradict himself. For if freewill was utterly ruined by the first sin, and afterwards remained so defective in the whole human race, that it could will nothing but evil, and could not turn itself at all to good ; if, being by the necessity subject to sin, it is compelled to obey the allurements of vice ; if the law of sin dwells in the members, and this has obtained its dominion over the image of God by marriage ; if the devil's bramble is grafted on man ; if this grows by natural increase, becomes green, and loaded with corrupt fruit ; if this, by Augustine's position, has been produced by the single crime of the first man, then it cannot be said of grace, that it frees from *many* offences, for, by this supposition, no sins at all would be committed by the proper movement of freewill. *One* infectious crime of the seed of the first progenitor, is then the cause of so great an evil ; and the grace of Christ does not cause justification by the pardon of *many* offences ; but its whole office is limited to freeing from one individual sin. II. 105 sqq.

Augustine replied . The sentence is from one sin to condemnation, because they were condemned in whom this individual sin is innate. But grace helps to justification from many offences, because it removes, not merely that innate sin, but also all the additional sins committed by freewill.*

---

* Such presentations as these, by our author, are for the most part nearly a literal though condensed translation from the originals to which he refers —TR.

From the two contrary propositions, " As by the offence of one, condemnation [was] to all, so by the righteousness of one, [was the free gift] to all men to justification," Julian inferred, that the question could not here respect any original sin to which all men are subject II. 135. For had Paul intended to say, that all are brought into condemnation by Adam, how could he have said that all are justified by Christ ? The universality of one proposition precludes the universality of the other. [Julian meant, they could not be all condemned and all justified, at the same time —Tr.]

Augustine replied, that there is here no contradiction. For no one is brought into condemnation except through Adam, and no one is freed from this condemnation, except through Christ. Hence the word *all* may be used in both propositions. All men died in Adam, and from them Christ makes as many alive as he will.

Julian remarked : Since, by the apostle's representation, grace is greater than sin, because he says, " the benefits abound to many more than the injury invades," (multo in plures abundasse beneficia, quam irrepsisse dispendia), and on the contrary, by the opinion that sin is propagated, sin must have injured more than grace has aided, it follows irresistibly, that Paul was not thinking of such a propagation of sin, but that, by his meaning, the traducians together with the Manichaeans are overthrown in their doctrines. II 142

Augustine answered · The apostle has not so expressed himself as Julian pretends He has said, " much more has grace abounded to many ," not " to many more," but " more abounded." In respect to the last, he remarks (De Pec Mer. I. 11), that this, as appears from the following, was said in the sense that, while Adam by his single transgression produced the guilty, Christ has also, by his grace, blotted out and forgiven the sins which men have added to original sin. In Op. Imp. II 205, it is said, " Grace much more abounds towards those, because they through Adam live for a time in a miserable and dying way, but through Christ they are to live most happily and forever " In respect to the following words of Paul, " where sin abounded, grace hath much more abounded," it is added as the reason, " because grace, in those who belong to it, blots out the guilt of all those kinds of sin, and affords, besides, the advantage that the love of sin is overcome by the love of righteousness, and afterwards extends to that life where there will be no sin at all " II. 217.

Julian observed further, that by the words, " as by the disobedience of one man, many were constituted sinners, so by the obedience of one many are constituted righteous," the apostle explained
what was before said He gave it to be understood, that *he* only
can venture to lay claim to the rewards of virtue who, after the incarnation of Christ, has sought to obtain them by imitating his holiness , and that he only can be called a sinner in Adam, who has
sinned by transgressing the law in imitation of the first man ; but
that the grace of Christ also refers to innocent children, to whom
Adam's guilt has no reference, and he therefore insisted, that God's
grace and the gift of the one man Jesus Christ, extend to a far
greater number   Hence it follows that the apostle is in opposition
to Augustine. The apostle says, that by one man's disobedience, not
all, but many became sinners ; that by one man's obedience, not all,
but many became righteous. Augustine, on the contrary, would
have all born liable to punishment through Adam, and some to be
freed by the grace of Christ. Augustine therefore opposed the
opinion of the apostle. Had Paul thought like Augustine, he must
have said, " By the disobedience of one, all became sinners, but by
the obedience of Christ, some of these have returned to righteousness." But with this declaration the other could not have been reconciled, that Christ's grace has benefited more than Adam's transgression has injured If, then, we did not know at all in what sense
many are made sinners by one man's disobedience, yet it would ever
remain decided, that what, according to the apostle's declaration, belongs not to all but to many, cannot refer to original sin. Op. Imp.
II. 146 sqq

Augustine replies . " He [the apostle] calls them all, and calls
the same *many*. By saying *many*, he does not deny *all*, unless he
is contrary to himself, as either your impiobity deceives or your
blindness is deceived. For the apostle said both all and many.—
But you, by calling them not all whom the apostle has called all,
are beyond doubt convicted of being contrary to the apostle," etc.

Finally, it is not true that the apostle has designedly taught, that
God's grace and the free gift of the one man Jesus Christ, are to a
far greater number, since in the Greek it is not πλεῖστοι most, but
πολλοί many, etc.

Julian also endeavored to prove from the connection with what
follows, that Paul, who must best have understood his own writings,

did not intend to teach an Augustinian original sin. Thus Paul speaks in Rom 6: 12 : " Let not sin therefore reign in your mortal body to obedience unto it." This admonition plainly proves, that Paul speaks of voluntary sins. If he were speaking of natural imperfection, he could in no wise admonish us to guard against it, for it were nonsense to warn against natural things. But the apostle has certainly commanded nothing which deserves censure He therefore meant voluntary sins, which he urges to avoid. The apostle proceeds (v. 13, 14) : " Neither present ye your members, the instruments of iniquity unto sin ; but present yourselves to God as alive from the dead, and your members as instruments of righteousness unto God ; for sin has not dominion over you ; for ye are not under law but under grace." The greater the freedom, says the apostle, which you now enjoy, the more faithful should you prove yourselves in God's service. When you still had to fear punishment for your transgressions, sin reigned over you ; but since you have obtained the highest benefits by the grace of God, and your sins are forgiven, you are bound to show yourselves grateful for this aid. When the apostle subsequently speaks of servants of sin, he gives it to be understood, that he means by them merely those who had voluntarily served vice, but that these afterwards changed their will and became the servants of righteousness. " I say what is human, because of the infirmity of your flesh ; for as ye have presented your members to serve uncleanness and iniquity unto iniquity, so now present your members to serve righteousness unto sanctification," adds the apostle, (v. 19). *What I say is human*, means nothing different from this, *what I say is easy, practicable.* I demand, says the apostle, nothing too hard, nor impossible ; I give you no new precepts. Pursue virtue with only just the same zeal with which you were before devoted to vice. Let us, therefore, adds Julian, believe the teacher of the Gentiles. For what he has enjoined is really human, that the will ought to reform itself and avoid freewill vices But that it ought to put away the other—something innate—hereditary—would be not only unhuman, but also wrong, nay insane It is therefore shown, that Paul, this venerable teacher of Christianity, thought of no natural sin, but rather inculcated, that we become the slaves of sin no otherwise than by the will ; and that by the same will, when it is reformed, we can serve righteousness. And thus it is made out, that Paul, on whom the traducians place their chief reliance, affords as little support to their opinions as do reason and the catholic church. II. 226, to the end.

What Augustine places in opposition to this reasoning, is extremely weak.* Paul, he remarks among other things. does not say, " *let* not sin *be* in your mortal body," but " let it not *reign.*" This presupposes the existence of concupiscence, which can only be in a mortal body That man can make himself righteous by his own freewill, the whole church denies, which prays publicly what she has learned from her good Master, " Lead us not into temptation," etc.

The words, " In the day ye eat, ye shall die the death," Julian as well as Pelagius referred merely to the death of the soul Op. Imp. VI. 10. The words, " Earth thou art and to earth shalt thou go," Julian regarded, not as words of the curse, but rather of consolation. But the curse which God pronounced on Adam and Eve, he supposed to embrace only the punishment of the first pair, not their posterity. From the words, " Multiplying I will multiply thy sorrows," he argued that even without Eve's sin, children would have been born with pain, for the increase presupposes the existence of a thing already. VI. 26, 27.

Julian also considered Rom. 7 14—25, as the language of a Jew living under the law. The " body of death," he considered as the sins committed, and grace as the pardon of them imparted to us in baptism. l. 67.†—He gave a new translation of Eph 2 3, in a way to differ from the explanation of Pelagius " We were *wholly* children of wrath"—making φύσει to mean *wholly* C. Jul. VI. 10 ; Op. Imp. II. 228. Augustine protested against this explanation, and maintained, that it was favored by no Latin manuscripts.

Besides the reasons derived from God's justice, an attribute inseparably connected with the existence of God, and by which he can

---

* In this discussion, as elsewhere, Augustine proves most fully our dependence on the divine spirit and our proneness to sin, and refutes all which Julian seems to imply to the contrary But professor Wiggers probably means only to say, that Augustine's reply was extremely weak when considered simply in reference to " natural sin," or involuntary sin, where the individual has no agency —Tr

† On this point, Augustine's refutation is as complete as his language is severe—showing most ably, from the passage itself, the absurdity of supposing it the language of a Jew still under the law, and also of its referring to past sins instead of present conflict, etc —Tr

punish those only who sin voluntarily, and can command nothing which one is not able by his nature to perform, and holds no one responsible for things natural, and by which therefore he imputes foreign sins to no one, and hence does not punish innocent children for the sins of their parents—besides these rational grounds, which made it clear how unjust it would be, if guilt were transferred by generation, (which reasons we find quoted by Augustine, Op Imp. I., and refuted by him as well as he was able from his position, and of which we have already treated above), Julian now sought to make it still further manifest, by particular *scripture* proofs, that it would be the height of injustice, if the sins of parents were imputed to their children. We find these scripture proofs (Op. Imp. III. 12 sqq) put together with great dexterity and acuteness, and it will not be uninteresting to see an outline of the use which Julian made of them, and of what Augustine replied, with dialectic art but often feebly enough.

Julian Among the laws which God gave the Israelites for the purpose of establishing a more perfect government among them, we find the following, in Deut. 24. 16. "The Fathers shall not die for the children, and the children shall not die for the fathers. Each one shall die in his own sin " According to this ordinance of God, by which the judicial process of the Israelites was regulated, parents were not to be punished for the crimes of their children, nor children for the crimes of their parents. This principle of justice was therefore established, that relationship should not injure the innocent, but punishment should fall on the individual person who had deserved it But this principle could find no place, if there were a connection between the will and the seed, or if a voluntary transgression passed by propagation to posterity. By this proof, therefore, the pernicious doctrine of original sin, is completely refuted. Those who maintain an original sin against this declaration, should also now abide by their opposition, and maintain likewise, that sin also extends back from children to parents ; for the scripture says that the transgressions of the parents should not injure the children as those of the children should not injure the parents.—But God cannot be the transgressor of his own law. If he wills that we should be just, and yet he acts unjustly himself, he wills that we should be more righteous than himself

Augustine. This passage treats of those already born, and not of the children condemned in their first father, in whom all have sinned and in whom all die And he gave this command for the direction of men, that the father should not die for the son nor the son for the father, if the father only or the son only should be found guilty   But God has not confined to the law the decisions which he may give by himself or by men whom he endows with the prophetic spirit.   For he did not separate the children who had not yet imitated their parents, when he destroyed all, by the flood, except Noah and his family ; and the fire did not consume the Sodomites without their children.   Had the Almighty willed this, he certainly could have done it And Achan was found as the only transgressor of the command, and yet he was put to death with his sons and daughters.   And of so many cities besieged under the command of Joshua, that man of God, were not all slain so that not one was left alive ? What evil had the children done ? Did they not, by the divine decision, suffer one common punishment for the sins of their parents, of whom they could know nothing, and whom they could not imitate ? God therefore judges in one way, and directs man to judge in another, though he is doubtless more righteous than man

In Lev 26 39, God says   " And those who remain of you, shall perish because of their sins and because of the sins of their parents." God says, Deut 5 9, " I will recompense the sins of the parents on the children," which he often repeats.   But he never says, " I will recompense the sins of the children on the parents," although parents may imitate their bad children ;—a plain proof that he punishes the faults (vitia) of generation, not those of imitation   God therefore deals in one way as God, and directs man as man in another   The higher divine righteousness is above human righteousness, so much the more unsearchable is it and so much the more removed from the latter.

Julian. That God's commands and his decisions do not contradict each other, and that he therefore does not impute foreign sins to men, and forbids them to impute them to others—for the establishment of this truth, the scripture proof is entirely irrefutable.   Thus the prophet Ezekiel, who was filled with the Holy Ghost, said (18: 2 sqq.) · " Why have ye this parable in the land of Israel, saying, The fathers have eaten sour grapes and the children's teeth are set on edge ?   As I live, saith the Lord Jehovah, this parable shall not be spoken any more in Israel ; for all souls are mine ; as the soul of the father, so also the soul of the son, all souls are mine. *The soul that sinneth it shall die.*" The prophet speaks to the Jews, who had brought captivity on themselves by their own vices, but who, in order to turn from themselves the odium of their own transgressions, ascribed the fault to the morals of their ancestors. God, to confirm the righteousness of his sentence, employed an oath, and also declared the reason why foreign sins are not to fall on relatives. All souls, says he, are mine, and therefore it is utterly unfit and unreasonable, that foreign transgressions should burden my image.

In the subsequent verses, the declaration is illustrated by examples. It is shown, that if one, who lives blamelessly and piously, begets a son that leads a bad life and forsakes the way of his father, the glory earned by the father with ever so much assiduity, can avail nothing to his justification. On the other hand, he presents the son of a sinner, who abandons the way of his father, and shows that the misconduct of his father does not injure him. Just such a comparison he instituted between righteousness and sin, thus asserting that the faults of the parents can be no more propagated by the seed than their virtues, but that all souls belong of right to him. By this, also, your assertion, according to which both soul and body are under the dominion of the devil, is shown to be impious. For the prophet proceeds (19, 20): "And ye say, Why is it that the son doth not bear the iniquity of the father? Because, saith he, the soul that sinneth it shall die; but the son shall not receive the unrighteousness of his father, neither shall the father receive the unrighteousness of his son. The righteousness of the righteous shall be upon him, and the wickedness of the wicked shall be upon him." Who of us could have presented this with such clearness?

He derives a still further reason in confirmation of his righteousness, from the acts of mercy, and makes the declaration, that even those who have voluntarily sinned, their past errors shall not injure, provided they repent and reform. "If the wicked," says he (21, 22), "turn from his iniquities which he hath done, and keep my commandments, all his faults, whatever he hath done, shall not be remembered. In the righteousness which he hath done, he shall live the life" That is, since I am so merciful as to pardon even the actual transgressions of those who repent, how is it possible that I should impute foreign sins to those who are born? From these as well as from the following words, it is manifest how God would judge. He will not im-

pute the sins of parents to the children, nor the sins of children to
the parents   And thus is it also shown from scripture proof, where-
in reason did not suffer us to doubt, that in his decisions, God ob-
serves the same righteousness which he has observed in his precepts.

Augustine.   This promise by the prophet Ezekiel, which you do
not understand, refers to the New Testament, where God distinguishes the regenerated from the begotten, by their conduct in riper
years.   For those of whom it is said, " The soul of the father is
mine, and the soul of the son is mine," are already living their own
lives.   But while the prophet veiled the secret, which in its time was
to be unveiled, he did not call it the new birth, by which every son
of man passes from Adam to Christ , but he intended that what he
did not then say, should be understood when the veil should be removed from those who pass to Christ.   I ask you, then, whether if
man performs all the works of righteousness which the prophet Ezekiel so often mentions, he shall live, even without being born again ?
If you say, he shall live, Christ contradicts it, when he says (John 6:
54), " Except ye eat my flesh and drink my blood, ye have no life
in you."   That *flesh* and *drink* here refer to the regenerated, yourself, willing or unwilling, must allow.   But if, borne down by the
weight of such an authority, you reply, that he who does all that
good, if not regenerated, does not live, then tell what is the cause,
and see, that not *imitation*, but *regeneration*, is put in opposition to
generation, when the apostle represents Adam on the part of sin,
and Christ on the part of righteousness.   On account of baneful
generation it is said (Deut. 5 9), " I will recompense the sins of the
fathers upon the children ;" and hence arose the proverb of the sour
grapes.   But the New Testament is promised on the ground of free
regeneration, where this shall no longer be said, because the condemned inheritance derived from Adam, is renounced through the
grace of Christ.   You therefore do not understand the proverb contained in the words of the prophet.

That also needs to be more accurately defined which, according
to your position, the prophet says, namely, that " children are benefited by no virtues of the parents."   For would you deny that
through the faith of the parents, the children of mother church are
presented for regeneration and baptized by the ministers of God ?
Shall not therefore the virtue of the parents aid the children at all ?
Or will you undertake to maintain that christian faith is no virtue ?

Are they not aided when they are brought into the kingdom of God by that regeneration ? Why, too, was it said to Isaac, of temporal benefits (Gen. 26. 24), " I will do it for thee on account of thy father Abraham ?" And on what ground was Lot, the son of Abraham's brother, benefited by the merits of his uncle, if the virtues of the fathers do not benefit their children ? The parable of the prophet, therefore, means nothing else but that the unregenerated father does not injure the regenerated son, in the attainment of eternal life, to which the expression refers, " he shall live the life ;" that the regenerated father does not help the ungenerated son in this; and that again the regenerated son does not help the unregenerated father, or the unregenerated son does not injure the regenerated father, so that the one dies and the other lives.

Thus much for the scripture proofs which Julian employed to show the *injustice* of imputing foreign sins.

Against the Augustinian assumption, that temporal death is a punishment of Adam's sin, the Pelagians brought the case of Enoch and Elias who, according to scripture, did not die, and that, at the coming of Christ, believers then alive will not die but will go to meet the Lord in the air ; and consequently bodily death can be no punishment of sin for all men, for those are free from it — In the prohibition therefore, " in the day thou eatest of the interdicted tree, thou shalt die the death," spiritual and not natural death is to be understood. Sin effects that, but not the seed ; in that transgression only occurs, and man can escape it only by repentence. Ep. 193. c. 3, 4. Comp. Lib de octo Dulcitu Quaestionibus, quaest. 3 ; Op Imp. VI 30.

Here Augustine knew of nothing satisfactory to reply, and came at last to the resort that, according to revelation (John 11: 7), it is probable that Enoch and Elijah would again return to this earth for a short time and die, in order that the punishment of Adam's sin might be also accomplished in them. Comp. De Gen. ad Lib. IX. 6. In respect to the words of Paul (1 Thess 4 15), " we which are alive —shall be caught up," etc., he confessed his ignorance and the difficulty of reconciling them with other passages of Paul in which he speaks of the universality of death or the universality of the resurrection. Yet he justly remarked that, allowing some to be freed from death, it does not follow that it is no punishment of Adam's sin. For if besides the sin, God wills also to forgive the punishment of sin to

40

some, what can we have to reply ? This would be a special grace. But how the universality of original sin would not hereby fail of proof —this doubt Augustine did not satisfactorily solve.

The passage in Wisdom 12 10, 11, Julian would not take in the strongest sense, but would understand as a comparison. The author would say, that the old inhabitants of the holy land had so despised God's long-suffering and had become so wedded to their vices, that it seemed as though these were born with them The expression, " cursed seed," he referred to Ham, on whom his father Noah had pronounced the curse

The scripture proofs of the freedom of the human will, could not fail the Pelagians, for they had only to adduce all the passages where the particular application of its power is ascribed to man and he is called to virtue and to a blameless life. And they ceased not to make use of these passages.

In the letter to Demetrias (c. 8), Pelagius proves from scripture, that sinners cannot exculpate themselves on the ground of any necessity in their nature, but fall always by voluntary inclination. Since in the same nature and amid the like circumstances, the deserts are different, the cause is to be sought simply in freewill. Pelagius further remarked, that it would conflict with the righteousness of God, to give man a law which he could not keep. 19 The apostle could not have said to Ananias, Why hath satan tempted thy heart to lie to the Holy Ghost ? if the devil, (whose influence on men Pelagius admitted, with all his cotemporaries), could have done this without the consent of the will of Ananias. 29. Pelagius further quoted, as a proof of freewill, Ps. 109· 18, where it is said, He delighted in cursing, and it shall come upon him ; and he refused blessing, and it shall be far from him. To cripple the proof of this passage, Augustine sought to help himself in a way which he had often tried in the like condition, but by which the very essence of freedom would be totally destroyed, namely, by the assumption that, after the fall, freedom for evil still remains to man. " In that passage," says Augustine (De Gest Pel 3), " the question regards the corruption, not of nature as God had formed it, but of the human will which is estranged from God. But if he had not indeed loved the curse and had willed the blessing, and if he had then denied that his will was in this very thing aided by grace, he would have been abandoned to his own guidance as ungrateful and impious ; so that without God's guidance, he would be hurled to the abyss and gone to his own punishment, as he could not have been regulated by himself."

Also from one of the apochryphal books of the Old Testament, of which Pelagius as well as Augustine made just the same use as of the canonical, Pelagius borrowed a proof for the moral freedom of man. " He has placed before thee water and fire," it is said in Ecclesiasticus 15: 16, 17, " stretch forth thy hand to which thou wilt. Before man, is good and evil, life and death. That which pleases him, shall be given to him." With this, he connected, in his epistle to Demetrias (2), the passage in Deuteronomy . " I have given before thy face, the blessing and the curse Choose life for thyself, that thou mayest live." In precisely the spirit of his system, Augustine also here remarked (ib.) " It is obvious, that if the man puts his hand into the fire, and evil and death please him, the will of man produces this. But if he loves good and life, the will does this not alone, but is divinely aided. For the eye is adequate of itself for not seeing, i. e for darkness but it is not competent of itself to see by its own light, if the aid of a clear light from without, is not afforded."

Julian also found in 2 Cor 5· 10, a striking proof of freewill. " Freewill, as we hold it, is that on account of which alone the teacher of the Gentiles writes, " We are to be manifest before the tribunal of Christ, that each one may receive what belongs to his body (propria corporis), according as he hath done either good or evil." Op. Imp. I. 96

The Mosaic law Julian also regarded as a witness for the freedom of the will. But according to Augustine, it was given, that man might see that he is evil ; that he cannot become better by the law ; and should hence long for the aid of grace. VI. 15.

Pelagius could find no proof of the want of freedom in the passage quoted for this purpose by Augustine from Rom. 7: 15, 19, " What I will I do not, but what I hate, that I do," etc In his commentary on Romans, Pelagius explained this passage as referring to the power of habit, by which one comes, as by intoxication, to forgetfulness of himself But he also proposed other interpretations which were different from the Augustinian. In the power of evil habit, freedom always remains entire ; for with Pelagius, the evil habit itself was something culpable. Still less could he find, in Rom. 6: 20, 21, " when ye were the servants of sin, ye were free from righteousness," what Augustine found in it, namely, that by the sin of Adam, man's freedom was lost as the "possibility of good and evil." "Ye were free from righteousness," was nothing else with Pelagius but, Ye did not serve righteousness. The fruit of it was death, i. e. temporal and eternal unhappiness. But now, as ye are freed from sin, and have become the servants of righteousness, ye have the fruit of living as consecrated by baptism. In this way Pelagius could bring the passage to harmonize with his system. In like manner Julian interpreted it. Op. Imp. I. 107 sqq.

In John 8. 36, If the Son shall make you free, ye shall be free indeed, Julian found that deliverance from punishment, which is granted to sinners through Christ. "In these words, the Lord promises pardon (indulgentiam) to the guilty who have lost by sin, not the freedom of will, but the consciousness of rectitude. But freewill is as complete (plenum) after sin as it was before sin, for by its operation, it comes to pass that most men abandon the hidden things of infamy (2 Cor 4: 2), and after forsaking disgraceful vices, they become adorned with the badges of virtue." Op. Imp. I. 91. Julian also quoted (93), in support of freewill, John 5. 43. Matt. 12: 33. 23. 37, 38. John 10. 38

The truth of the Pelagian opinion, that man can be without sin, —for which Jerome, though unjustly, reproached the Pelagians with teaching a stoical apathy—Caelestius sought also to prove from scripture passages; and placed these in opposition to Augustine's scripture proofs for the contrary position Augustine also, (De Perf. Just. Hom. 11 sqq), knew how to adapt them to his system.

In the letter to Demetrias, c. 8, Pelagius endeavored to make the goodness of human nature itself intuitively evident from the fact, that men were without the law for so many years before the time of Moses. God knew, said Pelagius, that he had so formed human nature that it might do without the law.

The passage in 1 John 2. 16, The lust of the flesh is not from the Father, and from which Augustine endeavored to prove that concupiscence is something sinful, was interpreted by Julian in another way. He explained "concupiscence of the flesh" by *luxury* (luxuria). To this Augustine replied, that as luxury is a bad thing, how can a desire which seeks what is bad, be a good thing? Op. Imp. IV 69

Finally, as respects the question of the origin and propagation of the soul, creationism was taken under patronage by the Pelagians. "We believe," says Pelagius in his confession of faith, " that souls are given by God, and say they are made by himself. We condemn connected with the bodies, or have resided in heaven."* They were the error of those who maintain that they have sinned before being inclined to creationism for precisely the same reason that Augustine could not adopt it, namely, because it would not harmonize with his assumption of original sin. C. d. Epp. Pel. II. 2. From Ezek. 18: 4, As the soul of the father so also the soul of the son, all souls are mine, Julian sought to prove, though not in a strictly demonstrative way, that the work of propagation can have no influence on the soul, which belongs to God. Op. Imp. III. 44

The words in Col. 1: 13, " Who delivereth us from the power of darkness," which Augustine brought as a proof that man in his natural state is found under the power of the devil, Pelagius in his commentary referred to ignorance or error Julian would at least not have them applied to infants

The Pelagians, having now defended their theory of the uncorrupted state of human nature, and of the moral freedom of the will, both by philosophy and scripture, and having wrested from the hands of Augustine the exegetical weapons for his original sin, needed no scripture proofs at all for their other doctrines in opposition to Augustine ; for these followed of course from that theory. If there is no original sin, then the pardon of it cannot be the object of infant baptism ; and then, too, the children that die before baptism, cannot be eternally damned ; for all ground for such a condemnation fails, and it is utterly opposed to correct ideas of God's holiness and justice. The passages particularly quoted by Augustine for his theory of infant baptism, could cause but little trouble to the Pelagians. We do not indeed find how they explained themselves respecting the passage in Mark, He that believeth not shall be damned ; but they needed only to understand it of unbelieving adults to whom the gospel is preached, in order completely to destroy all Augustine's argument. John 3: 5, Except one be born of water and the spirit, he cannot enter into the kingdom of God, they might aptly bring into harmony with their theory, by which they made a distinction be-

---

* Referring of course to the opinion of Origin, who supposed all souls to have existed in heaven and to have there sinned and merited their banishment to this earth —Tr

tween salvation and the kingdom of God.   According to that theory, none but the baptized enter the kingdom of God.   The words in Rom 6: 3 sq , Whoever of us have been baptized in Christ Jesus, have been baptized in his death (in morte), etc., Pelagius, in his commentary, referred to adults who had gone over to Christianity by baptism.   These were bound by baptism to die to sin and to renounce their previous sinful life.   And Julian found in this passage, not a proof of original sin, but a call to virtue   Op. Imp. II. 223.   And 2 Cor. 5· 14, One died for all ; therefore all were dead, etc , Pelagius explained thus : Christ was the individual who was presented as a spotless victim for all who were dead in sin.

What there was further in the Pelagian theory of grace that particularly differed from the Augustinian—for even supernatural influences of grace the Pelagians admitted in a certain sense—followed of itself from their theory of the incorrupt state of man and the moral freedom remaining to man after the sin of Adam.   Hence it followed that, by supernatural influence, the practice of virtue is rendered *easier* to man, but is not thus made possible ; that consequently many individual good acts may be performed without the aid of grace ; that we must seek to deserve this grace by the application of our own power ; and that grace is not irresistible.   Only in this way can a supernatural grace be brought to harmonize with the Pelagian view of man's moral nature, as well as the moral attributes of God.

The scripture passages by which man's freedom can be proved, were hence also proof texts for the Pelagian limitations under which alone their defenders admitted any supernatural influences of grace. From passages like Zech 1· 3, Turn unto me and I will turn unto you, they endeavored to prove, that grace is imparted according to our merits , against which Augustine could easily adduce declarations of the Bible which appear to have an opposite meaning. De Gr. et Lib. Arb. 5.

In his commentaries, Pelagius knew how to give a sense consistent with his theory, to passages in Paul's epistles in which to think and to will as well as to perform good, seem to be presented as the immediate effect of Deity.   Rom 8. 14, Those who are led by the spirit of God, are the sons of God, he explained as, Those who *deserve* to be ruled by the Holy Ghost ;—just as, on the other hand, they who sin are led by the spirit of the devil.   Or, they who live according to the teaching of the Holy Ghost, are those who are moved by the spirit of God.   1 Cor 12: 11, All these things worketh one and the same spirit, etc , he understood of miraculous gifts, among which he also reckoned faith, in as much as this is capable of working miracles, e g to remove mountains.   2 Cor. 3. 5, We are not sufficient to think anything as of ourselves, but our sufficiency is of God, he referred to the apostles who, without God's grace, could not save the world.   Paul intended to show that he did nothing by his own skill or power.   Phil. 1: 29, To you it is given, on Christ's account, not only to believe in him, but also to suffer, he explained thus : "The occasion of faith is given by God ; for if Christ had not come and taught, we should not believe at all.   In other respects, we find even faith to be voluntary in the acts of the law," i. e. in the books of the Old Testament.   "He therefore designs you should have not only the merit of faith, but also the reward of martyrdom ; while God suffers you to be tempted in order that you may conquer."   On Phil. 2: 13, For it is God that worketh in you both to will and to do of good will, he remarked : " The willing he produces by persuading and by promising rewards.—But the doing as well as the willing is ours, since by the limitation of the passage itself, both belong together."   The words, " of good will" (pro bono voluntate), he referred, not to God, but to man, and explained them thus : "If ye continue in the same (si in ea maneatis)."   Rom. 5. 5, The love of God is shed abroad in our hearts by the Holy Ghost, which is given unto us, he explained thus · "How God loves us, we know from this, that he has not only forgiven our sins through the death of his son, but has also given us the Holy Ghost, who now shows us the glory of things future."   In 1 Cor. 8: 1, he understands by " knowledge (scientia)" human knowledge. This puffeth up those who have not divine knowledge with it.   Passages like 1 Cor. 4. 7, What hast thou which thou hast not received ? he referred, not to an immediate, but an indirect operation of God. De Pec. Mer II. 18.   The Pelagians also quoted Prov. 16. 1, It belongs to man to prepare the heart (hominis est preparare cor) and, the answer of the tongue is from the Lord.   From this they argued, that man can commence virtue without the aid of grace. C. d. Epp. Pel. II. 9.

On the other hand, Augustine endeavored to show, from passages of scripture, that all which man does, takes place from God.   " Man

does no good things," says Augustine, " which God does not make
him do."

In opposition to the Augustinian belief of an impartation of grace
by which it does not depend and cannot depend on man's conduct,
and consequently as little on a resistance as on prayer or knocking,
the Pelagians endeavored to make Matt. 7 7, avail them, where it
is said, Ask and ye shall receive ; seek and ye shall find ; knock
and it shall be opened unto you, etc. On the contrary, Augustine
remarked, (C. Jul. IV 8), that grace must precede this knocking
and seeking; it must already have touched the man's heart. " Your
explanation" that it depends on man's will in seeking and knocking,
" infants themselves refute by their silence, who no more ask than
seek or knock ; but besides, when baptized, they cry and oppose and
struggle against it, and still they receive, and find, and it is opened
unto them.   And they go hence into the kingdom of God, where
they have the salvation of eternity and the reception of the truth,
while far more children are not received to that grace by him who
wills all men to be saved."   In what sense Augustine understood
the last passage, we have already seen.

Finally, as respects the Pelagian doctrine of predestination, it
stood in the closest connection with the other doctrines of the Pelagians. In his predestination to salvation, God must have had respect
to man's worthiness, for otherwise man would cease to be a moral
being. The application of the power which he has, must first make
him capable and worthy of salvation. And the redemption of Christ
must extend to the whole human race, because all have a like promise of salvation, based simply on the good use of their powers.

How the passages in Romans which seem to bear an Augustinian
import, would be explained by Pelagius, has been already shown
while presenting his view of predestination   It is here only needful
to remark further, that the words (c. 9), " Therefore it is not of him
that willeth nor of him that runneth, but of God that showeth mercy,"
to " why doth he yet find fault," were taken by Pelagius as an objection which Paul raises against himself, and in opposition to which
he maintains the freedom of man. But Augustine considered the
Pelagian explanation of those passages of Paul in which he saw his
" absolute," but they their " conditional predestination," to be totally
at variance with the connection. If God, said Augustine, loved Jacob and hated Esau, because he foresaw their future works, why did

he not say this, when he raised the objection to himself (Rom. 9: 14),
" What shall we then say ? Is there unrighteousness with God ?
God forbid." Here was the place to explain himself in so brief
and clear a manner as the following—" for God foresaw their works
when he said, the elder shall serve the younger," etc. Ep. 194. c 8.

Julian especially knew how to explain away, with great acuteness,
the unconditional decree which Augustine found so plainly asserted
in the apostle's declaration (Rom ix), He hath mercy on whomhe
will, and whom he will he hardeneth.

He commences with the remark, that the apostle was disputing
with the Jews, who, as they were so proud of their origin, could not
endure to have the Gentile believers enjoy equal privileges as Christians   Paul therefore taught and showed them, that it well comport-
ed with the justice and grace of God, for God first to distinguish the
Jews by the knowledge of his law ; and afterwards, by the preaching of Christ, to call the heathen also to the christian religion.   God,
says he, is not the God of the Jews only, but also of the Gentiles.
He gives to each his own, without defrauding him and without grace,
i. e. without respect of persons, (for in this sense is the word grace
to be taken in the definition of righteousness), and he will reward
Jews and heathen according to their conduct.   The teacher of the
Gentiles therefore endeavors to quell the pride of the Jews, and
shows, by the example of Jacob and Esau, that the preference of a
people rests, not on desert, but on moral conduct.

While the apostle carries this through the whole controversy, he
nevertheless speaks in some passages, in order to humble the arrogance of the circumcised, of the mere power of God under the name
of grace.   For instance, addressing these, who sought their glory in
the observance of ceremonies and the presentation of sacrifices, and
on this account believed that other nations, who were not bound to
the customs of the law, could not and ought not immediately to
come into communion with themselves, he says that, even if the sum
of righteousness consisted in those observances, still God had it in
his power to make a change among nations, so as to reject whom he
would, and adopt whom he would.   Hereupon, *he suffers a Jew to
make the objection*, So then nothing more can be required of the will
of man, since God has mercy on whom he will, and hardens whom
he will   Against this, the apostle subjoins, O man, who art thou that
repliest against God ? and introduces the testimony of Isaiah, Shall

41

the thing formed say to him that formed it, why hast thou made me thus? and adds of himself, Or·has not the potter power over the clay, of the same lump to make one vessel to honor and another to dishonor? That is to say; Because I have commended the will of God and set forth the authority of his grace by saying that he has shown mercy to him on whom he has had mercy, thou, O Jew, bringest the malicious objection against me, as though the commendation I have presented of the divine will and the divine power, undermined God's justice, and because I have said, He doeth what he will, thou inferrest that nothing more can be required of the will of man, if God doeth all according to his own will. But when I say of God, He doeth what he will, I say nothing else but that He doeth what he ought; because I show that he willeth nothing but what he ought. Both are the same. Where, therefore, will and justice are inseparably connected, there I have indicated both when I have mentioned one.

The apostle would therefore beat down the pride of the Jews, who glossed their inactivity with the varnish of necessity for the purpose of opposing the reception of the heathen to the privileges of the gospel and making but one community of both, and who urged, that either the heathen should not be admitted to share the promise, or else that freewill would be destroyed. Hence he said, If it were even as thou pretendest, still thou oughtest humbly to pray to God, and not to raise rebellion. And he does not push the matter further, but, as he commended the power of God, so he also defends the justice of God, in as much as in the sequel he says expressly, that the vessels, which are formed to dishonor or to honor, receive this as a punishment or a reward of their own will. "For if God, willing to show his wrath and make his power known in much patience, in the vessels of wrath completely prepared for perdition· And that he might make known the riches of his glory in the vessels of mercy which he has prepared for glory, whom he has also called, even us, not only of the Jews but also of the Gentiles." Here he says expressly, that God suffers those vessels only to feel his wrath, who are completely fitted for destruction, but that glory is awarded to those who are before prepared for it. But by *whom* such vessels are prepared for punishment or for salvation, the apostle plainly declares (2 Tim 2· 20, 21) "In a great house, there are not only vessels of gold and silver, but also of wood and earth; some indeed to honor, and others to dishonor. If one therefore shall cleanse himself from these things, he shall be a vessel sanctified unto honor, useful to the Lord, prepared for every good work." In the words, "If he shall cleanse himself," the work of freewill is recognized. By "vile vessels," are to be understood the vicious. These vessels are therefore prepared by their own efforts either for wrath or for salvation. But in both, God shows his power, as he either exercises his severity towards the ungodly, or bestows his blessing on the faithful. Op Imp. 1. 131 sqq.

By this explanation, Julian endeavored to wrest from Augustine Rom. ix, as favoring his doctrine of predestination. It was not the apostle, but a proud Jew who would grudge the proclamation of the gospel to the Gentiles, that would draw from the words of Paul the inference, "He hath mercy on whom he will," etc. This the Apostle would refute, and would show the harmony of God's justice and his power, by which man's freedom is saved. But what he says himself of the divine grace that has no respect to man's desert, has merely for its object to humble the arrogance of the Jews.

The passage in Isaiah also, from which the apostle had borrowed some words, Julian could bring into harmony with his view, as well as with other declarations of the prophet, in which the latter exhorts to abandon evil and do good, (Is. 1: 16 sq.).

Augustine, as may well be supposed, was not satisfied with this explanation of Julian. He therefore took all pains to show his own interpretation to be the only true one. God, said he, owes grace to none. He appealed to the example of Paul in order to refute the position of Julian, that God does what he ought, and that consequently his will is in accordance with justice, and therefore his grace is guided by man's desert. God brought Paul to himself by his power; and yet he had persecuted the Christians. He had therefore acquired no merits. He appealed to many passages of scripture, e. g. Rom. 11: 5, 6; Ezek. 36. 23, in which it is declared that grace is afforded not at all on account of good works.—He says of the patriarch Jacob, that he was not elected on account of his mild and good character and his obedience to his parents, as Julian would have it; but that he was made a good man *because* he was elected. He conceded, in regard to 2 Tim. 2· 21, that it may be said of a man, that he prepares himself for salvation; but he there made the remark, which again removes freedom, that the will must be before prepared by the Lord.—According to the Apostle's express declara-

tion, it depends not on the willing and the running of man, but on the
mercy of God   God therefore did not show mercy because Jacob
willed and ran ; but Jacob willed and ran because God showed
mercy   But God shows mercy according to grace, which is given
gratuitously, and is not awarded to merit; but he hardens in judgment, which is sent according to desert.   For out of a condemned
mass to make a vessel to honor, is manifest grace ; but to make a
vessel to dishonor, is a righteous judgment of God, etc.

The passage in Eph. 1· 4 sq , on which Augustine laid great stress,
Pelagius explains, in his commentary, in a manner agreeable to
his theory   On the words, As he chose us in him before the foundation of the world, that we should be holy and immaculate, he says,
in accordance with his conditional predestination, " Because there is
nothing new with him, all was with him before it takes place ; not
as some heretics dream, as though the souls had been assembled in
heaven."   And on the words, He predestinated us to the adoption of
sons, etc., " He decreed that men who would believe, should have
power to become children of God, as it is written, They spoke with
assurance to every one that would believe."   " According to the
purpose of his will," he explained as " Not according to our merit."

The words of Paul therefore contain a predestination , but precisely because it has respect to the conduct of man, it is in no contradiction with the freedom of the human will   On the other hand,
it is to be regarded as grace and not as merit, that God will permit
the salvation of Christianity to be imparted to man on the condition
of his own application of his power

Pelagius found the universality of redemption plainly enough declared even in Paul's epistles : " Christ died for all," (2 Cor. 3: 15),
means, according to Pelagius's interpretation, Christ was presented
as a spotless offering for all sinners   On 1 Tim 2· 4, Who would
have all men to be saved and come to a knowledge of the truth, he
remarked, that the objection from the hardening of Pharaoh· and the
rest of the objections of this kind, are removed.   God wills that all
should be relieved, if they will all only give ear to God's call.   On
verse 6, " Who gave himself as redemption for all," he remarked,
He has given himself for all if all would be redeemed.

Thus much for the reasons which Augustine, on one side, and Pelagius on the other, employed as proofs of the soundness of their theories. ·We are yet to cast a' searching glance on those proofs at the close of this work. But the question is first to be answered, how the fathers previous to Augustine thought respecting the contested doctrines, as it must not be passed over in a pragmatic history of the Augustinian and Pelagian controversies.

REMARK BY THE TRANSLATOR

Here our author closes what was more appropriately the result of his own investigation of the original sources of the history   For the matter contained in the ensuing chapter, he appears to have relied, in no small degree, on the labors of his predecessors in the same field,—Horn, Münscher, etc.

Nor is it to be expected that he should here show the same depth of research as in the previous portion which he had assumed as his more appropriate subject of investigation   Of course his individual opinion on any topic pertaining to this earlier period, though certainly worthy of regard, cannot justly challenge so high a degree of deference as on topics of the period he had so much more thoroughly studied. '

Here, too, he can no longer follow the *exhausting* method, but is compelled to give only a brief and compendious view of the opinions of the earlier fathers on the points in question.   In some cases, this view has indeed appeared to me so brief as hardly to convey, to one not previously acquainted with the subject, either a very clear or just conception of the matter presented : and in such cases I have felt it a duty to make room for considerably more extended extracts from the original sources, as well as for explanatory remarks.

CHAPTER XXII.

Examination of the question respecting the opinions of the fathers previous to Augustine, in regard to the contested doctrines of Augustinism and Pelagianism.

Such an investigation is certainly very important and interesting; but it is also very laborious and difficult, especially as the ecclesiastical writers do not always express themselves with sufficient precision.—Here we can of course refer only to the *results* which have been afforded by examining the opinions of individual fathers.

Vossius has collected much for this purpose, though he lacked the proper critical skill. Whitby also, in his Tractatus already quoted, has brought together much concerning the opinions of the early fathers on original sin and the imputation of it Horn's Commentatio de Sententiis eorum Patrum quorum Auctoritas ante Augustinum plurimum valuit de Peccato Originali (Goett. 1801—4), possesses great merit and facilitates the investigation respecting original sin and the doctrines more immediately connected with it This prize essay contains a tolerably complete exhibition of individual fathers in regard to the doctrine of original sin. Only it ought to have been more definitely shown in what the fathers placed the image of God that was lost by Adam's fall. That the works of Munscher, Wundemann, and others, contain much on this subject, needs not to be mentioned.

Here too we find, what is often enough met with in ecclesiastical history, that, in the rising contests, each party charged the other with departing from the doctrine of the church. It is worthy of remark that Augustine reproached the Pelagians abundantly with introducing a *new* doctrine. He calls the Pelagian heresy " the most recent heresy of all, originating from the monk Pelagius." De Haeresibus, c. 88. He never derives Pelagianism from any earlier heretic; and hence appears to have regarded Pelagius as the inventor of a new doctrine. This he might the more readily do as he was ignorant of the Greek fathers. Only once or twice does he express himself doubtfully; namely, in De Pec. Orig 22, where he says, respecting Pelagius and Caelestius, " They are either believed or even proved to be the *authors* of this perversity , or, if they are not the *authors* but have learned it from others, they are certainly the assertors and teachers of it," etc ; and in Ep 190. c. 6, where he calls them " either the authors or at least the most eager and notorious advocates of the new heresy."

Thus much however is certain, that Augustine regarded Pelagianism as a new doctrine, and was only sometimes doubtful as to its author.

[It may here properly be added that, when pressed by the Pelagians for more of positive proofs that his own doctrines were the same as those held by the previous fathers, Augustine urged, as asserted by Faber, that the reason why no more direct proof was to be found, was the fact, that those doctrines had always been held in the church *without being disputed*, and therefore the previous fathers had not been led to say much respecting them.

This plea has certainly the air of plausibility ; nor can I doubt that it contains much of truth. At the same time it is by no means enough to prove that those fathers thought *exactly* with Augustine on even a single subject—much less that his theory as a *whole* was precisely the same as theirs. Their mere silence, simply in itself, could indeed prove nothing at all in respect to their belief either way. It could only show that there was but very little if any dispute on the topics. Other evidence is therefore needed in order to show which way the general tide was flowing, if indeed there *was* then much tide of this sort in either direction. If, in such a case the *positive* proof, though scanty and not very decisive in its nature, should yet be all on one side, the argument from the comparative silence must lend whatever force it possesses (which may sometimes be very great) in further support of that side.

In the present case, the sources of argument are two. One of them is the actual state of belief in the church at the time when the Pelagian controversy commenced. If the church were then in the main on the one side or on the other, the inference must be that they had always been on that side, unless the fact can be sufficiently accounted for on special grounds.

And here the special cause that is chiefly worthy of consideration,

is that which has before been incidentally brought to view, though
in a different connection ; I mean the fact that the church were called upon to sustain a perpetual warfare against the doctrine of heathen fate, and thus to give a disproportionate prominence to those
doctrines that lie at the foundation of human responsibility   It is
morally impossible for such a thing as this to be done in a community, for any great length of time, without materially though perhaps
silently changing the faith of that community.   I am acquainted with
no important and extensive cause, of the opposite tendency, that can
fairly be assigned as a counterpoise to this.

But the further question of fact, and indeed the chief one on this
branch of the evidence, still remains: What *was* the actual state of
doctrinal belief in the church at the commencement of the Pelagian
disputes ?   And here, again, the evidence is twofold ; first, the testimony given and the doctrinal positions maintained by cotemporary
writers ; and secondly, the decisions on the controversy itself by the
councils held respecting it.   On the former of these two sources,
nothing further need here be added.   And on the latter, very little
can perhaps be suggested that has not already occurred to the reader
while tracing the progress of the events in the case.   I will recal
his attention here but to a single topic   It is the simple but great
fact, that the controversy was so generally decided against the Pelagians.   If this does not prove that the church in general were thoroughly Augustinian, as it certainly does not, it is nevertheless one
of the strongest proofs that they were at quite a remove from Pelagianism.   When all the abatements are made which candor would
require in view of the facts which our author has placed in so strong a
light—the influence of Augustine, the part taken by the civil rulers,
the supposed combination of the Alexandrian and Romish prelates,
etc.,—the great fact is still very far from a satisfactory explanation without supposing a strong and pervading, though perhaps not
very definite sentiment in opposition to the Pelagian opinion.   Had
the current been the other way, who can believe that the single man
Augustine, giant though he was, could so decidedly have changed it
in a single score of years—nay, in less than half that time so far as
the decision of the Latin church was concerned.

And then, again, if this was not substantially the general state of
belief, at least among the Latins, how could Augustine speak as he
continually does, of Pelagianism as being a novelty ?   And if it

was not nearly so in the east likewise, how could the more learned Jerome, who had now long been residing in Palestine, give such a view of the case as the one now immediately to be presented from him by our author?—TR.]

Jerome thought differently [from Augustine, as to the complete novelty of Pelagianism, though manifestly agreeing with him in the main position, that it was far from being the general faith of the church.—TR.] Besides attributing the Pelagian errors in part to several philosophers, he admits that they were brought forward by some teachers in the church, as Origen, Rufinus, or, as he generally calls him, *Grunnius* (a nick-name from *grunnire*), Evagrius of Pontus, Jovian, and others See the prologue to his Dialogue against the Pelagians, the preface to his fourth book on Jeremiah, and other passages. He calls the Pelagian doctrine "a twig of Origen" (Ep. 133), which in his view, at that time, was a great offence.

Marius Mercator derives the Pelagian heresy from certain Syrians, and particularly Theodore of Mopseusta, and makes Rufinus to have first brought it from Syria to Rome. Com. p. 63. Ap.

On the other hand, the Pelagians maintained that *their* doctrine was orthodoxy; that they had in their favor the sentiments of the fathers, among whom they often and joyfully quoted Chrysostom; and that their opponents departed from the doctrine of the church.

The reproach was very frequently retorted by the Pelagians, and particularly by Julian, that Augustine's doctrine was no better than what Augustine represented Pelagianism as being, i. e. nothing but Manichaeism.

Against this reproach, Augustine defended himself and sought, especially in his first two books against Julian, to prove that the doctrine of Adam's sin passing over to his posterity, had in its favor the most famous of the Greek as well as of the Latin fathers; and that therefore, if the doctrine was Manichaean, the reproach of Manichaeism fell also upon these fathers; but that Manichaeism rather received support from the Pelagian doctrine.

And in fact, as we have already seen, Augustine's doctrine was at a distance from Manichaeism. Its opposition to Manichaeism consisted mainly in Augustine's endeavoring to avoid the dualism of Manes by holding that original sin was not of man's substance, which, as created by God, he considered good in its nature. Au-

42

gustinism, however, in many of its parts, preserved an echo of Manichaeism. Among the most striking of these, may be mentioned what Augustine says of concupiscence in generation, by which man is subjected to the devil · only Manes went one step farther. He allowed the devil to be the *author* of man by concupiscence, and therefore regarded lust as something evil. See the letter of Manes to his daughter Menoch, quoted by Julian. Op. Imp. III. 180, 187.

But how did Augustinism and Pelagianism actually stand in relation to what the earlier fathers taught on the contested points ?

To facilitate our view of the various opinions of the fathers, before Augustine, on the contested doctrines, it will be expedient to distinguish the doctrine of original sin and what is directly connected with it, from the doctrines of grace, redemption, and predestination.   Therefore ·

I. *Opinions of the fathers, before Augustine, concerning original sin and the doctrines more immediately connected with it.*

Here we must first remark, that speculation among the fathers on the nature of man as changed by Adam's sin, first began in the time of Justin, and therefore not till after the time when the philosophers came over to Christianity, i e after the middle of the second century.   The apostolic fathers, so far as we can judge from the remnants that have reached us of their works, did not trouble themselves concerning this anthropological matter.   What they said respecting it may be reduced to the following simple and indefinite propositions.   Adam was created upright by God and destined to immortality   The cause of sin was external, namely, the devil ; the limits of whose kingdom do not extend so far that he can compel us to sin, but rather we can resist him.   When we are perfect, it is our work *and* God's.   See Horn's Comm. p. 8.

Hence when we speak of the opinions of the fathers before Augustine, we can refer only to those who lived after the middle of the second century, and consequently from the time of Justin.   And here it is manifest,

1. That almost all the fathers before Augustine, agreed with him in believing that man was originally made upright, possessed freedom of will ; and would not have died if he had not sinned.   They regarded the death of the body as a punishment of Adam's sin for

Adam himself, and as at best an evil proceeding from him to his posterity, and consequently as a hereditary evil Had Adam not transgressed God's command, as a reward of his obedience he would not have died. This opinion was maintained, with many modifications indeed, among the Greek fathers by Justin Martyr, Tatian, Theophilus of Antioch, Irenaeus, Clement of Alexandria, Methodius, Cyril of Jerusalem, Athanasius, Basil, both the Gregories, and Chrysostom ; and among the Latin, by Tertullian, Cyprian, and Ambrose. The passages on this subject, which might easily be increased by many others, have been collected by Horn. We need only further to remark, that several of these fathers, particularly Irenaeus, Methodius, Basil, Gregory Nazianzen, and Ambrose, and besides them Hilary of Poictiers, considered death so far a blessing from God as that an end is thus put to man's sinful state. Gregory of Nyssa thought death a physical consequence resulting from the use of the forbidden fruit, by which a kind of poison, destructive to man's nature, invaded human bodies. Orat Magna Catechet sec. 37. But in this he consequently differed from Augustine and many other ancient fathers, e. g. Theophilus.

Athenagoras does not express his opinion respecting Adam's fall and its consequences. Origen, Arnobius, and Lactantius differed from the other fathers by holding to some singular opinions, derived mostly from Platonism.

(a) Origen, as is well known, in accordance with the Platonic philosophy, supposes all souls to be connected with their material bodies by way of punishment for sins previously committed by them. He allowed, however, that souls were originally good and endowed with freewill. They are imprisoned as it were in bodies for sins before committed. He regarded bodily death as a punishment of the sins which each soul committed before the creation of the world.

(b) Arnobius, whose views were not the most popular, allowed that the human soul, which held a middle rank between the mortal and the divine nature, was not created by the supreme God, and therefore considered moral wretchedness, sin, and death as natural and inbred evils Hence immortality could be conferred only by the special blessing of God Disputatt. adv. Gentes II. c. 30 sqq. Parte prima ex ed. Orelli. Lipsiae 1816.

(c) Lactantius, a disciple of Arnobius, maintained that the human body, as being matter, is corrupt. And yet he says, that the soul of man is good, and that man must therefore strive to conquer matter and gain the mastery of it. Besides he also assumes, that Adam, if he had obeyed God's commands, would not have died; and therefore derived temporal death from Adam's sin. Inst. II 13; Munscher's Handbuch der Dogm. II. 172.*

The Pelagians, then, differed from all the orthodox fathers in maintaining that Adam would have died even if he had not sinned. The orthodox opinion had become so general perhaps in consequence of the threatening, In the day thou eatest thereof thou shalt surely die. The Pelagians explained this passage, as already shown, by spiritual death, or the moral punishment of sin.—The expressions *to be condemned* and *condemnation*, when used by the fathers before Augustine, as referring to the consequences of Adam's sin on his posterity, always relate to temporal death. Here the passage is in point which Augustine quotes (C. Jul. I. 6) from Chrysostom, but from which, as usual, he argues too much for his own theory : " When Adam committed that great sin and involved the whole human race in condemnation (in commune damnavit)," etc.

2. *All* the fathers differed from Augustine and agreed with the Pelagians, in attributing freedom of will to man in his present state. Thus Justin says, in his smaller apology (c. 7. ed, Ben. Hagae Comit. 1742), " Every created being is so constituted as to be capable of vice and virtue For he could do nothing praiseworthy if he had not the power of turning either way." In like manner Athenagoras expresses himself in his apology, e. g c. 24 Irenaeus, Gregory Nazianzen, and Chrysostom, expressly oppose in their writings the fate of the Stoics and triumphantly defend freewill. Clemens Alexandrinus and Origen very strongly maintain the same. The latter even sets it forth as a position of orthodoxy founded on apostolic tradition, that every rational soul possesses freedom of will. De Princip Prooem. p. 48. ed. de la Rue T. I. Paris, 1733.

[Here, however, the reader may be gratified by seeing the man-

---

* In the above statements, we may notice in passing, the deplorable tendency to gnosticism which pervaded even the whole ancient church from a very early period after the accession of the philosophers " Evil matter" was their ceaseless lament—and how to counteract it, their ceaseless cogitation. We might almost say, that *matter*, with them, took the place of Augustinian original sin.—Tr.

ner in which these masters in the early Greek church set forth the matter of human freedom, and also the relation which they considered it as holding to the decrees of God and to the influences of the Divine Spirit. There will be an advantage in giving the passages at some length, though a part of what they contain would be more appropriate under subsequent heads. It will be seen that these men had thought somewhat on these important topics.

"Now," says Clement, "anything is in our power when we are equally masters of that and its opposite; as to philosophize, or not; and to believe, or to disbelieve. And what is in our power, is found possible by our being equally masters of each of the opposite things." Strom. IV. 24. "The use which heathen philosophy had made of divine truth," (that is, in perverting the truth acquired from the prophets of the Old Testament), "was a sin, and one which God foresaw and yet did not prevent; and that because he had a good purpose for which he designed to overrule the sin, though the perpetrator had a different and a bad purpose. I know there are multitudes rising up among us and saying, that he who does not prevent is himself a responsible cause.—But non-prevention is not at all a cause.— Hence whoever *hinders* any one from doing a thing, is responsible for such hindrance; but he who does not thus interpose may justly sit in judgment on the choice of the soul, so that God is not the responsible cause of our sins. But since free choice and voluntary seeking are the commencement of sins, and a false notion sometimes prevails which we through ignorance neglect to abandon, punishments are therefore justly inflicted. For to be sick of a fever is involuntary; but when one brings a fever upon himself by his intemperance, we blame him. Thus the evil may be involuntary, as no one chooses evil merely as evil; but drawn away by the pleasure that surrounds it, supposing it good, he decides to embrace it. These things being so, it is in our power to be free from ignorance and from an evil though pleasing choice, and in spite of them to refuse our assent to these seductive illusions." Strom I. 17.

Still Clement held to our need of divine aid. For, as translated by Cave, he says, that "as there is a free choice in us, so all is not placed in our own power; but that by grace we are saved, though not without good works, and that to the doing of what is good we especially need the grace of God, right instruction, an honest temper of mind, and that the Father draws us to him, and that the powers of the will are never able to wing the soul for a due flight for heaven without a mighty portion of grace to assist it " Strom. I. 5.

Origen thus scientifically states his views on the subject. " In one place, the apostle does not ascribe it to God that a vessel is formed to honor or to dishonor, but refers the whole to us, saying, If any one shall purify himself he shall be a vessel sanctified unto honor and useful unto the master as prepared to every good work. In another place, he does not ascribe it to us but seems to refer the whole to God, saying, The potter hath power, etc Now the things spoken by him are not contradictory, and we must therefore reconcile both and derive from both one perfect sense Neither is our liberty without the wise efficiency of God, nor does this efficiency of God necessitate us to proceed in our course unless we also conduce somewhat to the good that is effected. Neither does freewill cause any one to be unto honor or unto dishonor without the efficiency of God and the disposal of what is according to the dignity of our freewill. Nor does the will of God only form any to honor or to dishonor, unless he have some matter of difference inclining the choice to the worse or the better." De Princ. I. 22.

In another place, when treating on the objection to prayer and effort which is so commonly presented as arising from foreknowledge and decrees, Origen states that there are three kinds of motion, that of inanimate things as of stones, which is motion from without ; that of the vegetable world, as of plants in their growth, which is motion by nature ; and that of living and rational beings, who have motion of themselves (δὶ αἰτῶν). He then proceeds in his argument against the fatalists, which I shall give, as I have given the preceding, in rather a free translation, but taking care to make the essential parts exactly literal. " If we take away from one his motion arising from himself (ἀπ᾽ αὐτοῦ), he can no longer be recognized as an animal but will be either like a plant which is moved only by nature, or like a stone which is impelled by something from abroad. But if any one follows his own motion, as we may call this being moved by himself, he is necessarily rational They, therefore, who will have nothing to be in our power, must necessarily admit this most foolish thing, that we are neither rational nor living beings ; but, as if moved by some one from abroad, and not moving ourselves, we may be said to do by him what we think ourselves to do. Besides, let any one understandingly inspect the things of which himself is

the subject, and see if he can shamelessly say that he does not himself will, and does not himself eat, and does not himself walk, nor himself assent to receive some opinions, nor discard others as false. As,
then, there are some dogmas to which a man can never be induced,
although ten thousand times over he artfully arranges the proofs for
this purpose and employs persuasive language, so is it impossible
that any one should be brought so to think of human things as though
nothing were left in our power. For who settles down in the belief
that nothing is comprehensible?—And who is there that does not
blame the son that fails in filial duty? and censure the adulteress as
base? For the truth impels and necessitates one, in spite of a
myriad of plausible things which he may invent, to break forth in
such cases, either in applauses or censures, as though there were
something still kept in our power as the foundation of praise and
blame. But if freewill is preserved to us, with its ten thousand
propensities to virtue or to vice, and again with all its propensities to
what is fitting or what is improper, all this, together with other things,
was necessarily known to God before it took place, that is, from the
creation and foundation of the world, just as it was to be. And in all
things which God foreordains accordingly as he foresaw respecting
each act of our freewill, his decree was according to what was requisite to each movement of our freewill, and what would be meet
for himself, on the part of providence, and what was to occur according to the connection of things which were to take place; yet, not
that the foreknowledge of God was the cause of all things that are
to take place and that are to be produced from our freewill according
to our spontaneous action. For even on the supposition that God
does not foreknow future events, we could not, on that ground, boast
that we should do these things and think these things. But this advantage, on the other hand, accrues from foreknowledge, namely,
that everything in our power receives an assignment in the arrangement of the universe which is beneficial to the condition of the world."
De Oratione, c. 6.

How far this ancient thinker was right as well as profound in all
this and much more that might be adduced from him on these topics,
and how far his speculations paved the way for Pelagianism,—
and how far too, if well studied, they might have held back both
Pelagius and Augustine from their wide extremes,—we have no time
further to inquire.—It may be well for the reader to bear in mind

the import of what has now been quoted from these writers, while following the necessarily rapid steps of our author through some of the subsequent topics.—Tr]

The manner in which Cyril of Jerusalem expresses himself on freewill, in his fourth catechetical lecture, and even in his chapter on the soul (περὶ ψυχῆς), is remarkable. "Know," he there says, "that thou hast a soul possessed of freewill (ψυχὴν αὐτεξούσιον),—which has power to do what it will. For thou dost not sin by birth (κατὰ γένεσιν), nor by fortune (κατὰ τύχην)," etc. We sin by free choice (ἐκ προαιρέσεως)."

All the Latin fathers also maintained that freewill was not lost after the fall; but they did not express themselves so strongly on the point as the Greeks and especially the Alexandrians Compare Keil, De Doctoribus veteris Ecclesiae Culpa corruptae per Platonicas Sententias theologiae liberandis. Comment. XIII. a. 1804 And even Augustine, as before remarked, declared in favor of freewill, while writing against the Manichaeans. Here we need not, with Wundemann (Gesch. der chrst Glaub II. 92), cite his book De Fide adv. Manichaeos. For as that is ascribed to Evodius, it is not safe *to* infer Augustine's opinion from it.

3 The greater part, at least the most famous, of the fathers, placed the image of God in understanding or perception and freewill; others, in corporeal resemblance to God, and immortality; others, again, in a very favorable state generally, to which they also added the dominion over all other creatures.

First, they perhaps placed it in a corporeal resemblance to God, and thus unquestionably hit in the best manner the sense in the first chapter of Genesis, however anthropomorphic was this presentation. Thus Irenaeus, for example, (who besides, like Theophilus, supposed Adam to come into the world, not in a perfect state, but as a child), placed it in the body (plasmate, Adv. Haer. V. 6, 1), to which he also added immortality. IV. 38, 4. On the contrary, the likeness (דמות), which he distinguishes from the image (צלם, imago), he placed especially in perception and freewill. IV. 4, 3 In like manner, Tertullian places the image in the body (De Resurrect. 6); and also in freewill. C. Marcion II 5.

On the other hand, Clemens Alexandrinus had before refuted those who would place the image in any corporeal resemblance to

God, and with more propriety placed it in understanding. With
him agreed his great disciple Origen. Both likewise distinguished
between the image and the likeness; but in a different way from
Irenaeus. Both placed the image (εἰκὼν imago) of God in the original capacity of man for good; but the likeness (ὁμοίωσις similitudo),
in the good habit acquired by their own assiduity. Clem. Alex. Strom.
II; Orig. De Princ. III. 6.

So must it also early have been placed in immortality, because
the loss of this was regarded as a punishment of Adam's fall.
This was done by Eusebius, but the other fathers of the fourth century, Macarius, the two Gregories, Cyril of Jerusalem, and others
went farther, and placed it in understanding and freewill. Some
of them, e. g. Gregory Nazianzen, *seem* also to have placed it in
immortality. This may be affirmed with certainty of Gregory of
Nyssa The latter also, in his tract on the formation of the first man,
considers him as being in a very happy state before the fall, free
from passions, exercising dominion over the rest of creatures, and
distinguished for personal beauty. But in treating on the image and
likeness, he makes both of them a representation of the mystery of
the trinity and of the incarnation, in as much as Adam may represent
the *unbegotten* God and Father; his son, the *begotten* Word of God;
and Eve, proceeding forth from Adam, the *proceeding* person, or the
Holy Ghost, etc. This view was refuted by Augustine, in De Trin.
XII.

In the work Contra Gentes, attributed to Athanasius, the image of
God is placed in man's being made according to the Logos (κατὰ λό-
γον). In connection with this, stood the idea which Irenaeus, Origen, and others had, and which most of the early Platonic fathers
adopted, namely, that something of the divine Logos was imparted
to men, and indeed to the wise in a higher degree.

Chrysostom placed the image of God in the dominion over the
whole earth which was given to Adam. Ambrose supposes the human soul before the fall, to have been adorned with all virtues, and
seems herein to have placed the image of God. In his book on
Paradise, he explains Paradise to mean the human soul, which was
planted in Eden, i e. where it found a life of joy and pleasure. The
stream which watered it, was Christ, from which four rivers issued,
i. e. the cardinal virtues of wisdom, temperance, valor, and justice.

On the other hand, Augustine, as before shown, placed it in the

43

intelligent and rational nature of man. De Gen. ad Lit. VI. 12 ; De Gen ad Lit. Lib. Imp c 16.

Consequently none but those fathers who placed the image in corporeal resemblance to God, in dominion over the rest of creation, and in immortality, could say that it was lost by the fall. But those who placed it in understanding and freedom of will, could not say that it was lost, since they, like Pelagius, allowed both to remain after the fall. And these again differed from Augustine, for he considered the intellect as weakened and freewill as lost by the fall.

4. A chief point in the Augustinian system, was the imputation of Adam's sin to all his posterity, the reatus peccati Adamitici. The fathers before Augustine never expressly taught this imputation, and consequently they thus far differed from him.

Almost all of them, indeed, considered temporal death as a consequence of Adam's sin and as an evil resulting from Adam's fall. And they accordingly called this evil a punishment of Adam's sin ; and on this account, Augustine appealed to the harmony of the catholic church in this particular De Civ. Dei, XIII. 15. But they never expressly say, that this evil or this punishment has come on Adam's posterity by the *imputation* of his sin.* Thus Tertullian, for example, says, in accordance with his idea of the traducianism of the soul, that Adam left the punishment of death as an inheritance to his posterity. De Test Anim c 3. In his work against Marcion, (I. 22), he says, " The man was condemned to death because he had tasted of one little tree. Hence sins grew with punishment, and all now die who had never known anything of Paradise." But he says nothing of an imputation.

Others indeed express themselves as if they had an imputation in view ; but they may have thought only of a participation in the punishment without imputation of the guilt. Thus Irenaeus, for example, (Adv. Haer. V 16, 3), says · " In the first Adam, we have offended God in not keeping his command ; but in the second Adam, we have again been reconciled with him, since we have become obedient in him even unto death." Basil, in his sermon on fasting as quoted by Augustine (C Jul. I. 5), says, " because we did not fast, we fell from Paradise." Gregory Nazianzen, (Orat. 38. in d. nata-

---

* Nor does Augustine say that it is by the imputation of *his* sin in distinction from its being truly their own sin, committed in him, as before shown.—Tr

lem Christi), in a passage also quoted by Augustine, (C. Jul. I. 5), says : " As in Adam we have all died, so in Christ let us all live. With Christ therefore let us be born, and with him be buried, that with him we may also rise to life. For it is necessary that we undergo this salutary and requisite change, in order that we, who have been brought from a good to a mournful condition, may be brought back from a mournful to a better. For where sin was mighty, grace becomes still more mighty, since those whom the use of the forbidden tree has condemned, the cross of Christ justifies with a richer grace."

Here it is to be remarked that, with the fathers, as Erasmus has suggested, the expression *to die* or *to die in Adam*, is synonymous with being driven out of Paradise, because they who were driven out of Paradise, were no more allowed to eat of the fruit of the tree of life. At least this is the common meaning. For us to have died in Adam, is nothing else than what Methodius, in a fragment in Epiphanius (Haer. 64), thus expresses, " We were driven out of Paradise in the first father." See Horn's Com. p. 51

Gregory of Nyssa, in his larger catechetical sermon (c. 8), says : " Since by the free exercise of will, we have drawn on ourselves a participation in the evil (τῷ αὐτεξουσίῳ κινήματι τοῦ κακοῦ τὴν κοινωνίαν ἐξεσπασάμεθα), since we have, along with a kind of pleasure, brought into our nature as it were a poison mingled with honey, we have thereby fallen from that blessedness which consisted in the absence of passion, and have been changed for the worse."

By Chrysostom, it is even said, that " Christ came and found our hereditary obligation which Adam had written." This passage Augustine quotes in the original from a homily to Neophites, by the famous orator, and uses it in support of his imputation. C. Jul. l. 6. Ambrose says, in his commentary on Luke, according to Augustine's quotation, " the death of all was Adam's guilt.—Adam was, and we were all in him; Adam perished, and all perished in him." C. Jul. I. 3 ; Op Imp. II. 36.

The Augustinian imputation might indeed be derived from such expressions, if the passages were considered aside from their connection and without regard to the other doctrines of the fathers. But they admit also of the explanation, that Adam's posterity share in the *punishment* of his sin, without any *imputation* of its guilt being supposed.

That this last is the sense of those fathers, admits of no doubt. They regarded death as a punishment of Adam's sin, which has extended to all men And as we must now share the punishment, it is just the same as if we had all sinned. Thus Cyril of Jerusalem expresses his opinion of the passage in Rom. 5 14, *death reigned from Adam to Moses.* "This Paul has given in order to teach that, although Moses was a righteous and wonderful man, yet the sentence of death denounced against Adam, came upon him and upon those who followed him. They did not, however, sin like Adam, and by disobedience (ἐν παραχοῇ) eat of the tree in Paradise." Catech 15. Cyril therefore here declares Adam's posterity free from his disobedience.

In this sense may be explained the passages already quoted and others of the like kind. No one of the fathers thought of conceiving of the matter as if Adam's sin was imputed to us.

As part of the curse, which some of the fathers supposed to come on all men, and partly as hereditary, they understood death. Chrysostom, in the passage already quoted, would say nothing more than that Adam first sinned and incurred a debt. This debt was an obligation upon him. He immediately adds · "Adam began the debt and we have increased the loan (τὸν δανεισμὸν) by subsequent sins." In this way the passage is in perfect harmony with other assertions of that father.

Finally, Ambrose explains the words quoted, "the death of all is the fault of Adam," thus. "We all die in Adam, i e. like Adam, because by one man sin came into the world, and death by sin, and so death hath passed through to all men," etc.—Consequently he referred the whole to temporal death as the punishment of Adam's sin. But he says nothing of an imputation of Adam's sin. And just as little does he say of any such imputation in other passages adduced by Augustine. In the passage quoted (De Pec Orig 41) from Ambrose's book on the resurrection, temporal death is spoken of as the punishment of Adam's sin, in which punishment we all share, but nothing is said of an imputation of his sin   "I fell," he says, "in Adam; I was driven from Paradise in Adam , I died in Adam. If he had not found me in Adam, he would not again call me forth as justified in Christ, in like manner as I was subject in Adam to that debt, liable to death." To this also refers what Augustine quotes from the seventh book of Ambrose's exposition of

Luke: "Adam received a deadly wound (lethale vulnus), by which the whole human race would have died if that descending Samaritan had not healed his doleful wound." C. Jul I. 3

Were the second apology of David genuine, a weighty passage might be adduced from it to prove that Ambrose held to an imputation of Adam's sin to all his posterity. For in the twelfth chapter, it is said . " We have all sinned in the first man, and by the consequence of nature the consequence of guilt has passed from one to all.—Adam is in each one of us. For in him, mankind (conditio humana) have sinned, because sin has passed through one to all." But as the Benedictines doubted the genuineness of that work, it is not to be regarded. And in fact a more important reason exists against its genuineness, as Augustine does not adduce it, who was so fond of recurring to Ambrose, and to whom nothing could have been more desirable than just this assertion of the famous bishop of Milan, greatly revered too as he also was by Pelagius

Besides this, passages may be adduced in which the fathers utterly repel any such imputation of Adam's sin, and express themselves directly against it. Particularly is this true of the fathers of the Greek church.

They denied, in part, that man is born infected with Adam's sin. Thus, e. g. Athenagoras says, in his apology (25), " man is in a good state (εἰ τάκτως ἔχει), both in respect to his Creator and also in respect to his *natural generation* (τῇ κατὰ τὴν γίνεσιν φύσει)," etc.

Clement of Alexandria inveighs against the conclusion which the encratites drew, from certain passages of scripture, in order to show that generation and marriage are objectionable Stromat. III. p. 468. ed. Colon. 1688 Here the passage from Job again comes up . No one is pure from defilement, not even though his life be of but one day ; and the passage, Ps. LI, I was conceived in sins and in iniquities did my mother conceive me. On this he properly asks, How can a newborn infant sin ? and how can the curse of Adam belong to him who has not yet done anything at all? Though David was conceived in sins, yet he still had in himself as a child no sin on this account David spoke as a prophet, and intended Eve by the term mother, as Eve was the mother of all living.

The passage in Job and similar passages, Clement referred, not to children, but to adults, whereby the greatness of their sin is shown. In his Protrepticon (p. 16), he explains the words in the epistle to

the Ephesians, We were by nature children of wrath, with entire
propriety, of the previous state of the heathen.

[Notwithstanding the explanations which Clement occasionally gave
of some passages of scripture, as mentioned in the last paragraph,
we are by no means to infer that he held to the *sinlessness* of infants.
This would be as great a mistake as to infer, on the other hand, from
certain expressions that he uses, that his views of native depravity
were the same as those of Augustine.

But that we may learn more exactly what were the views of so
early and so important a teacher in the Greek church, it may be
well to present the entire passage of which our author has just
given us quite too scanty a summary   It will in this way be manifest that the specific thing which he denies, instead of being all guilt
in children, is only the guilt of generation in opposition to the encratites   We shall also learn something further about the anthropological views of this philosophizing father.

He thus quotes from the Septuagint the passage in Job, and then
goes on with his argument against the encratites.   "No one is free
from pollution, says Job, not even though his life be but of one day
Let them tell us, whence was the new-born infant guilty of fornication ? or how has *he* fallen under the curse of Adam, who has done
nothing ?   It therefore remains for them, as it seems, to say that
generation is evil ; and not only the generation of the body, but of
the soul also, for the body is formed by the soul.   And when David
says, I was conceived in sins, etc , he speaks of mother Eve.   But
Eve was the mother of all living.   And if he was *conceived* in sin,
yet he was not himself *in* sin, nor was he *himself* sin.   But whether
every one who turns from sin to faith, turns from the custom of ha-
bitual sin, as from a mother, one of the twelve prophets shall bear
me testimony, who says, If I give my first-born for my impiety, the
fruit of my body for the sin of my soul.   He does not blame *Him* who
said, Be fruitful and multiply ; but *the very first motions* (ὁρμαί) *after
generation*, in which motions we know not God, he pronounces to
be imperfect " Paed III 12

Here is indeed *ante-natal* sin, though in a different sense from that
of Augustine.   And at no less a remove than this, was Clement from
holding to the sinlessness of children, though it is clear that he would
consider all their sin as consisting in their own individual action.

In the assignment of so early a period for moral agency, he is nearly if not quite alone. Most of the Greek fathers, however, appear to have held to the commencement of such agency as early as the first day, supposing this to be implied in the passage from Job, which they as well as the Latins were continually quoting.

Clement has also another passage on native depravity, in the same chapter, which is too striking to be omitted. " *To sin, is innate and common to all* (πᾶσιν ἔμφυτον καὶ κοινὸν) " And from what has just been adduced, it is sufficiently easy to perceive in what sense he regarded sin as innate, and what kind of sin it was that he had in view.

Origen appears to have considered all sin as voluntary ; and with his views of our having all sinned in a previous state of existence, he must of course have supposed us to come into the world sinners. But he appears to have wavered in his opinion respecting our continuing to sin during the stage of infancy, as he sometimes speaks of sin as then lying dormant within us.

The habit of applying the oft-repeated passage in Job as a proof of the sinfulness of infants, as may here properly be remarked, is to be traced back to the very age of the apostles, for Clement of Rome so quotes and applies it   And I think there can be but little doubt that the greater part of the earlier fathers considered man as in some sense a sinner from the earliest infancy   The Greek fathers seem much more disposed than the Latin to regard him as then a moral agent.   Indeed many of the Latins, as Tertullian, Cyprian, and Augustine expressly deny moral agency at that period.

Nearly all, both Greek and Latin, would probably have allowed, had the question been put to them in its modern shape, that infants are born with a disposition or a propensity to sin ; but it is equally probable that all the Greek if not quite all the Latin fathers would have denied the moral responsibility of the individual for anything previous to his own voluntary exercise of such disposition.—Tr.]

Cyril of Jerusalem, in his fourth lecture on the soul, shows, in opposition to Origen, that souls have not sinned before coming into this world.   We came into the world *without sin*, and sinned here of freewill.   According to him we should not come with the false interpretation of Rom. 7: 16 : What I would not, that I do ; but we should remember him who says, in Rom. 6: 19, As ye have yielded your members servants of uncleanness and iniquity unto iniquity, so now yield ye your members servants of righteousness unto sanctification.   And in his twelfth lecture, he says   "It is God that forms the children even while in their mother's womb, as Job says 10 10. —There is nothing defiled in the human formation (οὐδὲν μιαρὸν ἐστὶ ἐν ἀνθρωπίνη κατασκευῇ), if it does not defile itself by adultery and excess"

And Athanasius himself, who is still very orthodox, though not of Augustine's orthodoxy on the doctrine of original sin, declares, in his third oration against the Arians (T. I. Colon 1686 p 485), that "there have been many holy men who were pure from all sin. Thus Jeremiah was holy from his birth; and John, while yet in his mother's womb, leaped for joy at the voice of Mary the mother of our Lord   Nevertheless, death reigned from Adam to Moses, even over those who had not sinned like Adam himself"

Finally , Chrysostom, (who in general thought more philosophically than his predecessors, and always sought to save the idea of God's holiness and justice in the admission of evil and sin into the world), in his tenth homily on Romans, and while interpreting the passage, *by the offence of one*, etc , expressly declares it an absurdity to admit, that by Adam's disobedience any one else should be a sinner, for no one can deserve punishment who is not of himself (μὴ οἰκοθεν) a sinner.   He therefore directly rejects "the guilt of the Adamitic sin"

Many more passages might easily be adduced ; but these are sufficient, especially as we shall soon see that none of the Greek fathers knew anything of an Augustinian original sin.   I should, however, have a scruple about here adducing a well known passage from the work entitled Questions to the Orthodox, since its author, if not a Pelagian, was perhaps Theodore of Mopsuesta, which to me is not improbable ; at all events, he belonged to a later age.

5 Now as the fathers before Augustine held to no guilt of the Adamitic sin, they could not allow the forgiveness of a sin originating from Adam, or original sin, as an object of infant baptism, just as, on the same ground, they could not admit the condemnation of unbaptized children.   They therefore differed from Augustine on this latter point also.

We cannot here appeal to the old church formula—baptism is " for the remission of sins"—in order to prove original sin the object of infant baptism. It comes from that early period when only adults were baptized.* But in every adult actual sins might be presumed ; and so the formula had its full import.

Furthermore, Irenaeus, Basil, and others, indeed, express themselves strongly enough respecting the effects of baptism ; but they make no mention of a forgiveness of original sin. Tertullian says, " Why hastens the *innocent* age to the forgiveness of sins ?" De baptismo, c 18. Even Cyprian, who however, with his bishops, defended infant baptism, does not say, in his well known letter to Fidus (Ep 64), that original sin is forgiven in the newborn child through baptism The passage quoted by Augustine from that letter, (in which Cyprian, with the sixty-six bishops assembled by him, maintains that, in case of necessity, we must baptize a child before the eighth day, for, as much as in us lies, we must suffer no soul to be lost—nulla anima perdenda est), doubtless refers to the idea which appears to have been prevalent among the orthodox before Augustine, as well in the Greek as in the Latin church, namely, that salvation is conferred through baptism, although the unbaptized children of Christians would not be condemned for the want of baptism. C. d Epp. Pel. IV. 8 Comp. De Nupt. et Conc. II. 29, and other places. Here we have therefore again the *middle place* (medius locus) of Pelagius,† about which Augustine jeers so often in his

---

* Our author does not tell us exactly when that period was, nor does he refer us to any authority for the assumption that there ever was such a period in the christian church. And, what is a little remarkable, within the compass of two pages from this, we find him speaking of ' the custom, in *the early centuries*, of deferring the *baptism of children* and catechumens to easter week " The terms " early *centuries*," as there used, would seem to carry us back at least as far as the close of the first century, the time of the apostles, though possibly Dr W did not so intend them But whether he has or has not here made an opposite assumption to the first, I cannot help thinking, from the uncommonly loose manner in which he has spoken on the topic, that he has never made the early history of infant baptism a subject of much investigation, nor was it needful to his grand object —Nor would it here be deemed proper in me so far to divert the attention of the reader from that object as would be requisite for even the briefest epitome of the historical evidence which, at least in my view, disproves the first assumption —TR

† The premises just stated seem by no means to admit of this conclusion ; for Pelagius would be far enough from saying of his " middle place," that the soul which went there was lost, *ruined*. On the contrary, he contended

works against the Pelagians, though he himself, before the beginning
of the Pelagian controversy, seemed to incline to this idea. De Lib.
Arb III 23 Gregory Nazianzen, in his fortieth discourse (Colon.
1680 p 653), says, that unbaptized children do not indeed obtain
salvation (δοξασθήσεσθαι), because they are not baptized, though
they cannot be condemned by a righteous judge, because they are
innocent (ἀπόνηροι), and have rather *suffered* the loss of baptism than
caused it He therefore indeed attributes to baptism the effect of
conferring on those who receive it a share in the salvation of Christians, though he would allow none who do not receive it, to be condemned on this account;—here agreeing entirely with Pelagius.
For, he immediately adds, he who deserves no punishment, does
not on that account deserve distinction, just as he who is unworthy
of distinction, does not on that account deserve punishment. Gregory of Nyssa even says, in his work on children who are prema-
turely removed · " *The child free from all sin* (ἀπειρόνακον νήπιον)
finds itself in the natural state, and needs no purification for its
health, because it has as yet fallen into no disease of the soul " Opp.
T II. ed. Paris 1615 p. 361.

    Ambrose expresses himself, in a manner the most remarkable and
sorely offensive to the Benedictines, respecting the state of infants
dying before baptism. " No one," says he, " ascends into the king-

---

that it was *saved*, though not with the highest salvation Cyprian and his
bishops seem plainly to have thought that unbaptized infants must go to
perdition Nor was this opinion new. It had prevailed in Africa at least
thirty years before, as is plain from the declaration of Tertullian, who died
about the year 220. In his work on baptism, he says, not simply that it is
his own opinion, but ' It is *on acknowledged rule* that none can be saved
without baptism, grounded especially on that declaration of our Lord, Except a man be born of water, he has no *life* " And further on, in the same
work, and in justification of lay-baptism in some cases, he says, in effect,
that any one who should refuse to baptize, in case of extreme peril, would
be guilty of the perdition of the individual —All this is surely very far from
that good though minor salvation of unbaptized children, to which Pelagius
held, and which our author plainly enough shows was, at least in some
shape, held by many individuals before the time of Pelagius But the private opinions of individuals, and even of Tertullian himself at another time,
are not sufficient, on such a question of *general* fact, to balance his positive
testimony in regard to the "acknowledged rule," or at least this would
hold in respect to the general fact in Africa, where Tertullian and Cyprian
resided, if not in respect to the Greek church —Tʀ

dom of heaven unless by the sacrament of baptism For unless one be regenerated by water and the Holy Ghost, he cannot enter into the kingdom of God. He excepts no one at all, not the infant, not the person prevented by any necessity. But notwithstanding they may have that hidden immunity from punishment, I know not whether they can have the honor of the kingdom (habeant tamen illam opertam poenarum immunitatem, nescio an habeant regni honorem)." De Abrahamo, II. 11. This immunity from punishment is again nothing but " the middle place " To mark this as something much spoken of by the fathers, Ambrose adds the word *illam ;* and he adds *opertam,* because he would determine nothing as certain on the point. And besides, in his Consolatio de Obitu Valentini, he scrupled not to assign a signal salvation to the emperor, notwithstanding his dying without baptism. He regarded his *request* for baptism as itself sufficient to render him a partaker of its fruit

From the custom, in the early centuries, of deferring the baptism of children and catechumens to easter-week, we may conclude that the doctrine of the damnation of unbaptized children, was not prevalent.

In a discourse to Neophites (in Aug. C. Jul. I. 6), Chrysostom expresses himself in a manner altogether Pelagian respecting the object of infant baptism He there says, " We also baptize children, though they have no sin, that they may have holiness, righteousness, adoption as children, heirship, fraternity with Christ, and may also become his members." Of freeing from original sin, he says not a syllable.—In the like spirit—to add barely this—his disciple Isidore of Pelusium, expresses himself in the third book of his letter (Ep. 195). He answers minutely the question proposed to him, Why are children, *being without sin,* baptized (δὶ ἣν αἰτίαν τά βρέφη, ἀναμαρτητα ὄντα, βαπτίζεται) ? Some, he remarks, maintain very superficially, that infant baptism is administered that the corruption, imparted to nature by Adam's transgression, may be washed away (ὅτι τὸν διὰ τὴν παράβασιν τοῦ Ἀδάμ διαδόθεντα τῇ φύσει ῥύπον αποπλύνονται). This he indeed also believed ; but yet considered it of little importance ; and maintained that the benefits of baptism are much greater. The soul is regenerated, sanctified, redeemed, adopted, justified, and made a fellow heir with the Only-begotten. This is nearly the same as Chrysostom's view. We must not, however, conclude from Isidore's speaking of a defilement imparted to human nature by Adam's transgression, that he admitted an *impu-tation* of Adam's sin. For had he done this, how could he say, that the ablution of the defilement was of little importance.

Also the damnation of the virtuous heathen, which stands in close connection with the damnation of unbaptized christian children, was denied by many of the Greek fathers, particularly the Platonic. Thus Clement of Alexandria, in the second and sixth books of his Stromata, allows that not only the believers under the Old Testament, but also the well disposed heathen, are baptized in the future world, that they may share in the salvation of Christians.* It was otherwise, however, in the African church, where the dogma of salvation only in the church, was very early perfected, and by which we must consequently leave to condemnation the heathen, however highly prized for their virtues.

6. A transfer of Adam's sin by propagation, or original sin in the severest sense, was denied by all the Greek fathers, but not by the Latin. From the former, some have indeed been ready to except Justin Martyr, or the author of the dialogue with Trypho if they did not consider this as the work of Justin. But if we attentively read this production and without preconceived opinions, we shall find no original sin in it. It is indeed there said, that the human race from Adam downward, are subjected to death and the seduction ($\pi\lambda\acute{a}\nu\eta$) of the serpent, i. e. the devil; but nothing is here said of a *sin*. On the contrary, this is always attributed by Justin to the individual's own fault. When he calls Christ the only undefiled and sinless person ($\mu\acute{o}\nu o\nu$ $\mathring{a}\sigma\pi\iota\lambda o\nu$ $\varkappa\alpha\grave{\iota}$ $\mathring{a}\nu\alpha\mu\acute{a}\rho\tau\eta\tau o\nu$), this probably refers to the gnostic idea of the generation of man, which Justin also held. For he believed this to take place with an evil and unlawful lust. And as Jesus was begotten without this lust, he could call him in this view the only undefiled —In the case of Origen, we need not be perplexed by expressions like the following "We are all born to sin ($\pi\acute{a}\nu\tau\varepsilon\varsigma$ $\pi\rho\grave{o}\varsigma$ $\tau\grave{o}$ $\mathring{a}\mu\alpha\rho\tau\acute{a}\nu\varepsilon\iota\nu$ $\pi\varepsilon\varphi\acute{\iota}\varkappa\alpha\mu\varepsilon\nu$);" C. Celsum l. III. T. I. p. 491; "perhaps no one is pure from sins, though his life has been but a day, because of the mystery of birth ($\delta\iota\grave{a}$ $\tau\grave{o}$ $\tau\grave{\eta}\nu$ $\gamma\acute{\varepsilon}\nu\varepsilon\sigma\iota\nu$ $\mu\nu\sigma\tau\acute{\eta}\rho\iota o\nu$)," Com. in Matt. Opp. T III. p. 685; "by the sacrament of baptism, the impurity of birth is done away, for which children are baptized" Hom in Luc.

---

* Hermas, an apostolic father, and others after him, supposed Christ and the apostles to descend to *Hades* for the purpose of baptizing the patriarchs, prophets etc —Tr

XIV. Opp. T. III. p. 948.   For, by his hypothesis of the preexistence of the human soul, it is banished into the body as a punishment for sins previously committed; and in this sense, are these passages to be taken and others of like import.   They therefore imply no transfer of sin from Adam, as Augustine would have it.   Besides this, he held, as a Platonist, that the soul is defiled by its union with the body, and for this reason could call children unclean, and regard infant baptism as needful.

We must also make a distinction between the Greek and the Latin church.   And the Greek fathers, again, differ both in respect to the evil they derive from Adam's fall, and also the origin of man's sin. But they agree among themselves and likewise with the Latins, and also with Augustine and Pelagius, in placing the origin of the *first* sin in the abuse of freedom.

We have already seen, that Athenagoras considered human nature, even in its present state, as well disposed.   But the most remarkable of all, is the declaration of Athanasius respecting original sin, in his work De Salutari Adventu Jesu Christi (Opp. T. I. p. 639), where he pronounces the " propagation of sin" (διαδοχὴ τῆς ἁμαρτίας) an error of Marcion and Manes, in as much as they subjected the body and generation to an evil being and made man the slave of this being.   This error was renewed, in his time, by some who even subjected man's rational nature to an evil being, and maintained that it could not avoid sin.

Gregory Nazianzen, in his thirty-first discourse on Matt. 19: 12, expresses the opinion, that the spiritual and not the corporeal circumcision is meant in this passage.   For some seem circumcised by nature, i. e. inclined to good; others are purified by instruction, because it circumcises as it were their passions, teaches them to distinguish good from evil, and thus produces spiritual soundness (πνευματικὴν σωφροσύνην); while others circumcise themselves, who practice virtue without a teacher, spontaneously blow the spark of virtue, and acquire such a habit (ἕξιν) of virtue, that it is almost impossible they should turn to vice.—Such assertions, which stand in the most direct contradiction with the admission of an original sin, are everywhere found in this famous orator.

Gregory of Nyssa, (On the Soul and the Resurrection, Opp. T. II. p. 670), maintains expressly that the soul, since it is created by God, is not *necessarily* evil (ἔξω τῆς κατὰ κακίαν ἀνάγκης εἶναι); but it either of free choice (ἐκ προαιρέσεως) closes its eyes to good, or is blinded by the devices of the enemy of our life, or looks simply at the light of truth and keeps aloof from dark passions.

Furthermore, in respect to the *consequences* of Adam's sin, the Greek fathers *before Methodius* placed them in death as well as in many other physical evils, as diseases, pains of parturition, etc   It might seem as though Theophilus was an exception, since he derives death from Abel.   But by this he only means that Abel was the first man that died. Ad Autolycum II. 29.—But the Greek fathers *after Methodius* and therefore from the close of the third century, at least a part of them, added also a second consequence, an excessive susceptibility to sensual allurements or an increased sensuality * In this sense, Gregory Nazianzen, in a passage quoted by Augustine (C. Jul. I. 5), speaks of the stain of the first birth, with which we were conceived and born, and from which baptism frees us. In this sense, Basil (on Psalm xxix) ascribes to human nature a weakness, and says of generation, that it takes place " in the filth of sins." De Bapt. I 7.   In this sense, Gregory of Nyssa speaks of a natural propensity to evil (συμφύια πρὸς τὸ κακὸν)   Orat. m. Catech c. 35. Hence Chrysostom, in his eleventh homily on Rom vi speaks of the great power of the passions, by which our bodies, before the advent of Christ, were easily overcome by sin.   " In this dying state, a great swarm as it were of passions entered   Hence the body was not very fleet for the course that leads to virtue, because there was neither a spirit that could help, nor a baptism that was fitted for the dead."   To the same increased sensuality do the words of Chrysostom refer when, according to Augustine's quotation (C. Jul. II 6), he says of the first pair, " They were covered with fig-leaves in order to hide the form of sin (tegentes speciem peccati)."

Lactantius held a singular opinion, different from all the other fathers both before and after Methodius.   By Adam's sin—so he taught in his Oratio ad Graecos c. 7 sqq —we have lost the higher spirit, which is the source for a perfect understanding of truth.   The consequence is, that we have separated ourselves from converse with heavenly and have loved earthly things, and become subject to the temptations of demons.   Still there remains a spark of the perfect spirit within us, and it is in our power again to be united with it.

---

* *Sinnlichkeit—sensuousness*, Mr. Coleridge would have us say ,—and truly we seem now to need some distinct term for the thing —Tʀ

In respect to the *cause* of the sins which are committed by Adam's posterity, the Greek fathers before Methodius commonly adduce the evil spirit and the natural sensuality of man. Athenagoras expresses himself in a peculiar manner on this point, in his apology, c. 27. ed. Bened. Hagae Comit. 1742. p 305. According to him, the irrational and capricious movements of the soul derive idols from bodies, or invent them for themselves. This is done particularly when the soul of man no longer directs its view to heavenly things and the Creator, but fastens on earthly things. Then it receives the material spirit (ὑλικὸν πνεῦμα), and the demons avail themselves of this to infuse error into the human understanding.* Irenaeus placed the cause of sins in Adam's posterity, in the abuse of freedom and a forgetfulness which arises from great negligence (πολλὴν ἀμέλειαν). But no one is either good or bad by nature. Adv. Haer. IV. 37. The power of the devil he considers as entirely broken by Christ. V. 21. To this Clement of Alexandria added also ignorance, (Paed. I. 13); and Origen, perverse education and bad example (περιήχησεις). C Cels. lib. III. Opp. T I p. 493. To seek for the cause of sin in the state of the body, he pronounced irrational. De Princip. III. 5 Opp. T. I. p. 111.

The fathers after Methodius, indeed, in addition to the abuse of freedom, adduce the devil and sensuality as causes of sin : but they allow sensuality to have been increased by Adam's fall They regard a greater excitability of man, in the *human body*, to evil, as a consequence of the fall, which afterwards became a cause of sin.

In this view, the manner is characteristic in which Methodius (in Photius, Cod. 234) explains the triple law which, in his opinion, Paul admitted. One, says he, is the good implanted in us. This is νόμος νόος. Another is the law of evil (νόμος πονηροῦ, of the devil), which inwardly draws the soul in various representations addressed to the passions. Of this, Paul says, that it wars against the law of the mind. The third is that which hardens according to the sinful passions *in the flesh.* This is what Paul calls the law of sin, which dwells in the members.

Methodius therefore regarded the body, not the soul, as the seat

---

* From a view of the whole passage here referred to, it is at least doubtful whether Athenagoras intends at all to account for the sins of men in general, as he is treating only of the origin and vanity of idolatrous superstitions.—Tr.

of sinfulness. But Cyril of Jerusalem appears to have had a more refined idea. "Tell me not," says he in his fourth catechetical lecture on the body, "that the body is the cause of sin. For if the body were the cause of sin, why does not the dead body sin ?—The body does not sin of itself, but the soul through the body.—Defile not, then, this thy beautiful vestment "

Finally, in respect to the devil, several of the Greek fathers, especially of the fourth century, as Athanasius, both the Gregories, and Basil, represent his influence as very great over man after the fall. After that event, the devil, in their opinion, could use his seductive art far more extensively then before. They had already in part the Augustinian idea, that the devil has an acquired right (jus quaesitum) over men, and that God must in justice leave them to him. As however, with all the other fathers, they maintained the freedom of the human will after the fall, they had to limit the unconditional dominion of the devil over the human body ; on which he exercised his power by death.

But among the fathers of the Latin church, Tertullian and Ambrose assumed, that. as a consequence of Adam's sin, in addition to death and the power of the devil over men, there is an *actual vitiosity of the soul* (vitiositas animae) *propagated by generation.*

It will be worth the pains to quote the passages themselves of Tertullian and Ambrose, pertaining to this subject.

It cannot indeed be denied, that dark passages are presented in Tertullian, which seem to incline to other views But we need not wonder at this in an author who often expresses himself so confusedly and darkly. There are passages enough which place beyond all doubt his belief of a corruption of the soul propagated by generation.

In his treatise, De Testimonio Animae, c. 3, he says : " At the beginning man was circumvented by him (satan), so as to transgress God's command, and was therefore devoted to death, and thenceforward made the whole race, infected from his seed, the recipients and propagators of his condemnation (exinde totum genus de suo semine infectum, suae etiam damnationis traducem fecit)."

This may indeed be understood of death which is propagated by generation, especially as the word *damnatio* is used respecting Adam's condemnation to death according to the custom of speech among the fathers. But there are other passages from which the propagation of a vitiosity of the soul is manifest.

In De Anima, c. 41, he says : " The evil of the soul, besides what is built upon it by the intervention of the evil spirit, precedes from the corruption of origin, which is in a manner natural. For the corruption of nature is another nature (Malum animae, praeter quod ex obventu spiritus mali superstruitur, ex *originis vitio* antecedit, naturale quodammodo Nam naturae corruptio alia natura est)" Here we have plainly an *original evil*, which Tertullian calls in a manner natural or inborn. What is this but a fundamental corruption inherited from Adam ?

Another passage from the same book (16) is likewise plain, and serves to elucidate the one just quoted " Plato divided the soul into rational and irrational. This definition we indeed approve, but not so as that each is to be imputed to nature For the natural is to be regarded as rational, what is begotten in the soul from the beginning, namely, by the rational author For why should not that be rational which God has put forth by his command? to say nothing of what he has emitted by his breath. But that is to be considered as irrational which came afterwards, as being what took place at the instigation of the serpent, the committed act itself of transgression, and what then grew in and together with the soul as something now natural, because it happened immediately at the commencement of nature —The introduction of sin is from the devil. But all sin is irrational. Therefore the irrational is from the devil, from whom is also sin, which is extraneous to God from whom the irrational is foreign." According to this, the corruption of the soul became a second nature after the fall.

Finally, like so many fathers both before and after him, and of the Greek as well as of the Latin church, Tertullian considered human suffering, and the pains of parturition among the rest, as the consequence of Adam's sin, and to be denominated a kind of inheritance, after that sin ; which sin also propagated itself among his posterity. De Poenit. c. 2 ; De Habitu muliebri, c. 1 —The curse pronounced, according to Genesis, upon Adam and Eve, must certainly have contributed to the universality of this view

Ambrose also taught plainly enough a " vitiosity of the soul" propagated from Adam. Here I place no stress on the explanation of the complaint of Job, given by Ambrose in the third chapter of his first book De Interp. Job. We do not even see whether it contains the opinion of Ambrose on original sin, since it merely shows how

45

Job considered the unhappy condition of man; and then the explanation itself is obscure, and it rather appears to me that we are to refer the fault (culpa) which comes upon the child from the cradle, to bodily death. There are, however, enough of plain passages on the point. In the lost book of Ambrose De Sacramento Regenerationis sive De Philosophia, he says, in a passage quoted by Augustine (C. Jul. II. 6): "Eve brought forth unhappily, as she left travail to women as an inheritance, and every one produced by the pleasure of lust, et genitalibus visceribus infusus, et coagulatus in sanguine, in pannis involutus, contracts the contagion of sin before he draws vital breath." Here is manifestly the doctrine, that children are born already corrupt, and that this corruption comes from Eve and was propagated by her—Also in the *enarratio in Psalm* L. *Davidis*, which is likewise designated by the name of the *apologia prophetae Davidis* (in Aug c d Epp. Pel IV. 11; C Jul. I. 3), Ambrose says. "Before we are born, we are stained with contagion, and before we enjoy the light, we receive the injury of our origin, and are conceived in iniquity.—We are conceived in the sins of our parents and in their transgressions are we born. And even birth itself has its contagions, nor has nature herself merely one contagion."—Here it is manifestly taught, that we are conceived and born with original sin. Ambrose also says (De Poen. c. 2) · "All men are born under sin, whose birth itself is in vice" Aug C. Jul II 3; C. d. Epp. Pel IV. 11; Op. Imp II. 163. He says in another place, "The variance of flesh and spirit has, through the transgression of the first man, passed into our nature (in naturam vertit)" Ambros in Luc. l. 7, on Luke 12 52, in Aug C. Jul. II. 5. And he says of Peter (De Initiandis c. 6) whose feet the Master washed: "Peter was clean, yet he ought to wash the sole of his foot. For he had by succession the sin of the first man whom the serpent had beguiled and persuaded to err. Therefore the sole of his foot was washed, that hereditary sins might be removed."

Passages of like import we find everywhere in the works of Ambrose; and they are diligently enough quoted by Augustine We content ourselves with here presenting only one more, which leaves no doubt at all of his theory, and which is taken from his exposition of Isaiah, and is quoted by Augustine, De Nupt. et Conc. I 35; II. 5, "Every man is a liar, and no one is without sin except God only. It is therefore proved that no one, produced from man and woman,

i. e. by the mingling of their bodies, is free from sin. But whoever is without sin, is without this kind of conception." Hence he considered small children as recovered from the evil (malitia) by baptism at the commencement of their being Lib I. in Evang Lucae, in Aug. C. Jul I. 3. He considered Jesus alone as unpolluted, because begotten of uncorrupted seed Lib II in Evan Lucae, in Aug. l. c ; and in another passage from the book De Arca et Noe, now lost but quoted by Augustine, C. Jul. II 2. Ambrose must therefore have agreed with Augustine in holding generation as something in itself bad, as is manifest both from the passages already quoted and from others which Augustine has collected, C. d. Epp. Pel. IV. 11

The first germ therefore of the idea of an original sin or a conveyance of Adam's sin by propagation, is to be sought in Tertullian. In him also first appears the expression *tradux* in reference to the evil of sin propagated by generation, as also the expression *originis vitium.* In Cyprian also, a faithful disciple of Tertullian in most points, it has been maintained that the doctrine is found of a corruption of the soul propagated by generation. This, however, is not perfectly clear, although several passages, quoted in part from his works by Jerome and Augustine, seem to lead to this conclusion.

From Africa this view spread over the rest of the west It was plainly enough exhibited by Ambrose bishop of Milan. But in the hands of Augustine, it became wholly African. He carried it so far as to defend the total inability of man for good, which none of the earlier fathers intended ; nor could they with their assumption of human freedom after the fall.

But it is singular enough that Africa should become a pattern in religious theory for the whole west, and that the unphilosophical Tertullian should lay the first foundation for it ! We need not, however, wonder that Tertullian should derive " the vitiosity" of the soul from parents to children by propagation, since he taught the materiality of the soul and admitted that the soul is propagated by generation. He was also confirmed in this view by observing the agreement in disposition of the child with the parents. De Anima, 25.

Now those fathers who admit such an inborn vitiosity, also regard it as one of the causes of the sins which are committed by Adam's descendants. But they also ascribe to the devil a great power over men. How great it was generally supposed in the Latin church to be, is apparent from the *exsufflatio* and the exorcism, which were

such important rites in baptism   This power was supposed to have
been gained by the devil through Adam's fall   Ambrose expresses
himself very strongly on this point in his book De Tobia c 9   " Who
is that usurer of sins but the devil, from whom Eve borrowed the sin
which passed over to her posterity, and by the interest involved the
whole human race in debt (defoeneravit).   Finally, as a base usurer
he held the hand writing which the Lord afterwards blotted out by
his blood.   For what is written in letters of death must be blotted
out by death.   The usurer therefore is the devil."   See also other
places.   Ambrose therefore conceived of the power which the devil
exerts over men as a rightful possession of which he must be dispos-
sessed by the blood of Christ, if God would not be unjust towards
him.   " The price (pretium) of our liberation was the blood of Christ,
which *must necessarily be paid to him* to whom we were sold by our
sins."   Ep. 77.—The Latin fathers, as was in part the fact with
the Greek, might also allow the force of habit always to have an influence in aggravating the propensity to sin in Adam's posterity.

   Among the rest of the Latin fathers, a Gallic bishop, Hilary of
Poictiers (Hilarius Pictaviensis), whom Horn omits to mention, must
not here be overlooked.   He was cotemporary with Athanasius and
a zealous defender of him in the doctrine of the relation of the Son
to the Father.   But in the doctrine of original sin, he differed from
the Athanasian view.   He also admitted with Tertullian a propagation of sin by generation, a " vice of origin."   In Psalm cxviii. lit 14.
§ 20.   But he did not make sin to proceed from the soul but from
the body, by which he connected the increased sensuality which the
Greeks assumed, with the vitiosity of the soul which Tertullian
taught, and therefore, in a sort, orientalism with occidentalism.   For
though he attributed a perversity (malitia) to all men (in Psalm cxviii.
lit. 15. § 6), and by no means freed the soul from corruption, (comment, in Matt. x.),   yet he considered the body as the material of all
vices (omnium vitiorum materiem), by which (per quam) we, impure
and defiled, retain nothing of purity and innocence.   He supposes
the devil to avail himself of the infirmity of our flesh through which
he seeks to entice us to evil, to whose seductions we must oppose
the strength of the mind (firmitatem animi).   In this sense he speaks
of an " instinct of our nature," which impels us to vice, from which
the religion of faith must bring us back ; though even with the best
will, man must place his reliance in God's mercy, which will not

impute to man his trespasses. See the passages quoted from the writings of Hilary by Augustine, C. Jul. II. 8. Comp. In Psalm. cxviii. lit 11. § 5. Hilary also differed in an essential point from the Augustinian view of original sin, by assuming, with the other fathers before Augustine, the freedom of the will Hilary therefore did not hold to such corruption, as that man, without the supernatural aid of God's grace, can do nothing but evil. "The rich man in Hades might have been in Abraham's bosom by the liberty of will "* In Psalm. 51 62, 5; 118· 14. "There is not any necessity of sin in the natures of men ; but the practice of sin is derived (arripitur) from the appetite of the will and the delight of sins " In Psalm. 68: 9

Other fathers of the Latin church, belonging to the fourth century, though less renowned, are quoted by Augustine in support of his original sin. C. Jul I 3. Though they did not indeed teach an Augustinian original sin, yet they seem really to have taught a transmission of Adam's sin by propagation , and we hence see how widely Tertullian's doctrine had spread in the fourth century Thus Reticius, a bishop of Augustodunum (Autun) taught that baptism is a principal mode of remission (indulgentia principalis), by which we lay down the whole burden of the ancient crime (antiqui criminis omne pondus exponimus), and blot out the ancient transgressions of our ignorance, when we also put off *the old man with the inborn vices* (ubi et veterem hominem cum ingenitis sceleribus exuimus) Olympius, a Spanish bishop, expressed himself thus, in a discourse " If faith had remained uncorrupt on earth,—never would vice have

* Hilary does not here mean that the rich man possessed freedom of will in hell , for he is arguing directly the reverse though he asserts that we possess freedom on earth, as will be seen from the connection of the passage, which the student may think worth his inspection Non enim confessio peccatorum nisi in hujus saeculi tempore est *dum voluntati suae unusquisque permissus est*, et per vitae licentiam habet confessionis arbitrium Decedentes namque de vita simul et de jure decedimus voluntatis Tunc enim ex merito praeteritae voluntatis lex jam constituta, aut quietis aut poenae excedentium ex corpore suscipit voluntatem Cujus temporis non jam liberam, sed necessariam voluntatem ostendit propheta, cum dicit, Non est mihi in diebus illis voluntas Cessante enim voluntatis libertate, etiam voluntatis, si qua erit, cessabit effectus. Transire namque ad Abraham volens dives, chao medio non sinitur cum tamen per libertatem voluntatis in Abrahae sinibus esse potuisset. Interclusa est ergo libertas voluntatis, qua confessio nulla est mortuis In Psalm 51 23 —Tr

sprung up through the death-bringing transgression of the first man,
so that sin should be born with man." This seems to refer to a corruption of the soul.

7 Almost all the fathers before Augustine, besides regarding the
bodily death of Adam as a consequence of his transgression, as already shown, generally considered the physical state of man before
the fall as being better than Pelagius supposed it. He therefore differed from them on this point The toil of labor, the pains of parturition, and the subjection of the wife, constitute a part of the condemnation of the first pair for their transgression, according to Irenaeus, Adv. Haer III 23, 2 Consequently these evils could have
found no place in Paradise Chrysostom also derives from Adam's
fall the noxiousness of beasts to man, and their fear of him, according to a passage quoted by Augustine (C. Jul I. 6) from his ninth
homily on Genesis. The account in Genesis of the curse which
God pronounced on the earth, has plainly conduced to the universality of this view. Finally, the fathers, as soon as they assumed
that Adam would not have died if he had not sinned, must also have
considered him, previously to sinning, as free from all the evils
which could have death as their consequence.

Hence it is clear, that the fathers before Augustine agreed neither
with Augustine nor Pelagius on the points adduced. No one assumed, with Augustine, that the original freedom of the will was lost after the fall ; no one allowed with him that children are condemned
for Adam's sin ; no one assumed with him an imputation of Adam's
sin, and therefore also no one assumed any forgiveness of it in infant baptism Nor did any one assume with Pelagius, that Adam
would have died even if he had not sinned Especially were the
fathers of the Latin church at a remove from the Pelagian representation, by their assumption of an original sin, as also among the
Greek fathers, perhaps no one regarded man, in his present natural
state, as so uncorrupt in a moral and physical view as Pelagius
thought him. The fathers had therefore not the entire system of
Pelagius; and as little had they that of Augustine ; and generally
as yet no definite and consistent system at all on the now contested
doctrines. The opinions of the Greek fathers especially differed

immeasurably from Augustine's system in respect to the consequences of Adam's sin.

The striking difference of Augustinism from the previous doctrine of the fathers, will be still more apparent from the following investigation.

II. *Opinions of the fathers before Augustine respecting grace, predestination, and the extent of redemption.*

As the ante-Augustine fathers admitted no Augustinian original sin, i. e. no such moral debasement propagated from Adam, that man can will and do nothing but evil, but even those who came nearest to Augustine still always acknowledged the moral freedom of man, so, unless they would be guilty of the most palpable inconsistency, they could neither maintain any "irrisistible grace" nor any absolute predestination, nor therefore even any limitation of the redemption of Christ to the elect.—Individual fathers might lay ever so much stress on grace, yet an Augustinian grace they could not admit, if freewill was to remain to man. This, which might be expected beforehand, will be established in the following investigation.

1. Several of the fathers, both Greek and Latin, laid a great stress on grace; but they did not teach an Augustinian grace. Nor yet was it a Pelagian grace.

First, the Greek fathers. Irenaeus makes faith and the willing of good to depend on man, and then a greater and more perfect illumination of the understanding to be imparted by God. C. Haer. IV. 29.

[The following declaration, however, as given by Cave, is indicative of a very deep sense of our dependence in this spiritual grandson of the apostle John, however he might think as to the order of precedence in the human and the divine movement. " As well may the dry ground (says Irenaeus) produce fruit without rain to moisten it, as we, who are at first like dried sticks, be fruitful unto a good life without voluntary showers from above, that is (as he adds) the laver of the Spirit." Adv. Haer. III. 19 —Tr.]

In the same way Theophilus explains himself, Ad Autolycum, I. 7.

However strongly the Alexandrians Clement and Origen defend the freedom of man in his present state, they still by no means exclude divine grace. In De Princ. III. 2, Origen taught that the good purpose alone is not adequate to the accomplishment of good, but

that it is brought to completion only by divine grace   And in c. 1,
where he treats minutely of freewill, he states that the willing and
the running of man, are not sufficient for attaining the object, but
the grace of God is required.

Macarius and Basil express themselves with peculiar strength respecting grace, though the latter in other places so greatly exalts
man's natural powers for good, and the former also mentions the
application of one's own power as the necessary condition of enjoying grace.   The homilies of Macarius are full of passages which
assert, that the soul bereft of grace is dead; that without the help
of the Holy Ghost, it can accomplish nothing for its salvation; that
the soul is subjected to vice; and that as the bird cannot fly if the
wings are not restored which were taken from him, so men cannot
act without grace, which repairs the want of nature.   Among all
the assertions which we find in Basil respecting grace, that is perhaps the strongest which is quoted by Basnage (Histoire de l'E'glise
I. 628), in which it is said, with a rhetorical hyperbole indeed, that
we cannot utter a word to the honor of Jesus Christ, if the Holy
Ghost does not work in us.

Both the Gregories made the bestowment of grace dependent on
man's own strivings.   Grace must come as help in order completely
to change the heart of man.

Chrysostom thus expresses himself on the relation of grace to freedom, in his twelfth homily on Hebrews · " All is in God's power,
but so that our freewill is not lost —It depends therefore on us and
on him   We must first choose the good (ἐλέσθαι τὰ ἀγαθὰ), and
then he adds what belongs to him (τὰ παρ᾽ ἑαυτοῦ εἰσάγει)   He does
not precede our willing (οὐ προφθάνει τὰς ἡμέτερας βουλήσεις), that
our freewill may not suffer   But when we have chosen, then he
affords us much help —It is ours to choose beforehand and to will,
but God's to perfect and bring to the end."   He made faith to proceed from man, as might be supposed from what has already been
quoted. Homil II in Psalm L.   In another passage he says · " God
imparts to us power (ἐμερίσατο τὴν ἀρετὴν).   All does not depend on
us   To choose good, to will it, to prosecute it with zeal, to make
every effort, lies in our freewill; but to accomplish it, to not suffer
us to fail, and to reach the mark of good deeds, is the work of heavenly grace." T. VI. 164.

The fathers of the Latin church, especially Cyprian and Ambrose, (to whose authority Augustine very often, though erroneously, appeals in regard to his own theory of grace), speak in very strong expressions respecting the operations of divine grace. Respecting Cyprian, Augustine refers especially to his Exposition of the Lord's Prayer, and quotes several passages on the subject, in C d Epp. Pel. IV 9. Thus Cyprian writes · "We say, Hallowed be thy name, not as if we desired of God that it might be sanctified by our prayers, but because we ask of him that his name may be sanctified in us. Besides, by whom is God sanctified, who himself sanctifies? But because he himself says, Be ye holy, as I also am holy, we seek and pray, that we who are sanctified in baptism, may persevere in that which we have begun to be.—We add also and say, Thy will be done in heaven and in earth, not that God should do what he will, but that we may be able to do what God wills. For who shall withstand God, that he may not do what he will? But because we are opposed by the devil, so that our mind and conduct should not in all things be in subjection to God, we pray that God's will may be done in us That this may be done in us, there is need of God's will, i. e. of his aid and protection, for no one is valiant in his own strength, but is safe by the grace (indulgentia) and compassion of God." In a letter (Ep. 215) written about the year 427, Augustine also refers the Adrumetian monks, in respect to divine grace, to Cyprian's exposition of the Lord's prayer. Cyprian teaches, that everything pertaining to our morals whereby we live properly, must be sought from our Father in heaven Augustine also frequently refers to the words of Cyprian, " we are to glory in nothing, for nothing is ours." Testim III. 4.

Ambrose, likewise, in the second book of his Exposition of Luke (Aug. De Gr. Chr. 44), thus expresses himself respecting grace: " The power of the Lord always cooperates with human efforts, so that no one can build without the Lord, no one can guard without the Lord, no one can begin anything without the Lord." In other passages also, of which Augustine has quoted several (C. d. Epp. Pel. IV. 11), Ambrose lays great stress on the aid of divine grace for the practice of virtue. Thus, in De Fuga Saeculi, c. 1, he says · " The allurement of earthly desires steals in, and a flood (offusio) of vanities occupies the mind, so that you must think and revolve in your mind, what you ought to avoid , to guard against which, is difficult for man , to put away, impossible. That this is rather an object of

46

desire than of achievement, the prophet testifies by saying, Turn
away my heart to thy testimonies and not to avarice. · For our heart
and our thoughts are not in our power, which unexpectedly confound
our mind and spirit and draw them in a different direction from what
thou hast prescribed, recall us to secular things, mingle earthly things,
introduce pleasures, interweave allurements, and at the very time
when we prepare to elevate the mind, we are, by the insertion of
vain thoughts, for the most part cast down to earthly things.   But
who is so happy as always to ascend in his own heart ?   But how
can this be done without divine aid ?   Certainly in no way."   In his
Exposition of Isaiah, he says . " Also to pray to God, is a spiritual
grace.   For no man calleth Jesus the Lord except by the Holy
Ghost."   On the words of Luke 1 3, It seemed good to me, he
makes this note in his exposition of that evangelist : " What he declares to appear good to him, can appear good not to him only
For it appears good not simply by the human will, but as it has pleased Christ, says he, who speaks in me, who causes that what *is* good
should also *seem* good to us   For whom he pities he also calls.   And
therefore he who follows Christ, when asked why he wished to be a
Christian, may answer, *it seemed good to me.*   When he says this
he does not deny that it seemed good to God, for the will of men is
prepared by God ; for it is the grace of God, that God is honored by
the saint." Aug. De Nat et Gr 63 ; De Dono Persev 19   By Ambrose, therefore, even the will of man is made dependent on the influence of divine grace, on the nature of which, though the main
thing, he explains himself no farther.

On the other hand, Hilary Pictaviensis, who lived somewhat earlier, makes the commencement of good, the willing, to proceed from
man himself ; but ascribes to the aid of divine grace a part in com-
pleting the same, and in perseverance in faith.   This appears from
several passages of his *enarratio* in Psalm cxviii.   In the same way
thought his cotemporary Optatus of Mileve.

From what has been said, it is manifest that the ante-Augustine
fathers, both Greek and Latin, even on the doctrine of grace, thought
in accordance with neither Pelagius nor Augustine.   They did not
agree with Pelagius, because none of them denied the *necessity* of
God's grace to the completion of good purposes, however much individual fathers conceded to human power   The Pelagian Anianus
therefore unjustly appeals, in the preface to the translation of some

discourses of Chrysostom, to the agreement of his theory of grace with that of Pelagius. This is proved by the passages already quoted from the famous orator, in which he indeed makes the will, but not the execution, to depend on man alone. And especially must the Latin fathers have differed from Pelagius, as several of them taught an inborn vitiosity of the soul. And just as little did the ante-Augustine fathers agree with *Augustine* in regard to grace. No one of them admitted, that all the good which man wills and does, is merely the effect of an irresistible grace. And a preceding grace, Chrysostom even denied in express terms! As all assumed the freedom of the will, they must always have left something for the application of one's own power, if they would not fall into the grossest contradiction of their own principals. In all the assertions of particular fathers respecting the necessity of grace to the practice of virtue, they must at least have allowed to man the power of admitting or rejecting grace. For if not, where was left the moral freedom of man? But by this they were already semipelagians.

Finally, it is not to be mistaken and is undeniably apparent in the expressions of several of the fathers that, previously to Augustine, the idea of grace was extremely indefinite, and that between a mediate and an immediate grace of God, between its natural and its supernatural effect, there was not a sufficiently nice distinction. Now, the whole christian economy was called grace by them; now, baptism was so called by way of eminence, now, the forgiveness of sin; now, the influences of the Spirit of God, without their undertaking to define the mode of these influences. Hence the wavering and insecurity in their positions respecting grace; and hence also the ambiguity with which Pelagius could speak of it! But how freely one might express himself respecting the relation of freedom to grace as a divine influence on man in the production of good, before the commencement of the Pelagian controversy, is apparent from this, that even those fathers who were regarded as orthodox, could attribute ever so much weight to man's own power for good, without prejudice to their orthodoxy.

The doctrine of grace which was afterwards denied as semipelagian, might therefore have been the doctrine before and even up to the time of Augustine. Even Jerome, in a work against the Pelagians, written in 415, presents it as an orthodox doctrine, that the commencement of the good will and of faith comes from us. In his

dialogue (III. 10), he makes his catholic maintain against the Pelagians, that " freewill consists only in this, that we will and desire
and approve of things required (placitis).   But it is in God's power
that we are able, by his help and his aid, to accomplish that which
we toil and strive for (quod laboramus ac nitimur)."   Even Augustine himself, as we have seen in the exhibition of his theory of grace,
at first approached near to semipelagianism !

2 In respect to predestination, the fathers before Augustine differed entirely from him and agreed with Pelagius.   With Pelagius
they founded predestination upon prescience, upon Gods foreknowing him who would make himself worthy of salvation and him who
would not.   They therefore did not adopt the unconditional predestination of Augustine, but the conditional of the Pelagians.   Hence
the Massilians were entirely right when they maintained (Aug. Ep.
225), that Augustine's doctrine of predestination was contrary to the
opinion of the fathers and the sense of the church (ecclesiastico sen-
sui).   And furthermore, no father has explained the epistle to the
Romans in the Augustinian way, or so explained it as to educe a
grace which precedes the merits of the elect.   Augustine endeavored only to make it out by an inference, that Cyprian, Ambrose and
Gregory Nazianzen had known and adopted his predestination, as he
appealed to the agreement of this doctrine with their theory of grace
De Dono Pers. 19.

The Greek fathers were foremost in teaching a conditional predestination.

By Justin Martyr, in his larger Apology (c. 28), the salvation of
men is grounded on God's foreknowledge that they will repent.

[The following specimen from this very early and important father,
will show us more fully what he and many others after him thought
on this and some of the kindred topics.   It will be seen how they had
the doctrine of heathen fate continually before their eyes while treating of these matters.   I avail myself here of Reeve's translation
of Justin's larger Apology, p. 76

" Lest any should collect," says Justin, " from what has been said,
that we are assertors of fatal necessity, and conclude that prophecy
must needs infer predestination, we shall clear ourselves as to this
point also ; for we learn from these very prophets, that rewards and
punishments are to be distributed in proportion to the merits of man-

kind   And if it be not so, but all things are determined by fate,
then farewell freedom of the will.   And if this man is destined to
be good, and that evil, then, neither the one nor the other can be
justly approved or condemned ; since that unless we suppose man
has it in his power to choose the good and refuse the evil, no one
can be accountable for any action whatever   But to prove that men
are good or evil by choice, I argue in this manner :—We see in
the same person a transition to quite contrary actions.   But now,
were he necessitated to be either good or bad, he would not be capable of this contrariety, nor so often veer from one to the other. Besides, there would not be this diversity of virtuous and vicious in the
world : for either we must say with you, that destiny is the cause
of evil, and then destiny would act contradictorily to herself in being
the cause of good ; or else I must say, what I have said already,
that you conclude virtue and vice to be themselves nothing, but to
receive their estimate of good or bad from the opinions of men only,
which, according to right reason, is a consummate piece of impiety
and injustice.   But this, I will tell you, is destiny, inevitable destiny,
that those who choose to walk in the paths of virtue shall meet with
appropriate returns of honor , and those who prefer a contrary course,
shall be punished accordingly : for God has not made man like trees
and beasts without the power of election ; for he that has no hand
in making himself good or bad, but is born so ready made, is no proper subject for the distributions of justice, for neither the good nor
the evil are such by themselves but only as they are formed by the
hand of destiny."

To these topics of grace and predestination, as the reader may
recollect, belong also considerable portions of the passages adduced
on p. 332 sqq.—Tr]

Irenaeus teaches (C. Haer. IV. 39. § 4) that God who foreknows
all things has prepared habitations of light for those who seek the
light, but habitations of darkness for those who fly from the light.

Clement of Alexandria says expressly (Strom. VI. p. 652), that
predestination is directed according to the foreseen actions of men.
That Origen made the predestination to holiness or to damnation to
depend on the conduct of men, on which point he expresses himself at large, especially in the seventeenth book of his commentary
on the Romans, needs the less proof, as Beza himself, in his notes on

the same epistle, admits this. In his notes on the ninth chapter, we find the remarkable declaration   " This passage is diligently to be guarded against by those who make the foreknowledge of faith or of works the cause of election. Into which really most base error *Origen* led most of the ancients, both Greek and Latin , until at length the Lord, through the Pelagians, excited Augustine to the consideration and correction of this error."

Finally, Chrysostom expresses himself very strongly for a conditional predestination. In his fifty-first homily on Genesis, he refers the declaration of the prophet Malachi, The Lord says I have loved Jacob and hated Esau, to God's foreknowledge by which he foretold the virtue of Jacob and the wickedness of Esau   With this compare his sixteenth homily on Romans, where Chrysostom speaks still more fully respecting " the election according to foreknowledge" (ἐλλογὴ κατὰ πρόγνωσιν).

All the fathers of the Latin church were equally averse to the Augustinian predestination.

Tertullian teaches (C Marc. 2, 23), that God elects him who does well, and rejects him who does ill. Hilary of Poictiers says (in Psalm. lxiv. § 5) · " Election is not the cause of an *unconditional* decision (indiscreti judicii), but the election is made according to merit." And in his commentary on Matt xxii. that many were called but few chosen, because in the calling is manifested a kind regard for the general good, but in the election respect must be had to merit.

Ambrose says (De Fide V. 2) : " God did not predestinate before he foreknew, but he predestinated the rewards of those whose merits he foreknew (quorum merita praescivit, eorum praemia praedestinavit)." Augustine appeals (De Gr Chr. 46 ; De Dono Pers. 19 ; Op. Imp 135), indeed, to the words of Ambrose (lib. 7 in Luc. 9 58) : " God calls those whom he sees fit, and makes pious whom he will (Deus quos dignatur vocat, et quem vult religiosum facit) " But that Ambrose would not here maintain an absolute decree, but would rather teach in the sense of Paul, that in the proclamation of the gospel through Christ, God was not guided by the imaginary prerogatives of men who might be supposed to have a greater claim to it, is not only taught by the connection and the occasion of the passage but follows also from other positions of the Milan bishop. Thus he strongly inculcates the doctrine, (in the *enarratio in Psalm* xlviii), that God calls *all* men. But the calling of *all* men, was in plain contradiction to an Augustinian predestination! Augustine, however, could object, that Ambrose does not here speak of the calling according to purpose (vocatio secundum propositum), but of calling in general. But of such a distinction between a *calling according to purpose*, which should concern the elect, and a *calling* which pertained to all men, as *Augustine* sets it forth—a distinction which can be as little justified from the Bible as from philosophy*— we find no vestige in Ambrose.

Finally, even Jerome, who was so zealous an armor-bearer to Augustine in the Pelagian controversy, (though, as appears from his dialogue against the Pelagians, he was in no point purely Augustinian, and could by no means ever entirely have adopted Augustinism), in respect to predestination was a decided Pelagian. For he based this on foreknowledge. The proof passages on this point are collected by Vossius in great numbers, p. 738.

But the fathers, in respect to the means which God employs to lead one to salvation but does not afford to another, always allowed an unsearchableness of the counsels of God. Only they did not, through the hidden ways of God in the visible world, suffer themselves to err respecting a belief in the revealed benignity of God, which would have all men to be saved, as was the case with Augustine through fondness for his system.

3. As the previous fathers did not hold to the revolting *particularism* of Augustine respecting predestination, it might of course be expected that they would not confine redemption to the elect, but would in this respect profess the *universalism* of Pelagius. And this was in fact their general doctrine. No one of them had been impelled by speculation to explain away from the New Testament the universality of God's grace through Christ, who, according to Paul's doctrine, gave himself a ransom for all. So different did they also make the extent of redemption, and so little in their investigations did they enter into the *value* of the atoning death of Jesus, (about which the scholastics speculated so much), that they universally admitted, with Pelagius, that God would have *all* men to be happy, and that God sent Jesus into the world to redeem *all* men. The proof passages may be found collected by Munscher, (Handb

---

* Perhaps this remark was not intended against what is now meant by *effectual* calling, and if it was, I need not here spend time to refute it.—Tr

der Christl. Dogmengesch. II. § 198, 200; IV § 105); only we may be allowed to add one further passage from Ambrose which seems peculiarly conclusive. It is found in his *enarratio in Psalm.* xlviii. § 2. " Christ promises redemption to *all*, so that no one need tremble, no one despair, as no one is excepted, but every soul is invited to grace, that it may be redeemed from crime without price, and may obtain the fruit of eternal life."

From these doctrines of the ante-Augustine fathers respecting grace, predestination, and redemption, so different from Augustinism, we might infer, if there were still any need of such an inference, that they likewise differed from him on the doctrine of original sin.

From all this comes the result, that Augustine introduced into the ecclesiastical system several views entirely new. He was properly the first to set up a *system*, which he obtruded on the christian world as an old orthodox system. This system was *in part* new in respect to its *matter*, and must have been *wholly* new in respect to the form, or the connection, in which he placed the several doctrines with each other. For although some fathers before him, particularly in the Latin church, had some ideas analogous to his, and it may not unjustly be maintained that the germ of Augustinism is found in Tertullian and Ambrose, yet, from his doctrine of original sin, (which he modified in a manner wholly peculiar to himself, and placed in a systematic connection with the other doctrines), he developed consequences which were hitherto wholly unknown and unheard of in the christian church. Among them were the irresistibleness of divine grace, absolute predestination, and the limitation of redemption to the elect. Even the name *original sin* (peccatum originale), Augustine may have been the first to use, to which the term *vice of origin* (originis vitium) in Tertullian, is only similar. By the use of the former expression by the African national council at Carthage, 418, it became symbolic* for the African church.

Regarding the doctrine of the church so far as it was hitherto defined by symbols, Augustine might rather be called a heretic than

---

* *Symbolisch*, here used as an adjective from *symbolum* in the sense of creed or doctrinal formula —Tr

Pelagius For the former, as we have seen, departed from that doctrine in an essential point, as he denied the freedom of the human will after the fall. But we do not find that the Pelagians offended against " the faith" in any grand principle as settled, before anything was decreed by the synods through Augustine's management, respecting the contested doctrines The symbols generally defined but very little respecting anthropology. However widely therefore the Pelagians departed from all the fathers in their doctrine of the entire incorruption of human nature after the fall of Adam, yet, while they varied in no main doctrine from the " rule of faith," they could hardly be called *heretics*. Often as Augustine arrayed against them the declarations of the fathers, yet he could never bring against them one symbol. In this sense Caelestius was not wrong, when he called the errors imputed to him *questions aside from the faith* (questiones praeter fidem), and maintained respecting original sin propagated by generation, that the doctrine was the subject of investigation (questionis), but not of heresy.

It is worthy of still further remark, that the Pelagians never formed a sect, but always held to the catholic church, and that, although they and their opinions were condemned by the synods, still the Augustinian doctrine *in all its extent*, at least in its predestination theory, was never expressly pronounced *orthodox*, at any synod, even including the Ephesian.

[All this, in the manner above stated, may be true, while at the same time Pelagius was much farther than Augustine from the general views of truth that had prevailed in the church Decrees of councils in favor of any principles, are not to be looked for till those principles have been first assailed, and that in an alarming degree Pelagius might therefore be no heretic *in form*,—and hence Augustine did not venture to call him such, before the decisions—while he was deeply so *in fact*, as regarded the general sentiment.—TR.]

CHAPTER XXIII.

Concluding remarks.

The problem which I proposed to solve by writing this book, I may consider as solved. I have endeavored to exhibit Augustinism and Pelagianism in their limited period,—how each was historically developed and formed,—and also its internal coherency. I might therefore now lay down the pen. But the ensuing remarks, which in part follow as results of what has been said, and in part may serve as a review of the two contrasted systems, may still find a place.

The exhibition now given affords, I think, the most complete solution of the question, how Augustine could set up and defend such a system as his. It is found in Augustine's own natural disposition ; in his early training in the school of the Manichaeans ;* in his learning by his own experience how difficult it is to resist the power of sensuality, and how little he could effect in his own strength , in the African theology, which now, from Tertullian's time, was wont to predicate so much evil of human nature , and in his early acquaintance with the epistle to the Romans, which he read in the Latin translation and did not sufficiently understand for want of skill in the language

It was amid the Pelagian disputes, that he now formed his views and his present convictions *into a system.* It is therefore no mistake to suppose this system, as such, to have proceeded from this controversy ; for in it and from it, his views first acquired a congruity and coherence which they had not before   But in regard to the essen-

---

* This effect of his nine years trial of Manichaeism, as I have once before suggested, may well be doubted   For however natural such an effect might seem, at first view, the *opposite* effect is pretty clearly proved by the plain matter of fact, that immediately on leaving the Manichaeans and becoming a Christian, he advocated, in opposition to them, a much more liberal kind of anthropology than that to which he was afterwards gradually led. Nor was it, on the whole, at all unnatural that the deep disgust he now felt at Manichaeism, should have a much greater effect in the formation of his christian system, than could result from any remaining influence of his old Manichaean cogitations.—Tr

tial doctrines themselves which Augustine professed, they did not
have their source in the opposition he made to the Pelagians   In
their essential elements, they belonged to the fundamental convictions of Augustine, which had been settled with him from the commencement of his episcopate, as he then thought the true nature of
divine grace to be made perfectly clear by that declaration of Paul,
What hast thou which thou hast not received ?   And if even no
controversy had arisen between him and Pelagius, still all the distinguishing traits of the two men were so very different, that they
could not possibly have harmonized in their mode of thinking.   How
could the mysticism of Augustine have found warmth and nourishment in the rationalism of Pelagius ?

To Augustine's own inward experience I might allow no unimportant place, when treating of the reasons why he came to his system.   Augustine had fallen into the abyss of gross sensuality.   By
feeling a spontaneous impulse for the better, the wish arose within
him to return to virtue ; but he at the same time felt that this wish,
if not aided by a higher power, was in vain.   In the history of his
own conversion, he must have found the proof that man can do nothing of his own strength, and that in his reformation he is merely
passive.   So much the more inclined must he have been to derive
the practice of good from an influence superior to sense (von einem
ubersinnliche Einflusse).   But now as this *supersensual* influence
was distinct from all the proper power of human nature, man remained but a miserable creature, prone to sin and destitute of all
merit.   All the rest that Augustine thought, followed of course.

And from the foregoing exhibition, it may also be seen how the
authors and defenders of Pelagianism came to *their* view.   Pelagius,
a man so discreet and free from all mysticism, could be satisfied only
with such a system as his own, which left the most part to man's
own power ; a system which he developed with clearness and consistency.   As a monk also, who could admit no entire corruption of
human nature on account of the rigorous practice of virtue to which
he attained, he must have been averse to Augustinism.   Hence, too,
is explained the fact that, in the sequel, Pelagianism, though in a rather modified form, had most of its defenders among the monks.—
A perception of the great injury which the Augustinian system might
do to morality, and how greatly it might be abused as a cloak for the
neglect of duty, inspired Pelagius with the most implacable hatred

against it.   He burned with vehement zeal in his book De Natura,
(as Augustine himself informs us, De Nat. et Gr. c. 1), against those
who, instead of blaming the human will for their sins, rather blamed
the nature of man and exculpated themselves on account of it.

Julian also hated Augustinism because it destroys morality. C Jul.
III. 26.   He accounted in part for the approbation with which it was
received, from its favoring vice. Op. Imp. II 5 sqq.

Why Pelagianism likewise found many friends—Augustine himself granted, in his letter to Hilary (Ep 157, written about the year
414), that it had already found many disciples, as he could believe
—may be sufficiently comprehended from its internal structure, even
aside from the external relations in which its authors as monks,
though belonging to no particular community, stood to a fraternity
already so increased and widespread.   It must have been the way
of thinking of all those who regarded it as needful to the morality of
man to lay great stress on the exertion of his own power; of all
those who were not inclined to mysticism.   And besides this, Pelagianism contained the most direct contrast to Manichaeism, to which
the aversion had now become so great by the zeal of Augustine himself.   Can it be wondered at, that the number of the friends of Pelagianism was so great?

Augustinism and Pelagianism were therefore the two opposite
poles which were removed in hostile separation from each other and
whose union was not to be thought of.   Christian humility and religious resignation to God, were the best element in the former, only
it might easily, by a consequential application, become dangerous to
morality and rob man of alacrity in the discharge of his duty.   The
moral element was predominant in the latter; but Pelagianism might
as easily nurture the pride of human virtue and thus become prejudicial to genuine christian humility.*

---

* This statement of the case on both sides, has certainly the appearance
of candor, especially if we look at the *extreme* of Augustinism   And doubtless in many cases on both sides, it has been verified by facts, as in the case
of the Adrumetian monks, on the one side, in running into antinomianism
But " christian humility," if actually produced, is the best of all possible
safeguards against the vicious tendency of any system, while " the pride of
human virtue," if it may sometimes preserve a decency in external morality,
is a canker in the heart which consumes the whole spiritual man , and the
system which would foster this pride, must ultimately, one would think, be

Both Augustine and the Pelagians rested the truth of their opinions on reason and scripture; but in a totally reverse order. What Augustine thought he had found in the Bible, he also sought to defend with philosophic weapons. The Pelagians sought confirmation from the Bible for the opinions they had derived from reason and reflection on the moral nature of man. The former was a super-rationalist; the latter, rationalists. Julian, in several passages, declares the principle of his rationalistic interpretation of the Bible. Scripture can teach nothing against the plain decisions of reason (contra rationem perspicuam) Op. Imp. II. 53; IV. 136; VI. 41.

But as it respects the theological and philosophical verity of the two systems, a minute philosophical and exegetical examination of them, would far transcend the limits of this work. The following simple remarks, however, will be enough to show that neither the one nor the other can be biblically and philosophically sustained

Augustine had but poorly established his grand principle of original sin. An *Augustinian* original sin can never be at all sustained before the tribunal of reason. An Augustinian original sin by which man can do only evil, removes completely the freedom of the will, and consequently annihilates all accountability of human conduct, so that there can therefore be no morality at all. Such an assumption, at war with our moral nature and the demands of the law within us, cannot possibly be admitted by a sober philosophy. Besides, an *imputation* of Adam's sin to posterity, whereby God has punished the sin of the first man, is entirely unphilosophical. A crime, and of course anything moral, can by no means be inherited, but must come by the man's own conduct. The justice of God can impute no foreign sin to me, but merely my own. But I must regard every sin as foreign which is not committed by me as an *individual*, even though we should admit the traducianism of the soul. For to admit an imputation before I exist as an individual, and therefore before I am any more conscious of myself than of a law, has something contradictory in itself

All this has been so often and so forcibly said by the opponents of Augustine, and especially by Julian, that a more extended presentation is not here needful.

---

ruinous to the morals of a people at large, whatever might be the effect on some philosophic minds. But facts, after all, are the grand test for the tendencies of doctrines. What *classes* of men have actually been the most holy and moral? is the question. —TR

Nor can Augustine's original sin be exegetically sustained. It is not the doctrine of the New Testament; never the doctrine of Paul

To stop but a moment on that which Augustine considered the chief passage, Rom. 5 12 sqq His original sin is by no means taught in it. Paul there institutes a comparison between Adam and Christ, and maintains that, by the former, sin and death have come into the world, but that the latter has blessed the whole human race. That θάνατος is here to be taken for moral infelicity, as the newer expositors, after the example of Pelagius, commonly explain it, I have never been able to believe For that physical death is an evil which has come into the world and upon all Adam's posterity through his sin, is an idea which pervades all Judaism and christian antiquity, and is also certainly according to Paul. But what Augustine would educe from this passage, that the whole human race sinned in Adam, and consequently that Adam's sin, with all its consequences, is deservedly imputed to us, is not in it, and none but an unjust interpretation can find it there. The terms ἐφ' ᾧ, in the phrase ἐφ' ᾧ πάντες ἥμαρτον, cannot be referred to Adam. This would be an unexampled harshness. Ἐφ' ᾧ corresponds with the Hebrew בַּאֲשֶׁר, and like διότι and quoniam, quia, is to be translated because, just as Luther has correctly translated it Augustine, who used the Latin translation, found in quo (in whom), and was therefore pardonable in referring it to Adam But still it is a question whether the Vulgate has not put in quo for quia, since in quo, even in good Latin, sometimes stands for eo quod, quia —And furthermore, even if sin and death came into the world by Adam and passed over to all, because all sinned, still there is in this no total incapacity of man to good in his natural state. Such a representation was entirely foreign from the apostle and stands in contradiction to his express teaching Nay, he even allows that the heathen do by nature fulfil the precepts of the law (Rom 2 14); and just before, he says, that God will render to every one according to his works (2 6).

But the Pelagians also could no more justify from philosophy than from the Bible, their views of the uncorrupted state of human nature in its present condition.

Not philosophically. A philosophy that does not transcend its limits, cannot mistake the fact that, although it cannot explain the supersensual ground of evil in human nature, a propensity of nature to evil is found in man. That we are prone to the forbidden (nitimur in vetitum) is a complaint as old as history; nay older than that, as we find it in the mythic age. Discreet philosophers also have not denied a radical propensity to evil, which may not indeed very unfitly be called *original sin.* But that it is a doctrine of the Bible, not only of the Old but also of the New Testament, and of Paul in particular, that man is corrupt by nature, the unbiased expositor cannot deny. How many proof passages does not the single epistle to the Romans present? It only deserves to be noticed that Paul places the corruption, not in the soul, but in the body and consequently in the sensuality of man In me, i. e. *in my body,* says he among other things, dwelleth no good thing, to which also the antithesis peculiar to himself between the sensual and the spiritual man, refers.

As the doctrine of original sin is the central point from which all the rest of Augustine's anthropological doctrines proceed, the latter, at least on this side, must lose their support, if the former appears not well founded.

The necessity of infant baptism to the pardon of original sin, can no longer be inferred from this original sin, since the proof of the latter rests on so weak a foundation.—And no one not blinded in favor of his own system, could find in Mark 16: 16, the damnation of unbaptized children. For when the Redeemer pronounced condemnation on the unbelieving, he certainly did not intend children. For how then could the great friend of children say, If ye do not become as children, ye shall not enter into the kingdom of heaven?

The relation of human freedom to divine grace we should by no means be prepared exactly to define, but would consider it as a mystery; and this so much the more since even the New Testament decides nothing respecting it, but connects each with the other by admonishing to virtue and piety as well as also of the aid of grace, when it mentions its necessary aid without determining how much man does by his own strength and what God works immediately in man in the conversion of the sinner and the practice of virtue. When Paul (Phil. 2: 13) ascribes to God the willing and doing of good, he nevertheless summons the Christian, in the preceding verse as well as in other passages, to the utmost stretch of spontaneous effort; and furthermore, by connecting the two verses together by the particle *for,* he shows most plainly the close relation in which he regarded both [agencies], and how he considered the one as conditioned upon the other. The hope of divine help should rouse to greater effort How else could he well ascribe, in the seventh of Romans, the willing of good directly to man? But more nice delineations the Apostle does not afford. Such a relation however is not to be conceived of as a mechanism of nature!—The irresistible grace is nowhere to be found in scripture, not even where the higher influence of the Holy Ghost is most definitely spoken of.—At the same time the ambiguity of the Greek word χάρις, translated grace, gratia, allowed of several quotations of proof passages on the doctrine of gracious influences, but which, for want of investigating the Hebrew import of the expression, could by no means be satisfactory. Christianity, which wisely consults the practical wants of man, considered it enough for us to know that, by the conscientious application of our own powers, we may enjoy the higher aid of God. And this is indeed all it is necessary for us to know for our conversion and consolation !

In support of absolute predestination, Augustine was indeed able, with some plausibility, to adduce the ninth chapter of the epistle to the Romans. But even this support dwindles on close examination. Several expressions, it is true, are there presented, which may lead to an unconditional decree, if we press the words without noticing the connection and examining it with philosophical acuteness. But all the expressions in this passage must be judged of according to the object of the Apostle. This certainly was not to establish, with philosophical precision, the relation of the divine purpose to the moral conduct of man, but to meet those who were proud of their own merit and would confine the blessings of Christianity to the people to whom themselves belonged. In accordance with this object must the vivacity of the expressions there used be judged of. The main thought is this . Whatever of good accrues to man, he ought not to consider as in consequence of his desert, but the result of God's grace. The election to Christianity depends on God's free grace.— Paul therefore labored to oppose the *Jewish particularism* (particularismus), and for this, men would make him a *christian particularist* !

The other passages also of the Bible, which Augustine either did or could quote, bear on a close examination into the spirit and language of the Bible, a different sense from what Augustine was prepared to give them. According to the scripture use of language, all events are referred directly to God, and we shall plainly prove too much if we construe such expressions with philosophical strictness. How often is it said in the Bible, especially in the language of the Old Testament, God hardened the heart, when natural causes of the hardening are immediately assigned; and in other places, the hardening is attributed to the man himself, e. g. Ps. 95: 8. We are not therefore to prove the predestination system from solitary expressions of the Bible. It must rather be proved from the spirit of Christianity. But this is totally opposed to it. Christianity, by its *universalism* (universalismus), contained indeed the very opposite to the Jewish particularism.*

Nor are there wanting declarations of the Old Testament prophets in which is expressly declared the universal and paternal love of God, according to which he finds no pleasure in the death of the ungodly but wills that he should repent and live; and the bestowment of salvation is made to depend on the right conduct of man. Ezek. 18· 20 sqq. According to the New Testament, God has so loved the world as to give his only begotten son (John 3: 16); he wills not that any one should be lost, but that every one repent, etc. Matt. 18 : 14; 2 Peter 3 . 9. Paul, so greatly revered by Augustine, says, that Christ died for all (2 Cor. 5: 14, 15), that he gave himself a ransom for all (1 Tim. 2: 6), that every one shall receive according to what he has done, whether it be good or evil. 2 Cor. 5: 10. By him also (Rom. 2 5) is attributed to the man himself his hard and impenitent heart. And by this, does not the whole Augustinian particularism tumble to ruins at a blow? that is, the limitation both of the election of grace and also of what is most intimately connected with it, the extent of redemption, to the elect? not to mention that the scriptures teach expressly, that Christ died for those who will be eternally miserable

[In these remarks and citations of scripture our author seems to have confined his view to *Augustine's* unconditional predestination, as they are not at all applicable to the system which holds to the universality of the atonement, complete free agency, the bona-fide offer of salvation to all, and a judgment according to works, but which still admits an " unconditional election " Nor is it easy to see how our author

---

* These terms, as here and elsewhere used both in the original and the translation, are sufficiently intelligible from their connection Nor, however barbarous both in German and English, could they easily be avoided without a tedious circumlocution.—Tr

himself could object to God's *unconditional* purpose to do precisely
what he represents him as doing, in the bestowment of that spiritual
aid without which no one will repent and live, unless he would say
either that God's purpose is predicated on *impenitent acts*, or else
that both human and divine agency are so reciprocally conditioned
on each other that neither can be regarded as *unconditional*, and
neither as taking the lead even " in the order of nature " And
perhaps this *is* the view he intended to indicate on a previous page.
But if so, it is surely a view which stands in as much need of distinct proof and vindication, as do any of even Augustine's positions.
For though the final salvation of man, and even his conversion, may
be equally conditioned on both concomitant agencies, yet how do we
know that divine grace does not so take the lead in the great work,
that the purpose to bestow this grace may properly be regarded as
not predicated on man's act ?   And besides, how can we attach any
meaning at all to the specific declaration that God worketh in us *to*
will and *to* do, without supposing his agency to take the lead, at least
in the order of nature, just so far as it is the *cause* of our right agency.   Nor does this necessarily imply an *irresistible* grace, but only
one which will not in fact be resisted in the particular cases.—Tr]

What Augustine further said or at least indicated, with dialectic
plausibility, for his absolute predestination, and what has in later
times been repeated in its favor with a lavishment of philosophical
acuteness, that by the adoption of a conditional predestination the
will of God ceases to be an *almighty* will, because it is thereby admitted that something may take place which God has not willed—
vanishes on closer examination.   Man cannot fathom the depths of
the divine nature.   Every conception of the idea of Deity, is limited
by our finite powers of conception, and hence, however great our
struggle to be free from all anthropomorphism, a human idea always
remains.   But never may we venture to think of Deity in such a
manner as to destroy the moral action of man and the moral government of the world.   This is an absolute surrender of our whole moral nature.   But by every merely physical conception of divinity,
we encounter the danger of destroying the moral quality of man
and of exalting God's omnipotence at the expense of his holiness.
Hence we must admit that all the physical attributes of God stand in
the closest connection with his moral atributes.   And hence his almighty will must never be thought of as distinct from his holy will ;

and the belief in his holiness must hold us back, where the naked
idea of his omnipotence would ruin us.   But men always think of
God's almighty will apart from his moral attributes when an election
of grace, confined to merely a few as the elect, is adopted by them
for the reason that, if God had willed to save all men, they would
be saved, since nothing can resist his will.   If I may not think the
divine omnipotence physically limited I *must* think it morally limited, if I would not lose the proper idea of Deity.   And this moral
limitation takes place, to be sure, not by anything from without, but
from what is within God and has its origin from him.   But how can
the idea of his holiness, his righteousness, his wisdom, and his goodness, be connected with an unconditional decree which is based on
his almighty will ?*   His holiness is cast into the shade as soon as
his almighty will has only willed that a few should repent but all the
rest should remain in their sinful state ; his righteousness, if he refused to one what he imparts to another alike destitute of all merit ;
his wisdom, if he selected the most appropriate means only for the
salvation of some ,† his goodness, if all his rational creatures cannot
look up to him as the father of eternal love, but he excludes most of
them from his paternal heart.   And to what purpose, in the end, are
the admonitions to virtue and piety, if nothing depends on the free
decision of man but all on an unconditional decree of God, fixed
from eternity, and on that irresistible grace which stands in connection with it ?   Here, truly, the Adrumetian monks were in the right,
and Augustine was not able to refute them.   What a wide field is

---

* Mere omnipotence cannot make a wrong thing right   And if this is
all our author means, it may readily be granted without surrendering God's
right to decide, in a sovereign way, whom effectually to aid and whom to
leave without such aid —Tr

† Such assertions can only surprise the reader, from the pen of so discriminating an author   Had he forgotten the parable of the laborers ?   Or
would he think of asserting that God actually affords to every man the best
possible means for his conversion ? or that the people of Sodom would not
have repented if they had enjoyed the means afforded to Capernaum ?—Such
assertions, too, are equally against the Pelagian theory of grace ; and against
all other theories except that of the Gnostics and the Manichaeans, which
dethrones God   nor can they be at all needed in support of what he has
further to say in opposition to the extreme positions of Augustine ,—and
may therefore be regarded rather as one of those occasional meteoric *bolt-
ings* of the German mind, than an expression of his sober convictions —Tr

here opened for spiritual sloth, and for unconsolable despair! The absolute decree may therefore be ever so much veiled by dialectic art, the contradiction between it and a worthy though human idea of Divinity, can never be removed.

The Pelagians were also able to wrest from Augustine the argument which he derived from God's almighty will in support of unconditional predestination, by replying that, after all, he did not himself regard the fall of Adam as a matter of God's decreeing, but only allowed in it a foreknowledge of God, and since he ascribed freewill to Adam before the fall, he could not even admit of the decree. God had not willed the fall of Adam, and yet Adam fell. Consequently no almighty will of God was here even allowed, but on the contrary a limitation by a moral object. Now as Augustine conceded such a limitation before the fall of Adam, how could he derive a proof of unconditional predestination from the illimitable nature of the divine will?

By what has now been said, the appeal to "the depth of the wisdom of God," of which Augustine so often availed himself when he could not otherwise avoid the objections of his opponents, is reduced to its proper bounds. The mystery of the divine government and foreknowledge in the manner in which it is presented to our weak vision in the visible world, no mortal can unveil; and to this Paul directed his notable declaration. But this "depth" need never shake our faith in the holiness of his will and his righteousness, and hence too in his wisdom itself. The concealed God who, behind the veil of visible things, directs the fortunes of man, cannot be in contradiction with him who is revealed to us by scripture and reason. However unsearchable to us may be the means he employs, in the occurrences of life, for our perfection, the holiness of his object itself should never be a mysterious depth to us, if we would not lose all moral and religious consistency. And Augustine, when he had once assumed in this respect a mysterious depth in the Deity, never dared to try to make doctrines from this depth agreeable to human reason.

Finally, as to the rest of the Pelagian doctrines, they, as in the case of Augustine, flowed from the fundamental view which their defenders had of the state of human nature, or at least were in harmony with this view.

The Pelagian view of infant baptism, that it entitles to the kingdom of heaven, may well be considered the weakest among the Pelagian opinions. It exposed to Augustine a naked spot of which he availed himself, on every occasion, to distress the Pelagians; although he, as we have seen, had at an earlier period declared himself not altogether disinclined to that distinction, which was also adopted in reality, though not in words, by other teachers. For assuming such a distinction between salvation in general and the salvation of Christians in particular, there was no solid reason at all; and the difficult question, why God should allow baptism to be administered to one twin brother but not to the other, was now changed to the equally difficult question, why God should allow the salvation of Christians, and therefore a higher and more signal salvation, to be conferred through baptism on the one but not on the other. The declaration however of Jesus, Whoever is not born of water and the Spirit, cannot enter into the kingdom of God, (in which baptism is to be sure demanded as a necessary condition of participating in the kingdom of God preached by Jesus, and therefore in the salvation which he promises to his followers), does not authorize such an assumption. It may justly be supposed that the Redeemer referred only to those who wilfully declined an admission among his disciples by baptism, and not to small christian children who die before baptism. How much better would the Pelagians have done, had they avoided this rock, and indulged themselves in no definite assertions on a subject respecting which it might well be considered as rashness to decide anything.

What may be regarded as wrong in the Pelagian view of grace, flowed, at least in part, from their idea of the uncorrupted state of human nature. They did not deny the supernatural influence of grace, but its necessity for the practice of virtue. Divine grace was only to *facilitate* the practice, but not to be considered as indispensable to the practice. Here may easily be perceived the *one-sidedness* (einseitigkeit) of the man who relied too much on his own power, and the arrogance of a pride of conscious virtue which may at least be pronounced *not* Christian.

The conditional predestination which the Pelagians adopted, as well as their doctrine of the universality of redemption, is entirely conformable with the universalism of the New Testament, and equally accordant with a just idea of Deity. This universal aspect

is the happiest feature in Pelagianism   Viewed on this side, Pelagianism affords, to the aspirant for morality, a prospect which both
sustains him in the conflict with sensuality, and fills him with joy in
the performance of his duty.

Augustine, therefore, as well as Pelagius—this is afforded as the
result—both erred.   Whether the semipelagians afterwards took a
middle path between Augustinism and Pelagianism, with better success, the sequel of the history will show.

[Our author here refers to his continuation of the same general
history in another volume of nearly equal size with the present, in
which he gives a connected account of semipelagianism from its
commencement to the time of the second council of Orange in 529.
A translation of this latter work may possibly be given at a future
day, if there shall appear to be a call for it.   The period it embraces
is far less known to theologians of our own country, than the period
embraced in the present volume ; but it is one in many respects of
deep and solemn interest, and will doubtless hereafter receive a
greater share of attention than has commonly been bestowed upon it.
It embraces the first part of the long night of the dark ages ; and
one of the best safeguards against the recurrence of such ages to the
church, or of any of their besetting evils, is a good acquaintance
with the early history of those times, when the evils were in their
incipient stages and the causes were at work that produced still
greater evils   Nor was the period, though one of deep and complicated troubles, so destitute of wise and good men, especially among
the clergy, as many have been left to imagine.   It may then well
be supposed that, in the rapid increase of theological literature, such
works as the history of the origin and progress of semipelagianism,
will be demanded.   But whether the publication of an extended
work on that subject, would be warranted at present, is a matter of
some doubt.

It would here be an easy task, in closing the labors of this translation, to fill pages with additional remarks on the momentous topics that have been brought to view.   Nor would it be found an uninteresting theme, were we to dwell on the consequences of this
first grand controversy on the points in question, as developed in
different periods from that time to the present.   The christian world

is doubtless far different from what it would have been if no Augustine had lived, or no Pelagius had risen to call forth his gigantic powers on this then untried field.

But were one to embark on the tide of such reflections, where or when could he stop? A portion of them, too, would come more in place at the close of the history of the semipelagian controversy, should that hereafter be given to the public.

Should the present work be found to conduce to a better knowledge of the grand truths as well as of the history of the christian system, and thus to the greater usefulness of the reader in commending those imperishable truths to the acceptance of his fellow men, my highest aim in the protracted but cheerful labors of its preparation for the English reader, will be accomplished.—TR.]

END.

CPSIA information can be obtained at www.ICGtesting.com
Printed in the USA
BVOW09*0220110416

443758BV00009B/29/P